RUSSIAN-AMERICAN DIALOGUE ON
THE AMERICAN REVOLUTION

RUSSIAN-AMERICAN

DIALOGUES ON

UNITED STATES HISTORY

Volume 2

General editors:

Eugene F. Yazkov

Richard D. McKinzie

Louis W. Potts

RUSSIAN-AMERICAN DIALOGUE ON

THE AMERICAN REVOLUTION

Edited by

Gordon S. Wood and Louise G. Wood

UNIVERSITY OF MISSOURI PRESS

COLUMBIA AND LONDON

Library of Congress Cataloging-in-Publication Data

Russian-American dialogue on the American Revolution / edited by Gordon S.
  Wood and Louise G. Wood.
        p.   cm.—(Russian-American dialogues on United States history ; v. 2)
     Includes index.
     ISBN 0-8262-1020-1 (cloth : alk. paper)
     1. United States—History—Revolution, 1775-1783.   2. United States—
  Politics and government—1775-1783.   I. Wood, Gordon S.   II. Wood, Louise G.
  III. Series.
  E203.R86   1995
  973.3—dc20   95-35343
                                                                        CIP

Designer: Elizabeth K. Fett
Typesetter: BOOKCOMP
Printer and Binder: Thomson-Shore, Inc.
Typefaces: Times, Univers Condensed

In the memory of Richard D. McKinzie, 1936–1993

CONTENTS

JOINT PREFACE

In 1989 the initial volume of this series, as edited by Otis L. Graham Jr., appeared. The goal, as envisioned by the late Richard D. McKinzie, was to create a dialogue among scholars in the Soviet Union and the United States who shared interest in selected topics in American history. Soviet scholarship was then flourishing, especially in journals published in the USSR. Translated from Russian into English, eleven essays on the New Deal were critiqued by American scholars. Hence both sets of scholars could better comprehend the contours of their explanations. This publication was largely the product of three key developments: (1) the growth of American Studies in the Soviet Union from its inception in the 1930s to its blossoming in the 1970s, especially in the Department of Modern and Contemporary History at Moscow State University, the Institute of General History, and the Institute of U.S. and Canadian Studies; (2) the maturation of the Fulbright Program from 1974 onward, which enabled outstanding American scholars to lecture at Moscow State University each spring and to engage in lively discussions and methodological debates; (3) the thaw in the cold war, which led to cultural exchange agreements such as the 1986 pact between Moscow State University and the University of Missouri that established this publication.

Since 1989, events, large and small, have stymied the dialogues publication project. Nonetheless, these obstacles have been surmounted, and we are pleased to present this volume on the American Revolution. As volume editor Gordon Wood remarks,

> Both the United States and the Soviet Union were born in revolutions that had universalist aspirations; each claimed to be in the vanguard of history, leading the world toward its particular kind of future. It is natural therefore that Soviet scholars should have wanted to study the American Revolution of 1776, the source of the nationhood of the United States, just as many American scholars have studied the Russian Revolution of 1917 as the source of the existence of the Soviet Union.

These nine essays as selected by the editorial boards represent the current interpretations in Russia of this most significant episode in American national history, if not international history.

The dialogues project is being reviewed. A third volume, focusing on Russian-American relations prior to 1917, is being completed. The knowledge of past diplomatic and cultural relationships will offer lessons pertinent to the present and future. An additional volume, addressing the history of the two-party system in America, is in gestation.

We are pleased to acknowledge the cooperation and fortitude of a number of scholars who persevered with this project. University leaders at Moscow State University supported the Department of Modern and Contemporary History's laboratory for American history and conferences of scholars from both lands. We are especially obliged to Rector Victor Sadovnichy, Vice Rector Nikolai Koroteev, and Dean Yuri Kukushkin. At the University of Missouri we have been sustained by President George A. Russell, Chancellor Eleanor B. Schwartz, and Executive Dean Marvin Querry. Russian essayists and American commentators proved cooperative and patient. We trust this volume, and its successors, will augment the exchange of ideas among future generations of Russian and American peoples.

Eugene F. Yazkov
Louis W. Potts

EDITORIAL BOARD

RUSSIAN-AMERICAN DIALOGUE ON
THE AMERICAN REVOLUTION

INTRODUCTION

by

Gordon S. Wood and Louise G. Wood

The American Revolution is the single most important event in American history. It not only legally created the United States but also produced most of the persistent values and hopes of the American people. The noblest ideals and highest aspirations of Americans—their commitments to liberty, equality, constitutionalism, and the well-being of ordinary people—were first defined in the Revolution. The Revolution inspired Americans with the belief that they were a people with a special destiny to lead the world toward liberty, becoming, as Abraham Lincoln put it, "the last best hope" for democracy on earth. The Revolution, in short, gave birth to whatever sense of nationhood Americans as a whole have had.

It could not have been any other way; the United States could never be an ordinary nation. From the outset it was compelled to make political and social principles, rather than ethnicity and blood, the foundation of its existence. Only ideas, and not some form of tribalism, could make the people of the United States a single entity. A society composed of so many different races and peoples from so many different places could never be a nation in any traditionally understood sense. Only the ideals and beliefs of the Declaration of Independence could form what Lincoln called "the electric cord" linking the variety of Americans together and allowing them to claim a common nationality "as though they were blood of the blood, and flesh of the flesh" with each other.[1] The United States became in fact the first nation in the modern world to make ideology alone the source of its nationhood.

It is not surprising therefore that many Soviet scholars of American history should have devoted their energies to studying the American Revolution. Not only is the event crucial for understanding American history and the beginnings of the modern world, but also it is the Revolution that has linked the destinies of Americans and the peoples of the former Soviet Union through much of the twentieth century. For the Soviet Union too was a country of many different nationalities and ethnicities held together solely by ideology—an ideology that, like the American ideology of 1776, was created by a revolution. Indeed, the deepest sources of the Cold War and the great antagonism that immediately sprang up between the United States and the Soviet Union in the years following the Soviet Revolution of 1917 rested not simply on the exigencies of power politics or the circumstances of contrasting economic systems but, more important, on the world-historical competitiveness of two very different revolutionary traditions. Both the United States and the Soviet Union were born in

---

1. Roy P. Basler, ed., *Abraham Lincoln: His Speeches and Writings* (Cleveland, 1946), 688, 401–2.

revolutions that had universalist aspirations; each claimed to be in the vanguard of history, leading the world toward its particular kind of future. It is natural therefore that Soviet scholars should have wanted to study the American Revolution of 1776, the source of the nationhood of the United States, just as many American scholars have studied the Russian Revolution of 1917 as the source of the existence of the Soviet Union. The articles collected together in this volume represent the best of Russian scholarship on the American Revolution written during the Cold War.

Now not only has the Cold War come to an end but also the Soviet Union itself has disintegrated—the natural consequence of the failure of the ideology that held the state together. These world-historic events will in time make this collection of essays by leading Russian historians of the American Revolution something of a memorial for a traditional kind of Leninist-Marxist scholarship dealing with revolutions. The volume will eventually become a historical document in its own right, a reminder of just what Soviet scholarship about America was like at the height of the Cold War. Despite their apparent datedness, however, the papers brought together in this volume still stand as the latest and most highly regarded expressions of contemporary Russian scholarship on the American Revolution.

There may be new ideas and new thinking about the American Revolution present in the minds of some younger and maybe not so young Russian historians. But so far none of these new thoughts or new ideas about the American Revolution has been published. The confusion and financial crises stemming from the failure of communism and the collapse of the Soviet Union have seriously impaired the editing and publishing of Russian historical scholarship during the past decade. Consequently, we are assured by the best of Russian historians that nothing new of importance on the American Revolution has been published in Russia since the appearance of these various papers collected in this volume.

This is extraordinary, since all these Russian papers were written prior to *glasnost* and the world-shattering events of 1989–1991, many as long as twenty years ago. Nearly all appeared in the 1970s; only one was published in 1980. This is why most of their approaches and citations appear antiquated and dated to American historians today.

There is an inherent fascination in finding out what foreign scholars think of one's own national history, and this fascination is increased when the foreign scholars happen to be Russians, and Russians writing when they were citizens of the Soviet Union. Readers may be surprised at what they will discover or not discover in this volume. There is virtually nothing here of what Americans call the "new social history" or history from the bottom up, nothing on the collective culture of what Western historians call *mentalites,* nothing on women or slaves, and very little on the behavior of ordinary people or the lower orders; the closest to this last subject is the paper on Shays's Rebellion. It is readily apparent that these Russian Marxist historians did not go through the transformation that Western Marxist historians did in the 1960s and 1970s. During those years such Western Marxist historians as E. P. Thompson and Eugene Genovese, influenced by the work of Antonio Gramsci and Raymond Williams, shifted their emphasis from economic forces to culture. Suddenly it seemed to these Western Marxists that material strength alone was not what gave elites their power; such elites also needed to establish their cultural domination, in Gramsci's term, their "hegemony," over other social classes. Ideas were now regarded as being as important if not more important than the forces of production. Although these Russian historians are interested in ideas, particularly V. V. Sogrin in his analysis of the thinking of Thomas Jefferson, Benjamin Franklin, and Thomas Paine, it is ideas traditionally understood that they write about; it is not ideas as hegemonic culture.

But perhaps even more surprising than the Russian historians' traditional treatment of ideas is their general refusal to rely on the forces of production or other deep-lying structural economic determinants as explanations for events. Indeed, most of the Russian historians explain events of the Revolution much as American historians traditionally have—concentrating on the decisions and actions of royal governors, members of the Continental Congress, or other great men. In large part this is a consequence of the limited sorts of sources available to the Russian scholars— government printed documents and published letters of the leading participants. But it is not just the Russians' reliance on great men and headline events to explain the Revolution that makes their work similar to that of many American scholars; it is also their choice of subjects. Many of the Russian historians write about the same things that American historians have usually written about—the politics of the Continental Congress, the Articles of Confederation, Shays's Rebellion, and the ideas and activities of the principal Founding Fathers, such as Thomas Jefferson, John Adams, or Benjamin Franklin. Indeed, it is remarkable just how traditional their choices of subjects have been.

Nevertheless, despite these obvious similarities between Russian and American scholarship on the Revolution, there is a significant difference between the Russian and the present-day American approaches to the subjects and events of the Revolution, a difference that lies behind much of the American commentators' criticism. The Russian approach might be called a soft Marxist one. American historians, including many of the commentators in this volume, tend to identify this approach with the American school of Progressive historians writing during the first half of the twentieth century—historians ranging from Charles Beard to Merrill Jensen. These Progressive historians, influenced by the same desire to find the underlying determinants of social behavior that Marx had found, tended to assume that all revolutions, including the American Revolution, were driven by social class conflicts arising out of oppression or economic malaise. Thus, according to the Progressive historians, the American Revolution was more than a colonial rebellion; it was also a struggle among various social groups for dominance—merchants versus artisans, planters versus farmers, rich easterners versus poor westerners, creditors versus debtors. As Carl Becker, one of the most important of these early Progressive historians, once put it, the Revolution was not only about "home rule," it was also about "who was to rule at home." These early twentieth-century Progressive historians, like Marx, tended to assume that society was divided horizontally into mutually hostile layers of class, each united by a common occupation or a common source of income. In these social circumstances a revolution had to arise essentially out of a social struggle by members of a deprived and underprivileged class against members of an entrenched class above them.

Despite an extraordinary amount of research and writing during a good part of the twentieth century, however, the Progressive historians, like Beard and Arthur Schlesinger Sr., and their more recent neo-Progressive followers, like Jensen and Jackson Turner Main, and the still more recent "New Left" historians, like Gary Nash and David P. Szatmary, have not been able to make such a class conception of revolution persuasive to most Americans. The social reality of eighteenth-century America simply does not support this kind of class analysis. It seems awkward to conceive of slave-holding gentry-leaders like Thomas Jefferson and George Washington as bourgeois. And a downtrodden, wage-earning proletariat is hard to find. Certainly the existence of a half-million African-American slaves was an example of large-scale oppression, but the slaves scarcely constituted a class in Marxian terms, and they could not be major agents in the Revolution. Despite the presence of poor colonists here and there, poverty among white Americans was nowhere comparable to that existing in eighteenth-century England, where half the population was regularly or at least occasionally dependent on charity for subsistence. American historians have found it difficult to make the case for the white American colonists being an oppressed people. Most, in fact, have agreed that the British colonists were freer, more egalitarian, more prosperous, and less burdened with cumbersome feudal and monarchical restraints than any other part of mankind in the eighteenth century.

In the absence of these traditional kinds of class deprivations and oppressions— which, thanks to the influence of Marx, are presumed to be the usual impulses behind revolutions—explaining the Revolution in a Marxian or Progressive manner becomes something of a problem. Consequently, in the half century since World War II many other American historians have sought to find an explanation for the Revolution different from that set forth by the Progressive historians. Many presented what was in the 1950s called a "consensus" interpretation and since the mid-1960s has come to be called an "ideological" interpretation. If the Revolution could not be explained as a response to the poverty and economic deprivation that supposedly lie behind most revolutions, then some historians, represented in the 1950s by Robert E. Brown and Edmund S. Morgan, thought that the Revolution could best be explained as primarily an intellectual or constitutional struggle, undertaken not to change the society but to preserve it and to protect American liberties and rights. Thus the Americans' attachment to constitutional principles and their belief in "no taxation without representation" had to be taken seriously as causes of the Revolution.

In the mid-1960s historians, led by Bernard Bailyn, filled out and extended this "consensus" interpretation—largely by uncovering and describing more emotional and irrational moods of the culture—to the point where this interpretation is no longer put in terms of formal discourse and constitutional principles; it has become an "ideological" explanation. Beneath the surface layer of constitutional principles lay less formal, more inchoate currents of thought, thoughts about power and liberty, virtue and corruption, that gave meaning to the colonists' behavior in the Revolution.

Indeed, so heavily ideological has the explanation of the Revolution become that it can no longer be something free-floating and exclusively intellectual; it has become fully enmeshed in social and political circumstances, as any ideology must be. Where historians of the 1950s could discuss the Revolutionaries' constitutional principles apart from their political and social context, more recent historians have found it more difficult to separate the Revolutionaries' newly discovered ideology—its belief in conspiracy, its desire to root out corruption, its yearning for virtue—from its sources in the political and social circumstances of the day.

Most of the former Soviet Americanists represented in this volume write with little awareness of this recent "ideological" interpretation, and their failure to take it into account is often the source of much of the American commentators' criticism. Keeping up with American historical scholarship is not an easy matter. Indeed, so fast-moving, complicated, and sophisticated are the discourse and dialectics of American historical scholarship that it is nearly impossible for any foreign scholar, even for those whose native language is English, to participate fully and equally in that discourse and those dialectics. In America the print on the pages of newly published works of history is scarcely dry before refutations and counter-arguments are launched in conferences, journals, and newsletters. Sometimes these debates take place over works that have not yet been published. Under these circumstances one has to have a good deal of sympathy for foreign scholars who desperately try to keep up with what is going on in the United States in the writing of American history. These Russian students of American history, compared to, say, German or Italian students of America, have the added difficulty of the sheer unavailability of many American books and journals.

Thus any dialogue between Russian and American historians on American history is bound to be unequal. The American historians, like many of the commentators in this volume, will always say that everything is more complicated and complex than the Russian scholars realize: there are articles in journals they have not heard of, there are books, sometimes in press, that they have not read, and there are new ideas and new kinds of history that they are unaware of. So it is quite understandable that the Soviet scholars writing in the 1970s should not know about the new "ideological" or "republican" interpretation of the American Revolution. Actually, if they had known about it, they would not have found it totally incompatible with their own rather traditional soft Marxist explanations. Marx after all fully appreciated the importance and power of ideology in human affairs.

It is in fact through ideology and its implication in underlying social circumstances that we may be led back to a concern for social and political change. Only significant developments in the society and politics of the colonies can account for the emotional and frenzied character of the Revolutionaries' rhetoric. And so the peculiar nature of the ideology that American historians of the past several decades have uncovered may in the end drive us back to an examination of the underlying social forces that created such ideology, will drive us back, in other words, to doing once again what the Progressive historians tried to do in the first half of the twentieth century. As the collected papers of the Russian historians make clear, there is something at the heart of the old Progressive interpretation that will not go away. Despite all the devastating criticism leveled at it over the past generation, despite all the new and sophisticated refinements in social and political analysis that historians have applied to the Revolution, and despite the peeling away of a hundred and one of its false and misconceived aspects, the old Progressive interpretation still retains a core of truth, a basic accord with reality, that cannot be evaded. Not that the Revolution was caused by poverty or social deprivation, and not that coherent classes were pitted against one another: these views the past reality will not support. But that there were social circumstances lying behind the Revolution and that significant changes occurred in the society as a consequence of the Revolution are views that the past reality will support.

Every American historian knows that politics and society in the eighteenth century were fundamentally different from those of the early nineteenth century. One was a world of aristocratic and hierarchical pretension, family and oligarchic factionalism, underdeveloped economic behavior (at least compared to England), and limited popular participation in government. The other was a world of competitive electoral politics, political parties, rampant popular commercialism, and egalitarian democracy. How did Americans move from one world to the other except through the Revolution? The old Progressive historians were admittedly too rigid and too crude, too class-obsessed and too anachronistic, in their answers to this question. Despite the schematic ideological orthodoxies constraining much of their scholarship, the same might be said of many of the Russian contributors to this volume. Their concern for the radical social and political character of the Revolution alone makes the Russians' essays worth our consideration.

What the end of the Cold War and the disintegration of the Soviet Union will eventually mean for future historical scholarship in Russia and the other former Soviet republics is hard to calculate. But the collapse of communism and the discrediting of Marxism are bound sooner or later to have momentous effects on history written about the United States. We can perhaps get some sense of the implications of these awesome world-historical events for the future study of United States history by examining both the recent comments of several Russian historians of America and the proceedings of an international conference on "New Approaches to the Study of American History" held March 19–21, 1991, in Moscow and sponsored by the Institute of General History and the Department of American History of the Academy of Sciences of the former USSR.

N. N. Bolkhovitinov (who has the opening essay in this volume) is head of the Department of the History of the U.S.A. and Canada at the Institute of General History and is undoubtedly the Russian Americanist most known in the United States. During the past several years he has been extraordinarily critical of his fellow historians of America. Russian scholars, he wrote in 1991, had only themselves to blame for the isolation and parochialism of their scholarship; by their "rigid class approach" to history they had cut themselves off from the outside world. "In the last fifty years," Bolkhovitinov lamented, "we have not translated a single major work by an American historian, apart from the writings of two well-known Marxist authors,

Herbert Aptheker and Philip Foner. . . . Remaining enclosed in our own circle, we foredoom ourselves to a fiasco and waste our scientific potential on the investigation of long-known facts and truths."[2]

In an unpublished essay, but one widely presented in speeches in the United States in 1992, Eugene F. Yazkov, head of the United States Center at Moscow State University, has briefly surveyed the course of history writing about America since its beginnings in the 1930s. During the Stalinist era the situation was grim, and Yazkov has graphically described the political pressures imposed on Soviet historians of America. "From the very beginning," he says, "their entire research was aimed at proving basic theoretical statements," namely that "politics in America and other capitalist countries reflected a policy carried out solely in the interest of the corporate bourgeoisie."[3] Under Stalin those historians who deviated from the Communist party's views were intimidated and coerced into line, sometimes in the crudest ways. In the 1950s and 1960s, after the death of Stalin, conditions for researching and writing American history in the Soviet Union began improving, and Soviet scholars were actually allowed to visit archives in the United States. In 1974 the Fulbright program brought the first of what became a series of distinguished American historians who come each year to teach students at Moscow State University. Steadily the interest in American history has grown—to the point where by 1991 there were in the former Soviet Union nearly three hundred specialists working in various areas of American history. Yazkov believes that the American history written during the 1960s through the 1980s, the kind of historical scholarship, in other words, represented in this volume, is vastly different from the earlier work done in the 1930s, 1940s, and 1950s: it is based on a wider body of sources, less ideologically strict, and less flatly condemning of the United States. Yet, Yazkov admits, much of this more recent scholarship still retains strong traces of the original rigidity of Marxism, as readers of this volume may discover. Capitalism is still an evil that is in continual crisis, and big business still shapes the policies of the American government. "The presence of these and other dogmatic notions," says Yazkov, "often gives the works of even the best Soviet historians a certain flavor—of internal contradiction and predetermined conclusions." He sees the radical change that has taken place in the former Soviet Union as opening up new freedoms and opportunities for Russian historians. He notes, however, that some scholars are fearful that the pendulum is swinging too far in the other direction, that some Russian historians are celebrating American liberty and capitalism as uncritically as they had formerly condemned them. But in the end Yazkov is hopeful that historical scholarship in Russia can attain some kind of balance, that eventually it can throw off some "age-old dogmas and stereotypes" without, however, rejecting some beneficial "Marxist methods and conceptions, such as the analysis of class." "The future of American history in Russia," he concludes, "will involve expanding the scope of historical study, and employing—alongside some

2. N. N. Bolkhovitinov, "New Thinking and the Study of the History of the United States in the Soviet Union," *Reviews in American History* 19 (1991), 160.
3. Eugene F. Yazkov, "Teaching and Writing History in the New Russia," 3.

Marxist methods and conceptions—other methodological approaches and ideas."[4] Until this new more balanced scholarship is written and published, however, the kind of history represented in this volume remains the best of Russian scholarship.

The proceedings of the March 1991 Moscow Conference revealed a similar ferment in present-day Russian scholarship. As described by the American historian Marcus Rediker, the conference sought "to use *glasnost* (openness) and *perestroika* (reconstruction) to create new points of departure for the study of American history," including the history of the American Revolution. Bolkhovitinov had another opportunity to criticize his colleagues for their backwardness. He launched a courageous and basically liberal attack on the dogmatism of former Soviet writing about American history. Too much of Russian scholarship about America, he said, was devoted to issues of "exploitation" and "imperialism." He implored his colleagues to set aside their past denunciations of expansionist American capitalism. He denounced the ritualistic invocation of such communist cant as "bourgeois falsification" and "dictatorship of monopoly capital." And he urged all the Russian historians of America to strike out in new directions. They should try, he said, to appreciate American individualism, enterprise, and property-based freedom and should affirm "universal human values" and a "law-based state," both of which, he believed, are expressed and secured by the United States Constitution. Contrary to what Russian historians have said, following Charles Beard and the Progressives, the American Constitution, Bolkhovitinov declared, has met the needs of more than a tiny oligarchy; in fact, it has over the past two centuries well served the mass of the American people.[5]

Not all conference participants agreed with Bolkhovitinov. Most of the disagreement and the most heated criticism of the United States, however, appear to have come not from the Russian scholars but from the American historians who were present, such as Jesse Lemisch and Edward Pessen. Lemisch criticized the Russians' present "dream of capitalism," a widespread "mystical and magical belief in the capacity of the market to produce happiness." He found fault with the Russian historians for what he saw as their antipopulist tone, and he warned against their falling in with all those conservative American historians who describe the American Revolution as made by "great white men" without paying sufficient attention to "lower-class protest." While some members of the old guard cheered Lemisch's criticism of America, other scholars appeared to endorse a new emphasis on individual rights, the growth of a market society, and protection of private property in writing about the American past. Georgii Arbatov, director of the Institute for the Study of the U.S.A. and Canada called upon his colleagues "to de-ideologize our attitude toward American history." And A. O. Chubarian, the head of the Institute of General History of the Academy of Sciences, warned his fellow Russians that they must make fundamental changes in their history writing if they are to "join the world scientific community" of historians.[6]

4. Ibid., 12, 14, 15.

5. Marcus Rediker, "The Old Guard, the New Guard, and the People at the Gates: New Approaches to the Study of American History in the USSR," *William and Mary Quarterly,* 3d ser., vol. 48 (Oct. 1991), 580–97.

6. Ibid., 585–87, 592.

Everyone agreed that the free, excited level of debate at the conference was unprecedented for a Russian academic meeting on American history. Nevertheless, given the "wild dialectical swings of thought" taking place throughout the conference, predicting the future direction of Russian study of American history is not easy. As one Russian historian, Vadim Koleneko, has recently warned, "it is difficult for people immediately to reject dogmas and definitions convenient in the past." Yet enough prominent Russian scholars are presently calling for reform in the study of American history, calling for an end to the "self-induced isolation" and "dogmation" of American studies in Russia, that we can expect some major changes in Russian scholarship about the United States.[7] At least, we can hope that the past ideological rigidities in interpreting American history will become less dominant.

• • •

Each of the Soviet articles has appeared earlier in Russian in Soviet publications. The place and date of the original publication is noted at the beginning of the notes for each article. All the articles and nearly all of the Russian scholars' responses have been translated from Russian into English by Professor Richard Tempest of the University of Illinois. We are all indebted to him for his help in this project. Professor Patricia Herlihy of Brown University translated one of the Russian scholars' responses, and we are grateful for her help also. The project was initiated and originally overseen by the expertise of Professor Richard McKinzie of the University of Missouri–Kansas City. Sadly and suddenly, he died before the book could be completed, but his crucial role in the Russian-American Dialogues was gracefully assumed by Professor Louis W. Potts, also of the University of Missouri–Kansas City. Professor Potts not only helped to produce this volume but also worked tirelessly to keep the dialogues project alive. Everyone involved with the Russian-American series is deeply indebted to him.

Despite our best efforts, experts will probably find errors of fact and citation in the Russian articles. Many of these errors of fact we have left uncorrected, for they reveal the nature of the Russian Americanists' scholarship. As N. N. Bolkhovitinov has recently said, "one of the weakest points in Soviet works on American history is the scholarly apparatus," including "unpardonable mistakes in footnotes" and "carelessness" and "inaccuracies . . . in the presentation of facts." One of the reforms he expects from the "new generation of historians," who "must be fully free from the burdensome legacy of the past," is greater reliance on "the most ordinary objectivity and accuracy" in their history writing. In our super-sophisticated, postmodern Western world, saturated as it is with epistemological doubt and confusion, it is refreshing, to say the least, to find a scholar so concerned with such elementary matters as ordinary objectivity and accuracy.[8]

Nine different historians of the American Revolution, all experts in the field, have each commented on one of the Russian articles. Their comments in turn have been sent to the Russian scholars, who were invited to respond to the American historians'

7. Rediker, "The Old Guard," 586; Vadim Koleneko, "North American History in the USSR before *Perestroika* and Today," *Organization of American Historians, Newsletter* 19 (August 1991), 4; N. N. Bolkhovitinov, "New Thinking," 155–65.

8. Bolkhovitinov, "New Thinking," 162–63.

reviews of their pieces. Most of them have replied to the Americans' criticism, a few of them quite pungently, as readers will discover. All the exchanges reveal a desire on the part of scholars in both countries to get to know better each other's historical interpretations of the American Revolution. This by itself has made the Soviet-American Dialogue on the American Revolution worthwhile.

CHAPTER 1

Some Problems in the Historiography of the American Revolution of the Eighteenth Century

by

Nikolai N. Bolkhovitinov

As the bicentenary of the War of Independence approaches, preparations in the United States for the celebration of the national jubilee are growing in scale and intensity. A massive program of celebrations is being drawn up. As early as 1966 the U.S. Congress created a national commission consisting of government figures, members of Congress, and the representatives of various scientific, public, and private organizations.[1] At the time of writing, bicentennial commissions are active in all fifty American states. Special commissions have also been formed in the largest cities of the United States. An advisory group attached to Philadelphia Mayor Frank Rizzo has drawn up a program of festivities that will cost the city $291 million, of which $150 million will be provided by the federal government during a period of three years.[2]

In addition to the official celebrations in Washington and Philadelphia, there are also plans for a number of international congresses for American and foreign scholars to be held throughout 1976, a giant "Parade of the States," numerous exhibitions including a special "Freedom Train," etc. In view of the government's loss of standing and the disenchantment of American youth with national ideals, the approaching jubilee is seen by the leaders of the United States as an important incentive for the revival of American society and the strengthening of its moral spirit.[3]

The narrowly commercial and propagandistic nature of the bicentennial events has already on several occasions given rise to protests and criticism in the American

1. O. L. Stepanova, "Washington's Propagandistic Aims for the Bicentennial," *U.S.A.—Economics, Politics, Ideology* 1 (1972), 118–23. For more on the activities of the National Bicentennial Commission, see its reports to the President (of July 4, 1970), the U.S. Congress, etc.—*America's 200th Anniversary: Report of the American Revolution Bicentennial Commission* (Washington, D.C., 1970); *Report to the Congress of the United States* (Washington, D.C., 1971). This article by Nikolai N. Bolkhovitinov was first published in *Modern and Contemporary History* 6 (1973).

2. *Bicentennial Newsletter* 3, no. 10 (December 1972), 7.

3. *Liberty and Learning: The American Revolution Bicentennial Program of the Library of Congress* (Washington, D.C., 1970), 3; *Bicentennial Newsletter* 3, no. 6 (August 1972), 1–2.

press. Thus, for example, the radical young historian Professor Jesse Lemisch has observed that the national commission is chiefly interested in bicentennial parks, pies, and other commercial projects. Instead he proposed holding town meetings (similar to those that took place in New England at the time of the Revolution) where the people would be able to discuss freely the most critical issues of the day. Lemisch has also spoken in favor of holding a nationally televised discussion among historians about problems in the historiography of the American Revolution.[4] For a number of years now the *Progressive,* a radical journal, has been subjecting the activities of the national commission to sharp criticism, and in the middle of August 1972 the influential newspaper the *Washington Post* published a series of articles on this question. In March 1973, after another debate in Congress, the national commission was replaced by a new administrative body—the American Revolution Bicentennial Administration—attached to which is an advisory committee.[5]

A bicentennial commission, among whose members were such eminent scholars as Julian Boyd, Lyman Butterfield, John Alden, and Clarence Ver Steeg, had for several years existed within the American Historical Association. Later the composition of the commission underwent significant changes, with representatives of the younger generation of American historians such as Lemisch; Gordon Wood, the author of a major study of the creation of the American republic; and Cecelia Kenyon, an eminent scholar investigating the Revolutionary period becoming its members. Professor Richard B. Morris of Columbia University, a well-known specialist on early U.S. history who is the author of numerous studies of the American Revolution, became chairman of the commission.[6] Much is being done in connection with the impending jubilee by the National Commission for the Publication of Historical Documents, the U.S. Library of Congress, the National Archive in Washington, the state historical societies, individual universities, etc. From the Ford Foundation alone the U.S. Library of Congress received $500,000 for the publication of a new multivolume collection of the correspondence of the delegates to the Continental Congress.

Beginning in 1972, the Library of Congress has been holding yearly symposia at which individual problems of the American Revolution are discussed. The first of them, chaired by Richard Morris May 5–6, 1972, was devoted to the formation of revolutionary ideology in America. Among the participants in the symposium were such eminent historians as Henry S. Commager, Caroline Robbins, Jack P. Greene, and others. A second symposium was chaired by Julian P. Boyd and held May 10–11, 1973, at the Library of Congress; at this gathering papers were presented by Bernard Bailyn ("Common Sense"), Cecelia Kenyon ("The Declaration of Independence"), Merrill Jensen ("The Articles of Confederation"), and Richard Morris ("The Peace Treaty of Paris"), as well as by J. P. Wiggins, the former American ambassador to the United

---

4. *Chicago Tribune,* October 26, 1972.

5. A. N. Shlepakov, "The U.S.A. on the Eve of the Bicentenary of Independence," *Problems of History* 7 (1973), 196.

6. *The American Historical Review* 74 (April 1969), 1469 (henceforth referred to as *AHR*); *American Historical Association Newsletter* 9, no. 4 (September 1971), 8 (henceforth referred to as *AHA Newsletter*); ibid., 11, no. 1 (February 1973), 5.

Nations.[7] The Institute for Early American Culture and History held a symposium March 8–12, 1971, at Williamsburg, Virginia. Professor Bailyn of Harvard University gave the first paper, which was devoted to the central questions of the American Revolution. Professor Edmund S. Morgan, another major authority on seventeenth- and eighteenth-century history, discussed the general results and significance of the events of the Revolution. Richard M. Brown, Rowland Berthoff, Jack P. Greene, John Shy, and other well-known scholars specializing in the American Revolution also presented papers. In 1973 the proceedings of the symposium were published in a separate book.[8]

Just a list of the most important historical publications and events being conducted in connection with the approaching bicentennial celebration would fill up a whole article. The activities of the main centers of scholarship and the numerous publications of documents commemorating the coming anniversary are being carried out on quite a large scale. L. H. Butterfield is bringing out the papers of the Adams family in one hundred volumes. For several decades Julian Boyd has been preparing the publication of a fifty-volume collection of the writings of Thomas Jefferson (by 1972 fifteen volumes had appeared); other editions of writings include those of James Madison (seven volumes have appeared), Alexander Hamilton (by 1968 thirteen volumes had appeared), and other important figures of the American Revolution in the eighteenth century.[9] This year the publication of the papers of John Jay, on which Richard Morris has been working for many years, will begin. All these editions are of a high professional standard.

The publication of biographical studies of the Founding Fathers is being conducted on a vast scale. According to the calculations of James Flexner, George Washington's latest biographer, the New York Public Library catalog alone lists some three thousand books devoted to Washington. In addition to popular books about him, he is the subject of a seven-volume definitive study by Douglas S. Freeman,[10] as well as of a three-volume study by Flexner himself, in which he has so far reached the year 1793.[11] Also well known is the biography of Jefferson that Dumas Malone began to publish in 1948 (the fourth volume of this work, devoted to Jefferson's first term as president, came out in 1970).[12] Wide acclaim was won by Irving Brant's life of Madison.[13]

7. *Liberty and Learning,* 7; *New York History* 51 (July 1971), 324; Library of Congress, *The Development of a Revolutionary Mentality* (Washington, D.C., 1972).

8. S. G. Kurtz and J. H. Hutson, eds., *Essays on the American Revolution* (Chapel Hill, 1973).

9. National Historical Publications Commission, *Program for the Publication of Historical Documents: A Report to the President . . .* (Washington, D.C., 1954); National Historical Publications Commission, *Documentary Source Materials of the American Revolution: A Program for Their Publication Proposed by the National Historical Publications Commission* (Washington, D.C., 1970).

10. D. S. Freeman, *George Washington, a Biography,* 7 vols. (New York, 1948–1957).

11. J. T. Flexner, *George Washington,* 4 vols. (Boston, 1965–1972); for more details see N. N. Iakovlev, "The Labyrinths of Washingtoniana," *Problems of History* 5 (1972), 138–57.

12. Dumas Malone, *Jefferson and His Time,* 6 vols. (Boston, 1948–1981).

13. Irving Brant, *James Madison,* 6 vols. (Indianapolis, 1941–1961). Brant also published a one-volume synoptic study of Madison, *The Fourth President: A Life of James Madison* (Indianapolis, 1970).

As Jesse Lemisch has perceptively observed, until recently American historians and archivists directed their efforts toward publishing the papers of "Great White Men." The federal government, the Ford, Rockefeller, and Guggenheim foundations, the universities, historical societies, and publishing houses offered every assistance to the publication of the papers of Franklin and Jefferson, but not to those of Thomas Paine or Frederick Douglass. President Kennedy found the time to be present at the celebrations in Boston commemorating the publication of the first volumes of the John Adams papers. He not only spoke at this event but also wrote a detailed critique of the diary and autobiography of Adams for the *American Historical Review*. Of course nothing like that could have happened in the case of the Paine or Douglass papers; Philip Foner, who devoted considerable effort to arranging their publication, was never deemed worthy of a presidential congratulation. Lemisch was thus fully justified when he called on his colleagues finally to embark upon the systematic publication of the papers of those figures that were "neither great, nor white, nor men." He named as some of the most urgent tasks the publication of sources on popular protests in colonial America, documentary materials on Americans imprisoned in British jails, eyewitness accounts of the American Revolution, etc. In addition, Lemisch noted the racist tendencies in "elitist" historiography that does not concern itself with the history of blacks, Indians, or women.[14] Many American historians recognized the timeliness and importance of Lemisch's criticism. The leaders of the National Historical Publications and Records Commission did not in their statements oppose the program he had put forward. But for the time being, no significant changes in the type of books being brought out are being envisaged.

Let us now proceed to discuss in concrete terms the contemporary historiography of the American Revolution in the eighteenth century. V. I. Lenin spoke highly of the revolutionary traditions of the American people and called the colonists' struggle against England "one of those really liberating, really revolutionary wars, of which there have been so few compared to the vast numbers of the wars of conquest."[15] The total underestimation of the revolutionary traditions of the American people; an emphasis on unity and stability, "consensus" and "continuity" in U.S. history; and the direct or indirect denial of the revolutionary nature of the North American colonists' struggle for independence have become the most characteristic traits of postwar historiography in the United States.[16] It is no accident that the famous

14. Jesse Lemisch, "The American Revolution Bicentennial and the Papers of Great White Men," *AHA Newsletter* 9, no. 5 (November 1971), 7–21. A short review of this article was published by P. B. Umanskii in *Problems of History* 2 (1973), 174–75.

15. V. I. Lenin, *Complete Collected Works,* vol. 37, 48; ibid., vol. 28, 62.

16. For more about contemporary trends in U.S. historiography, the consensus theory, neoconservatives, young radicals (the New Left), cliometricians (new economic history), etc., see N. N. Bolkhovitinov, "Contemporary American Historiography: New Trends and Problems," *Modern and Contemporary History* 6 (1969), 116–29; Bolkhovitinov, "The U.S. War of Independence and Contemporary American Historiography," *Problems of History* 12 (1969), 73–88. For a general review of the development of the historiography of the U.S. War of Independence in the nineteenth century and the first half of the twentieth century, see the two-volume historiography textbook

book *Democracy in America* by the French aristocrat Alexis de Tocqueville, first published in 1835, has been the most popular historical work in the United States in the postwar period. Following in the tradition of Tocqueville, Louis Hartz, the well-known leader of the neoconservatives, stated that the Americans "did not have to endure a democratic revolution."[17] According to Hartz, the characteristic feature of the American Revolution was the appearance of "outright conservatism" or, more exactly, the consolidation in the United States of the unchallenged domination of "the liberal tradition of Locke."[18]

In the opinion of another leading neoconservative historian, Daniel Boorstin, "the most obvious peculiarity" of the American Revolution was the fact that "in the modern European sense of the word, it was hardly a revolution at all."[19] The Revolution, Boorstin further states, merely confirmed a belief in the old English constitutional system (trial by jury, freedom of speech, the slogan "no taxation without representation," etc.) and did not signify any radical changes.[20]

On the whole the leaders of the new movement, among whom one must include Robert Brown, Boorstin, Clinton Rossiter, and Hartz, tend to see the American Revolution in the eighteenth century as a conservative movement that defended freedom and property and found its logical conclusion in the Constitution of 1787.[21] The War of Independence, concludes the husband-and-wife team of Robert and Katherine Brown, was begun to preserve the existing order rather than to change it.[22] Professor Brown, in his book *Middle-Class Democracy and the Revolution in*

edited by I. S. Galkin, *Historiography of the Modern Period of the Countries of Europe and America* (Moscow, 1967), and also P. B. Umanskii, "Problems of the First American Revolution," *The Basic Problems of U.S. History in American Historiography* (Moscow, 1971), 61–110.

17. Louis Hartz, *The Liberal Tradition in America* (New York, 1955), 35, 38. Alexis de Tocqueville wrote that the great social revolution occurred in America simply and calmly and that the United States enjoyed the fruits of a democratic revolution without having experienced a revolution itself. Tocqueville, *Democracy in America* (Moscow, 1897), 9.

18. Hartz, *Liberal Tradition*, 6, 47, 50.

19. Daniel J. Boorstin, *The Genius of American Politics* (Chicago, 1953), 68. (By the early 1970s more than ten editions of this book had been published.)

20. Ibid., 66–98. Boorstin developed his views further in his works *The Americans: The Colonial Experience* (New York, 1958); *The Americans: The National Experience* (New York, 1965); and *The Decline of Radicalism in America* (Chicago, 1969).

21. Richard B. Morris, *The American Revolution Reconsidered* (New York, 1967), 44; G. A. Billias and G. N. Grob, eds., *American History: Retrospect and Prospect* (New York, 1971), 12, 55, 56, 68, 74, 79, 92–94, 100, 103; John H. Higham, *Writing American History* (Bloomington, 1970), 143–46, 173; F. O. Gatell and A. Weinstein, eds., *American Themes: Essays in Historiography* (New York, 1968), 438–40, 461–63; G. N. Grob and G. A. Billias, eds., *Interpretations of American History: Patterns and Perspectives*, 2d ed. (New York, 1972), 15–18. Yet certain differences exist among supporters of the consensus theory. If for Boorstin the ideology of Americanism, "consensus" and "givenness," represent the greatest of blessings, Hartz admits that "consensus" impoverishes the history of the United States. Boorstin, *Genius*, 8–35; Hartz, *Liberal Tradition*, 11.

22. Robert E. Brown, *Middle-Class Democracy and the Revolution in Massachusetts, 1691–1780* (Ithaca, 1955), 401; Robert E. Brown and Katherine Brown, *Virginia, 1705–1786: Democracy or Aristocracy?* (East Lansing, 1964), 308.

Massachusetts, 1691–1780, argues that there was no revolution in Massachusetts and there could have been none since there was nothing to change there. Democracy already existed in Massachusetts. Long before the Revolution, the majority of the adult male population in the colony already had the right to vote. In depicting Massachusetts colonial society as a "middle class democracy," Brown goes to absurd lengths by applying this view to almost the entire area between New Scotland and western Florida, which he claims was largely and indeed almost exclusively inhabited by independent farmers.[23] It was Brown who in the 1950s initiated the crusade against Charles Beard and who very recently, in 1970, published a book directed against another prominent "Progressive" historian, Carl Becker, accusing the latter of "the open advocacy of the Marxist philosophy of history."[24]

At one time (particularly in the 1950s) it seemed that the exponents of the "consensus" school of history had gained complete victory in the United States and had captured the leading positions in American historiography. It is revealing that although in the 1930s and 1940s Samuel E. Morison and Commager, the authors of the most widely used U.S. History textbook, regarded the Constitution of 1787 as a kind of "Thermidor," in the 1950s and 1960s the section dealing with the "Thermidor" and indeed the word itself were altogether missing from their textbook.[25] Even such a well-known "Progressive" historian as Arthur Schlesinger Sr. changed his views to a significant extent (although not completely) under the influence of the consensus theory, thereby earning special praise from Robert Brown in the pages of the *American Historical Review.*[26]

James Lemon's monograph on the life of small farmers in southeast Pennsylvania is another example of the influence of the consensus theory. The very title of his book—*The Best Poor Man's Country*—is already revealing. Lemon emphasizes the liberal orientation of the farmers of Pennsylvania, who were believers in the bourgeois ideology of liberalism and lived much better than their European counterparts.[27] The young scholar selected the richest and most fertile part of Pennsylvania for his analysis. This fact alone dramatically diminishes the significance of his conclusions not only for the country as a whole but also for Pennsylvania itself.

But American historiography began to undergo significant change as early as the 1960s. The serious flaws in the works of the exponents of "consensus" history became increasingly obvious. John Cary was the first to point out that Brown's conclusion

---

23. Robert E. Brown, *Reinterpretation of the Formation of the American Constitution* (Boston, 1963); R. F. Berkhofer Jr., ed., *The American Revolution: The Critical Issues* (Boston, 1971), 29–45.

24. Robert E. Brown, *Charles Beard and the Constitution* (Princeton, 1956); Robert E. Brown, *Carl Becker on History and the American Revolution* (East Lansing, 1970), 182, 191; *William and Mary Quarterly,* 3d ser., vol. 28 (April 1971), 338–40 (henceforth referred to as *WMQ*).

25. S. E. Morison and H. S. Commager, *The Growth of the American Republic* (New York, 1942), vol. 1, 277; S. E. Morison, H. S. Commager, and W. E. Leuchtenburg, *The Growth of the American Republic* (New York, 1969), vol. 1, 243.

26. A. M. Schlesinger Sr., *The Birth of a Nation* (New York, 1968); *AHR* 74 (April 1969), 1357–59.

27. J. T. Lemon, *The Best Poor Man's Country: A Geographical Study of Early Southeastern Pennsylvania* (Baltimore, 1972), xiii, xv, 227–28.

that 90 percent of the population of Massachusetts consisted of farmers generally owning their own plots of land was based on an analysis of the property of only eighteen individuals. Brown based his argument that 95 percent of the colony's adult male population had the right to vote on a study of only fifty wills, although he had in his possession several thousand such documents. After examining just one volume of wills, Cary reached an entirely different conclusion. He discovered that only 43 percent of the population had the right to vote and that only members of the "upper class" enjoyed that right. All farmers and craftsmen (100 percent) were in fact deprived of the right to vote. "Professor Brown's interpretation is not without interest," concludes Cary, "but it was an interpretation for which sufficient proof was lacking."[28]

A number of serious studies (by James Henretta, Alan Kulikoff, and others) showing the existence and intensification of social and property inequality in North America, including Massachusetts, subsequently appeared in the *William and Mary Quarterly* and other American historical journals. Particularly pertinent in this connection is an article by Alan Kulikoff, written from a radical perspective and based on a large volume of factual material, including meticulously verified statistical data. The author established that in 1771, 10 percent of all taxpayers owned approximately two-thirds of all property and held almost all important elective offices in Boston. Boston society did not become less stratified as a result of the Revolution: social inequality in the city actually increased further.[29]

On the whole the political and ideological climate of the stormy 1960s (the dramatic intensification of social antagonisms, the rise of the workers' and black people's movement, the wide scope of the antiwar demonstrations by young people, etc.) contributed to the weakening of the neoconservative consensus, which until recently had occupied a very firm position in American historiography. When the ice of the cold war started melting and a radical change began to take place in the relations between the USSR and the United States, the conservative historians were deprived of arguments in the field of foreign policy as well. What we are now witnessing is not merely criticism of some aspects of the theory of consensus or of errors in certain works by the proponents of "consensus" history, but a crisis of the neoconservative school as a whole.

In a number of cases the consensus theory has ceased to satisfy even those who until recently were among its firmest supporters. The evolution in the views of one of the most eminent American historians, the prematurely deceased Professor Richard Hofstadter (1916–1970) of Columbia University, is revealing. At one time Hofstadter initiated a revision of the history of the United States from the position

28. John Cary, "Statistical Method and the Brown Thesis on Colonial Democracy," *WMQ* 20 (April 1963), 251–76.

29. J. A. Henretta, "Economic Development and Social Structure in Colonial Boston," *WMQ* 22 (January 1965), 75–92; C. W. Roll Jr., "We, Some of the People," *Journal of American History* 56, no. 1 (June 1969), 21–40 (henceforth referred to as *JAH*); Alan Kulikoff, "The Progress of Inequality in Revolutionary Boston," *WMQ* 28 (1971), 375–412.

of the consensus theory, the fundamental principles of which he formulated in the introduction to his book *The American Political Tradition.* He wrote that the most important political tradition in America consisted in the recognition of the "rights of property, the philosophy of economic individualism, the value of competition."[30] And now, twenty years later, under the impact of the serious, one might even say radical, change in the general political situation—the dramatic aggravation of the Negro problem, the unprecedented rise in the student and young people's movement in the United States—the Columbia historian in his new monograph (1968) openly conceded that the consensus theory no longer seemed as satisfactory as ten or fifteen years before. "If we conclude that the American Revolution lacked a true revolutionary character because of the traditionalism of its *ideas,*" stressed Hofstadter, "we may miss a vital point."[31]

By the very title he chose for the final chapter of his study, "Conflict and Consensus in American History," Hofstadter emphasized the inadequacy of the old theory of consensus and recognized the important role of conflicts and antagonisms. And yet he did not completely reject the concept of "consensus" history but merely modified it—not radically revising his previous views but merely attempting to adapt them to new circumstances. While noting the inadequacy of the theory of coordinated interests and underlining the important role of conflicts and violence in U.S. history, he carefully avoided the issue of antagonistic contradictions and the class struggle. This is fully apparent in Hofstadter's introductory article to the collection of documents *American Violence.* "The United States," he wrote, "has thus been able to endure an extraordinary volume of violence without developing a revolutionary tradition, and indeed while maintaining a long record of basic political stability."[32]

The paper Edmund Morgan presented at the above-mentioned symposium in Williamsburg, in which he specifically addressed the issue of "conflict and consensus in the American Revolution," is in this connection also revealing. Understanding that many of the cardinal problems in the struggle of the United States for independence cannot be adequately explained within the framework of the consensus theory, the Yale professor tried to supplement this theory by acknowledging the existence of conflicts, but conflicts that are primarily regional (the West versus the East) or between new and old segments of the ruling class rather than between classes. Morgan above all regarded the movement of the Regulators in the Carolinas, the actions of the "Green Mountain Boys" in Vermont, and Daniel Shays's rebellion in Massachusetts as manifestations of the anger of the western settlers with the policies of governments controlled by the inhabitants of the East Coast.[33] In this way the

30. Richard Hofstadter, *The American Political Tradition and the Men Who Made It* (New York, 1948), viii.

31. Richard Hofstadter, *The Progressive Historians: Turner, Beard, Parrington* (New York, 1968), 459.

32. Richard Hofstadter, "Reflections on Violence in the United States," *American Violence: A Documentary History* (New York, 1970), 10.

33. E. S. Morgan, "Conflict and Consensus in the American Revolution," in Kurtz and Hutson, eds., *Essays on the American Revolution,* 297, 299–300.

existence of class antagonisms is either unjustifiably denied or else concealed. The American Revolution, concludes Morgan, led to consensus among the victors, but this consensus was not "static." American society gave birth not to Charles I and Cromwell but to Hamilton and Jefferson, Hoover and Roosevelt.[34]

In American historiography there have always been many liberal historians whom it is difficult and often indeed impossible to describe as members of a particular movement or school. The increase in their number and the growth of their standing in the late 1960s and early 1970s testify to the progressive weakening of the conservative consensus and reflect the strengthening of liberal and democratic attitudes in contemporary American society. The consolidation of old currents of opinion and the appearance of a number of new ones, whose representatives have resolutely declared their disagreement with the main principles of the "consensus" interpretation of history, are an important indication of the crisis in the neoconservative school. I am primarily referring to the large group of young radicals (the New Left) who in the 1960s embarked on an active struggle against the entire conservative-liberal leadership of the American Historical Association, the reappearance in modified form of old "Progressive" concepts (in the works of Merrill Jensen, Jackson Turner Main, and others) and finally, the emergence of an influential "ideological" or "new intellectual" school (Bernard Bailyn, Gordon Wood, and others).

Professor Jensen, of the University of Wisconsin, was until recently called almost the last representative of the dying "progressive school."[35] It has now become obvious that the traditions of Beard and Jameson live on in American historiography, while Jensen has trained a large and productive group of able disciples. "The American Revolution," he wrote in one of his best-known works, "was far more than a war between the colonies and Great Britain; it was a struggle between those who enjoyed political privileges and those who did not." The War of Independence was largely a democratic movement, and its significance lay in the raising of the political and economic status of the majority of the people of the thirteen colonies. The Articles of Confederation, wrote Jensen, "were the constitutional expression of the philosophy of the Declaration of Independence."[36]

It was Jensen's undoubted achievement to offer a well-argued critique of the notion advanced by the leader of the new conservatives, Robert Brown, that an "idyllic democracy, united in a struggle against British tyranny" had existed in the colonies and above all in Massachusetts. Jensen argued that the American colonies, including Massachusetts, were ruled by relatively small groups of "colonial aristocrats." In most of the colonies appointments to the upper chambers of the legislatures, the supreme courts, and other organs of power were made by the English king. "In short," writes Jensen, "colonial political society was not democratic in operation,

---

34. Ibid., 309.

35. Merrill Jensen, "The American People and the American Revolution," *JAH* 57, no. 1 (June 1970), 9.

36. Merrill Jensen, *The Articles of Confederation: An Interpretation of the Social Constitutional History of the American Revolution, 1774–1781* (Madison, 1940; rev. ed. 1948, 1959), 6–7, 15, 239.

despite the elective lower houses and the self-government which had been won from Great Britain."[37] Thus, for example, in 1760 in Massachusetts the government was dominated by a political machine headed by Thomas Hutchinson, who together with his friends and relatives exercised control over almost all important positions in the colony except the post of governor. Boston's political leaders used every means, from slander to mob violence, to capture control of the government of the colony, but only after the crisis created by the Stamp Act did they win a majority in the house of representatives. In the end Jensen concludes that "the American Revolution was a democratic movement, not in origins but in result"; that is, it only became democratic in the course of the War of Independence, a fact that found its expression in the Articles of Confederation.[38]

I should particularly like to mention Jensen's address of April 16, 1970, to the Organization of American Historians, which he gave as president of that body and which significantly bore the title "The American People and the American Revolution." Using his numerous studies and in particular his recent detailed monograph *The Founding of a Nation* (1968), as well as the works of his pupils (for example, Ronald Hoffman), Jensen adduced a number of important facts relating to the pressure exerted by the "lower orders" and their impact on the development of the events of the Revolution. In effect the scholar expressed his solidarity with the views of the New Left historians (Staughton Lynd, Jesse Lemisch, Alfred Young) on the role of the popular masses in the War of Independence and stressed that most previous studies dealing with the American Revolution in the eighteenth century were "elitist," that is, written from the perspective of its leaders. In Jensen's opinion the colonial aristocrats in the 1760s were forced simultaneously to deal with two challenges: "British policy, and the discontent of their fellow-Americans."[39] As early as 1765 the "lower orders," the mob, the "vulgar herd," etc., had become a constant factor in American political life. The intensity of the class struggle in the country was reflected in the fact that approximately as many troops were used to suppress internal disturbances in Maryland as had been employed in the War of Independence. But on the whole, according to Jensen, as a result of the Revolution the American people "acquired more power and more liberty" than they had before independence, and some of them acquired "a new spirit and a new attitude towards the society in which they lived."[40]

One of Professor Jensen's numerous pupils, Jackson Turner Main, the Director of the Institute for Colonial Studies at State University of New York at Stony Brook,

37. Ibid., 16–53; Jensen, "Democracy and the American Revolution," *Huntington Library Quarterly* 20 (August 1957), 321–41, quotation on 323 (henceforth referred to as *HLQ*).

38. Jensen, "Democracy and the American Revolution," 341; Merrill Jensen, "Historians and the Nature of the American Revolution," in R. A. Billington, ed., *The Reinterpretation of Early American History* (San Marino, Calif., 1966), 101–227.

39. Merrill Jensen, *The Founding of a Nation: A History of the American Revolution, 1763–1776* (New York, 1968), 32. For Jensen's book see also the reviews by W. W. Abbot and John A. Schutz in *WMQ* 27 (January 1970), 148–50, and *JAH* 56, no. 1 (June 1969), 124–26.

40. Jensen, "The American People and the American Revolution," 15, 32, 35.

has published four major monographs in the last ten years alone and has gained a solid reputation as one of the leading authorities on the American Revolution.[41] His book on the class structure of American society in the colonial age is of considerable interest. Although Main's definition of class is not a Marxist one (the most important criterion for him is property), his study of class differentiation in the United States has led to interesting results in a number of cases. Arguing against the neoconservative historians (Brown, Morgan, etc.) the author concludes that in American society there existed a "lower class" that embraced between one-third and two-thirds of the country's male population. Main includes in this class Negro slaves, white servants, landless farm laborers, and other persons who owned property in the value of less than £50. He does not include craftsmen, "free workers," and tenant farmers in the lower class, although he concedes that "many tenant farmers were also poor and in all probability about 30 percent of skilled craftsmen, particularly many weavers, cobblers, masons, and tailors left only very small estates after their death."[42] On the other hand, the "upper class," in which Main includes persons owning property in the value of between £2,000 and £4,000 (big landowners, rich merchants, jurists, etc.), made up about 10 percent of the white male population and controlled 45 percent of the country's national wealth.[43]

One cannot always agree with Main's conclusions, let alone with the general methodological principles he employed in his study. But the very fact that an eminent American historian has undertaken an analysis of the class differentiation of the population is highly symbolic. Let us recall that even recently the neoconservatives were still writing about the complete supremacy of "middle class democracy" in colonial America.

In another major study by Main, *The Upper House in Revolutionary America, 1763–1788,* which is dedicated to Jensen, the author, analyzing the composition of the upper chambers, described a "tendency towards democratization."[44] Even earlier, in an article published in the *William and Mary Quarterly,* Main used statistical data to trace changes in the composition of the lower houses and concluded that in the course of the American Revolution a tendency emerged for persons of "lower socio-economic status" to be elected to the state legislatures. In this connection a complaint voiced in one of the Boston newspapers is revealing. Starting in 1786 the states, declared the complainant, were "worse governed" than before; "men of sense and property," he said, "have lost most of their influence by the popular spirit of the war." Although previously the people had respected the governors, clergy, and judges and had obeyed them, since the war "blustering men, who started into notice during the

41. J. T. Main, *The Antifederalists: Critics of the Constitution, 1781–1788* (Chapel Hill, 1961); Main, *The Social Structure of Revolutionary America, 1763–1788* (Princeton, 1965); Main, *The Upper House in Revolutionary America* (Madison, 1967); Main, *Political Parties before the Constitution* (Chapel Hill, 1973).
42. Main, *Social Structure,* 272.
43. Ibid., 276.
44. Main, *Upper House,* 99.

troubles and confusion of that critical period, have been attempting to push themselves into office."[45]

Behind the class hostility of an obscure New England resident toward "ignorant men" from the lower classes one may clearly see glimpses of the social changes that took place during the American Revolution. This subject was the topic of special discussion at one of the panels at the annual meeting of the Organization of American Historians in April 1973 in Chicago.[46] As we have already seen, the "Progressive" traditions of Carl Becker and Charles Beard not only survive but have been further developed by contemporary American historians and in some cases have undergone modification. Thus, for example, it may appear that by undertaking a study of the history of colonial New York Patricia Bonomi was directly following the tradition of Carl Becker who had studied New York. And yet the conclusions the young historian draws differ significantly from the model proposed by her eminent predecessor. Analyzing the intense political struggle in New York, Bonomi concludes that what was at stake was not "which class would rule," as Becker once thought, but merely which "factions" and subsequently "parties" would later form part of "a stable and continuing order."[47] In this case the theory of consensus is not broadened by the inclusion of conflicts and antagonisms, but rather the "Progressive" concepts of Becker and Beard are being supplemented on the basis of the fashionable idea of consensus.

The strongest positions at present are held by the old "imperial school" represented by followers of Charles M. Andrews, such as Leonard Labaree, Lawrence Gipson, and others. For several decades Gipson has been working on a multivolume history of the British empire on the eve of the American Revolution, but unfortunately only a few scholars have found the time for a close study of the whole of this work. As early as 1954 Gipson, unwilling to rely on the modern reader's laboring through his large work, brought out a general synoptic book that contained a relatively concise statement of his views.[48] In accordance with the traditions of the "imperial school," Gipson regarded the British possessions as a whole and found weighty reasons to justify the actions of the government of the mother country, which was guided by the idea of creating a "self-sustaining empire." At the same time, like Andrews, he devoted much attention to the American "environment" in which the settlers found themselves and saw it as the cause that led to the development in the colonies of local interests distinct from those of England.[49]

45. J. T. Main, "Government by the People: The American Revolution and the Democratization of the Legislature," *WMQ* 23, no. 3 (July 1966), 391–407.

46. "Political and Social Change during the American Revolution," Organization of American Historians, Program, 1973. Among the papers presented at this panel, let us note in particular the one by Ronald Hoffman (University of Maryland), "Popularizing the Revolution: Internal Conflict and Economic Sacrifice in Maryland, 1774–1780," 26.

47. Patricia U. Bonomi, *A Factious People: Politics and Society in Colonial New York* (New York, 1971), 286.

48. L. H. Gipson, *The British Empire before the American Revolution,* 15 vols. (Caldwell, Idaho-New York, 1936–1969); Gipson, *The Coming of the Revolution, 1763–1775* (New York, 1954).

49. J. P. Greene, ed., *The Reinterpretation of the American Revolution, 1763–1789* (New York, 1968), 7.

In addition to the old "imperial school," a group of young scholars (Thomas Barrow, Michael Kammen, John Shy, and others) have introduced certain corrections and modifications into the Andrews-Gipson model. Professor Kammen of Cornell University has published two monographs on the internal factors determining the policy of England on the eve of the American Revolution.[50] If Gipson sees the American Revolution as the result of the "great war for empire of 1759–1763," Kammen argues that the political problems that became apparent after 1763 were linked to the "economic and social changes which occurred so rapidly after 1748."[51]

The works of Professor Barrow of Clark University, the author of a study of the British customs service in colonial America, are revealing.[52] It was not, however, his book *Trade and Empire* that won the scholar wide renown, but his article in the *William and Mary Quarterly*, "The American Revolution as a Colonial War of Independence." Editors of collections of historiographical articles hastened to include this article in their new anthologies on the American Revolution and thus guaranteed the relatively young scholar (born in 1929) additional publicity.[53] In Barrow's opinion, the comparisons American scholars drew between the U.S. War of Independence and the classic revolutions of the French or Russian type led them to a distorted understanding of the initial stage in the development of the United States. If comparisons are to be made, the American Revolution should be compared to the revolutions in the colonial and developing countries in the twentieth century. "The French Revolution," the author stressed, "is first of all destructive; a colonial revolution, first of all, constructive." The aim of the colonial revolution lies "in the achievement of self-determination," "in the fulfillment of an already existing society, rather than its destruction."[54]

The political significance of this concept (with its patent distortion of the character of the French Revolution) is clear. The American Revolution is being put forward as a "model" and an "example" for the developing countries of Asia, Africa, and

50. M. G. Kammen, *A Rope of Sand: The Colonial Agents, British Politics and the American Revolution* (Ithaca, 1968); Kammen, *Empire and Interest: The American Colonies and the Politics of Mercantilism* (Philadelphia, 1970).

51. L. H. Gipson, "The American Revolution as an Aftermath of the Great War for Empire, 1754–1763," *Political Science Quarterly* 65 (March 1950), 86–104; D. L. Jacobson, ed., *Essays on the American Revolution* (New York, 1970), 69–81; Kammen, *Empire and Interest,* 172. In addition to Gipson, a strong influence on the formation of Kammen's views was exercised by Bernard Bailyn and also by the well-known English historian Lewis Namier (1888–1960). American historiographers have also discerned the influence of the "atomistic picture" of British policy in the works of Kammen, Thomas Barrow, John Shy, and others. Billias and Grob, eds., *American History: Retrospect and Prospect,* 83. For more on the Namier school see N. A. Erofeev, "L. Namier and His Place in Bourgeois Historiography," *Problems of History* 4 (1973), 76–89.

52. T. G. Barrow, *Trade and Empire: The British Custom Service in Colonial America, 1660–1775* (Cambridge, Mass., 1967).

53. T. G. Barrow, "The American Revolution as a Colonial War for Independence," *WMQ* 25, no. 3 (July 1968), 452–64; G. A. Billias, ed., *The American Revolution: How Revolutionary Was It?* 2d ed. (New York, 1970); Berkhofer, ed., *The American Revolution: The Critical Issues.*

54. Barrow, "The American Revolution as a Colonial War for Independence," 462–64.

Latin America,[55] leading to the obvious confusion of completely different eras and national traditions. And if in the eighteenth century the War of Independence truly sounded the tocsin for the European bourgeoisie, the United States today, torn as it is by internal contradictions and racial conflicts, has long ceased to be an example to revolutionary peoples. Proof of this fact is the support extended by the United States to reactionary regimes, its imperialist intervention in a number of countries, and its economic enslavement of them.

When speaking of the newest tendencies in the historiography of the United States, it is necessary to mention also the nature of the "ideological interpretation" of the American Revolution contained in the numerous works by Bailyn and his pupils. If Boorstin and some other neoconservative authors altogether deny that the ideas of the eighteenth-century European Enlightenment seriously influenced the American colonists in any way, Bailyn and other representatives of the modern "intellectual" or "ideological" school devote their main attention to the formation of revolutionary ideology and see its sources primarily in the old traditions of radical thought in Great Britain.

The founder of the modern "intellectual" school was Morgan. Even quite recently (the 1950s) Morgan was still regarded as perhaps the most important representative of the neoconservative tendency among scholars of the American Revolution; his book *The Birth of the Republic* and his study of the Stamp Act, written with Helen Morgan, were written precisely from this position.[56] Extensive knowledge both of the period of the War of Independence and the history of the early American settlements (Morgan is the author of several studies of the Puritans and of biographies of John Winthrop, Ezra Stiles, and others) led him to conclude that the Revolution caused a fundamental change in the intellectual climate: religion was replaced by politics. "In 1740 America's leading intellectuals," writes Morgan, "were clergymen and they thought about theology; in 1790 they were statesmen and thought about politics."[57] Using concrete historical material, the author shows that during the Revolution religious doctrines were replaced by notions of natural right and equality, while in social life political argumentation came to play the leading role.

Caroline Robbins has made the ideological roots of the American Revolution the object of extensive study.[58] She meticulously traced the development of English

55. R. B. Morris, *The Emerging Nations and the American Revolution* (New York, 1970), ix-x, 222–23.

56. E. S. Morgan and H. M. Morgan, *The Stamp Act Crisis: Prologue to Revolution* (Chapel Hill, 1953, 1963); E. S. Morgan, *The Birth of the Republic, 1763–1789* (Chicago, 1956).

57. E. S. Morgan, "The American Revolution Considered as an Intellectual Movement," *Paths of American Thought,* ed. A. M. Schlesinger Jr. and M. M. White (New York, 1963), 11; D. L. Jacobson, ed., *Essays on the American Revolution,* 28.

58. Caroline Robbins, *The Eighteenth-Century Commonwealthman* (Cambridge, Mass., 1959). The European roots of republicanism were traced by Robbins in the paper she presented at the first symposium on the American Revolution held by the Library of Congress in 1972. Robbins, "European Republicanism in the Century and a Half before 1776," *Development of a Revolutionary Mentality,* 31–55.

radical thought that, as Bailyn subsequently showed, had a direct bearing on the American Revolution. This connection did not escape Robbins either. She noted that the activities of the "Real Whigs" preserved the revolutionary tradition and served as a link between the struggle against tyranny in seventeenth-century England and the Americans' struggle for independence in the eighteenth century.

Bailyn's latest works, particularly his book on the ideological origins of the Revolution, which won the Pulitzer and Bancroft prizes,[59] were decisively important in forming the modern "ideological interpretation" of the American Revolution. Unlike the neoconservatives, Bailyn not only does not deny the revolutionary significance of the U.S. War of Independence but indeed stresses it, though he sees this significance as mainly lying in the realm of ideas. In his view, "the American Revolution was above all else an ideological, constitutional, and political struggle, and not primarily a controversy between social groups undertaken to force changes in the organization of society or the economy." Ideas and the experience of the preceding 150 years gave the American Revolution its "peculiar force and made it so profoundly a transforming event."[60]

While not denying the well-known social changes that took place during the War of Independence, Bailyn emphasizes that the Revolution was not the product of dissatisfaction with the "structure of society" but rather an attempt "to preserve a free way of life" from the encroachments of the mother country.[61] In the course of the Revolution, he argues, ideas and principles that were already forming became fully crystallized. Following John Adams, he stresses that the Revolution occurred "in the Minds and the Hearts of People."[62]

Bailyn's views differ from those of the neoconservatives, but in many instances this difference is not one of principle. The inner contradictoriness in the views of the Harvard professor was fully manifested in the paper he presented at the first colloquium of Soviet and American historians in Moscow in October 1972. While not denying in principle the existence of an *ancien régime* in America, Bailyn devoted his entire attention not to an analysis of the elements of feudalism but only to the development in the colonies of a "unique way of life" that differed radically from the one in Europe.[63] Thus, having in effect begun by arguing against Hartz, Bailyn in

---

59. Bernard Bailyn, *The Ideological Origins of the American Revolution* (Cambridge, Mass., 1967). This book is a somewhat altered version of Bailyn's introduction to the first volume of *Pamphlets of the American Revolution,* ed. Bernard Bailyn (Cambridge, Mass., 1965). Somewhat later Bailyn published his lectures at Brown University as a small book, *The Origins of American Politics* (New York, 1968).

60. Bailyn, *Ideological Origins,* vi-vii; Bailyn, "Political Experience and Enlightenment Ideas in Eighteenth-Century America," *AHR* 67, no. 2 (January 1962), 339–51.

61. J. A. Garraty, *Interpreting American History, Conversations with Historians* (New York, 1970), pt. 1, 82. For a critique of R. E. Brown's thesis of the existence of a "middle-class democracy" in the colonies as an anachronism, see ibid., 85–86; Bailyn, "Political Experience," 346–47.

62. John Adams to H. Niles, February 13, 1818, in *An American Primer,* ed. Daniel Boorstin (Chicago, 1968), 248–49.

63. Bernard Bailyn, "A Study of the Historical Importance of American Towns in the 18th Century" (Moscow, 1972, rotaprint), 4, 12, and others.

the main part of his paper agreed with Hartz's views by continuing to adhere to the erroneous notion of American exclusiveness.

Bailyn's views were expanded upon in a monograph written by his pupil Gordon Wood. Initially, Wood expressed some doubt as to whether a "purely intellectual interpretation" could successfully supplant the socioeconomic approach of the "Progressive" generation,[64] but later, when working on his monograph *The Creation of the American Republic, 1776–1787,* he mainly concentrated on the dramatic change in American political thinking that occurred in the course of the Revolution. As a result of the Revolution, the Americans created not only "new forms of government but an entirely new conception of politics."[65] In Wood's view, "the ideology of republicanism" radically transformed American society.[66]

Bailyn's school today occupies the leading position in the study of the American Revolution. It is therefore not surprising that the first symposium on the American Revolution, which was conducted May 5–6, 1972, by the Library of Congress, was specifically devoted to the formation of revolutionary ideology and that Bailyn's young pupils Pauline Maier and Mary Beth Norton presented papers at this meeting.[67] The first day of the symposium at the Library of Congress in May 1973 was devoted to a discussion of Bailyn's paper on Thomas Paine's pamphlet *Common Sense* and Cecelia Kenyon's paper on the Declaration of Independence.[68] As is known, Marxist scholars do not deny the important role of ideas and revolutionary ideology in eighteenth-century America. It is agreed that the traditions of the "Real Whigs" in England are of great importance for the understanding of the American Revolution. Of course, not all colonists spent their evenings reading Francis Hutcheson's *System of Moral Philosophy,* but some did. Others learned about revolutionary ideas from their local newspapers. In any case, the writings of the "Real Whigs" helped the colonists to understand the events taking place and provided "a logical thrust towards revolution and independence."[69] While correctly noting the liberal character of Locke's ideas, which were espoused by the leaders of the American Revolution, Bailyn and his pupils studiously try to obscure the difference between the "liberalism" of the elite and the "radicalism" of the lower classes. And yet such a difference did exist in America. Here reference can be made to an early article by Jesse Lemisch published in

64. Gordon S. Wood, "Rhetoric and Reality in the American Revolution," *WMQ* 23, no. 1 (January 1966), 3–32; F. O. Gatell and A. Weinstein, eds., *American Themes: Essays in Historiography,* 55–80.

65. Gordon S. Wood, *The Creation of the American Republic, 1776–1787* (Chapel Hill, 1969), v, viii, 594–615.

66. Gordon S. Wood, "Republicanism as a Revolutionary Ideology," in *The Role of Ideology in the American Revolution,* ed. J. R. Howe Jr. (New York, 1970), 91.

67. Pauline R. Maier, "The Beginnings of American Republicanism 1765–1776," *Development of a Revolutionary Mentality,* 99–117; M. B. Norton, "The Loyalist Critique of the Revolution," ibid., 127–48.

68. "Symposia on the American Revolution," Program, Organization of American Historians, May 10, 1973; see also Paul H. Smith, ed., *English Defenders of American Freedoms, 1774–1778* (Washington, D.C., 1972).

69. Pauline R. Maier, *From Resistance to Revolution: Colonial Radicals and the Development of American Opposition to Britain, 1765–1776* (New York, 1972), xiv-xv, 27–48.

October 1965 in the journal of the New York Historical Society.[70] A bitter ideological struggle between avowed conservatives and supporters of the Revolution took place,[71] although on the whole political thought in eighteenth-century America was clearly dominated by the liberal tradition of Locke, a fact that left its imprint on the entire subsequent development of the United States.[72] As R. R. Palmer observed, it was not the strength but the weakness of the conservative forces that explains the moderate character of the American Revolution in the eighteenth century.[73]

Any picture of contemporary American historiography would be incomplete if it did not take into account the writers of the "new economic history" or the cliometricians, who widely use quantitative measurements, mathematical statistics, and various theoretical models. The cliometricians are especially known for their revision of traditional ideas about the unprofitability of plantation slavery, the decisive role of the railroads in the economic development of the United States in the nineteenth century, the importance of the Civil War of 1861–1865 in accelerating industrial development of the country, etc.[74] While stressing in every way possible the significance of the purely "quantitative" method, the cliometricians frequently lose sight of the fundamental social aspects of historical development. This becomes particularly clear in their revision of the role of the Civil War in the industrialization of the United States. It is true that from a purely statistical point of view the American people suffered considerable destruction and distress as a result of the Civil War of 1861–1865. In the 1860s the rate of industrial development was much lower than in the 1840s or 1880s. But does this mean, as Thomas Cochran has argued, that the Civil War actually slowed down the industrialization of the United States?[75] It would seem that in this case what was decisively important was not the quantitative but the qualitative side of things—the social results and consequences of the radical reforms carried out during the Civil War (the abolition of slavery, the adoption of the law regarding homesteads, etc.). In his "Letter to the American Workers" V. I. Lenin wrote: "In 1870 America, if one is to consider just the 'destruction' of some branches

70. J. Lemisch, "New York Petitions and Resolves of December 1765: Liberals vs. Radicals," *New York Historical Society Quarterly* 49, no. 4 (October 1965), 313–26.

71. S. Bernstein, "The Subject of Revolution in Post-Revolutionary America," *Studien über die Revolution,* ed. Manfred Kossok, 2. Aufl. (Berlin, 1971), S. 177–97.

72. A. Guttmann, *The Conservative Tradition in America* (New York, 1967), 3–4.

73. R. R. Palmer, *The Age of Democratic Revolution* (Princeton, 1959; repr. 1971), vol. 1, 189.

74. See *Modern and Contemporary History* 6 (1969). Among the latest American surveys, let us mention the article by T. C. Cochran, "Economic History, Old and New," *AHR* 74, no. 4 (June 1969), and also the new synoptic book edited by R. Fogel and S. Engerman in which all the major works by representatives of the school of "new economic history" are included: *The Reinterpretation of American Economic History* (New York, 1971). Ralph L. Adreano, ed., *The New Economic History: Recent Papers on Methodology* (New York, 1970), includes several methodological articles by cliometricians. For a critical analysis of these works, see also V. G. Nokhotovich, " 'New Economic History' and Problems of the Industrial Development of the United States," *American Annual, 1973* (Moscow, 1973), 186–207.

75. T. C. Cochran, "Did the Civil War Retard Industrialization?" *The Mississippi Valley Historical Review* 48, no. 2 (September 1961), 205.

of industry and the national economy, had fallen behind the level of 1860. But what a pedant, what an idiot, one would have to be to deny on this basis the tremendous, world-important, progressive and revolutionary significance of the American civil war of 1863 [sic]-1865!"[76] Lenin's words demonstrate the theoretical unsoundness of the "newest" discoveries regarding the Civil War made by cliometricians in the United States. This can be of some methodological importance when discussing the writings of the school of "new economic history" on the period of the American Revolution in the eighteenth century.

In 1930 the belief that the American Revolution freed the colonists of the "fetters of the English Mercantilist System" gained wide currency in U.S. publications.[77] In his calculation of the cost to the Americans of the mother country's Navigation Acts, Lawrence Harper estimated that the damage inflicted on the colonies was between $2.5 million and $7 million, and concluded that British legislation in the area of transatlantic trade placed a "heavy burden" on the colonies.[78] Curtis Nettels described British policy toward the colonies after 1763 as restrictive, injurious, and unfair.[79] Relatively recently, Robert Thomas, a young economic historian at Washington University, published an article in which he showed on the basis of the most intricate statistical analysis that the damage suffered by the colonies as a result of the Navigation Acts was altogether insignificant. According to his calculations, in 1763–1772 that damage totalled $2,255,000, or $1.20 per person. At the same time, the benefits derived by the colonists from the protection the British navy gave their trade equaled $1,775,000, or 94 cents per capita in monetary terms. In Thomas's opinion, a difference of 26 cents cannot serve as a basis for arguing that the colonies were exploited by England.[80]

Guided by Thomas's conclusions, as well as by those drawn by some other scholars, one of the leaders of the cliometricians, Douglas North, has in effect denied that the American Revolution was the product of economic laws and has questioned the benefits derived by the colonists as a result of the War of Independence. In his critical

76. Lenin, *Complete Collected Works,* vol. 37, 58.

77. L. H. Hacker et al., *The United States: A Graphic History* (New York, 1937), 28.

78. L. A. Harper, "The Effect of the Navigation Acts on Thirteen Colonies," in R. B. Morris, ed., *Era of the American Revolution* (New York, 1939), 3–39; Harper, "Mercantilism and the American Revolution," in Grob and Billias, eds., *Interpretations of American History: Patterns and Perspectives,* vol. 1, 108.

79. C. P. Nettels, "British Mercantilism and Economic Development of the Thirteen Colonies," *Journal of Economic History* 12, no. 2 (Spring 1952), 114 (henceforth referred to as *JEH*).

80. R. P. Thomas, "A Quantitative Approach to the Study of the Effects of British Imperial Policy upon Colonial Welfare: Some Preliminary Findings," *JEH* 25, no. 4 (December 1965), 615–38. Like many other "most recent" discoveries by the cliometricians, Thomas's conclusions in many ways duplicate ideas that were already known and that had been explored, for example, in the works of the "imperial" school. At the turn of the century G. L. Beer was already developing a detailed "pro-English" interpretation of the system of mercantilism, according to which the advantages and disadvantages were distributed equally between the mother country and the colonies, and in our own day the same was done by L. H. Gipson. See Gipson, *The Coming of the Revolution,* xi–xiv; Grob and Billias, eds., *Interpretations of American History: Patterns and Perspectives,* 88–90, 94–95.

analysis of the above-mentioned study by Harper, North is inclined to conclude that the extent of the damage inflicted by British policy on the American colonies must be "dramatically reduced." In the late 1780s export revenues were no higher than in 1770–1773, while the level of prosperity in the independent United States in the "critical period" was at best the same as that enjoyed by the colonists immediately before the Revolution.[81]

Many of the arguments the cliometricians put forward are correct. Having won independence, the colonists not only freed themselves of their onerous obligations toward the mother country but also lost the advantages of membership in the British imperial system, which had guaranteed them military protection and a large, protected market. But when applied to the period of wars and revolutions, pure quantitative analysis clearly shows its profound flaws. The cliometricians do not take into account what is most important—the basic social and political factors that exerted a durable influence on the entire subsequent development of the country. The War of Independence not only severed the links to the mother country but also led to major socioeconomic reforms within the United States; it not only destroyed but also created and, most importantly, it laid a firm foundation for future construction. It would be difficult to measure this construction statistically, yet if it is not taken into account, the picture is distorted.

It is obvious that quantitative analysis must be used skillfully. When the task has been correctly formulated and quantitative analysis is used in combination with other methods of socioeconomic analysis, it can give excellent results. Although we sometimes criticize the cliometricians' methodology, we cannot doubt the achievements and the potential of this powerful method. We should not adopt a negative attitude toward specific conclusions drawn by cliometric historians if they were made on the basis of reliable statistical material and by means of an impeccable research technique. By employing the methods of socioeconomic analysis and introducing into scholarly use new kinds of sources (certificates of birth, marriage, and death, wills, data regarding births and deaths, tax statistics, and information pertaining to land holdings), historians can learn much more about the life of the society as a whole—not only about its upper stratum but also about the main part of the "iceberg" that is hidden underwater and that earlier escaped their attention.[82] James Henretta provides an example of how this research technique can be applied to the historical period prior to the American Revolution. Making a subtle economic and mathematical analysis of the lists of Boston taxpayers for 1687 and 1771, Henretta concluded that social inequality among the colonists was increasing. In particular, he discovered that the have-nots amounted to 14 percent of the adult male population in 1687 and 79 percent in 1771.[83]

81. D. C. North, *Growth and Welfare in the American Past: A New Economic History* (Englewood Cliffs, N.J., 1966), 49; G. C. Bjork, "The Weaning of the American Economy: Independence, Market Changes and Economic Development," *JEH* 24, no. 4 (December 1964), 541–60.

82. G. B. Nash, *Class and Society in Early America* (Englewood Cliffs, N.J., 1970), 13.

83. Henretta, "Economic Development and Social Structure in Colonial Boston," 85; Fogel and Engerman, eds., *Reinterpretation of American Economic History,* 54–63. Using material pertaining

The most convincing evidence of the crisis in "consensus" history is the appearance and rapid growth in the last decade of a school of young radical scholars—the New Left.[84] Although the methodology of the New Left historians clearly suffers from eclecticism and their conclusions are often distinguished by excessive simplicity, the ablest representatives of this school—Staughton Lynd, Jesse Lemisch, Alfred Young, and others—have made a noticeable contribution to the study of the American Revolution.

Lynd's book *Class Conflict, Slavery, and the United States Constitution* comprises all his major scholarly articles, which earlier had appeared in various historical journals. Lynd adopts a critical approach not only to his predecessors but also to his own work. He admits that initially he had uncritically followed Becker, Turner, and Beard. If he corroborated Becker's conception in the history of the tenants' struggle in Dutchess County, in neighboring Albany County, where the land was owned by the pro-independence Livingstons, he found that the tenants in 1777 became Loyalists and supported the British troops advancing from Canada.[85] In the course of studying documentary materials, Lynd became convinced that in the debates that took place during the drawing-up of the Constitution of 1787 the main issue concerned slavery, whereas Beard and Turner had ignored this important problem. The ruling camp in the Revolution, notes Lynd, was not united. It consisted of northern capitalists and planters from the South. The Constitution of 1787 did not represent a victory by one section of the ruling circles over the other but instead amounted to a compromise between the two.[86] Beard had ignored the possibility that the Constitution was simultaneously an "economic document" and a republican manifesto.[87]

As a result of their broad approach to these events, Lynd and Alfred Young were able to understand the complex changes in the position of the New York craftsmen from 1774 to 1801 and to explain the apparent paradox of the resolute support the "mechanics" of New York gave to the Constitution of 1787 and to such conservative figures as Robert Livingston, John Jay, and James Duane: "A characteristic feature of the political demands of the mechanics during the entire period 1774–1788 was the fact that they combined a concern for democracy with uncompromising support

---

to the period of the Revolution, Alan Kulikoff in his study further developed Henretta's conclusions. Kulikoff, "Progress of Inequality."

84. For more see *Political Affairs* (August-September 1968); B. J. Bernstein, ed., *Towards a New Past: Dissenting Essays in American History* (New York, 1968); I. Unger, ed., *Beyond Liberalism: The New Left Views American History* (Waltham, 1971); see also R. E. Kantor, " 'The New Left' in the American Historical Association," *Problems of History* 9 (1971), 181–91; S. S. Salychev, *"The New Left": With Whom and Against Whom* (Moscow, 1972).

85. Staughton Lynd, "Who Should Rule at Home? Dutchess County, New York, in the American Revolution," *WMQ* 18, no. 3 (July 1961), 330–59; Lynd, *Class Conflict, Slavery and the United States Constitution: Ten Essays* (Indianapolis, 1967), 8, 25–62, 63–78.

86. Lynd, *Class Conflict*, 11, 14, 185–213.

87. Staughton Lynd, "Capitalism, Democracy and the United States Constitution: The Case of New York," *Science and Society* 28, no. 4 (Fall 1963), 386.

for the policy of endowing the central government with the authority necessary for prosecuting the struggle with the British."[88]

Today Lynd's interests have shifted to the 1930s, and he has begun to take an active part in the political struggle waged by contemporary American radicals. His latest major work relating to the history of the eighteenth century is his monograph on the intellectual roots of American radicalism. In this book Lynd devoted his main attention to the Declaration of Independence, which for almost two hundred years has served as a source of inspiration for democratic and revolutionary movements both in the United States and abroad. This document was cited by the nineteenth-century abolitionists, and by prominent figures in the American labor movement such as Eugene Debs, Daniel de Leon, William Z. Foster, and many others. Lynd notes that the young American radicals of today, who refuse to surrender the heritage of the Revolution to "liberalism and reaction" and insist that "only radicalism could make real the rhetoric of 1776," also trace their intellectual origins to the Declaration of Independence.[89]

Another radical scholar active in the study of the Revolutionary period in American history is Jesse Lemisch. Although this young scholar (he was born in 1936) has yet to produce a monograph (Lemisch's doctoral dissertation on the role of New York seamen on the eve of the War of Independence did not see the light of day),[90] the original articles he has published have made an important contribution to the historiography of the American Revolution in the eighteenth century. In particular, his study "The American Revolution Seen from the Bottom Up," which is devoted to the part played by the popular masses during the struggle of the United States for independence, is of major importance. The young scholar accuses his predecessors and colleagues, and not unjustly, of looking at the American Revolution only from the perspective of the elite. "The history of the powerless, the inarticulate, the poor has not begun to be written because they have been treated no more fairly by historians than they have been treated by their contemporaries," concludes the scholar.[91] The "elitist" historians were unreceptive to the issues that agitated the "inarticulate" lower classes above all others. They ignored the press-ganging of American sailors into the British navy. Nor was this problem reflected in the documents of the leaders of the "upper classes,"

88. Staughton Lynd and Alfred Young, "After Carl Becker: The Mechanics and New York City Politics, 1774–1801," *Labor History* 5, no. 3 (Fall 1965), 243–45. Alfred Young's study *The Democratic Republicans of New York: The Origins 1763–1797* (Chapel Hill, 1967) deserves particular attention. At present this scholar is preparing a new study dedicated to the history of the "lower classes" in early America.

89. Staughton Lynd, *Intellectual Origins of American Radicalism* (London, 1969), 7. For a shorter version see this anthology: Alfred Young, ed., *Dissent: Exploration in the History of American Radicalism* (Dekalb, Ill., 1968).

90. Jesse Lemisch, "Jack Tar vs. John Bull: The Role of New York's Seamen in Precipitating the Revolution" (Ph.D. diss., Yale University, 1962).

91. Jesse Lemisch, "The American Revolution Seen from the Bottom Up," in Bernstein, ed., *Towards a New Past,* 29.

since it was of little concern to them personally. And yet between twenty thousand and thirty thousand American sailors were imprisoned in English jails. Little was known about these "inarticulate" patriots. But during the War of Independence men such as William Widger took the side of the insurgents. "The nationalism of the seamen was as authentic as the nationalism of a Jefferson, an Adams, or a Franklin; in this sense the Revolution happened from the bottom up as well as from the top down."[92]

Of course not everyone among the "inarticulate" and the unfortunate necessarily turned out to be a patriot and a revolutionary. The opponents of the New Left historians immediately drew attention to this, and one of them, James Hutson, published an article in which he argued that prior to the War of Independence the mood of the ship carpenters of Philadelphia, the so called "White Oaks," was quite conservative.[93] Replying to him, Lemisch and John Alexander stressed that every group among the "inarticulate" must become the subject of special research. "We need studies of all kinds of groups: radical seamen as well as conservative ship carpenters."[94] The latter group, as was pointed out by one of the participants in the journal discussion, probably belonged to the most privileged segment of American craftsmen.[95]

Developing the concept of the "inarticulate," Lemisch observed that in the past American historians have "too often chosen to conclude that their inability to hear means that people were actually inarticulate."[96] And yet, as Lemisch has shown with his own works, the "inarticulate" can be heard if their participation in the events of the Revolution is traced not only in word but also in concrete deed.[97] The voice of the "inarticulate" was clearly heard during open demonstrations by the people, town meetings, street processions, and other actions by Revolutionary "mobs." The discovery of the "mob" as an important element in American political life promises to exert major influence on the interpretation of historical events. It is therefore no accident that this topic has become the subject of special attention and heated discussion.[98]

92. Jesse Lemisch, "Listening to the 'Inarticulate': William Widger's Dream and the Loyalties of American Revolutionary Seamen in British Prisons," *Journal of Social History* 3, no. 1 (Fall 1969), 7, 28.

93. J. H. Hutson, "An Investigation of the Inarticulate: Philadelphia's White Oaks," *WMQ* 28, no. 1 (January 1971), 3–25.

94. Jesse Lemisch and J. K. Alexander, "The White Oaks, Jack Tar and the Concept of the 'Inarticulate,' " *WMQ* 29, no. 1 (January 1972), 109.

95. S. J. Crowthart, "A Note on the Economic Position of Philadelphia's White Oaks," *WMQ* 29, no. 1 (January 1972), 134–36; James H. Hutson's Rebuttal, ibid., 136–42.

96. For the concept of the "inarticulate" see *WMQ* 29 (January 1972), 129–34.

97. See in particular Jesse Lemisch, "Jack Tar in the Streets: Merchant Seamen in the Politics of Revolutionary America," *WMQ* 25 (July 1968), 371–407.

98. Gordon S. Wood, "A Note on Mobs in the American Revolution," *WMQ* 23 (1966), 633–42; Wood, *The Creation of the American Republic,* 319–28; Pauline R. Maier, "Popular Uprisings and Civil Authority in Eighteenth-Century America," *WMQ* 27, no. 1 (January 1970), 3–35; T. R. Frazier, ed., *Underside of American History* (New York, 1971), vol. 1, 73–100. George Rudé, Jesse Lemisch, Pauline Maier, David Grimstead, and Leonard Richards were the official discussants of the role of the "mob" in American history. Program, Organization of American Historians, 1973, 46.

While justly noting the need for a comprehensive study of the role of the popular masses in the War of Independence, Lemisch and other New Left critics forget to mention the achievements of their predecessors and, above all, those of American Marxist historians. Nor are the latter's works always taken into consideration in the writings of Soviet Americanists, as they should be. As a result, many studies are presented to the reader as the "first" discussion of, or the "first" Marxist statement about, this or that question of American history. And yet Marxist historiography in the United States has existed and developed successfully for many decades. As early as 1937 Jack Hardy published a book in which he attempted to give a general Marxist interpretation of the U.S. War of Independence as a bourgeois revolution. The importance of this work consisted "not so much in the material offered as in the way that material has been presented."[99] And though today's reader will find certain omissions and shortcomings in Hardy's book, the importance of this work in formulating the Marxist concept of the American Revolution should not be underestimated.

One must emphasize that it is American Marxist historians who largely deserve the credit for raising the issue of the role of the urban and rural lower classes in the Revolution, as well as for undertaking a concrete study of the labor, Negro, and farmers' movements in the United States (see the well-known works of Herbert Aptheker, H. Morais, A. Rochester, W. Z. Foster, Philip Foner, and others). In the foreword to his fundamental history of the labor movement in the United States, Philip Foner stresses that "out of the working class have come great heroes and heroines" who made a notable contribution to the development of democracy. Their lives, however, "remained out of the history that has been handed down to us." The urban lower classes were very active during the early stage of the revolutionary movement against the mother country. They made up "the bulk and formed the backbone of the great street demonstrations of the day, and in addition furnished the forces necessary to circulate petitions, distribute handbills, fight British troops, and dump tea into the harbours."[100] In his overall evaluation of the War of Independence, Foster described it as a bourgeois revolution "in which the democratic element was very strong."[101]

The achievements of Marxist-Leninist historiography are vividly reflected in Herbert Aptheker's synoptic book. The Revolution in America, the author believes, was the result of the interaction of three trends: "A fundamental clash of interests between the ruling circles of the colonial power and the vast majority of the population of the colonies; class stratification in the colonies themselves and the class battles engendered by it . . . [;] the developing feeling of American nationhood." The universal significance and impact of the War of Independence on contemporaries, notes Aptheker, was first of all determined by the fact that "it was the first victorious colonial revolution in the entire history of mankind."[102] The concept of the War of

99. Jack Hardy, *The First American Revolution* (New York, 1937), 14.

100. Philip Foner, *The History of the Labor Movement in the United States* (Moscow, 1949), vol. 1, 22, 56; H. Morais, "Artisan Democracy and the American Revolution," *Science and Society* 6 (Summer 1942), 236.

101. W. Z. Foster, *Outline of the Political History of the Americas* (Moscow, 1953), 177.

102. Herbert Aptheker, *The American Revolution, 1763–1783* (Moscow, 1962), 38–41.

Independence as both a colonial and a social revolution has significantly enriched scholarly thinking, has allowed us to consider the dramatic events of the 1770s and 1780s from a broader perspective, and has enabled us to determine more accurately and correctly the role and significance of these events in the history of both the United States and the world.

In particular, very enticing vistas have opened up before scholars investigating the agricultural question. Let us recall that at the end of the eighteenth century more than 90 percent of Americans were farmers and that the fortunes of a significant part of the urban population were also directly linked to agriculture. And yet, surprising as it may seem, American scholars have mainly concerned themselves with the towns and not the villages; they have meticulously studied commercial interests rather than agrarian ones. Relatively recently, Jensen drew attention to this fact;[103] even earlier, in October 1968, a short article by Wallace Brown was published,[104] but on the whole the general situation has remained the same. "The role of the farmer in the Revolution is not easy to ascertain and the number of works treating that role in detail is correspondingly small," concedes D. Bowers of the U.S. Department of Agriculture, the author of the most recent bibliography on this subject.[105]

Soviet scholars are in a position to make their own contribution to the study of agrarian problems during the period of the American Revolution, particularly since they possess the relevant traditions and experience. The discontent caused in the colonies by the publication of George III's proclamation prohibiting the colonization of land to the west of the Allegheny Mountains (1763), the activities of the land companies, the concrete history of the confiscation of lands belonging to the Loyalists, the land grants received by the veterans of the War of Independence, etc., are all important subjects of research.

Until now even agrarian specialists did not fully realize the fundamental importance of the resolutions adopted in the 1780s by the Continental Congress concerning the question of the western lands. And yet it was during those years that the decision to nationalize the western territories and to create a stock of government land was made, creating the basis for developing a system of agriculture in the territories to the west of the Alleghenies that was American, that is, farm-based in character. The resolution of the Continental Congress of October 10, 1780, already stated that the lands that would be given to the individual states were in the future to be used for "the common benefit of the United States." On these lands "Republican States, which shall become members of the Federal Union," were to be formed.[106] By a succession of special acts passed from 1781 to 1802, the western territories occupying the area

103. Merrill Jensen, "The American Revolution and American Agriculture," *Agricultural History* 43, no. 1 (January 1969), 107–24.

104. Wallace Brown, "The American Farmer during the Revolution: Rebel or Loyalist?" *Agricultural History* 42 (October 1968), 327–38.

105. Douglas Bowers, comp. and ed., *A List of References for the History of the Farmer and the Revolution, 1763–1790* (Davis, Calif., 1971), 11.

106. W. C. Ford et al., eds., *Journals of the Continental Congress, 1774–1789*, 34 vols. (Washington, D.C., 1904–1937), vol. 18, 915.

to the north of the Ohio River and to the east of the Mississippi River, as well as those occupying the area of the present states of Alabama and Mississippi, were transferred to the federal government. Of the entire territory of the continental United States today (slightly more than 1.9 billion acres) only 463 million acres initially belonged to private individuals or the states. The other 1.44 billion acres were transferred to federal ownership during the period from 1781 to 1853.[107]

Thus agriculture in the United States developed under conditions in which more than three-fourths of all land was nationalized. Of course, transferring western lands to the federal government and creating a stock of government land were only initial measures that made it possible in principle for capitalism to develop along an American path. The actual manner of distributing the stock of land and the identity of the interests that would benefit from the land legislation depended to a large degree on the concrete correlation of forces and the degree of political activity among the working masses. As V. I. Lenin observed, nationalization of land is an indication of bourgeois progress. Its likelihood is greater "in a 'young' bourgeois society that is yet to develop its forces and whose contradictions are yet to evolve."[108] "The struggle for land, the struggle for freedom, is a struggle for the conditions necessary for the existence of a bourgeois society, because capital retains its supremacy in even the most democratic of republics, whatever the type of 'transfer of all land to the people,' " wrote Lenin.

Those unfamiliar with the teaching of Marx may consider such a view strange. But it is not difficult to become convinced of its correctness: one should recall the great French Revolution and its results, the history of the American "free lands," etc.[109] It is revealing that Lenin compared the history of the free lands, that is, the American path of development in agriculture, with the outcome of the great French Revolution. As a result of the U.S. War of Independence, agriculture was only beginning to follow a farm-based path of development (and that only in the northern part of the country!); the long struggle to democratize access to the western lands, homestead rights, and the abolition of slavery still lay ahead.[110]

We can learn much that is interesting and instructive by studying the influence of the American Revolution on the urban population, and in particular the merchant class. Although on the eve of the War of Independence those merchants who enjoyed close ties with England held the dominant positions in the colonies, in the course of

107. *Historical Statistics of the United States: Colonial Times to 1957* (Washington, D.C., 1960), 231, 236.

108. Lenin, *Complete Collected Works,* vol. 16, 298, 299.

109. Ibid., vol. 15, 205.

110. For more on the struggle for the western lands in the eighteenth and nineteenth centuries, see G. P. Kuropiatnik, "Concerning the Manner of the Development of Capitalism in U.S. Agriculture in the Pre-monopoly Period," *Modern and Contemporary History* 4 (1958); N. N. Bolkhovitinov, "Concerning the Pattern of Operation of the 'Safety Valve' in the History of the United States," *Modern and Contemporary History* 4 (1970) (English translation in *Soviet Studies in History* 10 [Summer 1971], 45–69); M. V. Demikhovskii, "The Colonization of the Western Territories and Aspects of the Development of Capitalism in the United States," *Problems of History* 5 (1973).

the Revolution new entrepreneurs who specialized in internal consumption by the American towns and the army came to the fore. These merchants obtained needed goods in nearby rural areas and were able to use the wartime situation to their advantage. It was during this period that the Appletons and Cabots, who earlier had not been among the most important merchant families and who later, in the nineteenth century, came to occupy a dominant position in Massachusetts trade, rose to prominence in Boston. In the Connecticut Valley the Wadsworths and Trumbulls began to play an important role, and so on.[111]

When emphasizing the importance of the socioeconomic changes that took place during the course of the American Revolution, one should bear in mind that this revolution was primarily a colonial one, a struggle by the insurgent colonists against the mother country, a war of the United States for independence. The main differences between the American Revolution and the classic French Revolution lay in the facts that America had never known an *ancien régime* and that feudalism did not exist in the country as a system and only some of its elements—fixed rent, entail, large estates, etc.—were present. The development of the colonies took place after the bourgeois revolution in England. Therefore the American Revolution, as I see it, was of the intra-formation type, and its gestation within the bowels of what was already a capitalist and bourgeois order was hastened by the national or, more exactly, the national-liberation factor, which from the very beginning imparted an anticolonial character to the whole independence movement. It should be noted that V. I. Lenin invariably underlined precisely the liberation aspect of the War of Independence and only then stressed its revolutionary character.[112]

In this connection, an important characteristic of the American Revolution was a certain conservative tendency inherent in it from the very beginning. We refer not only and not so much to the presence in the American Revolutionary movement of conservative groups and currents, or to the fact that Revolutionary events in the United States developed along Whig-Girondin rather than Jacobin lines, or to the fact that from the viewpoint of the scope and intensity of the class struggle the Revolution in America never attained the level of the Great French Bourgeois Revolution. We refer primarily to the conservative character of some of the aims of the insurgents, who fought not only for freedom and independence, not only to destroy the vestiges of feudalism, but also to preserve and strengthen the already existing system in America and the already existing freedoms and privileges from the encroachments of the British crown and parliament. "The United States were modern and bourgeois from their very conception. . . . They were founded by petty-bourgeois and peasants who fled European feudalism in order to establish a purely bourgeois society."[113] This had tremendous impact on the entire subsequent development of the United States, which was determined not only by the country's revolutionary tradition but also and above all else by its bourgeois-liberal tradition.

111. Garraty, *Interpreting American History,* 81–82.
112. See Lenin, *Complete Collected Works,* vol. 37, 48, 56; vol. 38, 344.
113. [Karl] Marx and [Friedrich] Engels, *Works,* vol. 39, 128.

The conservative tendency in the American Revolution manifested itself with particular clarity in the preservation and indeed widest development in the United States of that most reactionary of institutions, Negro slavery, at a time when blacks constituted one-fifth of the country's population! In his address of April 6, 1972, to the Organization of American Historians, Edmund S. Morgan, the organization's president, admitted that in the past American historians (himself included) had regarded slavery as merely an "exception," a kind of "dark spot" in the general bright picture of the development of the United States.[114] And yet, far from being an exception, slavery was one of the most important formative factors in the whole of American history. Morgan called slavery "the American paradox," but in fact he failed to explain it adequately.[115] It is difficult to find an explanation for this "paradox" within the parameters of traditional thinking. How could the Americans, having risen up to fight for freedom and independence and for the natural rights of man, at the same time have preserved and sanctified in law (the Constitution of 1787) Negro slavery? The whole point is that they fought not just for freedom but also for property, which at the time was regarded as a concept almost synonymous with freedom. In the Americans' view only property gave freedom, and only in the protection of their "sacred" property from English encroachments did the colonists see their freedom. But by fighting for the preservation of freedom and property they were at the same time fighting for the preservation of Negro slavery. It is no accident that almost all prominent American revolutionaries, including even men like George Washington, Thomas Jefferson, and James Madison, were also slave owners.

When speaking of the historical significance of the U.S. War of Independence, Karl Marx observed that it "sounded the tocsin for the European bourgeoisie."[116] It was in America during the War of Independence that "the idea of an indivisible great democratic republic" emerged, "the first declaration of the rights of man" was officially issued, and "the European revolution of the eighteenth century first received an impetus."[117] As a result of the Revolution, the American people freed themselves from the colonial yoke of the mother country, defended their political independence, and removed the shackles hindering the free development of capitalist relations. The remnants of feudalism in the country were destroyed, the western territories nationalized, and the estates of the Loyalists confiscated.

At the same time, the American Revolution in the eighteenth century led to an enormous increase in the power of the ruling bloc of bourgeoisie and planters. Although the masses of the people were the main motive force of the Revolution, the bourgeoisie and slave-owning planters remained the leaders of the Revolution. If in France, in the words of Chateaubriand, "the patricians started the revolution and the plebeians finished it," in America the "elite" that started the Revolution preserved its

114. E. S. Morgan, "Slavery and Freedom: The American Paradox," *JAH* 59, no. 1 (June 1972), 5–29.

115. Ibid.

116. Marx and Engels, *Works,* vol. 23, 9.

117. Ibid., vol. 16, 17.

authority until the end.[118] On the one occasion (Shays's Rebellion) when the masses of the people attempted to intensify the Revolution by their own plebeian methods and to question the actions of the leaders of the young republic, their movement was suppressed with relative ease. The power of the central government extended and strengthened with the Constitution of 1787. In later years while the revolutionary tradition in the country continued to exist, the conservative, defensive tendency to protect the power of the triumphant bourgeoisie grew increasingly stronger.

118. For a detailed comparative analysis of the American and French revolutions, see the article by A. A. Fursenko in *Problems of History* 11 (1972), 62–81.

COMMENT BY JACK P. GREENE

The two decades before the bicentennial of the Declaration of Independence in 1976 were years of enormous excitement in the study of the American Revolution. For the first time in more than a generation, scholars looked anew at the issues in contention between Britain and the colonies; examined variations in local responses to those issues; dissected the nature of political divisions and the socioeconomic basis of public life in Britain, the colonies, and the new Revolutionary states; analyzed the process of creating new republican state governments and a national political system; and sought to recover the underlying mental and material worlds that had shaped the responses of the participants. By bringing a new and more refined level of understanding to our knowledge of the late-eighteenth-century Anglophone world, the large body of work produced on these and related subjects effectively challenged older interpretations and themselves raised a host of new questions about the era of the Revolution.[1]

Professor Bolkhovitinov's remarkably comprehensive and perceptive essay captures much of the ferment associated with this scholarship as it had developed by the early 1970s. More fully than those of most American scholars at the time or since, his analysis is informed by an implicit appreciation of the important extent to which the revival of historical attention to the American Revolution was a response to a new interest in the phenomenon of revolution. This interest had developed out of the efforts of political leaders and social scientists to understand—and control—the wave of anticolonial revolts and revolutionary upheavals that swept the globe during the decades after World War II.

Some of this growing scholarly concern with the nature of revolution was explicitly oriented toward contesting prevailing definitions of revolutions held by many contemporary revolutionaries and students of revolution. In challenging the existing world order, many advocates of revolutionary change seemed unquestioningly to assume the paradigmatic character of the French and Russian revolutions. In response, many Western scholars, to one degree or another all opponents of the totalitarian regimes that were then arising in so many postrevolutionary states, touted the American Revolution as an alternative model for revolutions, one that seemingly had involved less violence and managed to preserve far more individual liberty.

Among those whose interest in the American Revolution was largely a product of such an impulse were some of the people Professor Bolkhovitinov identified as "neoconservatives"—Louis Hartz, Daniel Boorstin, Clinton Rossiter—as well as Hannah Arendt, Richard B. Morris, Irving Kristol, Martin Diamond, Robert Nisbet,

---

1. These developments are analyzed in the following works by Jack P. Greene: *The Reappraisal of the American Revolution in Recent Historical Literature* (Washington, D.C., 1967); "Revolution, Confederation, and Constitution, 1763–1787," in William H. Cartwright and Richard L. Watson Jr., eds., *The Reinterpretation of American History and Culture* (Washington, D.C., 1973), 259–96; and "Beyond the Neo-Whig Paradigm: Recent Trends in the Historiography of the American Revolution," in Cedric B. Cowing, ed., *The American Revolution: Its Meaning to Asians and Americans* (Honolulu, 1977), 35–62.

and many other social scientists and philosophers.[2] Except for Rossiter, Morris, and Diamond, however, none of these people played a significant role in the revival of scholarly interest in the American Revolution. They built on the new understanding that was developing out of that revival, but their interest in the Revolution was at most casual and their characterizations correspondingly simplistic.

In these respects they contrasted sharply with the principal contributors to the new literature on the American Revolution. However much those contributors' understandings of their subject may have been sharpened by the perspectives supplied by contemporary revolutions, they were all centrally concerned with explaining the American Revolution as an event in late-eighteenth-century history, and the questions they brought to their investigations were to a very large extent shaped by two other conditions. First were the new, more analytical standards and approaches to historical studies developed over the previous generation by scholars such as Sir Lewis Namier, Perry Miller, Marc Bloch, Lucien Febvre, George Lefebvre, Peter Geyl, and Johann Huizinga.

Second, and even more important, was the received wisdom about the Revolution. Far less concerned to demonstrate the peculiarity of the American Revolution in relation to other modern revolutions than to test the validity of long-accepted views, post–World War II students of the Revolution were determined to move beyond the simplicities they had inherited from earlier historians and to achieve a deeper and more multidimensional comprehension of the Revolution. Thus, they successfully challenged the views that Americans had no substantial grievances against the metropolitan government and constantly shifted their constitutional arguments merely to avoid paying Parliamentary taxes; that late colonial American societies were tightly controlled by hegemonic aristocracies and political participation was limited to a small segment of the adult male population; that political divisions everywhere and throughout the Revolutionary era revolved around a broad socioeconomic cleavage between conservatives and radicals, aristocrats and democrats, haves and have-nots; and that the outpouring of polemical literature during the Revolution could be dismissed as propaganda that masked the deeper material interests that underlay the controversies to which it spoke.

The cumulative effect of this wholesale scholarly reappraisal was a view of the Revolution that was strikingly similar to that of its Whig leaders. No one of the advocates of the emerging interpretation, not even Robert E. Brown, depicted American society and public life during the Revolutionary era as "conflictless." But even those who, like Cecelia M. Kenyon, Bernard Bailyn, and Gordon S. Wood, stressed the radicalizing effects of the Revolution, especially as it stimulated

---

2. While Hannah Arendt's *On Revolution* (New York, 1963) is certainly the most sustained and compelling expression of this impulse and Richard B. Morris's *The American Revolution Reconsidered* (New York, 1967) is probably the best informed, the symposium organized by the American Free Enterprise Institute to celebrate the bicentennial of the Revolution and published as *America's Continuing Revolution: An Act of Conservatism* (Washington, 1975) is in many ways more representative.

a reconsideration of traditional social and political conceptions, downplayed the importance of social class as an ingredient in political conflict and minimized the social affects of the Revolution.

As the civil rights struggles, the women's rights movement, and the antiwar protests of the 1960s and early 1970s exposed basic divisions within late-twentieth-century U.S. society, several historians, some of whom referred to themselves as "New Left," began to challenge this developing neo-Whig view. They denounced it for emphasizing ideological over material factors, for ignoring the role and feelings of non-elite groups, and for not paying sufficient attention to internal social tensions. They called for a more inclusive understanding of the Revolution that would consider the role and aspirations of common as well as gentle folk, radical as well as conservative patriots, outsiders as well as insiders. Most of all, however, they advocated an approach that would focus on internal conflicts of the kind emphasized by the old Progressive interpretation of the Revolution, conflicts among sections, races, ethnic groups, and, especially, socioeconomic classes.[3]

Professor Bolkhovitinov's judgment that the "new intellectual" school represented by Bailyn and Wood and the radical view championed by New Left and other historians demanding a broader approach to the Revolution were the most powerful "new" currents in Revolutionary historiography and represented the wave of the future was shared by many American historians at the time. From the perspective of the early 1990s, it would appear that he was at least half right.

The ideological dimensions of the Revolutionary era have indeed continued to engage the attention of historians and have yielded a large volume of outstanding work. Using as either a foundation or a foil the contemporary linguistic and conceptual worlds depicted by Bailyn, Wood, and J. G. A. Pocock, whose highly influential *The Machiavellian Moment: Florentine Political Thought and the Atlantic Republican Tradition* appeared in 1975,[4] scholars have explored in considerable detail many of the ways in which language and ideas shaped developments not just in the political but also in the cultural realm, including religion, belles lettres, historical writing, the lives of women, family relations, education, and the emerging debate over slavery.[5]

3. Alfred F. Young, *The American Revolution: Explorations in the History of American Radicalism* (Dekalb, Ill., 1976), provides a succinct distillation of this view.

4. (Princeton, 1975).

5. Among the most significant of the works published in this booming area since 1976 are Catherine Albanese, *Sons of the Fathers: The Civil Religion of the American Revolution* (Philadelphia, 1976); James West Davidson, *The Logic of Millennial Thought: Eighteenth-Century New England* (New Haven, 1977); Nathan O. Hatch, *The Sacred Cause of Liberty: Republican Thought and the Millennium in Revolutionary New England* (New Haven, 1977); Lance Banning, *The Jeffersonian Persuasion: Evolution of a Party Ideology* (Ithaca, 1978); Joseph J. Ellis, *After the Revolution: Profiles of Early American Culture* (New York, 1979); Morton White, *The Philosophy of the American Revolution* (New York, 1978), and *Philosophy, the Federalist, and the Constitution* (New York, 1986); Garry Wills, *Inventing America: Jefferson's Declaration of Independence* (Garden City, N.Y., 1978), and *Explaining America: The Federalist* (Garden City, N.Y., 1981); Drew R. McCoy, *The Elusive Republic: Political Economy in Jeffersonian America* (Chapel Hill, 1980); Lester H. Cohen, *The Revolutionary Histories: Contemporary Narratives of the American Revolution*

Several other areas mostly involving older subjects have attracted a degree of attention that few would have predicted in the mid-1970s. These include especially the constitutional and legal dimensions of the Revolution, an interest that long preceded but was doubtless stimulated by the bicentennial of the Constitution, the problem of working out a viable federal system, and the creation of a military establishment during and after the War of Independence.[6]

But the radical or New Left approach that seemed so promising to Professor Bolkhovitinov during the early 1970s has been far less productive. Disappointingly few monographs written explicitly from this point of view and emphasizing the importance of class conflict during the Revolution have been published during the past fifteen years. These include Gary B. Nash's account of the political manifestations of social relations in Boston, Philadelphia, and New York during the seventy-five

---

(Ithaca, 1980); Linda K. Kerber, *Women of the Republic: Intellect and Ideology in Revolutionary America* (Chapel Hill, 1980); Mary Beth Norton, *Liberty's Daughters: The Revolutionary Experience of American Women, 1750–1800* (Boston, 1980); Willi Paul Adams, *The First Constitutions: Republican Ideology and the Making of the State Constitutions in the Revolutionary Era* (Chapel Hill, 1980); Donald S. Lutz, *Popular Consent and Popular Control: Whig Theory in the Early State Constitutions* (Baton Rouge, 1980); Jay Fliegelman, *Prodigals and Pilgrims: The American Revolution against Patriarchical Authority* (New York, 1982); Melvin Yazawa, *From Colony to Commonwealth: Familial Ideology and the Beginnings of the American Republic* (Baltimore, 1984); Joyce Appleby, *Capitalism and a New Social Order: The Republican Vision of the 1790s* (New York, 1984); John Patrick Diggins, *The Lost Soul of American Politics: Virtue, Self-Interest and the Foundations of Liberalism* (New York, 1984); Daniel Epstein, *The Political Theory of the Federalist* (Chicago, 1984); Albert Furtwanger, *The Authority of Publius: A Reading of the Federalist Papers* (Ithaca, 1984), and *American Silhouettes: Rhetorical Identities of the Founders* (New Haven, 1987); Ruth H. Block, *Visionary Republic: Millennial Themes in American Thought, 1756–1800* (New York, 1985); Forrest McDonald, *Novus Ordo Seclorum: The Intellectual Origins of the Constitution* (Lawrence, Kans., 1985); Ralph Lerner, *The Thinking Revolutionary: Principle and Practice in the New Republic* (Ithaca, 1987); Michael Lienesch, *New Order of the Ages: Time, the Constitution, and the Making of Modern American Political Thought* (Princeton, 1988); Robert H. Webking, *The American Revolution and the Politics of Liberty* (Baton Rouge, 1988); and Cathy D. Matson and Peter S. Onuf, *A Union of Interests: Political and Economic Thought in Revolutionary America* (Lawrence, Kans., 1990). Many of these and other works in this genre are discussed briefly in Jack P. Greene, *A Bicentennial Bookshelf: Historians Analyze the Constitutional Era* (Philadelphia, 1986). See also Robert E. Shalhope, "Republicanism and Early American Historiography," *William and Mary Quarterly,* 3d ser., 29 (1982): 334–56.

6. The early phases in the emergence of the literature on the constitutional and legal dimensions of the Revolution are discussed by Jack P. Greene, "From the Perspective of Law: Context and Legitimacy in the Origins of the American Revolution, A Review Essay," *South Atlantic Quarterly* 75 (1986): 56–77. More recent contributions include John Phillip Reid, *Constitutional History of the American Revolution: The Authority of Rights* (Madison, Wisc., 1986), *Constitutional History of the American Revolution: The Authority to Tax* (Madison, Wisc., 1987), and *The Concept of Representation in the Age of the American Revolution* (Chicago, 1989); Jack P. Greene, *Peripheries and Center: Constitutional Development in the Extended Politics of the British Empire and the United States, 1607–1789,* (Athens, Ga., 1986); and Shannon C. Stimson, *The American Revolution in the Law: Anglo-American Jurisprudence before John Marshall* (Princeton, 1990). On working out a viable legal system, see in particular Jack N. Rakove, *The Beginnings of National Politics: An Interpretive History of the Continental Congress* (New York, 1979), and Peter S. Onuf, *The Origins*

years before independence; John K. Alexander's study of upper-class treatment of the poor in Philadelphia; David P. Szatmary's treatment of Shays's Rebellion; Edward Countryman's account of the impact of the Revolution upon New York political society, and Steven Rosswurm's analysis of the participation of non-elite groups in Philadelphia during the war years.[7] All of these studies have contributed in significant ways to our knowledge of the era of the Revolution, and Rosswurm has been particularly successful in recovering the behavior and ideology of Philadelphia's lower sort. So far, however, advocates of the radical approach have failed to show that class conflict within the free white population was a central, much less a ubiquitous, phenomenon during the Revolution.

If, however, class conflict has turned out to be a concept of relatively limited utility as a tool for the analysis of the Revolutionary era, the broader and more long-range social approach represented by the new social history would seem to have far more potential. Demands by radical historians for a more inclusive history of the Revolution were at least in part the reflection of this much broader movement that began to develop in early American studies in the mid-1960s and that was associated with earlier and similar movements in French and English history. Focusing on the settler societies that developed in Anglophone America during the colonial era, this still expanding movement quickly became one of the most vigorous developments in American historical studies. Increasingly during the 1970s and 1980s the colonial era gradually replaced the Revolution as the most absorbing concern among early American historians. In both volume and inventiveness the literature produced by this movement considerably exceeded even that growing out of the continuing fascination with the ideological and cultural dimensions of the Revolution.[8]

The result of this development, the rich potential of which was only just becoming fully evident at the time Professor Bolkhovitinov composed his essay, has been a

---

of the Federal Republic: Jurisdictional Controversies in the United States, 1775–1787 (Philadelphia, 1983). See also Rosemarie Zagarri, *The Politics of Size: Representation in the United States, 1776–1850* (Ithaca, 1987). On the creation of a military establishment, see especially Charles Royster, *A Revolutionary People at War: The Continental Army and American Character, 1775–1783* (Chapel Hill, 1979); Lawrence D. Cress, *Citizens in Arms: The Army and the Militia in American Society to the War of 1812* (Chapel Hill, 1982); and E. Wayne Carp, *To Starve the Army at Pleasure: Continental Army Administration and American Political Culture, 1775–1783* (Chapel Hill, 1984).

7. Gary B. Nash, *The Urban Crucible: Social Change, Political Consciousness, and the Origins of the American Revolution* (Cambridge, Mass., 1979); John K. Alexander, *Render Them Submissive: Responses to Poverty in Philadelphia, 1760–1800* (Amherst, Mass., 1980); David P. Szatmary, *Shays's Rebellion: The Making of an Agrarian Insurrection* (Amherst, Mass., 1980); Edward Countryman, *A People in Revolution: The American Revolution and Political Society in New York, 1760–1790* (Baltimore, 1981); Steven Rosswurm, *Arms, Country, and Class: The Philadelphia Militia and "Lower Sort" during the American Revolution, 1775–1783* (New Brunswick, N.J., 1987).

8. Many of the findings of this literature are discussed in essays in Jack P. Greene and J. P. Pole, eds., *Colonial British America: Essays in the New History of the Early Modern Era* (Baltimore, 1984), and John J. McCusker and Russell R. Menard, *The Economy of British America, 1607–1789* (Chapel Hill, 1985). See also Greene, *Pursuits of Happiness: The Social Development of the Early Modern British Colonies and the Formation of American Culture* (Chapel Hill, 1988).

sweeping revolution in early American historical studies. Although some of the new social historians have examined such subjects as the social impact of war, the nature of political divisions, and the social basis of religious conflict, probably the main characteristic of the historiographical revolution they have created is a shift of focus away from the political arena and the public realm. In seeking to reconstruct the nature of family and community relations; the workings and effects of emerging economic structures, social processes, and cultural systems; and the experience of nondominant groups such as women, slaves, servants, and nonwhites, including Amerindians, they have rather directed attention at the dynamic and complex scenes of private life and the social arrangements that sustained them.

The early American world this scholarship has revealed was one that in many ways differed radically from those on the eastern side of the Atlantic. The widespread availability of land and the need for commerce, labor, and other services offered wide scope for individual activity and gave the private sphere an extraordinary dynamism. They also led to the development of societies in which the independent—the possessing—proportion of the population was unusually high and the concern for the protection of private property and the independent status it sustained was enormously powerful, precisely because it was so widely shared. With a vibrant and expanding commercial order emerging early in their history of settlement and with no legally privileged social order, their social structures were, by European standards, everywhere still truncated and volatile, an increasingly differentiating social system not yet having brought those at the top either much security or much authority. Black slaves comprised an important source through which significant numbers of free people in many of these societies both acquired and expressed their independence. The population's resistance to paying high taxes meant that the bureaucracy was tiny, coercive power weak, and fiscal resources sparse. For these reasons, government was necessarily consensual and derived its energy and effectiveness from the force of community opinion. With such a small public sphere and with so large an independent population intensely preoccupied with the pursuit of personal and family independence and the social improvements that would guarantee and enhance their individual and social achievements, the scope for public activity was sharply limited.

Perhaps because social historians have concentrated so heavily on the colonial era and have been relatively unconcerned with politics, however, no one has yet examined in a sustained and systematic way the problem of how these and other sociopolitical characteristics of the societies of colonial British America affected the American Revolution. Of course, many of their more obvious effects have long been understood, at least among those who have resisted the impulse to try to assimilate American to European history by fitting the American Revolution into the mold of the French and other modern revolutions. As Professor Bolkhovitinov, with the benefit of his perspective from outside American culture, emphasized in the closing pages of his article, the absence of a powerful old regime and the corresponding weakness of conservative forces, the presence of a well-formulated "capitalist . . . bourgeois" and essentially "modern" socioeconomic order in the colonies well before the Revolution, and the overwhelming commitment of American revolutionaries to the sanctity of private property—all operated to differentiate the American Revolution from the French Revolution by limiting its social impact and ensuring that there would be no sweeping or sustained challenge to the authority of the possessing classes.

But the findings of the new colonial social history would seem to have even deeper and much less understood implications for the American Revolution. A fuller comprehension of those implications will have to begin with an awareness of the profound preoccupation of Americans with activities in the private sphere. As Billy G. Smith has recently shown in his superb social history of Philadelphia's laboring people during the last half of the eighteenth century, even those who belonged to the most economically disadvantaged segment of the free population were too preoccupied with their private concerns to permit politics to become a "paramount concern." Like generations of Americans before them, even during a major political upheaval like the American Revolution they evidently sought their futures primarily through their individual efforts in the private sphere rather than through collective activities in the public realm.[9]

This same private orientation may also help to account for the inability of Americans to sustain the public spiritedness of 1775–1776, the many centrifugal tendencies in public life at both the national and state levels, the widespread popular resentment at both the enlargement of the public sphere during and after the war and the rising levels of government intrusion into private affairs, the demonstrable reluctance to attack problems or pursue objectives that required significant public expenditures and higher taxes, the peculiarly noncivic definition of American republicanism that emerged during and after the war, and the systematic privileging of liberty over equality in the operation and continuing construction of social politics.[10]

As early American historians begin to grapple with these and other questions, we can perhaps look forward to a period of renewed excitement in the ongoing project to recover in all its complexity the history of the American Revolution.

9. Billy G. Smith, *The "Lower Sort": Philadelphia's Laboring People, 1750–1800* (Ithaca, 1990), 3.

10. For a fuller discussion of some of these issues, see the introduction and many of the chapters in Jack P. Greene, ed., *The American Revolution: Its Character and Limits* (New York, 1987).

RESPONSE BY NIKOLAI N. BOLKHOVITINOV

Today, almost twenty years after I wrote my article on the historiography of the American Revolution, I naturally see its flaws and limitations (they are clearly more numerous than my kind reviewer has indicated). My readers, however, should bear in mind that the article was published in 1973, when almost all Soviet writings on history, and particularly on historiography, had to reflect the demands of the ideological struggle. The texts of Soviet books and articles were saturated with terms like "bourgeois falsifiers of history," "the crisis of bourgeois historiography," and other ideological clichés. That is why at the time I considered it my modest achievement to have avoided such terminology, my chief aim being, as I saw it, to acquaint Soviet readers with the complex and multicolored spectrum of studies on the American Revolution that existed in the United States by the early 1970s. Today's readers might find it interesting that at the time of its publication in the USSR my article was seriously criticized for its lack of "a detailed evaluation of the positions and achievements of American Marxist historians." As might be expected, it was suggested that the title should refer to "bourgeois historiography." (I quote the official review signed by I. S. Galkin, the Head of the Department of Modern and Recent History at Moscow State University, which is preserved in my archive. To be fair, the review was, on the whole, quite professional and, considering the tenor of the times, its tone may even be described as moderate. Professor Galkin did not insist on the obligatory incorporation of his corrections into the text of the article, and its publication in the journal *Modern and Recent History* took place without further complications).

Professor Jack P. Greene's comments substantially supplement and amplify the contents of my article, mainly because of his knowledgeable and expert analysis of the writings on the American Revolution published in the late 1970s and in the 1980s. While agreeing with my conclusions, he cites the large number of excellent studies on the ideology of the revolutionary period and at the same time observes that over the last few years the radical historians' approach to analyzing the Revolution has proved to be "considerably less productive." Among the small number of works by radical scholars to which Professor Greene makes reference are the books by Gary B. Nash, John K. Alexander, David P. Szatmary, Edward Countryman, and Steven Rosswurm. He is right to emphasize that in the last fifteen years the historians of early America have increasingly shifted their attention from the period of the Revolution to the colonial period, as a result of which the study of "new social history" has experienced a veritable flowering. I can only say that I share his opinion, although I should also like to mention the small but active group of radical scholars who are pupils of Professor Nash: Billy G. Smith, Sharon V. Salinger, Marcus Rediker (the author of an interesting monograph on American seamen in the first half of the eighteenth century)[1] and some others.

However, this is not the crucial issue. As I see it, although the radical historians failed to achieve the kind of prominence that seemed possible in the late 1960s and

---

1. Marcus Rediker, *Between the Devil and Deep Blue Sea* (Cambridge, 1987).

early 1970s, several of their ideas in one way or another gained currency among today's historians, albeit in a different form or, to be more precise, on the basis of a "new synthesis." In 1968 Professor Richard Hofstadter concluded his book on the progressive historians with a chapter entitled "Conflict and Consensus in American History." The author, one of the founders of the "consensus" theory, thereby acknowledged the important role conflicts and antagonisms have played in the history of the United States.[2] In the 1980s scholars have written much about "post-revisionism," in particular in the historiography of the cold war, in which certain elements of the radicals' concepts were incorporated into the "new synthesis." To a greater or lesser extent, the radicals' ideas have also found expression in the contemporary historiography of early American history, including the Revolutionary period, although in a revised form. However, this is a phenomenon that deserves separate study.

It is on only one subsidiary point that I cannot altogether agree with Professor Greene. When citing Richard B. Morris's book *The American Revolution Reconsidered,* he mentions its author in a context that might suggest that the views of the late Columbia professor were close to those of Louis Hartz, Daniel Boorstin, and Clinton Rossiter. In his book Professor Morris does indeed speak of "consensus," "continuity," etc. But at the same time, in emphasizing the complex nature of the events of the period that are susceptible to a number of interpretations, he notes that the American Revolution was characterized by "liberative currents, class conflicts, and egalitarian urges."[3] Sometimes it is difficult to place a major historian within a particular school or group. His worldview and opinions are formed, and may change, under the influence of a variety of ideas. The evidence of a single monograph or a single set of facts may easily lead us to a completely arbitrary conclusion.

For instance, the very same Professor Morris taught Herbert Aptheker and Philip Foner, and later Jesse Lemisch. In 1979 he wrote the introduction to Foner's study of the "democratic republican societies" of the 1790s;[4] yet this fact cannot of course be taken as proof he was a Marxist! Morris's views were formed in the 1930s and were influenced by the ideas of the "progressive" school of history; in our own time his book *Government and Labor in Early America* (New York, 1946, 1965, 1981) influenced the radical historians of the colonial period.[5] I do not mention these facts in order to define Professor Morris as a member of a particular school of historiography. His scholarly activities are complex and many-sided, which makes it impossible to say that he belonged to one particular school, although perhaps he could be described as a liberal in the broad sense of the word.

Finally, I should like to say this. The policy of *perestroika* in the Soviet Union has led to substantial changes in the study of history in our country.[6] Many years ago,

2. Hofstadter, *Progressive Historians.*

3. Morris, *The American Revolution Reconsidered,* 84.

4. Philip C. Foner, ed., *The Democratic Republican Societies, 1790–1800* (Westport, 1976).

5. *Labor/Le Travailleur* 10 (Autumn 1982), 124.

6. For further details see N. N. Bolkhovitinov, "New Thinking and the Study of the History of the United States in the Soviet Union," *Reviews in American History* 19 (June 1991), 155–65.

under the direct impact of Lenin's doctrines, Soviet historiography became dominated by a concept that entailed the simple glorification of the policy of revolutionary terror and the Jacobin dictatorship and that extolled the leaders of that dictatorship (Marat, Robespierre, and Saint-Juste) as knights without fear and reproach. Monuments to Marat and Robespierre were erected in our country, and ships and factories were named after them. It was only in the late 1980s that it became possible to revise this concept, and this possibility offered prospects for a more objective analysis of both the American and the French revolutions by Soviet scholars.

Such an analysis may produce especially interesting and valuable results if it is conducted in a way that takes into account the accomplishments of the exponents of "new social history" in the study of the colonial period, which were described by Professor Greene in his illuminating and fascinating comments.

CHAPTER 2

The Land Question and the Revolutionary Situation in North America before the U.S. War of Independence

by

Gennadi P. Kuropiatnik

It is well known that the origins of the revolutionary situation in the English colonies in North America prior to the War of Independence were strongly influenced by a number of problems relating to agriculture. Yet until recently historians studying this period have concentrated on the actions of the town-dwellers. The "inarticulate" farmers, who constituted more than 90 to 95 percent of the colonies' population, have been mostly ignored.

American bourgeois historiography did not of course adopt the Marxist approach to the revolutionary situation. Nevertheless, a number of studies devoted to the political actions of the farmers on the eve of the War of Independence were published.[1] These studies are of some value because of the factual material they contain. Yet their authors attempt to gloss over the extent of property differentiation among the farmers (particularly in the West), the class nature of their struggle, etc.

Herbert Aptheker devoted some attention to the political actions of the farmers in the colonial period,[2] and William Z. Foster has advanced the extremely important proposition that "the main . . . influence on the course of the Revolution was exercised

---

1. J. S. Bassett, "The Regulators of North Carolina, 1765–1771," *The Annual Report of the American Historical Association for the Year 1894* (Washington, D.C., 1895); Irving Mark, *Agrarian Conflicts in Colonial New York, 1711–1775* (New York, 1940); Lee N. Newcomer, *Embattled Farmers: A Massachusetts Countryside in the American Revolution* (New York, 1953); Robert M. Brown, *The South Carolina Regulators* (Cambridge, Mass.; 1963); Richard D. Brown, *Revolutionary Politics in Massachusetts: The Boston Committee of Correspondence and the Towns, 1772–1774* (Cambridge, Mass., 1970); Charles Jellison, *Ethan Allen—Frontier Rebel* (New York, 1969); Ralph H. Records, *Land as a Basis for Economic and Social Discontent in Maine and Massachusetts to 1776* (Chicago, 1947). This article by Gennadi P. Kuropiatnik was first published in *Problems of History*, no. 8 (1976).

2. Herbert Aptheker, *The Colonial Era* (Moscow, 1961), 76–96; Aptheker, *The American Revolution of 1763–1783* (Moscow, 1962), 322–30; Aptheker, "On the Class Character of the American Revolution," *Problems of Peace and Socialism*, no. 7 (1975), 78.

by the small farmers, who constituted a majority of the population." "They also," Foster says, "constituted the bulk of the armed forces of the Revolution."[3] As for Soviet scholars, it was Alexander A. Fursenko who offered the most detailed analysis of the role of the farmers' rebellions in the democratic movement in the colonies, particularly in North and South Carolina and New York prior to the War of Independence.[4]

The society that the white colonists established on the Atlantic Coast of North America in the seventeenth century was not encumbered by societal accretions left by the earlier slave-owning and feudal historical epochs. Yet the rulers of the British empire pursued the deliberate policy of creating a strong ruling class in the colonies and actively tried to implant feudal practices in America.[5] However, the desire of the crown and the landed proprietors to organize life in the colonies according to the feudal model met with stubborn resistance on the part of the newly arriving colonists[6]—"the petty bourgeois and the peasants fleeing European feudalism in order to establish a purely bourgeois society."[7] After a certain decrease in the level of oppression exercised by the large landowners at the end of the seventeenth century, it became apparent as early as the second quarter of the eighteenth century in all the colonies, from New York in the north to South Carolina, that the old feudal obligations were being reimposed on landholders in the domains of the landed proprietors. The landlords wished to use their privileges to increase the revenues from their estates as much as possible. This had not been the case in the more patriarchal seventeenth century.

In the mid-eighteenth century the landowning lords intensified their oppression by rigorously collecting fixed rent and rent arrears and by increasing fixed rent. It was during this period that Lord Grenville, the proprietor of much of North Carolina, once again subjected the farmers to compulsory taxation. By the 1760s fixed rent alone brought him an annual income of £5,000, an enormous sum at that time.[8] Compared with what had been the case at the beginning of the eighteenth century, the revenue that the family of Lord Baltimore received from their lands in Maryland increased a hundredfold and by 1760 totaled £30,000.[9] Between 1740 and 1771, receipts from

3. W. Z. Foster, *A Study of American Political History* (Moscow, 1953), 175.

4. A. A. Fursenko, "The Farmers' Political Actions on the Eve of the U.S. War of Independence," *Modern and Contemporary History* 5 (1975), 92. See also A. V. Efimov, *U.S.A.: The Paths of the Development of Capitalism* (Moscow, 1969).

5. For more about this see A. S. Samoilo, *The English Colonies in North America in the 17th Century* (Moscow, 1963); G. P. Kuropiatnik, "The Struggle for Land in the Colonial Period of U.S. History (17th–early 18th c.)," *Problems of History,* no. 8 (1974).

6. In the years 1690–1770 the population of the colonies increased more than tenfold, from 210,000 to 2,148,000 people. *Historical Statistics of the United States: Colonial Times to 1957* (Washington, D.C., 1961), 756.

7. K. Marx and F. Engels, *Works,* 50 vols. (Moscow 1955), vol. 39, 128.

8. Rowland Berthoff and John M. Murrin, "Feudalism, Communalism and the Yeoman Free-holder: The American Revolution Considered as a Social Accident," in *Essays on the American Revolution,* ed. Stephen G. Kurtz and James H. Hutson (Chapel Hill, 1973), 268.

9. Ibid., 267n27; Ronald Hoffman, *A Spirit of Dissension: Economics, Politics, and the Revolution in Maryland* (Baltimore, 1973), 45; see also Charles A. Barker, *The Background of the Revolution in Maryland* (New Haven, 1940), 143–44, 148.

feudal rent in Virginia increased twofold.[10] By 1770 the collection of fixed rent and other revenues from the land provided the proprietor of Pennsylvania with more than £30,000, that is, three hundred times more than the Penns had received in the first thirty years of the eighteenth century. Moreover, the fixed-rent arrears owed by Pennsylvania farmers to the landed proprietors amounted to the enormous sum of £118,500.[11] Thus in the mid-eighteenth century the oppression and exploitation of the broad masses of farmers had greatly increased in the majority of England's North American colonies.[12]

Another source of worry for the bulk of the colonists was the appearance of large-scale land ownership on a new, nonfeudal basis. Wheeler-dealers and land speculators bought huge tracts of land with a view to reselling them later in small parcels. By the mid-eighteenth century speculative land acquisition schemes had increased to such an extent that individuals were no longer capable of carrying them out, and land companies began to be established for that purpose, among them the Ohio Company (two hundred thousand acres), the Loyal Company (eight hundred thousand acres), and some thirty other smaller companies.[13] The Seven Years' War of 1756–1763 interrupted the land speculation boom and the beginning of migration of colonists to the West. After the end of the war and the suppression of Pontiac's Indian uprising of 1763, western migration resumed and proceeded with even greater momentum and on an even larger scale.[14] The economic depression that followed the war forced many returning veterans, newly freed indentured workers, and impoverished craftsmen and factory hands to think of journeying beyond the mountains in search of land and a new place to live.

At the same time the number of land companies grew, and their petitions to the king for land grants were now for millions rather than thousands of acres. They set their sights on the territories stretching from the Appalachians to the Great Lakes and the Mississippi River. The bitterest rivalry was over the lands in the Ohio River valley.[15] Many prominent colonists, who later were to play a major role in the War of

10. Marshall D. Harris, *Origin of the Land Tenure System in the United States* (Ames, Iowa, 1953), 239.

11. William R. Shepherd, *History of Proprietary Government in Pennsylvania* (New York, 1896), 88; see also Berthoff and Murrin, "Feudalism, Communalism, and the Yeoman Freeholder," 268. In North America only one stratum in society—the proprietary lords, who by means of repressive measures had resurrected and strengthened the feudal forms of exploitation in their domains—received revenues comparable with those of the four hundred richest families in England, the most powerful and affluent capitalist country of the period. The average annual income of those families amounted to £6,000. The profits of the largest British traders were far smaller than the revenues received by the American lords. See ibid., 267n27.

12. For more about the feudal reaction in North America in the mid-eighteenth century see G. P. Kuropiatnik, "Feudal Rent in the North American Colonies of England in the Seventeenth–Eighteenth centuries (Regarding the Question of the Preconditions for the First Bourgeois Revolution in America)," *American Annual, 1975* (Moscow, 1975).

13. Shaw Livermore, *Early American Land Companies* (New York, 1939), 75–81.

14. See Howard Peckham, *Pontiac and the Indian Uprising* (New York, 1961); John R. Alden, *A History of the American Revolution* (New York, 1969), 111–15.

15. George O. Virtue, *British Land Policy and the American Revolution* (Lincoln, Neb., 1953), 3.

Independence—Benjamin Franklin, Thomas Jefferson, George Washington, Patrick Henry, Thomas Lee, and others—had a personal interest in the success of several of the land companies. The land companies already in existence (the Ohio Company and others) petitioned the king in London to recognize their new land claims. At the same time new land companies were formed, hoping to be in existence in time for the division of the land riches of the West. The most prominent among them was the Mississippi Company, which consisted of large planters and land speculators from Virginia and Maryland. The most influential members of this company were the Washingtons and Lees and the families of Adam Stephen and Thomas Bullitt. The company's plans called for the appropriation of a 2.5 million acre tract of land at the confluence of the Ohio and Mississippi rivers.[16]

Tens of thousands of colonists who wanted to acquire land in the West were ready to move into the territories recently conquered from France. Prominent among the would-be settlers was a large group of veterans of the Seven Years' War from Washington's regiment, who had been promised land as a reward for their military service. They expected the authorities to keep their promise. One of the officers, George Mercer, wrote to Washington, "We shall stop at nothing to secure these lands." Even as the Seven Years' War was still going on, Francis Fauquier, the governor of Virginia, reported to London that the colonists were very eager to settle on the fertile lands captured from the French. At the end of the war he again drew the attention of the English government to the fact that "the affairs of granting lands on the Ohio grows every day of more importance."[17] But the hopes of the colonists and land speculators were to be left unfulfilled. The Royal Proclamation of 1763 prohibited them from occupying and settling lands beyond the line of the Appalachian Mountains. All those who earlier had intentionally or unintentionally moved on to lands in that area were ordered to leave them immediately.

Because of the increasing oppression exercised by landlords, the postwar depression, and the closing of the "safety valve" (and thereby the possibility of migrating to the West), the situation of the small farmers and tenant farmers sharply deteriorated, leading to an intensification of the class struggle between them and the land barons. Consequently all the colonies—from New York to South Carolina—were engulfed in a wave of farmers' riots and uprisings. In Pennsylvania, land hunger, the rise in taxes exacted for the benefit of the landowners, and the governing elite's complete disregard of the farmers' demands for equitable demarcation of land, lowering of taxation, representation in the assembly, adoption of measures to defend the settlements from Indian raids, etc.[18] led to an explosion of anger among the settlers as well as organized mass action. In 1763 small farmers and leaseholders, who called themselves the

---

16. Jack M. Sosin, *Whitehall and the Wilderness: The Middle West in British Colonial Policy, 1760–1775* (Lincoln, Neb., 1961), 136–37; "Documents Relating to the Mississippi Land Company, 1763–1769," ed. Clarence E. Carter, *The American Historical Review* 16, no. 1 (1911), 311–19.

17. Sosin, *Whitehall and the Wilderness,* 44n32.

18. *American Colonial Documents to 1776,* ed. Merrill Jensen, vol. 9, *English Historical Documents* (New York, 1955), doc. #98, 640–42; doc. #96B, 614–17.

"Paxton Boys" after the county where the uprising was centered, formed armed detachments. They directed their anger first of all against the Indians, who were defending their lands from foreign invasion. Twice the white colonists attacked an Indian settlement and carried out savage reprisals against its inhabitants, massacring every single one. At the end of January 1764 an armed group of farmers marched on Philadelphia, the capital of Pennsylvania, terrifying the colonial authorities. The frightened rulers, lacking sufficient armed force at their disposal, promised to consider the demands of the "Paxton Boys," who took them at their word and returned to their farms. The promises, however, were not kept, and the disturbances among the farmers of northeast Pennsylvania continued up until independence was declared. From time to time the Paxton Boys would blockade British forts.[19] Governor John Penn launched a number of punitive expeditions against them. Fearing that where the provincial troops were concerned, "the militia would stand by these lawless settlers rather than against them," he asked General Thomas Gage, the commander of the English army, to send some of his troops to Pennsylvania.

The farmers' actions were spontaneous and uncoordinated. This fact alone doomed them to defeat. The failure of the farmers' attempts to secure ownership of the land they cultivated led them to contemplate migration to the West. But their path was barred by regular troops from the king's army, which for the first time in peacetime had grown to a considerable size (ten thousand men).[20] The English commander was given categorical orders to ensure compliance with the Proclamation of 1763.

The maintenance of troops overseas was enormously expensive; during the Seven Years' War, moreover, the debt of the British treasury had grown from £73 million to £137 million. Just the annual interest payments on the debt amounted to £5 million.[21] Nevertheless, England continued to keep its army in America. The search for new sources of revenue for the treasury led in 1763 to the establishment of stringent control over the collection of customs duties. A large number of additional ships were sent to American waters to assist the royal customs officers.[22] Revenues immediately increased, but they were still insufficient. Then the English government decided to shift the burden of maintaining the royal troops in America to the colonies. The colonists, who had come to America to acquire land, were now obliged to cover the costs of maintaining the royal troops that prevented them from settling on the lands of the West!

19. *English Historical Documents,* doc. #96A, 609–13; Gage to H. S. Conway, May 6, 1766, *The Correspondence of General Thomas Gage with the Secretaries of State, 1763–1775,* ed. Clarence E. Carter, 2 vols. (New Haven, 1969), I, 91.

20. Lord Halifax to S. Amherst, October 11, 1763, *Correspondence of Gage,* vol. 2, 2; E. V. Tarle, *Studies on the History of the Colonial Policies of the Countries of Western Europe (from the End of the 15th to the Beginning of the 19th Century)* (Moscow-Leningrad, 1965), 235.

21. Gage to Thomas Whately, November 7, 1764, *Correspondence of Gage,* vol. 2, 246; Sosin, *Whitehall and the Wilderness,* 82.

22. These measures outraged the American merchants, whose profits had been much reduced because of them. But the merchants were still at a stage when they did not dare to ask for the people's help, and they continued to pay the duty punctiliously. Neil R. Stout, "Goals and Enforcement of British Colonial Policy, 1763–1775," *The American Neptune* 27 (July 1967), 213–15, 218.

Eventually the English Parliament, after adopting a quartering act, for the first time in the colonies' history introduced direct taxation in the form of the so-called stamp duty,[23] the receipts from which were intended to pay for the cost of maintaining the English army. The army's main forces were stationed over a vast expanse of territory—from the St. Lawrence River to the Mississippi along the line described in the Proclamation of 1763—and were also performing garrison service in the forts. The news that a stamp duty would be introduced on November 1, 1765, reached the colonies by the middle of that year and led to fairly widespread protests in the larger towns (those with a population of five thousand to fourteen thousand). The protests were organized by members of the merchant bourgeoisie, and in the south by the planters as well.

In the course of these developments a society called the "Sons of Liberty" was formed; this group began to agitate against the measures of compulsion to which the mother country had resorted. The movement was centered in Massachusetts and its capital, Boston. Here the Sons of Liberty, led by the lawyer Samuel Adams, held meetings and demonstrations. Crowds of townspeople sacked the offices where the stamp duty was to be collected and burned the stamped paper that had been brought from England. Samuel Adams attached great importance to the attitude of the small farmers, regarding them as a major "force in any society," and conducted a single-minded propaganda campaign in the rural areas. One pamphlet published during this period warned the farmers that the English Parliament, having levied the stamp tax, was perfectly capable of imposing a tax on the land ("and on the light of the sun, the air that we breathe, and the earth in which we shall be buried"). In their struggle against British oppression, Adams and his followers among the Sons of Liberty looked for support mainly from the "two venerable orders of men stiled Mechanicks and Husbandmen . . . whose firm patriotism must finally save this country" from British domination.[24]

Many governors, finding themselves without adequate force to suppress the actions by the town dwellers, requested assistance from the mother country. Royal troops from the border zone and the interior areas recently conquered from France were sent to the rebellious cities. In the western regions the local authorities and royal plenipotentiaries also asked for troops. The British statesmen found themselves in a quandary:[25] should they dispatch troops to the East or leave them in the West? Meanwhile the situation in the colonies further deteriorated. Echoes of the protest in the East against the stamp duty had reached the remote agricultural settlements of the West. And although neither the duty stamps themselves nor the officials dispensing them had yet reached these areas, the anti–stamp tax movement of the craftsmen,

---

23. *English Historical Documents,* docs. #101, 102, 655–58; Philip Foner, *The History of the Labor Movement in the U.S.A.,* (Moscow, 1949), I, 46, 48.

24. John C. Miller, *Sam Adams—Pioneer in Propaganda,* (Boston, 1936), 139, 302.

25. Gage to H. S. Conway, August 10 and September 23, 1765, *Correspondence of Gage,* vol. 1, 64–68; Gage to H. S. Conway, February 22, 1776, ibid., 84; H. S. Conway to Gage, December 15, 1765, ibid., II, 30.

workers, shopkeepers, and merchants provoked a new series of political actions by the poor farmers, carried out under the slogan of "free land" and directed against the feudal magnates and land companies. In those areas where the measures employed by the landowning lords to resurrect and strengthen their privileges were particularly harsh, the farmers offered bitter and stubborn resistance.

This phenomenon may be seen in the case of the farmers' movement of the mid-1760s in the colonies of New York and North and South Carolina. The epicenter of the popular disturbances now once again shifted from the coastal towns, where the protests against the stamp tax had by that time died down, to the farming regions, where the authorities responded with the vigorous use of military force. Although demonstrations and meetings in the cities during this period still ended without casualties, in rural areas the passions engendered by the struggle had already led to the use of weapons and to bloody clashes. The rural workers in New York defied their landlords, proclaiming the natural right of the poor to equal ownership of the land with the rich. Their actions were immediately aimed at securing the abolition of fixed rent and rent payments to the landlords. In the autumn of 1765 the tenant farmers of Philips Manor not only suspended the payment of rent but also began to take over the landowner's land. Their example was followed by the farmers who rented allotments in the other manors in the Hudson valley. The judges, who were the faithful servants of the land magnates, ordered the sheriffs to expel the farmers from the land they had occupied. In response the rebels declared the allotments they had cultivated to be their property and no longer subject to the payment of fixed rent. To defend themselves, the settlers began to form armed detachments and, following the lead of the townspeople, adopted the name of Sons of Liberty.[26] The tenant farmer William Prendergast became their leader.

By January 1766 the movement for "free land" had spread to all the large manors. Extant data show that in two counties alone (Dutchess and Westchester) there were more than two thousand armed farmers. The authorities declared those taking part in the movement to be dangerous conspirators and "levellers."[27] After three of the rebels were arrested, the rural Sons of Liberty marched on New York. Their appearance in the streets of the city alarmed the city fathers. Distrusting the local militia, the authorities summoned a regiment of royal troops. In a proclamation issued by the provincial governor the farmers' leaders were accused of "high treason." The farmers hoped that the Sons of Liberty in the city would support them. But the organization was controlled by conservative merchants and lawyers, the latter dependent on the landlords, and its leaders prevented the formation of a united front of urban and rural Sons of Liberty. Deprived of help from the townspeople, the farmers' detachments were scattered by

26. A. A. Fursenko, *The American Bourgeois Revolution of the 18th Century* (Moscow-Leningrad, 1960), 48; Mark, *Agrarian Conflicts,* 137; D. R. Dillon, *The New York Triumvirate* (New York, 1949), 166.

27. Herbert M. Morais, *The Struggle for American Freedom: The First Two Hundred Years* (New York, 1944), 170; Irving Mark and Oscar Handlin, "Land Cases in Colonial New York, 1765–1767: The King vs. William Prendergast," *New York University Law Quarterly Review* 19 (January 1942), 167.

the king's soldiers and their leaders imprisoned. But other groups of rural Sons of Liberty arriving in New York crushed the resistance of the prison guards and royal soldiers, stormed the jail, and freed their leaders and the other rebels.[28]

To suppress the New York rebels, General Gage sent the 28th regiment, which he had summoned from Quebec, into the rebel strongholds of Dutchess and Albany counties. The bloody battles between the British battalions and the farmers' detachments ended when the rebel leaders, including Prendergast as well as a number of rank-and-file rebels, were captured. Some sixty trials of the rebels took place. At his trial Prendergast made a speech in which he declared his solidarity with the Sons of Liberty in New York, even though they had failed to come to the aid of the rebellious farmers. Prendergast was sentenced to be drawn and quartered; his remains were to be exhibited in the areas where the rebellion had taken place to deter the farmers. The court that pronounced this cruel sentence consisted of representatives of the large landowners and land speculators, including the relatives of Robert Livingston, the very landlord to whose lands the rebels had laid claim. Prendergast's sentence was also signed by one of the leaders of the urban Sons of Liberty, the lawyer John Morin Scott, who served the landlords and hoped to obtain an estate in the area where land use by squatters was prevalent. Several months later the governor of the colony, who was cognizant of the fact that "the spirit of Riot was too high amongst the People" and who feared new disturbances, obtained a royal pardon for Prendergast.[29]

But the disturbances continued, although the movement itself appeared to have passed its high point. When the English battalions returned to Livingston and Philips manors, the clashes between the feudal magnates and the tenant farmers led to a bloody slaughter. General Gage ordered that field guns be used against the rebels, who were building barricades and erecting obstacles, and that anyone firing on the royal troops was to be shot on the spot without mercy. "You will give them a good Dressing, and beat these Sons of Liberty into Loyal subjects," ordered the general.[30] In the summer of 1766 the English soldiers combed the manors in their pursuit of the insurgents, while the Sons of Liberty, adopting guerrilla tactics, constantly attacked them from the most unexpected places. The English soldiers, infuriated by the rebel attacks, destroyed the settlers' farms and crops.[31] Deprived of their homes and means of existence, the tenant farmers and squatters began joining the bands of the Sons

---

28. Staughton Lynd, *Class Conflict, Slavery, and the U.S. Constitution* (Indianapolis, 1967), 36, 66; Gage to H. S. Conway, June 24, 1766, to the Duke of Richmond, September 13, 1766, *Correspondence of Gage,* vol. 1, 95, 99, 108; Mark and Handlin, "Land Cases in Colonial New York," 166; Morais, *Struggle for American Freedom,* 170; Merrill Jensen, *Founding of a Nation* (New York, 1968), 32; Mark, *Agrarian Conflicts,* 133, 145; John Shy, *Towards Lexington* (Princeton, 1965), 218, 357.

29. John Morin Scott was one of the founders of the Sons of Liberty society in New York. His ornate speeches against the collection of stamp duty were popular and enabled him to play a leading role in the organization. See Thomas C. Cochran, *New York in the Confederation: An Economic Study* (Philadelphia, 1932), 86; Dillon, *New York Triumvirate,* 167.

30. Gage to the Duke of Richmond, August 26, 1766, *Correspondence of Gage,* vol. 1, 102; Shy, *Towards Lexington,* 220.

31. Gage to the Duke of Richmond, August 26, 1766, *Correspondence of Gage,* vol. 1, 103.

of Liberty. The most popular among these groups was the squatters' detachment led by Robert Noble, which had begun to partition land among the settlers living in the Livingston manor.

Trying to fulfill the landlords' wishes and eradicate the threat to their manors, the royal troops waged a war of attrition and annihilation against the farmers' bands. They mercilessly burnt down the squatters' shanties. In their pursuit of the insurgents the English soldiers made deep incursions into Massachusetts and Connecticut and by their operations against the squatters and their families provoked the anger and hostility of the local colonists. They behaved "more like a number of Banditti than like troops of the King," and the population of the areas they occupied "was afraid to lodge in their Houses or work in their fields."[32] In some of the centers of the uprising outbreaks of violence continued right up to the Revolution.[33] And although with the help of the English troops the land magnates were able to preserve their estates and privileges, the rebellion of the tenant farmers of New York contributed to the development of the settlers' struggle for land in the other colonies.

In the 1760s the movement of the farmers of South Carolina assumed a particularly violent character. From the very start squatters had been settling on territory of the colony that by royal charter belonged to proprietary lords. On the orders of the landlords, detachments of mercenaries moved into the area where squatting was rife and carried out reprisals against those farmers who refused to pay fixed rent. Their fields and settlements were laid waste. Frequently the local Indian tribes were induced to attack them.[34] In desperation the Carolina farmers in the winter of 1766–1767 formed associations of "Regulators" to defend themselves against the landlords and Indian raids. A petition addressed to Lord Charles Montagu, the royal governor of the colony, which was signed by some four thousand Regulators, described their most urgent needs and demands: official exemption from the payment of rent and recognition of their status as owners of the land they cultivated, the granting of the same rights and the same representation in the colonial assembly as those enjoyed by the inhabitants of the coastal regions, and the adoption of measures aimed at protecting the settlements from the Indians.[35] The Regulators threatened to march on Charleston, the capital of South Carolina, if their petition was rejected. The authorities responded by arresting their leaders. Royal soldiers and units of the colonial militia, which included many of the mercenaries hired by the lords, were sent to suppress the farmers' movement.[36]

The transfer of some British regiments to the East to put down the rebellions against the stamp duty and crush the farmers' movement weakened the royal army, which was dispersed over a huge area beyond the Appalachian Mountains.[37] The

32. Newcomer, *Embattled Farmers,* 23.
33. Mark, *Agrarian Conflicts,* 136–37.
34. Brown, *South Carolina Regulators,* 13–17.
35. *English Historical Documents,* doc. #95A, 592–604.
36. John R. Alden, *The South in the Revolution, 1763–1789* (Baton Rouge, 1957), 151; William R. Smith, *South Carolina as a Royal Province, 1719–1776* (New York, 1903), 337–41.
37. Gage to H. S. Conway, September 23, 1765, *Correspondence of Gage,* vol. 1, 68.

squatters and land companies were quick to take advantage of this. As soon as Pontiac's rebellion was defeated and Sir William Johnson, the British commissioner in America responsible for Indian affairs, had signed a peace treaty with the Indians, frontier pioneers from Pennsylvania, Maryland, Virginia, and other provinces began to cross the Appalachians without obtaining anyone's permission. The migration, which until the Seven Years' War had been sporadic, now became an awesome avalanche that swept everything in its path. As early as the summer of 1764, General Gage sent soldiers to chase the squatters off lands in the western areas of Georgia and South Carolina. But the English troops, scattered as they were across a vast expanse of territory, were unable to close all the paths along which the settlers were making their way west. One of the regular reports on the situation in the colonies being sent from General Gage's headquarters to London (the report was compiled in early June 1765) spoke of the urgent necessity of establishing control over the farmers on the border.[38] In the late 1760s the Holston area in North Carolina quickly filled up with people. Population growth in the area of Virginia beyond the mountains led to the formation of two new counties. In the northern Ohio River valley, where the ban on unauthorized occupation of land was enforced with particular strictness, thirty thousand squatters' farms sprang up in the course of several years.[39]

By the end of the summer of 1765 the reports sent by General Gage and the colonial governors describing the mass violations of the 1763 ban by the squatters and land companies had deeply alarmed the ruling circles in England. The London Chamber of Commerce condemned the illegal settlement of the western lands and advised the government to adopt urgent measures to evacuate the squatters. In October 1765 the Privy Council ordered the governors of Virginia and Pennsylvania to evict immediately the squatting farmers who had settled on lands in the Ohio River valley. In a dispatch to Gage, England's secretary of state for the colonies expressed his confidence that the governors and town councils in the provinces would collaborate with him in punishing "the border people" for their "scandalous Disorders, and preventing the like for the future."[40]

In the middle of the winter of 1766–1767 the commander of Fort Pitt conveyed to the squatters Gage's "advice" not to plant corn, for if by springtime they were not gone for good, troops would "drive away those who are already settled upon Indian lands & . . . destroy their habitations." Indeed, with the coming of spring the squatters were evicted from Redstone Creek. Their shacks and the first crops they had planted were burned and razed to the ground. The colonists were forced to submit. But in November 1767 they and several new groups of settlers returned to the same area. In other localities where organized groups of squatters offered armed resistance, bloody clashes took place, and Gage's soldiers were not always victorious. In the

38. Gage to Halifax, August 10, 1764; Gage to Halifax, June 8, 1765, *Correspondence of Gage,* vol. 1, 34, 61.

39. Peter Marshall, "Lord Hillsborough, Samuel Wharton and the Ohio Grant, 1769–1775," *English Historical Review* 80 (October 1965), 717–39; Virtue, *British Land Policy,* 33.

40. H. S. Conway to Gage, October 24, 1765, *Correspondence of Gage,* vol. 2, 27.

Cheat River valley the squatters, together with a party of new settlers consisting of fifty families from Virginia, managed to repel all attacks and remained on the land they had captured.[41]

It was here in the West that the powerlessness of the colonial authorities and their punitive organs first became evident. Eloquent testimony of this is provided by the reports Gage sent to London in 1765–1766, stressing that the inability of the authorities to punish "the lawless Ruffians" (as the English general called the squatting farmers) was inciting the other settlers to "every excess." The attempts to close off the lands of the West by means of armed force were becoming less and less successful. As a result, Gage became convinced that "the Reins of Government are too loose to enforce an Obedience to the laws" designed to make the colonists observe the border line of 1763.[42]

After reading the reports of the civil and military authorities in America, Lord Shelburne, England's new secretary of state for the colonies, concluded that the Proclamation of 1763 had failed in its purpose. Shelburne believed that the best way to cover the cost of maintaining the English troops in the colonies was to enforce rigorously the payment of quitrents and to sell land at the highest price. In his view, revenues from those sources would in a few years not only pay for the cost of maintaining the troops but also create an "American fund," the money from which could be used for other purposes. But neither England's empty coffers nor the troops stationed in the colonies could wait until the receipts from quitrents had increased. In June 1767 Charles Townshend, the chancellor of the exchequer, announced the introduction of customs duties on several types of goods imported into the colonies. The Townshend Acts led to a new wave of protests.[43]

At the height of the campaign to boycott the Townshend Acts, some of the farmers of North Carolina rebelled. The main struggle between the farmers and the landlords in that colony—a struggle that had gone on for a quarter of a century before the Revolution—took place in Lord Grenville's estates, which occupied two-thirds of the territory of the colony.[44] As in the other colonies, the struggle to obtain land that would be free of all feudal obligations was the main factor behind the growth of the farmers' movement in North Carolina. As a result of being in arrears on their rent and defaulting on their loans, the actual producers and cultivators of the land suffered the confiscation of their means of sustenance and production: their plots as well as their draught animals and farms. The highest price the farmers' property received when put up for auction normally amounted to no more than one-tenth of its real value. The merchants, planters, lawyers (many of whom were at the same time engaged in land speculation), sheriffs, and royal officials made a handsome profit out of these

41. Gage to Shelburne, April 29, June 13, August 24, 1767, ibid., vol. 1, 139, 142, 148.

42. Gage to H. S. Conway, May 6, 1766, ibid., 91.

43. R. A. Humphreys, "Lord Shelburne and the British Colonial Policy," *English Historical Review* 50 (1935), 260; Shelburne to Gage, September 13, December 11, 1766, *Correspondence of Gage,* vol. 2, 45, 49–50; *Documents of American History,* ed. Henry Steele Commager (New York, 1963), vol. 1, 63–64.

44. See Donald E. Becker, *Settlers in North Carolina, 1754–1763* (Chapel Hill, 1971).

auctions. The expulsion of the farmers from their land became massive and led to organized resistance.[45]

The associations of Regulators that were created in North Carolina in imitation of the ones in South Carolina demanded the abolition of feudal rent, the forgiveness of debts, the issuance of paper money, a more equitable system of taxation, and an end to the corrupt practices of the sheriffs.[46] When these demands were rejected, the farmers' associations adopted stronger measures. They began capturing judges, sheriffs, and rent and tax collectors, subjecting them to public floggings, and expelling them from the county in which they had operated. Those among the oppressors and bloodsuckers who inspired the most hatred received even harsher treatment, their estates and granaries being put to the torch. On a number of occasions William Tryon, the royal governor of North Carolina, sent troops into the rebel areas. When he managed to capture the farmers' leaders and put them in prison, armed bands of Regulators, following the example of the rebellious farmers of New York, stormed the North Carolina jail and freed their leaders. A veritable civil war ensued, lasting for more than three years. The uprising was suppressed only when Tryon sent against the farmers an entire army of mercenaries paid for by the landlords, merchants, and planters. The decisive battle took place on May 16, 1771, at Alamance near Hillsboro. The bands of Regulators suffered heavy losses and were defeated. They were subjected to cruel reprisals: seven of their leaders were executed, and many other insurgents were put in prison.[47]

At the same time as the North Carolina rebellion, the fighting in the West between the squatters and the royal troops resumed, redoubling in intensity. Under these circumstances, those within the ruling circles in England who favored transferring troops from the West and concentrating them in the Atlantic provinces prevailed. Lord Hillsborough, who had replaced Lord Shelburne, immediately blocked any new land grants to the American companies; this at once earned the mother country the bitter enmity of the largest shareholders—the colonial merchants, planters, and lawyers. The British government then issued new instructions confirming the ban on Americans' settling on the lands of the West under any circumstances, thus angering the settlers and speculators.[48] Yet despite its new decisiveness England's agricultural policy completely ignored the actual situation in North America. The entire previous history of the struggle of the squatters and land companies for the unoccupied lands clearly showed that the colonists would not be meek and passive in their response. Both the squatters and the land companies threatened to resort to armed force to achieve a radical change in British land policy in the West. General Gage came to realize this and in April 1770 concluded that it would never be possible to keep the people of the western frontier within the limits established by the border line.[49]

45. "The Origin of the Regulation in North Carolina (Documents)," ed. Archibald Henderson, *American Historical Review* 21 (January 1916), 325–31.

46. *English Historical Documents,* doc. #95B, 604–6.

47. Bassett, "Regulators of North Carolina," 197–205; *English Historical Documents,* doc. #95C, 606–9.

48. *English Historical Documents,* doc. #118, 704–7.

49. Gage to Hillsborough, April 24, 1770, *Correspondence of Gage,* vol. 1, 253–55.

England's rigid land policy and the farmers' unceasing struggle against the landowning lords and the land companies for unoccupied land gained the support of the central and western farmers for the radical wing of the Whigs and the Sons of Liberty. The Sons of Liberty in Boston, led by Samuel Adams, continued to carry out a large-scale propaganda campaign. They pointed out that there was a real danger that the powers-that-be might introduce heavy land taxes and begin to exact exorbitant rents, followed inevitably by the confiscation of land and a "horrid slavery." They used the pages of the *Boston Gazette* and the *Country Journal,* as well as pamphlets and booklets specially published for the purpose, to inform the rural population of the struggle of the townspeople against the new oppressive measures adopted by the colonial power. Addressing the farmers in 1772, Samuel Adams wrote: "But the breath of a British House of Commons can originate an act for taking away all our money; our lands will go next or be subject to back rents from haughty and relentless landlords who will ride at ease, while we are trodden in the dirt."[50]

The propaganda activities of Adams and his radical supporters contributed to the awakening of the political consciousness of the masses of farmers and helped them join with the urban poor in the approaching revolution. It was the farmers who aided the urban Sons of Liberty in carrying out the second boycott of English goods of 1769–1770 as a protest against the Townshend Acts. At a town meeting in Boston in November 1772, Samuel Adams suggested that a committee be formed to maintain contact with the population of the province. The new committee called upon all those in the towns of Massachusetts and in the other colonies who were dissatisfied with England's policies to create similar committees and establish permanent correspondence among them. By the summer of 1773, following the call from Boston, similar committees had appeared in the majority of farming settlements in Massachusetts. In 1773–1774 the same sorts of organizations were formed in the other colonies as well. Two planters, Patrick Henry and Thomas Jefferson, who were interested in acquiring land in the West, played a prominent role in the Virginia provincial committee. In their letters to Boston many of the correspondence committees of farmers bitterly condemned England's attempts to use every means to deprive the people of the fruits of their labor and station the royal garrisons on the most fertile lands. The Boston committee remained in permanent correspondence with the committees in the farming areas, requesting their opinion and seeking their advice on important matters. Samuel Adams, the leader of the Boston committee, referred to the farmers as "our friends in the country."[51]

In the early 1770s, while the squatters in the West were waging their struggle for the unoccupied lands, the clashes between the farmers and feudal landowners in the eastern and central areas of the country grew increasingly violent. By this time the lands in New Hampshire and Massachusetts to which the New York landlords

50. Newcomer, *Embattled Farmers,* 30; Herbert M. Morais, "Artisan Democracy and the American Revolution," *Science and Society* 6 (Summer 1942), 231; *The Writings of Samuel Adams,* ed. Harry A. Cushing, 4 vols. (New York, 1968), vol. 2, 350–59.

51. Brown, *Revolutionary Politics,* 92–121, 189; *English Historical Documents,* doc. #132, doc. #133 A, B, 762–65; Adams to Charles Thomson, May 30, 1774, *Writings of Samuel Adams,* vol. 3, 123.

had suddenly laid claim were being cultivated by a second generation of settlers. To defend their rights the farmers banded together, armed themselves, and formed rebels' clubs. Disturbances broke out across the whole of western Massachusetts and New Hampshire. At first the land speculators took advantage of the situation. Shady dealers from New Hampshire and their competitors from New York were selling the same lands in the area of the Green Mountains even before their claim to them was sanctioned by the king. A bitter quarrel ensued between the New Hampshire speculators, who had taken their cut from the actual settlers, and the clique around the governor of New York, which had granted thirty-six thousand acres of the same land to the landlords and their lawyers. In both cases the lands in what is now the southwestern part of Vermont were at stake.[52] The two parties took their dispute to the crown court in London.[53] The ones to suffer as a result of this squabble were the settlers of New Hampshire, Massachusetts, New York, and Connecticut, who had paid the New Hampshire speculators in full for the plots they had purchased. However, the land barons of New York, with the support of the governor, declared these land purchases invalid. The settlers' indignation was tempered only by their hope that their grievances would find a just resolution in London and the colonial courts.

Fearing a repetition of the farmers' "great rebellion" of 1766, the ministers in London were obliged to restrain the impetuous New York landlords. The king decreed that the decisions of the cabinet were to be strictly adhered to and ordered that all land grants in the disputed area were to cease.[54] But the landlords of New York ignored the king's command. At their insistence Governor Cadwallader Colden hastened to sell more than half a million acres in the disputed area to the most influential of the lawyers and landlords.[55] The conflict grew into an open struggle between the landed aristocracy and the small farmers. In northeastern New England (in the colonies of Massachusetts and New Hampshire) the conflict eventually involved not only the mass of settlers but also those elected officials who defended their interests. When the feudal magnates of New York sent their sheriffs (who as early as 1764 had managed to capture and arrest New Hampshire's official representatives) to expel the real settlers from their lands, the settlers were left with no choice but to take up arms. Ethan Allen assumed command of the armed detachments of the settlers, which in the history of the American Revolution came to be known as the "Green Mountain Boys." The ranks of Allen's army were swelled by destitute leaseholders and tenant farmers from New York as well as from New Hampshire, Connecticut, Massachusetts, and the other colonies of New England.[56]

52. Amelia C. Ford, *Colonial Precedents of Our National Land System as It Existed in 1800* (Madison, 1910), 33–34.

53. *The Documentary History of the State of New York,* ed. E. B. O'Callaghan, 4 vols. (Albany, 1850–1851), vol. 4, 348–52, 354–55. Henceforth referred to as *DHSNY*, ed. O'Callaghan.

54. Governor of New York H. Moore to Shelburne, June 9 and 10, 1767, ibid., 365–75; "Order of the King in Council of 24 July, 1767," ibid., 376.

55. Among those who thus acquired land were the landowning lords and the lawyers that served them: William and Robert R. Livingston, O. B. Cortland, W. Smith, D. M. Smith, and others.

56. *DHSNY,* ed. O'Callaghan, vol. 4, 356–57.

The governor of New York unsuccessfully sought the support of the authorities in New Hampshire. The land surveyors who had been sent from New York to determine the borders of the DeLancey manor were met by armed settlers from the Green Mountains; the governor ordered the arrest of the settlers.[57] Meanwhile the New York landlords—in other words, the land speculators—again resorted to litigation to evict the settlers from the areas in dispute. The subservient judges reached the verdicts desired by the landlords. Allen responded by declaring that "the gods of the valleys are not the gods of the hills." The area around the Green Mountains became the scene of a guerrilla war. Beginning in 1771, the Green Mountain Boys repelled the attacks mounted by armed detachments led by New York sheriffs. After a two-year struggle, having expelled the court officials and the other servants of the crown, they in effect established an independent system of government. The rulers of New York issued proclamations urging the apprehension of the rebel leaders, but to no avail. And when New York attempted to place its own manager in the Green Mountains district, the Boys torched his residence and expelled him. They also beat and threw out the land surveyors that had been sent from New York and confiscated their surveying equipment.[58]

In the summer of 1771 a large punitive expedition was sent to the area of the uprising. But the Green Mountain Boys put it to flight. This event initiated the mass movement of the peasants against the landowning lords and land speculators. Its leaders used the experience of the "Great Rebellion" of the New York tenant farmers in 1766. Wherever the Green Mountain Boys appeared, the authority of the crown officials was overthrown. They freed the farmers who had been arrested for defaulting on their debts, gave them back the lands, property, and cattle that had been confiscated from them, and burnt the court files containing the records of the farmers' liabilities. Here and there the manor houses belonging to the lackeys of the landowning lords—the lawyers, sheriffs, rent-collectors, and others—went up in flames. As these lackeys were sent packing off to New York, they were told, "Go you may now & complain to that damned scoundrel your governor. God damn your Governor, Laws, King, Council and Assembly."[59] William Tryon, who had now become the governor of New York, responded by issuing a proclamation offering a reward of £20 per head for the capture of Ethan Allen and the other leaders of the insurgency.[60] The reports from General Gage's headquarters describing the large-scale nature of the rebel movement led London to order Tryon to reach a mutually agreeable settlement. The ensuing talks centered on the cessation of military

57. "Proclamation of New York Lieutenant-Governor Cadwallader Colden of 12 December 1769," ibid., 379–80.

58. Ibid., 391, 394, 397–405, 406–11, 412–14, 433–35, 422, 456, etc.; Jellison, *Ethan Allen,* 39–60.

59. *DHSNY*, ed. O'Callaghan, vol. 4, 442–43, 446–55, 461–65, 472–73, 475.

60. "Order in Council for the Arrest of Ethan Allen and Other Rioters, 27 November 1771," ibid., 456. The Green Mountain Boys responded by issuing their own proclamation. The bounty they offered for the heads of the large landowners of New York—£10 and £15—was smaller.

operations, while the resolution of the land problem was left to the discretion of the king.[61]

The settlers had been unable to plant their crops and gather their harvest and were in need of breathing-space. The representatives of the poor farmers and Tryon, who the year before had drowned the uprising of the South Carolina Regulators in blood, failed to find a common language. The centers of the rebellion in the Green Mountain valley became active once again. In November 1772 Tryon asked London for military assistance but was refused. The New York landowners had no choice but to rely on their own forces. In the spring of 1773 they reinforced the colonial army with detachments of mercenaries and sent it to the Green Mountains. Hundreds of settlers were evicted from the lands they cultivated, and many were arrested and put in jail. In August 1773 the rebels received help from several groups of Green Mountain Boys, who saw to it that justice was done. Allen declared that after the actions taken by the landlords and the New York authorities, the farmers "valued not the government nor even the Kingdom; . . . force was force in whatever hands, and," said Allen, "they had force and power sufficient to protect themselves against either."[62] In the eyes of the insurgents, the governor and his political machinery no longer existed. The local authorities were totally unable to back up their orders and proclamations. Once more they turned for help to the English commander who, however, rejected their request, explaining that the dispatch of regular troops would only serve to demonstrate to the people the weakness of the New York city council and might have unfortunate consequences. Yet Tryon, a zealous defender of the interests of the landed aristocracy, refused to make any concessions. The detachments of Green Mountain Boys, having acquired a sense of their power, continued their struggle against the landowners for a land free of rent.[63]

In a number of places clashes occurred between the squatters and the representatives of the crown guarding the safety of the royal forests, which were intended as a source of ship timber for the British navy.[64] In both the North and the South, attacks by farmers on rent collectors and bailiffs engaged in debt collection, reprisals against judges and sheriffs, and in some localities the burning down of the estates of the most detested landlords became common. The authorities responded by arrests, the confiscation of property, and eviction.[65] Alarming reports came from everywhere.

61. *Correspondence of Gage,* vol. 1, 274–77; "Report of the Committee on the Disorders at Bennington, 1 June 1772," *DHSNY,* ed. O'Callaghan, vol. 4, 481.

62. "The Bennington Mob Erect Their Judgment Seat," *DHSNY,* ed. O'Callaghan, vol. 4, 521.

63. Ibid., 494, 500–501, 511, 512, 518, 521. Tryon complained to London that the "rebellious rabble" was preventing the landlords from taking possession of lands that were "lawfully theirs." He proposed granting the rebels thirty-acre plots elsewhere on land that was vacant and even agreed to defer collecting the fixed rent they owed. The disputed lands, however, were to become the sole property of the landlords. W. Tryon to Lord Dartmouth, July 1, 1773, ibid., 504–10.

64. Ibid., 383–89.

65. Harry A. Cushing, "Political Activity of Massachusetts Towns during the Revolution," in *Annual Report of the American Historical Association for the Year 1895* (Washington, D.C., 1895), 108; *Diary and Autobiography of John Adams,* ed. Lyman H. Butterfield (Cambridge, Mass., 1961), vol. 2, 35.

Such was the situation in North America at the end of 1773, when the famous Boston Tea Party took place. News of the repressive, retaliatory measures taken by the British at the end of March 1774 arrived at a time when the bulk of the colonists was already excited by reports of England's new land policy, described in the royal decree of February 3, 1774. The decree ordered the local authorities to survey all allotments in the colonies that were between one hundred and one thousand acres in size, number them, and mark them on the map. Those allotments that were found to be unoccupied were to be sold at auction at the highest price offered. The proprietor of the land thus purchased would have to pay an annual quitrent, which was to be five times the current one and which was to be paid not in produce, but in silver; he would also be obliged to hand over to the crown all precious metals and stones found on his allotment, rather than one-fifth of them as had been the case until then.[66] All previous royal decrees concerning the demarcation and distribution of land were abrogated. Also abolished was the right of every settler who paid his own way to the colonies to a personal plot of land—a right that still survived in some places.

But the crown not only raised the amount of quitrents to be collected from the allotments sold at auction but also became more aggressive in recovering rent arrears for the preceding years; this new policy directly affected the interests of the farmers, squatters, tenant-farmers, and planters, that is, the overwhelming majority of the colonists. The desire of the ruling circles in London to fill the exchequer by collecting rent and arrears stirred up the population and provoked a new wave of mass protests and disturbances among the farmers in all the colonies, presaging a new explosion of the people's wrath. Even Tryon understood this. "I took the liberty to assure Lord Dartmouth," he wrote, "that these new Crown orders could not have any operation."[67] Even in New England, where the institution of fixed rent was quite unknown, people feared it might be introduced.[68]

Meanwhile the laws passed by the English Parliament against "divers ill-affected persons" reached North America. The colonists termed these laws the "Intolerable Acts." Nominally they applied only to the population of Boston and the colony of Massachusetts.[69] A sea blockade was imposed on the Port of Boston, while additional royal regiments entered the city. The activities of the Sons of Liberty, as well as of the committees of correspondence and other revolutionary organizations, were banned, and the town meetings were abolished. All power became vested in the person of the governor, a position now held by General Gage. The real danger that armed force might be used stirred up all the colonies. The farmers of Worcester declared that the use of force against the citizens of Boston was a blow aimed via Boston at all American freedoms.[70] Farming settlements and communities not only held meetings but also

66. *Royal Instructions to British Colonial Governors, 1670–1776,* ed. L. W. Labaree (New York, 1935), vol. 2, 533–37.
67. Cochran, *New York in the Confederation,* 107.
68. Virtue, *British Land Policy,* 40n37.
69. *Documents of American History,* ed. Commager, vol. 1, 71–74.
70. Aptheker, *The American Revolution of 1763–1783,* 101.

rushed to help the Bostonians: Quebec and New Jersey sent wheat; the colonies of New England, meat and fish; South Carolina, rice. The farmers' solidarity played a large role in raising the spirits of the besieged citizens of Boston.[71]

When evaluating the political situation existing in 1774, the Massachusetts Committee of Correspondence took into account the attitudes of the different groups in society, including the declarations issued by the rural committees of correspondence in support of its actions. The resolve of the masses of farmers and their readiness to fight for their rights convinced the radical leaders in Boston that they could rely on the settlers in the interior and the West. As early as May 1774 the members of the Boston committee concluded that it was "the yeomanry whose virtue must finally save this country."[72] The committees of correspondence and the Sons of Liberty responded to the establishment of the Gage dictatorship in Boston by starting a campaign to overthrow the local British authorities. Though expelled from Boston, the provincial committee of correspondence and the popular organization that was the most mass in character—the town meeting—continued to function outside the city limits. Gage's proclamations and orders were ignored. Everything indicated that real power was slipping from the general's hands.[73]

And just when the colonists were suffering from a wave of "intolerable" repressions, London decided to change the temporary provisions concerning the land question in the Proclamation of 1763. In fact, the withdrawal of many of the interior garrisons from the West was in no way an indication of England's repudiation of its claims to those lands. On the contrary, the growing pressure from the squatters and land companies had led Whitehall to look for a solution guaranteeing England's control in the West without requiring the dispatch of large contingents of troops from the cities of the Atlantic coast. The government of the empire intended to transfer the western lands to the jurisdiction of the sparsely populated Canadian province of Quebec. This idea formed the basis of the Quebec Act,[74] which greatly contributed to the creation of a revolutionary situation by profoundly offending the Americans' nascent sense of nationhood. But of course the main factor was that the Act struck a blow at their economic interests. It extended the borders of Quebec by annexing an area of 11.5 million acres to the west of the Appalachians and to the north of the Ohio River (this territory had never been a part of French Canada). And it was these lands that were attracting thousands of migrants, many of whom, despite the prohibition of 1763, had already settled in the upper Ohio valley. The land companies also hankered after these lands.

The provisions of the Act were a very heavy blow to the hopes the farmers, tenant-farmers, indentured workers, craftsmen, and day-laborers had of obtaining their own piece of land. At the same time the Quebec Act had a negative effect on the extensive economy of the southern planters. One of the most influential planters in Virginia

---

71. *Correspondence of Gage,* vol. 1, 357, 361.
72. Adams to Charles Thomson, May 30, 1774, *Writings of Samuel Adams,* vol. 3, 125.
73. *Correspondence of Gage,* vol. 1, 370.
74. *Documents of American History,* ed. Commager, vol. 1, 74–76.

called this statute the most intolerable of all the Intolerable Acts.[75] With this act the English irretrievably lost the support of what was at that time the most affluent and influential stratum of the American bourgeoisie. As a result, most of the slave-holding planters joined the ranks of the rebel colonists.[76] These planters provided a galaxy of bourgeois revolutionaries that included George Washington, Thomas Jefferson, Patrick Henry, and others.

The leadership of the committees of correspondence and the Sons of Liberty in New England indignantly criticized the Intolerable Acts, seeing them as a new attack on their freedoms. Those who tried to justify the Quebec Act were given the contemptuous sobriquet "Tory." Even the First Continental Congress, which was distinguished by the conservatism of its views and the moderate nature of its demands, regarded the new measure of Parliament as an attempt to "hem in" the colonies. The common people in the farms, settlements, and towns, whose hopes and plans for happiness were linked to the acquisition of a piece of land, considered the Quebec Act a declaration of war against the colonists.[77] The English menace forced the colonists to close ranks. In the South the owners of commercial plantations assumed the leadership of the movement against the mother country.[78] The southern colonies began to form a militia. In the North the committees of correspondence and other Whig clubs and organizations established stores of arms and gunpowder and formed units of Minutemen (volunteers) staffed by farmers and craftsmen. Farmers, tenant farmers, and craftsmen commanded the regiments, battalions, and companies of volunteers.[79]

The swift development of events reflected the emerging revolutionary situation. Here and there spontaneous clashes occurred between the Tories—the followers of the crown—and the colonists. Having ceased paying quitrents, taxes, and debts, the farmers began to dismantle the machinery of royal authority: they closed the courts and town councils and expelled the judges, sheriffs, prosecutors, and other servants of the crown, many of whom had held sway in the colonies for decades.[80] By the autumn of 1774 the farmers in the western part of Massachusetts had overthrown the king's representatives and had begun to exercise power themselves through the local correspondence committees.

As a result of the constant terrorism of the rebellious farmers, the royal government of New York in March 1774 ordered the arrest of their leaders. Every week bloody clashes took place in different localities. The number of reports of insults and beatings suffered by those supporting the landlords and the royal authorities kept growing. In Charlotte County the Green Mountain Boys built two timber fortresses, instilling fear in the owners of the neighboring manors. The actions of the insurgents led the New York authorities to request military assistance for the third time. But Gage, taking

75. *University of Nebraska Studies,* New Series, #11 (1953), 45.
76. See N. N. Iakovlev, *Washington* (Moscow, 1973), 109.
77. Newcomer, *Embattled Farmers,* 50; Lynn Montross, *The Reluctant Rebels* (New York, 1950), 54; Harris, *Origin of the Land Tenure System,* 367.
78. Iakovlev, *Washington,* 119.
79. Lynd, *Class Conflict, Slavery, and the U.S. Constitution,* 35.
80. *Correspondence of Gage,* vol. 1, 365–72.

into account the tense situation, would not risk sending his troops into the Green Mountains district. In April 1775 the rebellion of the Green Mountain Boys was caught up in the unfolding struggle of the colonies against the mother country. In July 1775 Ethan Allen assured the new provincial congress of New York that the battalion of the Revolutionary army formed from the Green Mountain Boys "will retaliate this favor by wholly hazarding their lives, if need be, in the common cause of America." In this way the Yankee farmers who dreamed of acquiring plots of free land joined the Revolution in the ranks of the patriots.[81]

In the other colonies too, real authority was increasingly shifting to the county and village committees. Because the provincial congresses and conventions, with the exception of Maryland, were still very weak, the correspondence committees exercised overall control of the new local authorities. The First Continental Congress opened in Philadelphia on September 5, 1774, in an almost full-fledged revolutionary situation. Even though it submitted a loyal address to the English king, it acted as the chief intercolonial revolutionary institution by adopting two documents of historic importance. The "Declaration and Resolves of the First Continental Congress" contained along with a demand for the repeal of the "Intolerable Acts" the statement that the colonists "are entitled to life, liberty and property." The document that bore the title the "Association" declared that the colonies were prepared to sever all commercial links with England and called for the development of agriculture, the crafts, and local industry. The task of fulfilling these decisions was given to the local congresses and correspondence committees.[82]

However, the boycott of British goods met with the hidden and stubborn resistance of an even larger number of merchants than the earlier boycott provoked by the Townshend Acts. This resistance was crushed only after the rural correspondence committees appealed to the masses to "refrain from any commerce with Great-Britain & the West India Islands." It was the refusal of thousands of settlers to buy and use goods of English manufacture that forced the merchants to stop trading with Great Britain and join the third boycott of English goods. An anxious Gage reported to London that the siege of Boston had been relieved with help from farmers from other provinces, that the province was arming itself, and that a volunteer militia consisting of the farmers of Massachusetts, Connecticut, and Rhode Island was undergoing military training.[83]

At the same time the royal troops built up their strength. The situation had become so tense that any small clash was capable of leading to a general explosion. Gage clearly understood this. Taking a sober view of the forces under his command and realizing they were insufficient for suppressing a general uprising, he tried to prevent any outbreaks of armed violence. In September 1774 thousands of farmers from

81. *DHSNY*, ed. O'Callaghan, vol. 4, 526–27, 529–30, 534, 535, 554.
82. *Documents of American History*, ed. Commager, vol. 1, 82–84, 85–87; see V. N. Pleshkov, "The First Continental Congress (1774)," *Problems of History* 6 (1976).
83. *English Historical Documents*, doc. #141 A, 790–91; Gage to Dartmouth, September 12, 1774, *Correspondence of Gage*, vol. 1, 374.

various parts of western Massachusetts marched on the city of Boston after hearing that royal troops had carried out a bloody massacre there and that British ships had bombarded the city. The news turned out to be false, but the farmers' martial spirit was undiminished. The British battalions in Boston were in danger of being attacked at any moment. A similar situation arose in the southern colonies. When Lord Dunmore, the governor of Virginia, suddenly moved a quantity of gunpowder out of a depot, hundreds of farmers from the western districts marched on the provincial capital.[84]

It was only by accident that another false alarm in November 1774 failed to lead to an outbreak of hostilities. The correspondence committees received news that Gage's soldiers had marched out of Boston to requisition the powder stores of the patriots. Immediately the alarm was raised throughout the whole of New England. Armed groups of Minutemen and companies of volunteers consisting almost wholly of farmers set off for the Boston area. Meanwhile the English soldiers, who had marched several miles away from Boston, unexpectedly turned back. On this occasion no battle took place. The volunteers, full of martial spirit, were disappointed.[85] This upsurge of popular indignation showed that the rank-and-file members of the movement had adopted a more radical position toward England than many of their Whig-patriot leaders. The farmer volunteers were bursting to go into battle and reproached their leaders for being cautious and indecisive. "The People get after us for our hesitancy," wrote one of those leaders.[86]

Analyzing the events unfolding in the summer and autumn of 1774 and the reports sent in by local Tories, the headquarters of the royal commander-in-chief concluded that the spirit of rebellion was strongest in the rural areas and among the common people. As Gage wrote, those who demanded decisive action "are numerous, worked up to a fury, and not a Boston rabble but the Freeholders & Farmers of the Country."[87] The events of the stormy year of 1774 clearly demonstrated that the lower strata could no longer live as they had done before and that the upper strata could no longer govern as they had done before. A revolutionary situation had arisen in the colonies of North America. It led to armed conflict between two hostile camps that continued for eight years (1775–1783). During that period the American people, in the words of V. I. Lenin, were to give the world "an example of a revolutionary war against feudal enslavement."[88]

84. Jensen, *Founding of a Nation,* 546–50; Jensen, "The American People and the American Revolution," *The Journal of American History* 57 (June 1970), 22.
85. Adams, *Diary and Autobiography,* ed. Butterfield, vol. 2, 277–87.
86. Newcomer, *Embattled Farmers,* 55, 182.
87. *Correspondence of Gage,* vol. 1, 371.
88. V. I. Lenin, *Collected Works,* vol. 37, 49.

COMMENT BY JAMES A. HENRETTA

What was the "land question" in British North America prior to the American War for Independence? Was it the armed struggle between Scotch-Irish settlers and native Americans in central Pennsylvania? The uprising of German and English tenants against the manor lords of the Hudson River valley? The violent conflict in the Carolinas between backcountry farmers and royal officials? The confrontation in Vermont between settlers and land speculators from New York and those from New England? The machinations of capitalist land companies for title to the Ohio Valley? Or was it the struggle over quitrents in New York, Pennsylvania, Maryland, and the Carolinas?

G. P. Kuropiatnik assumes that most, if not all, of these disputes were essentially similar. He suggests that their central motif was the "political action" taken by petty-bourgeois farmers against an oppressive feudal class supported by the British imperial government. As initially "spontaneous and uncoordinated" uprisings, Kuropiatnik's argument continues, the farmers' movements were suppressed by governmental officials, hired mercenaries, or royal troops. Then the balance of social forces shifted. British policies of taxation and control sparked a resistance movement led by the urban merchant bourgeoisie and by southern slave-owning planters. This movement won the support of urban artisans and workers. Then, thanks to Samuel Adams and the committees of correspondence, it spread into the countryside. Farmers actively supported the boycott movement of 1769–1770 and by 1774 were "bursting to go into battle." Demanding "land free of quit rent," rural smallholders joined with urban craftsmen and the merchant and landholding bourgeoisie in (as Kuropiatnik quotes Lenin) a "revolutionary war against feudal enslavement."

This interpretation is flawed in two respects. In the first place, it fails to consider the unique array of social forces in each colony. Kuropiatnik cannot (and does not) explain why some disadvantaged rural groups refused to join the independence movement but instead threw in their lot with the Loyalist forces of feudal reaction. Second, the interpretation does not give sufficient emphasis to class division within the patriot movement. It fails to comprehend the very different interests and values of the patriot planters and landlords (the bourgeoisie), the yeomanry (petty bourgeois), and the landless tenant farmers and workers (the agricultural proletariat).

Kuropiatnik is not responsible for some of these weaknesses. He published this article in 1976, drawing primarily on original sources and secondary accounts written by American scholars before 1970. Since the publication of his essay, "new social historians" have developed a more complex and ambiguous interpretation of American rural development.[1] Specifically:

1. Jack P. Greene and J. R. Pole, eds., *Colonial British America: Essays in the New History of the Early Modern Era* (Baltimore, 1984) offers good historiographical summary and analysis of this literature. Synthetic surveys based on this work include Gary B. Nash, *Red, White, and Black: The Peoples of Early America* (Englewood Cliffs, N.J.; 3d ed., 1992); Edward Countryman, *The American Revolution* (New York, 1985); James A. Henretta and Gregory H. Nobles, *Evolution and Revolution: American Society, 1600–1820* (Lexington, Mass., 1987); and Jack P. Greene, *Pursuits*

There was not a single land question but a variety of distinct disputes over land ownership and tenure. Many involved ethnic rivalries or religious animosities. Scotch-Irish immigrants in the Pennsylvania backcountry had petty-bourgeois conceptions of property rights. Families demanded complete and undivided ownership of the land. They expressed open hostility to Native American forms of communal land tenure and usufruct rights. Therefore they opposed both the pacific Indian policies of the Pennsylvania assembly, which was dominated by English Quakers, and the accumulation of landed estates by the Penn family and its Anglican merchant allies.

These antagonisms—racial, ethnic, and religious as well as economic—determined the course of the Revolution in Pennsylvania. Scotch-Irish Presbyterians were the driving force behind the radical-democratic constitution of 1776. The new government instituted new (petty bourgeois) land policies. It seized much of the Penn family's unsettled land and ignored Native American land claims. The Presbyterian-dominated assembly also imposed loyalty oaths on Quakers and passed strict moral legislation. Ultimately ethnic rule and religious legislation led to the overthrow of the Presbyterian party and the enactment of a new conservative constitution in 1790.[2] To discuss the "land question and the revolutionary situation" in Pennsylvania only in economic terms is to offer an incomplete and ultimately a misleading analysis of its inner dynamic.

The course of events in the North Carolina backcountry was likewise more culturally and economically complex than Kuropiatnik allows. European migrants to the region were initially subsistence-plus farmers. They grew enough food to feed their families and bartered the surplus for imported salt, sugar, cloth, and farm implements. Beginning in the 1750s, some enterprising farmers sought to become full-fledged southern planters. They invested heavily in slaves to take advantage of rising market prices for wheat and tobacco. In Anson County the number of slaves increased fourteenfold between 1754 and 1767. As production rose, so did the planters' reliance on British mercantile credit. To buy slaves, land, and equipment, they went into debt to newly arrived Scotch traders.

The depression following the Seven Years' War brought a collapse in tobacco prices. As Kuropiatnik indicates, it also led to "an intensification of the class struggle." This confrontation began in the legal arena as creditors used the courts to seize the property of delinquent farmers. Merchants brought an average of ninety suits per year in Orange County between 1763 and 1765, a dramatic increase from the seven suits per year during the previous decade. Legal conflict prompted political upheaval. Backcountry farmers formed the Regulator movements. One of its leaders was Herman Husband, an aspiring entrepreneur with investments in milling, land speculation,

---

of Happiness: The Social Development of Early Modern British Colonies and the Formulation of American Culture (Chapel Hill, 1988).

2. See Eric Foner, *Tom Paine and Revolutionary America* (New York, 1976) and Owen S. Ireland, "The Ethnic-Religious Dimensions of Pennsylvania Politics, 1778–1779," *William and Mary Quarterly,* 3d ser., 30 (1973), 423–48 and "The Counter-Revolution in Pennsylvania, 1784–1786," (unpublished paper, 1987).

and iron production. Between 1768 and 1771, Regulators closed courts, harassed lawyers and judges, destroyed merchants' stores, and challenged the authority of the provincial government. Finally, Royal Governor William Tryon mobilized the eastern militia and suppressed the Regulation with armed force.

The facts are clear enough, but what was their inner logic? Again Kuropiatnik ignores the ethnic aspects of this struggle, even though these concerns bulked large in the consciousness of the historical actors. Regulators identified their enemies as "Scotch merchants," showered them with verbal abuse, and threatened "to kill all the Clerks and Lawyers" who were their political allies.[3] This hostility against "foreign" merchants raised the emotional level of the debt crisis, enhancing the prospect of armed violence.

Kuropiatnik likewise minimizes the "capitalist" causes of the Regulation. Scotch traders came to Carolina (and the Virginia Piedmont) as the agents of British commercial capitalism. They sought to expand the production of tobacco for export (to Europe, via Scotland) and the consumption of imported English manufactures. Their activities meant that the North Carolina Regulation was not only a struggle "to obtain land that would be free of all feudal obligations" (as Kuropiatnik argues) but also a populist petty-bourgeois battle against capitalist creditors. Depicting themselves as "poor families" and "industrious peasants," many yeoman farmers supported the Regulation because of their experiences with the new circuit court system. Governor Tryon's suppression of the Regulation was as much a defense of British mercantile capitalism as of Lord Granville's feudal claims.

Nor does the alignment of social forces in New York fully support Kuropiatnik's thesis of a bourgeois revolution against an imperially supported feudal regime. Leading New York patriots, such as the Livingston family, enjoyed feudal land rights in the form of quitrents, long-term leases, and manorial court privileges. Moreover, these aristocratically inclined patriots captured control of the new state government and wrote a constitution that safeguarded traditional property rights. Article XXXVI of the New York constitution of 1777 explicitly upheld the legitimacy of all "grants of land, within this state, made by the authority of the King (of Great Britain) or his predecessors."[4] Angered by this provision and by past oppression, many Hudson Valley tenants refused to support the patriot movement. Some remained neutral while others became Loyalists. In New York as in North Carolina, not all Loyalists were feudal landlords and not all patriots were bourgeois revolutionaries.

Moreover, the land question had a contradictory impact on the cohesion of the patriot movement. On the one hand, British imperial policies prompted an alliance

---

3. My account draws upon James P. Whittenberg, "Planters, Merchants, and Lawyers: Social Change and the Origins of the North Carolina Regulation," *William and Mary Quarterly*, 3d ser., 34 (1977), 215–38 and Marvin L. Michael Kay, "The North Carolina Regulation, 1766–1776; A Class Conflict," in Alfred F. Young, ed., *The American Revolution: Explorations in the History of American Radicalism* (DeKalb, Ill., 1976), 71–123.

4. See, in general, Edward Countryman, *A People in Revolution: The American Revolution and Political Society in New York, 1760–1790* (Baltimore, 1981).

among land-hungry tenants, ambitious yeomen, and acquisitive speculators. As Kuropiatnik indicates, the Royal Proclamation of 1763, and especially the Land Decree and the Quebec Act of 1774, created widespread rural discontent and prompted southern land speculators to join "the ranks of the rebel colonists." On the other hand, Americans were divided among themselves on many land issues. Inheritance-poor sons, tenants, artisans, and day laborers fought bitterly with patriot speculators over land prices and squatters' rights. Indeed, President George Washington's forcible suppression of the Whiskey Rebellion in 1793 stemmed in part from his anger at settlers who refused to honor his own western land claims.[5] Kuropiatnik has unwisely ignored Carl Becker's famous injunction that the American Revolution was a struggle both for home rule and over who should rule at home. Consequently, he has failed to recognize that the land question united and divided the American patriot movement.

The lack of interpretative complexity in Kuropiatnik's account raises doubts about his analytic categories. Here it is necessary to proceed with caution since Soviet and American scholars usually begin from different methodological premises. As Kuropiatnik notes, "bourgeois historiography did not of course adopt the Marxist approach to the revolutionary situation." How then can a bourgeois critic speak constructively to a Marxist-Leninist scholar?

There are two alternatives. The first, which I have employed thus far, is to accept Kuropiatnik's categories of analysis and to suggest weaknesses in his argument. Thus I have asserted that a rigorous Marxist examination of the land question in North Carolina must confront the impact of British commercial capitalism. I have argued further that Kuropiatnik has not given sufficient weight to class divisions within American rural society and has therefore misconstrued the Revolutionary movement and its goals. Beyond that, I have suggested that a thorough materialist explanation should comprehend ethnic and racial antagonisms as well as economic conflicts. Considered on its own terms, Kuropiatnik's interpretation does not fully comprehend the complexity of the land question.

A second alternative is to propose that Kuropiatnik revise or refine his analytic framework. This suggestion is hardly radical. Marxist scholarship outside Russia (and increasingly within it) is not monolithic. Socialist-minded scholars are as internally divided over issues of method, theory, and interpretation as their bourgeois counterparts. Some American scholars have contributed explicitly to this debate among Marxists. Others have framed their arguments in terms that are comprehensible to both socialist and bourgeois historians. And still more continue to produce studies that, as Kuropiatnik acknowledges, "are of some value (to those writing in the Marxist tradition) because of the factual material they contain."

In particular, recent American scholarship addresses an issue that Kuropiatnik's analytic framework cannot explain: why Massachusetts farmers "were bursting to go into battle" by 1774. They certainly were not victims of an established feudal

---

5. Thomas P. Slaughter, *The Whiskey Rebellion: Frontier Epilogue to the American Revolution* (New York, 1986), chap. 5.

regime. Freehold tenure (without quitrents) had been the norm in New England from the beginning of English settlement. To be sure, there were other class divisions and tensions. The region had its share of wealthy land promoters and speculators, such as Ethan Allen of New Hampshire. But as Kuropiatnik's treatment of the Green Mountain Boys demonstrates, these profit-minded entrepreneurs often commanded the support of middling and poor farmers. Finally, there was little hostility between backcountry settlers in Massachusetts and royal officials before the 1770s.

Why then did Massachusetts farmers respond so positively to Samuel Adams's propaganda even before the Intolerable Acts? Was their revolutionary activism essentially an affair of the mind, an idealist response to potential oppression in the future? Or did it proceed more immediately from their present political and material circumstances?

The "new social history" has revealed the fragile and perhaps deteriorating material base of New England rural society. Some scholars have posited a full-scale demographic crisis in eastern New England by the mid-eighteenth century. For example, Andover, Massachusetts, had a population of 435 in 1680, but grew to 1,435 residents in 1730 and no fewer than 2,900 in 1780. Faced with the pressure of population on landed resources, some farmers migrated to central and western Massachusetts. Other yeoman families provided for their many offspring by dividing their estates into small farmsteads. Still others urged their sons and daughters to accumulate cash for land purchase—through service in the military, working as house servants and day laborers, or by manufacturing nails or shoes in the quickly expanding capitalist putting-out system.[6] The variety of strategies testified to the pervasiveness of the crisis. A century and a half of rapid population growth threatened the traditional yeoman family economy.

American scholars writing in the Marxist tradition have given new theoretical form to this empirical data. They describe the New England economy in terms of a "household mode of production."[7] Most farm households, they point out, operated primarily outside of the labor and commodity markets. Yeoman producers normally relied on their own labor—and that of their wives, sons, and daughters—as they set

6. See Christopher M. Jedrey, *The World of John Cleaveland: Family and Community in Eighteenth-Century New England* (New York, 1979); Fred Anderson, "A People's Army: Provincial Military Service in Massachusetts during the Seven Years' War," *William and Mary Quarterly*, 3d ser., 40 (1983), 499–527; Daniel Vickers, "Nantucket Whalemen in the Deep Sea Fishery: The Changing Anatomy of an Early American Labor Force," *Journal of American History* 72 (1985), 277–96; and James A. Henretta, "The War for Independence and American Economic Development," in Ronald Hoffman et al., eds., *The Economy of Early America: The Revolutionary Period, 1763–1790* (Charlottesville, Va., 1988), 45–87.

7. Michael Merrill, "Cash Is Good to Eat: Self-Sufficiency and Exchange in the Rural Economy of the United States," *Radical History Review* 9 (1977), 42–72; Robert E. Mutch, "Yeoman and Merchant in Pre-industrial America: Eighteenth-Century Massachusetts as a Case Study," *Societas— A Review of Social History* 7 (1977), 279–302. The data on Massachusetts comes from Bettye Hobbs Pruitt, "Self-Sufficiency and the Agricultural Economy of Eighteenth-Century Massachusetts," *William and Mary Quarterly*, 3d ser., 41 (1984), 333–64. See also Allan Kulikoff, "The Transition to Capitalism in Rural America," ibid., 3d ser., 46 (1989), 120–44.

farm tasks. Moreover, most farmers in New England sent less than 10 percent of their total output into the market system. They lived within largely self-sufficient town economies, exchanging scarce resources and farm products among themselves—perhaps out of inclination and increasingly out of necessity. One-half of the nineteen thousand farms inventoried on the Massachusetts valuation list for 1772 did not have plows or oxen; 40 percent lacked enough cultivated acres to be self-sufficient in grain; and two-thirds did not have enough pasture for their livestock. Mutual interdependence was a condition of existence.

Cooperative exchange among neighbors created a productive system and cultural values that were resistant to market incentives. "The farmers have the game in their hands," an exasperated Alexander Hamilton complained in 1781 while trying to amass food for the Continental army; "they are not obliged to sell because they have almost every necessary within themselves."[8]

Yet New England's "household mode of production" was under attack by the 1770s, both from within and without. The demographic crisis drove some farmers to the frontier and others (or their sons and daughters) into the nascent capitalist putting-out system. Simultaneously, new British legislation deprived the provincial assembly and the town meetings of their traditional powers over taxes and governmental salaries. The authority to tax rested increasingly in the hands of Parliament or royal appointees. "If Parliament can take away Mr. Hancock's wharf and Mrs. Rowe's wharf," Samuel Adams reasoned, "they can take away your barn and my house."[9] To many hard-pressed yeomen families, Adams's warnings reaffirmed their own perception of declining control over their economic and political lives. They gravitated toward independence and republicanism to preserve personal and communal autonomy. As the Northampton town meeting put it during a debate on the Massachusetts constitution of 1780, no man should have "any degree or spark of . . . a right of dominion, government, and jurisdiction over (an)other."

Like all major historical events, the American Revolution was a complex experience. It involved, as G. P. Kuropiatnik claims, a repudiation of existing "feudal" rights and privileges. The new American social order had neither kings nor titled aristocrats nor a pervasive quitrent system. Yet the patriot movement was both something less and something more than a bourgeois uprising against a feudal regime. Something less, because this schema cannot explain events in New York, where leading patriots came from the old gentry class and successfully defended their ancient property rights until the 1840s, or in North Carolina, where royal Governor Tryon suppressed the Regulator movement on behalf of British commercial capitalists. Something more, because the Revolution in rural New England was the product, at least in part, of a corporatist (and not a bourgeois) society and ideology, and because the upheaval exposed deep class and ethnic divisions among patriots.

---

8. Quoted in Michael Merrill, "The Anti-Capitalist Origins of the United States," *Review: The Journal of the Fernand Braudel Center* 13 (1990), 465–97.
9. See Richard L. Bushman, *King and People in Provincial Massachusetts* (Chapel Hill, 1985), 198 and chap. 5.

To write a theoretically coherent history of these diverse events is a challenging task whether the scholar writes in the bourgeois or the Marxist tradition. I hope G. P. Kuropiatnik will again accept this challenge. His goal, I hope, would be to construct an analytically innovative Marxist interpretation that does full justice to the historical complexity revealed by bourgeois empiricism.

RESPONSE BY GENNADI P. KUROPIATNIK

Russian scholars have always tried to keep informed about the achievements of their colleagues in other countries. As Professor Henretta points out, the article he reviewed was published in 1976; and naturally when writing it, I could not have anticipated the research carried out by American historians in the late 1970s and 1980s and the new insights and concepts they developed as a result. I am, however, very interested in these new developments.

The article read by Professor Henretta was merely one of a number I published at the time of the U.S. bicentennial celebration. In these other works I discuss the two problems which Professor Henretta says I failed to analyze in the article in question. For example, in my book *The War for the Independence and Formation of the United States of America* (Moscow, 1976), I explain why some groups of small farmers and tenant-holders in New York state and the Carolinas joined the Tory camp (214–15).

The differentiation of the social forces in the British colonies and the class structure of the patriotic movement are discussed in my works "The Struggle for Land in the Colonial Period of U.S. History" (*Problems of History* 8 (1974), 68–86); "Feudal Rent in Britain's North American Colonies" (*The American Annual* [Moscow, 1975]); "Popular Uprisings in Britain's North American Colonies" (*Problems of the History and Ethnography of North America* [Moscow, 1979]); "The Struggle of the Two Tendencies of Capitalist Development in the United States in the Age of Bourgeois Revolutions" (*Modern and Contemporary History,* 2 [1976], 77–89); *The Problems of a Scientific Concept of Modern U.S. History* (Moscow, 1983).

Some of Professor Henretta's comments go beyond the chronological framework of my article. I refer to the question of the state constitutions of Pennsylvania (1776), New York (1777), and Massachusetts (1780).

However, I should like to stress that what he says about the issues I discuss in my article is a matter of profound importance to me, as are his views concerning the possibility and desirability of a constructive dialogue between the historians of our two countries. I quite agree that a "thorough materialist interpretation [of history] should comprehend ethnic and racial antagonisms, as well as economic conflicts," and in addition deal with "the complexity of the land question."

CHAPTER 3

John Adams during the Struggle of the American Colonies for Independence

by

B. A. Shiriayev

The American historical literature devoted to John Adams is very rich in scope and variety. Detailed information about the life of Adams during the struggle for the liberation of the colonies may be found, for instance, in Catherine Drinker Bowen's study, *John Adams and the American Revolution* (1950). This book is written in a popular style, yet it contains much factual material on Adams's childhood and youth and especially on his activities during the struggle for independence. Although the work portrays Adams as above all a committed American patriot, it fails to analyze the causes that determined his place and role in the revolutionary events of the age.

Steven Hess, in *American Political Dynasties from Adams to Kennedy* (1966), attempts to show Adams's position and significance in relation to the whole of American history. He paints an idealized and laudatory portrait of Adams and does not pay sufficient attention to the evolution of Adams's views.

Many studies have been devoted to particular periods and aspects of Adams's career. In *The Diplomacy of the American Revolution,* the well-known historian Samuel Flagg Bemis discusses at length Adams's diplomatic role during the era of the War of Independence. Bemis praises his diplomatic abilities and argues that American historians have underestimated Adams the diplomat. The rich legacy of writings John Adams left behind consists of his journals, voluminous correspondence, and works on the political issues of the day. They currently are being published in the United States in a series entitled "The Adams Papers." The journals and letters of Adams not only contain a great deal of information about his activities but also are a valuable source for the personalities, events, and atmosphere of one of the crucial periods of American history. His works, such as "A Dissertation on the Canon and the Feudal Law" and "Thoughts on Government," which were written during different periods of the struggle for independence, present fully and vividly his attitude toward the events in which he actively participated.

While not aiming to offer a detailed analysis of the activities of Adams, I shall discuss in this article certain aspects of the life and activities of this important U.S. politician and statesman. John Adams lived a long and eventful life. He was born in 1735, more than forty years before the Declaration of Independence, and died on

July 4, 1826, on the fiftieth anniversary of the founding of the United States. His life and work reflected an entire historical era—the stormy, conflict-filled, complex era of the formation of bourgeois ideology and the establishment of new political and social relations in America. The aspirations, ideological contradictions, and fears of the rising American bourgeoisie found what was perhaps their fullest expression in Adams's worldview.

Adams belonged to a wealthy family that lived in the small town of Braintree, Massachusetts, not far from Boston. Unlike Franklin, he never had to work hard to earn a living. At the same time, he was not, like Washington or Jefferson, the owner of a large fortune. Adams came from the typical New England bourgeois milieu, an environment that reflected the distinctive traditions, customs, and norms of Puritan morality, where diligence and frugality were valued and idleness and dissipation scorned. He wrote in his autobiography that his father had increased his fortune, acquired prestige, and become a respected figure in his native town "by his Industry and Enterprize."[1] Adams received what was regarded at the time as an excellent education. He first attended a private school and then studied at Harvard. In spite of the strict discipline prevailing at the college, Harvard was known for the liberal spirit of its instruction and offered its students the opportunity to learn about the advanced ideas of the age.

The outlook of the young Adams was formed at a time when significant changes were taking place in America. The various strata in society were becoming restless, economic activity was increasing, and the young American bourgeoisie was coming into its own. The atmosphere of social and political excitement that surrounded Adams in his youth aroused his interest in current events and political problems. "Be not surprised that I am turned politician," Adams reported in a letter written in 1755, when he was still at the university. "The whole town is immersed in politics. The interests of nations, and all the *dira* of war, make the subject of every conversation. I sit and hear, and after having been led through a maze of sage observations, I sometimes retire, and by laying things together, form some reflections pleasing to myself."[2] Adams was strongly influenced by two prominent Boston politicians, James Otis and Samuel Adams, who in the 1760s spoke out against the colonial policy of Great Britain. Adams's wide erudition and early interest in politics enabled him to understand contemporary issues and the spirit of the time. These abilities, together with his pragmatism, sense of purpose, and the unyielding pursuit of his goals—all qualities inculcated in him by the Puritan atmosphere of New England—made him stand out among his contemporaries. It is no accident that from an early age he began to devote his main attention to the problem of exercising power in society—a problem that for the American bourgeoisie of the

1. *Diary and Autobiography of John Adams,* ed. Lyman H. Butterfield, 4 vols. (Cambridge, Mass., 1961), vol. 3, 256. This article by B. A. Shiriayev was first published in *American Studies Annual for 1975* (Moscow, 1975).

2. Adrienne Koch, ed., *The American Enlightenment: The Shaping of the American Experiment* (New York, 1965), 179.

mid-eighteenth century was of not only theoretical interest but also considerable practical importance.

After graduating from Harvard, Adams decided to become a lawyer. The upsurge in business activity in the colonies and the growth in trade and manufacturing had increased the demand for those with expert knowledge of the law and put them in a very advantageous social position. So Adams rejected the career of a minister, which was his father's preference, and entered a well-known law practice as an apprentice. Having completed a two-year course of legal studies, he was admitted to the Boston bar and in 1758 began to practice law.

Adams became politically active as a result of the events in 1765 during the campaign against the Stamp Act. Massachusetts became the center of the disturbances, which spread throughout the American colonies. Reacting to these developments, Adams published in the *Boston Gazette* a series of articles entitled "Dissertation on the Canon and the Feudal Law." In this work he defended the concept of popular sovereignty and the idea that a government should be "founded only on natural and sensible principles." Adams sharply criticized the Catholic Church and the feudal system of oppression, which together had kept the people "in a state of servile dependence." "Since the promulgation of Christianity, the two greatest systems that have sprung from this original, are the canon and the feudal law."[3] He stated openly that in England the ecclesiastical and feudal system was still in existence and that it represented a threat to the freedom and privileges of the colonies.

Adams contrasted the old feudal order with the new developments and the new system emerging in America. That new system in his view had been formed "in direct Opposition to the Canon and the feudal systems." He believed that the very settlement of the New World represented a challenge to oppression. "I always consider the settlement of America with Reverence and Wonder—as the Opening of a grand scene and Design in Providence, for the Illumination of the Ignorant and the Emancipation of the slavish Part of Mankind all over the Earth," wrote Adams in one of the drafts of his "Dissertation on the Canon and the Feudal Law."[4] This statement, like many others, was in keeping with the spirit of Puritan maxims about the special role of America in God's plans. Adams shared many of the Puritans' beliefs, and this was reflected not only in his political views but also in his behavior in everyday life.

The "Dissertation on the Canon and the Feudal Law" was a perfect expression of the attitudes prevailing in the American colonies at the time. Adams began to attract the attention of businessmen and social and political figures in Massachusetts. A special committee created in his native town of Braintree to fight the Stamp Act asked him to compose a proclamation condemning that law. Adams produced a text that became known as the "Braintree Instructions"; it declared the Stamp Act unconstitutional and generally denied that the English Parliament had the right to impose taxes on the colonies without their consent. The "Instructions" were sent to the Massachusetts

3. Loren Baritz, *Sources of the American Mind: A Collection of Documents and Texts in American Intellectual History* (New York, 1966), vol. 1, 114.

4. Adams, *Diary and Autobiography,* ed. Butterfield, vol. 1, 256–57.

legislature, which approved them and stated that the Stamp Act was unlawful. The events in Massachusetts impressed all of America. The "Braintree Instructions" were published first in Boston and then in the newspapers of every colony. The name of the Boston lawyer became widely known; Adams was now one of the leading political figures in the city. "The Year 1765 has been the most remarkable Year of my Life," he wrote in his diary, summing up the events he had experienced.[5]

During the rise of the liberation movement Adams was a member of the revolutionary wing of the American bourgeoisie. His position on the question of the colonies' relations with England was very radical. In the 1760s and early 1770s the issue of independence had not yet arisen, but Adams always supported the idea of autonomous development of the colonies, arguing in his writings that England's attitude toward the American colonies was illegitimate. Adams believed that the American colonies did not belong to England because the settlement and development of the new lands in America had been carried out by independent colonists rather than by the British government. The first settlement occurred "on a Territory belonging [neither] to the People nor the Crown of England."[6]

Adams was convinced that the colonies should form a political commonwealth that would be England's equal in law. Though he considered the laws of England ideal, he nevertheless understood the difference between the social and political systems of Britain and the colonies. Adams regarded the colonization of America as a counterweight to the order that existed in England and the other countries of Europe. He believed that the views of the Puritans were the source of the existing American political system. In his opinion, the Puritans after coming to America "formed their plan, both of ecclesiastical and civil government, in direct opposition to the canon and the feudal systems. . . . *They knew that government was a plain, simple, intelligible thing, founded in nature and reason, and quite comprehensible by common sense.*"[7]

The policy of the British government following the events of 1765 convinced Adams that a worsening of the relationship between the colonies and the mother country was inevitable. In 1768 government troops entered Boston. The presence of the English garrison in the city confirmed him in his predictions. The very appearance of the troops in Boston, wrote Adams, "was a strong proof to me, that the determination in Great Britain to subjugate Us, was too deep and inveterate ever to be altered by Us."[8]

At the same time the struggle against the stamp duty law showed that the colonists were becoming politically active and that the masses were becoming more willing to resist the policy of the mother country. "The People, even to the lowest ranks," Adams concluded, "have become more attentive to their Liberties, more inquisitive about them, and more determined to defend them."[9]

5. Ibid., 263.
6. Ibid., 283.
7. Koch, ed., *The American Enlightenment,* 238.
8. Adams, *Diary and Autobiography,* ed. Butterfield, vol. 3, 290.
9. Ibid., vol. 1, 263.

Adams was now a prominent figure in the patriotic party in Massachusetts, although he did not take part in the mass movement and spoke out against "exciting public opinion." As a rule he declined to join in debates in the political clubs and taverns and was reluctant to take part in meetings and rallies. While being aware of the need to resist British policy, Adams feared political action by the people. Revolutions, he believed, were harmful to the cause of freedom. "I had read enough in History," wrote Adams in one of his passages devoted to contemporary events, "to be well aware of the Errors to which the public opinions of the People, were liable in times of great heat and danger, as well as of the Extravagances of which the Populace of Cities were capable, when artfully excited to Passion, and even when justly provoked by Oppression."[10]

Yet because he realized the inevitability of the conflict with the mother country, Adams could not remain a simple observer of events. Whatever his wishes, by virtue of his writings and all his other activities he was effectively helping to lay the moral, legal, and political basis for resisting the policy of Great Britain. Not only did Adams enjoy a growing political reputation, but he was also becoming better known as a jurist; his legal practice was now Boston's largest, as he himself acknowledged. "In the Years 1766 and 1767 my Business increased, as my Reputation spread, I got Money and bought Books and Land," he wrote in his autobiography.[11] His services were sought by well-known traders and industrialists from Boston. His clients included figures such as John Hancock, the city's wealthiest man. A prominent merchant, Hancock wielded great influence in Massachusetts business and political circles.

From 1766 to 1768 Adams took part in many court cases involving conflicts between the colonial administration and the merchants of Boston. He defended the merchants with considerable success, thereby increasing his popularity among traders and industrialists in all the colonies. Adams proved himself to be not only a brilliant and experienced litigator but also a man of definite political convictions; he attempted to show that the actions of the colonial authorities were unconstitutional and amounted to violations of the rights of man. The trials in which he took part thus always amounted to political jousts and were followed with great interest by the whole of Boston.

By taking legal action, Adams was able to secure the abolition of the duty charged on the goods imported by Hancock. At the court hearing he showed that the law on which the duty was based had no validity in the colonies: "My client, Mr. Hancock," declared Adams, "never voted for it and he never voted for any man to make such a law for him."[12] Statements such as this reflected attitudes that were current at the time among the inhabitants of the colonies, who were demanding "no taxation without representation." Excerpts from Adams's speeches were published in the newspapers and quoted at political meetings. His popularity grew even further when he saved from hanging four American sailors who had been accused of the murder of an English

10. Ibid., vol. 3, 290.
11. Ibid., 286.
12. Catherine Drinker Bowen, *John Adams and the American Revolution* (New York, 1950), 330.

officer. Thereafter the patriots of Massachusetts regarded Adams as one of their own, a defender of the enemies of Great Britain.

Adams's standing and popularity induced the governor of the colony to try to win him over. In 1768 he was offered the position of chief attorney in the admiralty court of Massachusetts. Adams was well aware that such a post would open the prospect of a brilliant career for him in the British administration. Yet strong ties bound him to the milieu from which he came and which was almost always hostile to the king's officials. Moreover, he had been a witness of the events of 1765 and was keenly aware of the growing tension in the political atmosphere around him. More than anyone else he was aware of the inevitability of the coming clash with England. That is why he rejected the tempting offer. "The Governor . . . knows who my friends are," was Adams's reply.[13] Across the spectrum of society the public reputation of the Boston jurist continued to grow. In 1770 he was elected to the Massachusetts legislature as a representative from Boston. Although Adams had long been a participant in the political struggle, he reacted to this new advancement with considerable doubt and hesitation, for as a member of an elected body he would now be engaged in political activity of a qualitatively different kind and would have serious new obligations and responsibilities.

His doubts were largely due to the events that had taken place in Boston in March 1770 when a clash between the townspeople and English soldiers had resulted in the death of five people. This incident provoked an unprecedented wave of indignation that spread from Boston to the surrounding areas. Calls to arms were heard everywhere, and the resulting tension threatened to erupt into armed violence. Not only did this crisis frighten the royal officials but it also caused concern among the movement's leaders, who did not want to see armed action by the masses. The disturbances subsided only when the governor withdrew the troops from Boston and ordered that the English officer responsible for the shooting of innocent civilians be put on trial. No one doubted that the officer would be severely punished. But to the surprise of many people, Adams, the most famous lawyer in Massachusetts, agreed to defend him in court at the request of the governor. In spite of the Bostonians' vociferous demands that the perpetrator of the crime be sentenced to death, Adams, employing his superb professional skills and his oratorical talent, was able to convince the jury that the officer was acting in self-defense, and the court found him not guilty.

Adams claimed that he had agreed to take part in such an obviously unpopular affair because of his "supreme professional duty." Yet it was clear that Adams was endeavoring to restore the balance in the relations between the colony's inhabitants and the royal administration, for the execution of a British army officer as the result of a jury trial in the colony could have had serious repercussions. First, it might have excited the masses even further, which was not something the leaders of the movement desired. Second, it might have led London to respond with measures that would have been harmful to the colonial bourgeoisie. The colonial leaders were not

13. Ibid., 318.

yet contemplating a break with the mother country and still hoped to strengthen their rights by reaching a peaceful agreement with the British government. Undoubtedly the existing situation and the mood of the masses put Adams in a difficult position. Political activity promised to bring him and the numerous members of his family a great deal of trouble. During this time he thought hard about the path he should choose, agonizing over whether he should immerse himself completely in the political struggle or stand aside and devote himself solely to his legal practice. In April 1771 he clearly felt inclined to abandon his public activities and "avoid politics, political clubs, [and] town meetings."[14] However, the increase in England's repressive measures and the upsurge in the national liberation movement in the colonies clearly showed that a bitter struggle was unavoidable. Like many other prominent political figures, Adams understood the necessity of resisting British colonial policy. He fully supported the action taken by the people of Boston that came to be known as the "Boston Tea Party." "Most people in America now think the destruction of the Boston tea was absolutely necessary, and therefore right and just," wrote Adams.[15]

The events in Boston stirred the whole of America. As had been the case during the controversies over the stamp duty in 1765 and the shooting of peaceful citizens by the British in 1770, the city again captured the attention of all the colonies. Boston once more became the center of the struggle against British repression. Adams knew well the significance and likely consequences of the actions taken by the patriots of his city. Yet he had no doubts of their determination to fight and to resort to extreme measures. He considered the Boston Tea Party a major step on the path leading to a break with England. "It must have so important Consequences, and so lasting, that I cant but consider it as an Epocha in History," he wrote.[16]

The stormy year of 1773 put an end to Adams's doubts and hesitations. He finally decided to devote himself completely to political activity. In his diary Adams gave the following answer to the question of whether he should or should not be a politician, a question that had preoccupied him for a long time: "I was not sent into this World to spend my days in Sports, Diversions and Pleasures. I was born for Business; for both Activity and Study. I have little Appetite, or Relish for any Thing else."[17] Adams was not yet demanding a clear break with England, but in his writings he was preparing politically and ideologically for the approaching severance of relations. Adams's statements in the newspapers and in his articles made him a dangerous radical in the eyes of the royal officials. In May 1773 the Massachusetts General Court elected Adams to the Council, the upper house of the commonwealth's legislature. However, the governor, who had to approve appointments to the Council, crossed Adams's name off the list presented to him.

The British government was not slow in responding with harsh measures to the Bostonians' actions. In 1774 the colonies became subject to the so-called Intolerable

14. Ibid., 419.
15. John Adams, "Novanglus," quoted in Koch, ed., *The American Enlightenment,* 245.
16. Adams, *Diary and Autobiography,* ed. Butterfield, vol. 2, 86.
17. Ibid., 82.

Acts, which, although they infringed on the interests of all the colonies, were primarily directed against Massachusetts. The port of Boston was closed. Massachusetts was deprived of its right to self-government and its legislative assembly was dissolved. These British actions caused indignation throughout the colonies. In the spring of 1774 colonists in different parts of America began to demand that a congress of the colonies be called to discuss the situation. The colonies elected delegates to what became the First Continental Congress meeting in Philadelphia. The delegates were chosen in different ways: in some colonies they were elected from among the members of the local legislatures; in others special conventions were organized to select the delegates. In Maryland, for example, the delegates were chosen by a "Meeting of the Committees appointed by the several Counties," while in Delaware they were chosen by a meeting of "Representatives of freemen . . . chosen and appointed . . . by the freeholders and freemen."[18] Adams was chosen as a member of the Massachusetts delegation, which included several well-known political figures. The membership of the Congress that assembled in Philadelphia consisted of landowners, merchants, and jurists—men who represented the elite of American society. There were no representatives of the democratic strata at this gathering, for the method of delegate selection was designed to exclude the people from taking part.

In Philadelphia, Adams found himself in the midst of a sea of political activity. The events of 1770–1773 in Boston were widely remembered, and the Massachusetts representatives were at the center of everyone's attention. "The Spirit, the Firmness, the Prudence of our Province are vastly applauded, and We are universally acknowledged the Saviours and Defenders of American Liberty," wrote Adams while the Congress was taking place.[19]

Although the First Continental Congress, opening on September 5, 1774, did not take up the issue of independence, from the very beginning it was split into two factions: a conservative group, which sought to achieve a reconciliation with the British government, and a group that sought actively to resist the policy of Great Britain. The conservative camp was dominated by the delegations from Pennsylvania and New York, while among the advocates of resistance the most active were the members of the Massachusetts and Virginia delegations. After protracted debate the Congress reached a compromise: it decided to draw up a bill of rights or "Declaration of the Rights of the Colonies" and to present the king with a petition, a "Loyal Address," as the members of the Congress called it. Adams was a member of the committees that were charged with composing the Declaration of Rights and the draft of the petition to the king. Although he did not insist on a break with England, he wanted the Congress to resort to stronger measures: namely, imposing a complete ban on trade with England; drawing up an address to the English people and an address to the American people, as well as sending a petition to the king; adopting a law creating a militia in each colony; collecting a sum amounting to not less than £500,000 and

18. Edmund C. Burnett, *The Continental Congress* (New York, 1941), 21.
19. Lyman H. Butterfield, ed., *Adams Family Correspondence,* 2 vols. (Cambridge, Mass., 1963,), vol. 1, 155.

mobilizing not fewer than twenty thousand men; and securing funds for building a navy.[20] However, the proponents of a compromise with England predominated at the Congress, and Adams's proposals, like those made by other advocates of firmer measures, failed to win support. Having adopted the "Declaration of the Rights of the Colonies" and having sent a petition to the king, the First Continental Congress concluded its work on October 26, 1774.

The time Adams spent in Philadelphia and his participation in the Congress proved to be of great significance in his political career. He established personal contacts with many political figures and had the opportunity to learn about the other colonies. The journey itself impressed him enormously, for hitherto he had never been to any other colony. "It would take a Volume to describe the whole," wrote Adams in a letter from Princeton, New Jersey, to Boston. "We have had Opportunities to see the World, and to form Acquaintants with the most eminent and famous Men, in the several Colonies we have passed through."[21] Adams was undergoing a transformation from a provincial politician to a figure respected in the other colonies as well. He described the role played by the Congress in increasing his prestige in these terms: "I left . . . Philadelphia in October 1774, with a Reputation, much higher than ever I enjoyed before or since."[22]

Although the Congress had failed to satisfy some colonists, the very fact that it was summoned was seen by the people as a signal for decisive action. After it ended, the colonists' liberation movement expanded. The population, particularly the working people, began to prepare for war without waiting for instructions; everywhere stores of weapons were established and volunteer detachments were formed. The battles of Lexington and Concord in 1775 showed that England was determined to crush the colonies' resistance by force. The battles also showed, however, that the bourgeoisie might lose control of the spontaneously erupting armed struggle; the revolutionary movement threatened to become an independent force guided only by the masses and their leaders.

The people's movement had a great impact on the attitudes and views of the delegates to the Second Continental Congress, which met on May 10, 1775. This time the delegates' mandates were much more specific, containing demands for the reestablishment and strengthening of the rights of the colonies "on a secure and legal basis." But even these mandates did not yet include a demand for independence. The American bourgeoisie was afraid of taking that essential step. Even after Lexington many of the patriots hesitated. Adams was irritated by the way the Congress had begun its work, as may be seen from these comments: "I have found this Congress like the last. When We first came together, I found a strong Jealousy of Us, [of] New England, and Massachusetts in Particular. . . . Our Sentiments were heard in Congress, with great Caution—and seemed to make but little Impression."[23] The leader of the

20. Adams, *Diary and Autobiography,* ed. Butterfield, vol. 2, 145.
21. Butterfield, ed., *Adams Family Correspondence,* vol. 1, 144.
22. Adams, *Diary and Autobiography,* ed. Butterfield, vol. 3, 313.
23. Butterfield, ed., *Adams Family Correspondence,* vol. 1, 216.

opponents of independence was John Dickinson, an influential conservative politician. Under pressure from the conservatives, the Congress attempted to reconcile with the king and addressed another petition to him. Dickinson believed that the colonies should strive for full autonomy but remain within the British empire.

However, the members of the Second Congress, unlike those of the first one, had assembled under revolutionary conditions. The armed struggle taking place served to strengthen the pro-independence tendencies. Under the pressure of events many political figures were beginning to realize that decisive measures had to be taken in response to England's repressive policy.

Adams was among the first to realize that the only alternative to independence was complete submission. His phrase "only independence will save us" became popular among the radical members of the Congress. He called on the Congress to act in a way appropriate to the wartime situation and insisted that necessary measures be adopted, in particular that a regular army under single command instead of local militia detachments be created.

On June 15, 1775, the Congress established a regular army and created the position of commander-in-chief. At the suggestion of Adams and with his active assistance, Colonel George Washington, a planter from Virginia, was appointed commander-in-chief. Adams supported the Virginian even though John Hancock of Massachusetts wanted the position and was supported by many delegates from the northern provinces. Indeed, as a resident of Boston, Hancock was linked to Adams by many personal ties. Yet Adams's long-range strategy was to try to avoid friction between the bourgeoisie of the North and the planters of the South, who looked upon the activities of the delegates from the northern colonies with a certain amount of suspicion.

Among the delegates to the Second Continental Congress, Adams was undoubtedly one of the most influential. He sat on ninety committees and was the chairman of twenty-five. He worked from seven in the morning until midnight. "I was incessantly employed, through the whole Fall, Winter and Spring of 1775 and 1776 in Congress during their Sittings and on Committees on mornings and Evenings, and unquestionably did more business than any other Member of that house," Adams later recalled.[24]

The advocates of a compromise with England were very strong. They consistently argued against the adoption of decisive measures, placing great hopes on the petition that had been sent to the king. "Every important Step was opposed, and carried by bare Majorities, which obliged me to be almost constantly engaged in debate," wrote Adams.[25]

Bitter controversy surrounded not just the major issues of principle; even the phrasing of certain statements provoked heated debate. Adams supported Paine's suggestion that in the congressional documents the American colonies should be referred to as "states." He was able to convince the members of the Congress that in these documents they should write "Great Britain" instead of "the mother country," as had been the case before. However, the majority of members refused to describe the

24. Adams, *Diary and Autobiography,* ed. Butterfield, vol. 3, 335.
25. Ibid., 327.

state of relations between England and colonies as amounting to war, and insisted on using in the documents the more diplomatic term "conflict." Realizing the importance of naval power in the struggle with England and for the defense of the American coastline, Adams spoke out in favor of creating not just a unified regular army but also a navy. But the most important measure that Adams demanded was the creation in each colony of its own government to replace the royal administration. "Almost every day, I had something to say about Advizing the States to institute Governments," wrote Adams.[26] Such a measure was vitally urgent, for in some of the colonies there was no organized form of government, while in others governmental functions were performed only by the legislatures, and in others the royal governors still remained in authority. The conservatives were frightened of adopting this measure, for the next logical step would have been the proclamation of independence. But if many of the members of the Congress hesitated, the English government had no doubts as to how to deal with the recalcitrant colonies. In August 1775 the colonies were declared to be in a state of rebellion. On December 22, 1775, a parliamentary decree deprived the American colonies of the protection of British laws, banned all trade with them, and authorized the capture of American ships on the open seas. In effect these actions by Parliament amounted to a declaration of war, and the policy adopted by Britain made its intentions toward the colonies abundantly clear.

The measures taken by Parliament increased the desire of the masses to secede from the mother country. The demand for independence now became central to social and political life. The newspapers openly discussed the subject, and posters in the streets of virtually every city called for independence. Adams and his supporters now saw secession from Great Britain as inevitable. He insisted that the colonies should take the following three steps: declare independence; form a confederation, that is, a union of the colonies; and conclude an alliance with certain foreign powers, primarily France. Despite hesitations and continuing discussions about independence, the pressure of circumstances forced the Congress to respond to Britain's actions with actions the proponents of independence had wanted. In March 1776 the Congress decided to arm American vessels "for the struggle with the enemies of the united provinces" and to establish naval ports and bases to defend the American coast from the Royal Navy. These measures laid the foundation for the creation of the U.S. Navy.

Adams's notes for the beginning of 1776 show that he was preoccupied with plans for declaring independence. In February of that year he added the following proposals to the list of measures to be adopted by the Congress: to draft an agreement establishing a confederation of the colonies; to form an alliance with France and Spain; to establish governments in all the colonies; to conclude trade treaties with France, Spain, Holland, and Denmark; to declare independence; and to declare war on England.[27] Moreover, Adams suggested reinforcing American troops in Canada and New York, strengthening the positions on the banks of the St. Lawrence and Hudson rivers, establishing powder-making factories in each colony, and attacking British merchant vessels at sea.

26. Ibid.
27. Ibid., vol. 2, 231–32.

During this period Adams's attention was mainly centered on the most controversial questions, those that related to the manner in which the American governments were to be formed, their structure, and the principles that should guide their policies. Many at the time saw the Congress as the prototype of the future governments. As the war spread, the character of the Congress changed. From a provisional assembly it turned into a permanent institution that combined legislative and executive authority. On the basis of this experience many political figures were now inclined to believe that in the future all power should be vested in a similar single-chamber representative assembly.

Adams spoke out forcefully against such views. In March and April of 1776 he wrote a pamphlet known by the title "Thoughts on Government." This pamphlet had grown out of several letters he had written to southern congressmen. With this pamphlet he became the first member of the Congress to state publicly his ideas about the state and its political structure. While his views on independence were radical, Adams's positions on social issues were fairly conservative.

Adams argued that a system of full popular sovereignty was inadvisable. He believed that it was impossible for the masses to take part in governing the country and be involved in the drawing up of laws. However, to avoid contradicting the theory of the social contract, which was popular at the time, Adams suggested that it would be necessary "to depute power from the many to a few of the most wise and good."

At the same time Adams supported a republican system of government. Although his republicanism was elitist and conservative in character, in the mid-eighteenth century, when the monarchical form of government was universally dominant, even his moderate republican principles represented a challenge to the existing political status quo.

Adams also argued for the doctrine of the separation of powers. He believed that to allow all power to be concentrated in a unicameral assembly like that of the Second Continental Congress would be intolerable. He thought that "a people cannot be long free, nor ever happy, whose government is in one assembly."[28] Adams clearly understood the relationships among the different groups within the bourgeoisie, and he suspected that these factions would engage in a struggle for control of the institutions of government. If all power were entrusted to a single-chamber assembly, that body would be in real danger of being controlled by one of those groups. Adams argued that a representative assembly, being a legislative organ, was not suited to performing executive functions. And a representative assembly would be even less qualified to wield judicial authority, for "it was too numerous, too slow, and too ignorant of the law." In his view all authority in the state should be divided into three mutually independent branches: the legislative, executive, and judicial. Legislative authority would be entrusted to a two-chamber parliament, known as the assembly, which would elect from among its members a council made up of twenty to thirty persons. This body would form the upper chamber of the assembly. The council would have the right to veto the decisions of the lower house. Both houses would annually elect the chief

28. John Adams, "Thoughts on Government," quoted in *The American Enlightenment,* ed. Koch, 247.

of the executive branch, known as the governor, who would enjoy the right of veto over the decisions of the legislature. The judiciary would be independent of both the legislative and the executive branches and would exercise control over them, while they in turn would control the judiciary. Such were Adams's plans for the political and governmental structure of the new state. They reflected the principle of strict separation and equality of powers, that is, the idea of "balanced government." Adams believed that a government based on the separation of powers would ensure a balance among the different factions of the bourgeoisie and be a reliable guarantee against democracy. Throughout his political and public career he vigorously promoted this principle, hoping that it would form the basis for the emerging system of government in America.

Adams first had the opportunity to realize his ideas in 1779, when he drew up the Massachusetts constitution. The document he composed became one of the chief models for the other state constitutions and influenced the federal Constitution. The constitution that Adams drew up contained the principle of "balanced government"; it provided for a two-chamber assembly, a strong executive, and an independent judiciary. The constitution stipulated that "in the government of the Commonwealth of Massachusetts the legislative, executive, and judicial power shall be placed in separate departments, to the end that it be a government of laws, and not of men."[29] This constitution was moderately conservative in character. Unlike the Declaration of Independence, it stated that ownership of property was man's inalienable right.

The struggle being waged by the colonies against Great Britain convinced growing numbers of the bourgeoisie and the planter class that independence was inevitable. At the beginning of 1776 the provincial legislatures of several of the colonies decided to instruct their delegations to the Congress to demand a declaration of independence. Some colonies were prepared to declare themselves independent countries without a decision by the Congress. John Winthrop, a member of the Massachusetts legislature, informed Adams that the inhabitants of Massachusetts awaited with impatience a declaration of independence by the Congress, and if the Congress did not hurry up, he would not be able to guarantee that Massachusetts would refrain from publishing its own declaration.[30] Reports like this made a great impression on the Congress. The pressure of events forced the delegates to take the necessary steps toward independence.

On May 10 the Congress adopted a resolution recommending that the colonies should form their own governments, abolish all institutions embodying colonial rule, and assume full power. The resolution held that "the respective assemblies and conventions of the United Colonies . . . [should] adopt such government as shall, in the opinion of the representatives of the people, best conduce to the happiness and safety of their constituents in particular, and America in general."[31]

29. Adams, *The American Enlightenment,* ed. Koch, 252.

30. Robert E. Brown, *Middle-Class Democracy and the Revolution in Massachusetts, 1691–1780* (Ithaca, 1955), 376.

31. Burnett, *Continental Congress,* 157.

As a member of all the most important committees of the Congress, Adams actively worked toward preparing the ground for declaring independence. He sat on the committee charged with drafting the Declaration of Independence. Although the actual draft of the Declaration was written by Jefferson, Adams played a major part in defending it when it was debated by the Congress. On July 1 during the debate over the Declaration of Independence John Dickinson put forward the views of the opponents of independence, arguing that the colonies were not yet ready to adopt such a document. Adams challenged him and urged the members of the Congress to vote for the Declaration.

The adoption of the Declaration of Independence was a major victory for the revolutionary wing of the American bourgeoisie, one of whose leaders at the time was Adams. "Yesterday the greatest Question was decided, which ever was debated in America," wrote a happy Adams on July 3, 1776.[32] But at the same time he expressed regret that during the protracted debates on independence many opportunities had been missed: "Had a Declaration of Independency been made seven Months ago, it would have been attended with many great and glorious Effects. . . . We might before this Hour, have formed Alliances with foreign States.—We should have mastered Quebec and been in Possession of Canada."[33]

Adams did much to shape the foreign policy of the new government. At the sessions of the Second Continental Congress he firmly advocated negotiating with the countries of Europe, particularly those that were in a position to help the colonies in their struggle with England. In June 1776 Adams became a member of the committee responsible for drafting treaties with foreign powers. At the committee's request he composed the so-called model treaty—a document that established the basis for U.S. foreign policy in the eighteenth century. Aware of the weak diplomatic position of his country, Adams proposed that the United States avoid direct participation in European affairs; the country should refuse to undertake any commitments that might involve it in a European war. Adams suggested in the model treaty that relations between the independent American states and the countries of Europe be based on trade.

Adams pressed for the conclusion of an anti-British alliance with France. He advised that the negotiations with France should be conducted "with great caution"; the United States should not enter into a close political alliance with France and should keep its distance from European affairs, while taking advantage of the antagonism between France and England:

> We ought not to enter into any Alliance with her, which should entangle Us in any
> future Wars in Europe. . . . It never could be our Interest to unite with France, in the
> destruction of England, or in any measures to break her Spirit or reduce her to a
> situation in which she could not support her Independence. On the other hand it could
> never be our Duty to unite with Britain in too great a humiliation of France. . . . Our
> real if not our nominal Independence would consist in our Neutrality.

32. Butterfield, ed., *Adams Family Correspondence,* vol. 2, 27–28.
33. Ibid., 29.

Adams said in one of his speeches to Congress, "If We united with either Nation, in any future War, We must become too subordinate and dependent on that nation, and should be involved in all European Wars."[34] The ideas expressed in the model treaty subsequently provided the basis for the American isolationism that for many years shaped the attitude of the United States toward European affairs.

Adams took an active part in the creation of the armed forces of the United States. In 1776 he was elected chairman of the military committee of the Congress and became one of the founders of the American army and navy. Adams occupied the position of chairman until November 1777, when he was given a diplomatic assignment. The duties of the military committee were numerous; in fact, this body acted as a ministry of defense. The military committee appointed the highest-ranking officers, controlled war supplies, and carried out all the Congress's decisions on military matters. Adams played a major role in the creation and strengthening of the armed forces. He devoted a great deal of energy to uniting the separate military detachments raised by the colonies into a regular army under a single command. Adams followed the course of military operations closely and spent time studying military science in order to be able to offer the generals informed advice and to see their mistakes and miscalculations. "I . . . contributed my Share towards the Creation of the Army, and the Appointment of all the Officers: and as President of the Board of War it was my peculiar Province to superintend every thing relating to the Army. I will add without Vanity, I had read as much on the military Art and much more on the History of War than any American Officer," Adams later wrote, not without pride.[35]

After the Declaration of Independence, Adams devoted his main attention to the issue of confederation. The problem of bringing the colonies together was being resolved only gradually, for parochial interests and the individual colonies' fear that they would lose their rights and privileges constituted an obstacle to the sensible desire for unification. "The great Work of confederation, drags heavily on," wrote Adams to Jefferson in May 1777. "The great and small States must be brought as near together as possible: and I am not without Hopes, that this may be done, to the tolerable Satisfaction of both."[36]

However, Adams's participation in the activities of the Congress soon came to an end: in November 1777 the Congress decided to send him to Paris as a member of the ambassadorial mission, which also included Benjamin Franklin and Arthur Lee. For ten years thereafter, with the exception of four months in 1779, Adams lived abroad as a diplomatic representative of the United States.

In February 1778 Adams boarded a naval vessel and sailed to Europe; after a long and perilous voyage he arrived in Paris. France amazed him by the noise of its cities, the affluence of its aristocracy, and the poverty of its lower classes. He met many figures who held liberal views and who expressed their sympathy and support for the American Revolution. Yet although he was himself by birth

34. Adams, *Diary and Autobiography,* ed. Butterfield, vol. 3, 328–29.
35. Ibid., 446.
36. *The Adams-Jefferson Letters,* ed. Lester J. Cappon, 2 vols. (Chapel Hill, 1959), vol. 1, 5.

a member of the third estate, Adams showed no desire to understand the feelings and moods of the third estate in Europe. Besides, he did not wish to be seen as a rebel or a representative of a revolutionary country. He had a different task: to be a trustworthy and respected diplomat and above all, to strengthen his country's standing in Europe. He did not share the European liberals' hostility to high society, believing that the bourgeoisie in Europe was threatened more "by the mob" than by the aristocracy.[37] Adams encountered great difficulties in France. He did not know the language and was not really familiar with the country's political customs and traditions. Moreover, his relationship with Vergennes, the French foreign minister, who disliked the resoluteness, independence, and outspokenness of the new American diplomat, was an unhappy one. Vergennes and Adams distrusted one another. The French minister believed that the colonies' main aim should be to win the war, while France should exercise control over the diplomatic activities of the alliance. Adams suspected that the French court intended to conduct the war solely in its own interests. Adams found that the American diplomatic mission was not operating successfully. Friction between Franklin and Lee was a serious obstacle to cooperation among the mission's members. Adams concluded that a committee of three ambassadors was not the best arrangement. In his opinion the embassy should be headed by a single envoy with plenipotentiary powers. He informed the Congress of his views. Eventually the Congress agreed with him and abolished the ambassadorial mission, leaving only Franklin as its plenipotentiary in Paris. In the summer of 1779 Adams returned to Boston.

As noted, Adams did not stay long in America. In September 1779 the Congress again sent him to Paris for the purpose of opening peace talks with England. Adams believed that to carry out his mission he had to enter into direct contact with London. Paris, however, insisted that the negotiations should be conducted through intermediaries; Austria and Russia were prepared to act in such a capacity.

Adams did not want the peace talks with England and the question of American independence to become entangled in the intrigues of European diplomacy. He did not trust his allies, and he had good reasons for not trusting them. He was wary of the equivocal position adopted by Spain, which although in a state of war with England did not wish to recognize the independence of the American colonies. He knew of the existence of a secret treaty between Spain and France, of which the United States had not been informed. Finally, he could guess at the intentions of France, which was eager to drag out the war in order to weaken England and acquire new possessions at England's expense. The United States, however, wished to end the war, for they had in effect already achieved their goal—independence.

All this led to sharp disagreements between Adams and Vergennes. Adams tried to establish relations with other countries to offset France's dominant influence over the foreign policy of the United States. When he was a member of the Congress, he had seen Holland as a possible and indeed a desirable partner for the United

37. Edward Handler, *America and Europe in the Political Thought of John Adams* (Cambridge, Mass., 1964), 13.

States. In July and August of 1780 Adams traveled to Amsterdam and The Hague where, without waiting for appropriate instructions from the Congress, he began talks with Dutch bankers and later the Dutch government.[38] The French foreign minister, using his influence in American political circles, insisted that the Congress should force Adams to listen to the advice of the French court, or replace him with a more compliant envoy.[39] In June 1781, under the influence of the French government, the Congress replaced Adams as a single envoy in the negotiations with England with a five-member delegation including Adams, Benjamin Franklin, John Jay, Henry Laurens, and Thomas Jefferson; at the same time Adams was officially authorized to conduct talks in Holland. The delegation received new instructions to strive to "secure the interests of the United States, *in such a manner as circumstances may direct and as the state of the belligerent and the disposition of the mediating powers may require.*"[40] On every point except the recognition of the independence of the United States, the instructions placed the American delegation at the peace talks in a position that obliged it to defer to Paris.

Adams objected strongly to these instructions and demanded that they be changed. He was annoyed that Congress had forced the American delegation to obey the French court and had in effect "surrendered their own Sovereignty into the Hands of a French Minister." "It is Glory, to have broken such infamous orders," he openly proclaimed.[41] Adams also demanded that an American envoy be sent to London to begin direct peace talks with England. Of the five men the Congress appointed to the delegation only three—Franklin, Jay, and Adams—were able to begin performing their duties. Moreover, at the time the delegation was created Jay was in Madrid and Adams in Holland, so the negotiations were conducted by Franklin alone and progress was slow at first. Adams's mission to the Netherlands continued for almost two years. He had two aims: to bring about Holland's recognition of U.S. independence and to obtain a loan from Dutch bankers.

At first his mission enjoyed little success. The Dutch government gave him a cold reception; although in 1780 it had declared war on England, it did not show any interest in recognizing the United States. The bankers were even more reluctant to offer the United States a loan. "I can represent my situation in this affair of a loan, by no other figure than that of a man in the midst of the ocean negotiating for his life among a school of sharks."[42] However, as the fortunes of war began to smile on the Americans, the mission to The Hague began to achieve results. Finally, in April 1782, after protracted and difficult negotiations, Adams was recognized as the ambassador plenipotentiary of the United States to Holland; this meant that the Dutch government had officially recognized the independence of the United States. Soon thereafter Adams secured a loan from a consortium of Amsterdam bankers in the

---

38. Steven Hess, *America's Political Dynasties from Adams to Kennedy* (New York, 1966), 23.
39. Samuel Flagg Bemis, *The Diplomacy of the American Revolution* (Bloomington, 1957), 178.
40. Ibid., 189–90.
41. Adams, *Diary and Autobiography,* ed. Butterfield, vol. 3, 108.
42. Thomas A. Bailey, *A Diplomatic History of the American People* (New York, 1950), 26.

sum of five million guilders.[43] It would be difficult to overestimate the importance of this loan for the almost bankrupt U.S. Treasury. In October 1782, thanks to Adams's efforts, Holland and the United States signed a treaty of peace and friendship. This was a major diplomatic success for the young nation. Holland became the second European country after France to conclude an agreement with the United States. The treaty made it possible for the United States to obtain Dutch loans, reduced their dependence on France, and began the process that led other European countries to recognize the independence of the United States.

American victories in the War of Independence, particularly the British defeat at Yorktown in October 1781, transformed the atmosphere at the peace talks. The military successes won by the Americans enabled their representatives in Paris to adopt a more independent position vis-à-vis their allies, and in March 1782 Franklin opened direct peace negotiations with the British. By the time Adams returned to Paris in late October the draft of the peace treaty between England and the United States was nearly completed; it was signed by the two sides in November 1782. Adams and Jay, who had arrived from Madrid somewhat earlier, persuaded Franklin not to consult with the French government in the future and indeed not to inform it of the progress of the talks. Fearing that the negotiations would result in haggling between England and France that might sacrifice the interests of the United States, the American envoys openly disobeyed the instructions of the Congress. During the negotiations the two sides agreed that England's recognition of the independence of the United States should form the basis for the peace treaty and that if Spain and France demanded concessions in Asia, Africa, or Europe, and as a result continued the war, England and the United States would sign a separate peace.[44]

Owing to a number of internal and external circumstances, the allies of the United States had to agree to the peace terms worked out by England and the United States. On September 3, 1783, England and the United States signed a peace treaty in Paris that recognized U.S. independence and defined the borders of the new state. Adams played a prominent role in developing the ideas of the American bourgeoisie, and he contributed greatly to the governmental and sociopolitical principles that were to guide the policies of the United States. He did much to strengthen the diplomatic position of his country. Adams devoted a great deal of attention to the theory of the bourgeois state and to bourgeois legal theory and thus may be considered one of the founders of bourgeois political science in the United States.

The path that Adams traveled in the course of his long political life was a tortuous one. In the beginning, like most of his contemporaries, he shared the progressive views of the Age of Enlightenment and spoke out in favor of the inalienable rights of man. Many years later, however, he completely rejected the progressive principles of eighteenth-century thought, having concluded that they were based on "false principles" of human nature. The evolution of his views reflected the complex events of the age and the changes in the views of the entire propertied class, whose members

43. Adams, *Diary and Autobiography,* ed. Butterfield, vol. 4, 264.
44. Bemis, *Diplomacy of the American Revolution,* 204.

quickly doffed the garb of revolutionary defenders of freedom and became chiefly concerned with defending their privileges. An exponent of the interests of this class, Adams was both its defender and one of its first theoreticians throughout all the stages of the struggle of the American bourgeoisie for power and for the consolidation of its rule.

COMMENT BY RICHARD ALAN RYERSON

Boris Shiriayev's "John Adams and the Struggle for the Independence of the American Colonies" is a clear, accurate, and perceptive treatment of Adams's career up to the Peace of 1783 between Great Britain and the United States of America. Shiriayev effectively discusses each of Adams's major beliefs and ideas that contributed to America's achieving its independence from the British empire and briefly recounts each of Adams's major public roles in meeting that goal: as patriot spokesman in provincial Massachusetts, key member of the Continental Congress, president of Congress's Board of War, diplomat to the courts of France and Holland, and finally as head of the American negotiating team that secured peace with Great Britain. For anyone seeking a clear and succinct statement of John Adams's importance to the establishment of America's independence from the perspective of an intelligent foreign observer, as of the mid-1960s (the most recent date of the essay's published primary and secondary sources), Shiriayev offers a fairly satisfactory starting point.

As an analysis of John Adams's career in historical context, however, Shiriayev's argument is seriously flawed by his general conception of early American society and by his view of Adams's relationship to that society. Shiriayev sees the American Revolution as the triumph of America's bourgeoisie over certain, largely unnamed, opposing classes, both those above them in the Anglo-American class structure, residing primarily in Great Britain, and those below them, in America. And he considers John Adams to be an archetypal spokesman, perhaps even the archetypal spokesman, for the values and aspirations of that bourgeoisie. Both of these contentions are open to serious question.

A belief in the ubiquity of class conflict and in the central historical role of the bourgeoisie is not a major obstacle to a perceptive analysis of the American Revolution or of its key players, such as John Adams. Nor are interpretations that are based on these assumptions confined to scholars who have been trained in a Marxist historical tradition or have lived in societies organized on Marxist principles. Several prominent scholars who were active in America's Progressive era at the beginning of the present century shared these convictions as they looked back at the American Revolution, and in the 1970s this perception, then labeled "neo-Progressive," had a certain revival. Indeed, in that decade the present author wrote a study that has a strong "neo-Progressive" character.[1]

Moreover, given John Adams's position in American society at his birth, the nature of his education, the function of his profession, the membership of his social circle, the income that he earned and enjoyed, and the content of his political and social

---

1. Progressive-era studies include most notably: Charles H. Lincoln, *The Revolutionary Movement in Pennsylvania 1760–1776* (Philadelphia, 1901); Carl Lotus Becker, *The History of Political Parties in the Province of New York, 1760–1776* (Madison, Wisconsin, 1909); Charles A. Beard, *An Economic Interpretation of the Constitution of the United States* (New York, 1913); and Arthur M. Schlesinger, *The Colonial Merchants and the American Revolution 1763–1776* (New York, 1918). The author's study is Richard Alan Ryerson, *The Revolution Is Now Begun: The Radical Committees of Philadelphia, 1765–1776* (Philadelphia, 1978).

ideas, labels such as "middle-class," "upper middle-class," and "bourgeois" can all describe him accurately. They only do so, however, when they are related clearly to the society he lived in. Shiriayev's bourgeoisie is too broad and ill defined to characterize either Adams's socioeconomic circle or any class within eighteenth-century American society. More to the point, Shiriayev's bourgeoisie is anachronistic; to the degree that the term is defined at all (indirectly by statements about Adams and about eighteenth-century America), it appears more suitable to a discussion of late-eighteenth-century England and to nineteenth-century Europe. In making John Adams a product and spokesman of the bourgeoisie presented in this essay, Shiriayev does not so much have the wrong man as he has the wrong century and the wrong country.

Consider certain interpretative emphases that appear early in the essay. Shiriayev begins describing Adams by stating that he "belonged to a wealthy family." This was hardly the case. Adams's father, "Deacon" John Adams, was a Braintree farmer and, during the cold winter months when farming activity was slow, a shoemaker. He spent his entire life in manual work. He was able to hire a few wage servants to assist him, and he did have the means to send his eldest son John to college, but he never became wealthy, and his two younger sons followed him into farming.

Shiriayev next states that "unlike Franklin, [John Adams] never had to work hard to earn a living." Unless Shiriayev includes only manual labor as work, this statement too is flatly wrong. Adams became a prosperous lawyer only by constant work and by traveling to county courts throughout the province of Massachusetts. He never stopped practicing law until he entered full-time public service in the First Continental Congress. Thereafter he was largely dependent upon his public salary for his income; in return for that salary, he often worked twelve or more hours a day.

Shiriayev also misunderstands the nature of the legal profession of which Adams was a member and the economic system in which he worked. He states that Adams "entered a well-known law practice as an apprentice," where he "completed a two-year course of legal studies." In eighteenth-century Massachusetts, however, there were no legal firms. Nor was there any "course of legal studies"; one could read law books, quite informally, with an established lawyer, and this Adams did. Shiriayev's terms, however, suggest developed legal institutions, like London's Inns of Court, and a highly organized legal profession. Such institutions and such a profession did exist in eighteenth-century England, but not in America.

Finally, Shiriayev says that Adams's services "were sought by well-known traders and industrialists from Boston." The image projected by the term "industrialists" fundamentally mischaracterizes eighteenth-century Boston. The city did have a few fairly large-scale manufacturers, primarily rum distillers and sugar bakers, ship builders, and rope and sail makers. Their numbers and their influence, however, were minuscule compared with Boston's merchants, who formed the core of the city's upper classes.

Individually these errors are minor, but together they suggest a view of early America that is fundamentally anachronistic. The world into which John Adams was born, in which he grew to maturity, and which he came to lead, was largely rural and preindustrial, and even to some extent precapitalist, located between the mercantilist world of the early British empire and the capitalist-industrialist world of the nineteenth century. Early American society was not classless, of course, any more than contemporary American society is classless, whatever many Americans have wanted, and still want, to believe. It did have, and does have, its wealthy and poor, its upper, middle, and lower classes, and these were and are defined, less rigidly than in most European societies, by several factors, notably income and education, and especially in the eighteenth century by family connections.

What early America did not have was a unified bourgeoisie of fundamentally the same character and with the same objectives throughout the several distinct colonies spread along the Atlantic seaboard from Nova Scotia to Georgia. Because America did not have a proper bourgeoisie in the eighteenth century, it is meaningless to portray the major events and institutions of the Revolution as essentially bourgeois achievements or to view John Adams as a representative spokesman for that class. Yet this is just what Shiriayev does.

A prominent example is his characterization of the First Continental Congress. He begins with the perfectly valid point that it was composed of "the elite of American society," but then finds it necessary to add: "There were no representatives of the democratic strata at this gathering, for the very method of delegate selection was designed to exclude the people from taking part." Shiriayev evidently believes that the "democratic strata" and "the people" were clamoring to participate in the Congress but were kept out.

In a society that had a more fully developed class consciousness than did eighteenth-century America such demands from below could be expected, and elite groups would indeed attempt to frustrate them. Up to 1774 in America, however, the "democratic strata" (assuming that the term includes manual laborers, persons without property, and all those with low incomes) played a subsidiary role in the politics of every province, and they did not expect ever to play a large role. The "elite of American society," therefore, had no need to exclude members of the lower classes from either the Continental Congress or from their provincial legislatures, and the only elites who got into serious trouble with classes below them in the coming of the Revolution were those who, as in New York and Pennsylvania, refused to lead their provinces out of the British empire.

Shiriayev's second argument is that John Adams was both an important and an archetypal spokesman for America's bourgeoisie. A striking example of this view is the need that he feels to explain Adams's apparent lack of interest in Europe's "third estate" when he served as a diplomat in France and Holland. Shiriayev, following the argument of Edward Handler, assumes that Adams, "himself by birth a member of the third estate" in America, must feel a deep sympathy for members of his own class in Europe. Yet because "he did not wish to be seen as a rebel or as a representative of a revolutionary country," but as "a trustworthy and respected diplomat," he ignored his class brethren and associated largely with Europe's titled aristocracy.

Now it is certainly true that John Adams quite consciously placed his duties as a diplomat—a public servant who was dedicated to advancing the fortunes of his country among all nations—above his personal feelings for or against any particular nation, class, or cause within Europe. This was for him a matter of personal conviction, but his neutrality was also expected and appreciated by both Congress and the American public. Adams's private writings, however, show that he was generally not much impressed with Europe's titled aristocracy, or with European society as a whole. Like several other Americans, Adams found Europe to be too urban and materialistic, and with too great a concentration of wealth within the titled aristocracy and the upper classes generally, to be fertile ground for the simple republican virtue that he saw as America's glory and that he hoped to preserve in America.

At the same time Adams saw Europe, like America, as having a less rigidly hierarchical social order than the concepts of first, second, and third estates would imply. As his political thought developed, his own definitions of aristocracy became increasingly idiosyncratic, even within America. For Adams, an aristocracy was any alliance of powerful and talented members of society for their own advantage and to the disadvantage of the general public, whether their power was based on wealth, family, or sheer ability and drive. Such an aristocracy could include any member of the French third estate who achieved any prominence, whatever the condition of his birth; that is, for John Adams the French bourgeoisie itself either was, or was on the verge of becoming, an aristocracy.

Beginning even before the American Revolution, however, and with increasing concern after the creation of an independent American nation, Adams argued that aristocracies were not to be suppressed in a sound republic because they never could be suppressed under any form of government whatsoever.[2] Instead their power should be limited and harnessed for the public good through a constitution of checks and balances that yoked together a popularly elected, powerful executive, an aristocratic upper legislative house, and a more democratic lower house.

Moreover, if Adams ignored Europe's—particularly France's—third estate as a distinct social class because he did not see it as a distinct social class, he did not in fact remain unmoved by the political struggles of many Europeans who usually would be thought a part of that third estate. Even after negotiating peace with Britain, it would have been easier for Adams the diplomat, and more in keeping with his and America's policy of neutrality toward European political and social issues and classes, to have ignored all such struggles. In 1786, however, he took an intense interest in

2. John Adams's writings, particularly in the years 1786–1790, make it clear that he thought the French court nobility under the ancien régime, Britain's Parliament (the House of Commons fully as much as the House of Lords), and the state legislatures and the Congress of the new American nation were all aristocracies. So too, in the present era, the members of Congress in twentieth-century America and the members of various Western European parliaments, the party bureaucrats in the Soviet Union under Leonid Brezhnev and Mikhael Gorbachev, and the vast army of officials left behind by Chairman Mao in China would all qualify as aristocrats, whether "republican" (that is, functioning within a republic), monarchical, or oligarchical, or, to use terms largely unknown to Adams, socialist, communist, or totalitarian. What determined the proper adjective to place before any particular aristocracy, in John Adams's view, was not so much the character of the members who composed it (which, he believed, varied little from one country or century to another, whatever the culturally determined moral nature of the members' daily behavior), as it was the character of the form of government and of the political culture in which the aristocracy functioned.

the republican reform, or Patriot, movement in the Netherlands, and he was deeply disappointed in the following year when elements of the Dutch nobility joined the reigning Prince of Orange and Prussian troops to suppress that movement. It was probably his initial hopes and fears for the Netherlands, combined with a recently published French criticism of America's state constitutions,[3] rather than any alarm over such popular uprisings in America as Shays's Rebellion in Massachusetts, that drove Adams to write his longest political treatise, the *Defence of the Constitutions of the United States of America* (1786–1787).

John Adams's *Defence* lies beyond the chronological boundaries of Shiriayev's portrait. But the essential argument of this massive work, which consists largely of European historical illustrations of the political themes that Adams had been developing in his writings since the 1760s, as well as the argument in several shorter pieces that Adams wrote shortly after his return to America in 1788,[4] casts considerable doubt on Shiriayev's final connection of John Adams with the term "bourgeois."

At the end of his essay Shiriayev contends that "Adams devoted great attention to the theory of the bourgeois state and bourgeois legal theory, and he may be considered one of the founders of bourgeois political science in the United States." But was John Adams properly a "bourgeois" political thinker at all? Important work on the political thought of the American Revolution done in the 1960s and 1970s, notably in Gordon Wood's *The Creation of the American Republic* and J. G. A. Pocock's *The Machiavellian Moment* suggests that Adams occupies a quite different point in the Western political tradition.[5]

After the War for Independence, as before it, Alexander Hamilton, Thomas Jefferson, and James Madison, and their respective supporters and admirers each in different ways largely accepted the political thought of English, Scottish, and French Enlightenment thinkers. Some, like Hamilton, looked ahead to a liberal, commercial America that would seek its glory in the economic achievements of its small but rising urban capitalist classes. Others, like Jefferson, saw an equally liberal and only slightly less commercial nation that would be more attuned to rural and agrarian values. And all concurred with Madison in seeking political stability in the balancing of

3. The text that impelled Adams to begin writing his *Defence* was Baron Turgot's letter of March 22, 1778, to Dr. Richard Price, which Price first published in his *Observations on the Importance of the American Revolution* in 1784. In this letter Turgot roundly criticized all those American state constitutions that provided for two-house legislatures and the careful separation and balance of powers—that is, just those constitutions to whose composition John Adams's *Thought on Government* (1776) had so greatly contributed. See Zoltan Haraszti, *John Adams and the Prophets of Progress* (Cambridge, Mass., 1952), chaps. 8 and 9.

4. See the correspondence between John Adams and Roger Sherman, July 1789, and between John Adams and Samuel Adams, September–November 1790, in *The Works of John Adams,* ed. Charles Francis Adams (Boston, 1851), vol. 6, 427–42 (with Sherman), and 405–26 (with Samuel Adams).

5. Gordon S. Wood, *The Creation of the American Republic, 1776–1787* (Chapel Hill, 1969), especially chap. 14, "The Relevance and Irrelevance of John Adams"; and J. G. A. Pocock, *The Machiavellian Moment: Florentine Political Thought and the Atlantic Republican Tradition* (Princeton, N.J., 1975).

competing economic interests in what they liked to imagine was a relatively classless society.

John Adams's thought was different from all of this. His *Defence of the Constitutions of the United States* was, in Pocock's words, "perhaps the last major work of political theory written within the unmodified tradition of classical republicanism."[6] Adams's most important political teachers, unlike the mentors of Hamilton, Jefferson, and Madison, were all of much earlier eras: James Harrington, Niccolo Machiavelli, and indeed Polybius and Aristotle. They taught, among many other things, that social classes—distinct social groups based primarily upon their relationship to the ownership of or the labor upon agricultural property—were eternal, and that sound governments must ultimately rest upon a balance of social classes.

This "classical republican" system of thought was the central component in the rise of republican theory in Europe and America from the fifteenth to the eighteenth centuries, and it is of obvious importance, particularly in the figure of Harrington, to the development of nineteenth-century class-conflict models of society by several thinkers, most notably Karl Marx. The classical republican tradition was not, however, a particularly bourgeois system of thought; indeed, after 1780 it was no longer in the mainstream of the bourgeois political tradition. The thought of Harrington in the 1650s and of his student John Adams in the 1760s and 1770s was by the 1780s too oriented toward the medieval and classical past, too committed to a rural, agrarian life that incorporated an organic, traditional view of society, to further the interests of an increasingly urban and commercial society in which class would be determined largely by money rather than by family background or even by education.

And while it was not until the 1960s and 1970s that historians such as Pocock began to sort out the complex differences between the historical lineages of John Adams's thought and the quite different intellectual genealogies of his American contemporaries, those contemporaries had no difficulty in perceiving that in his view of governments and social classes, Adams was not one of them. From his more urban and democratic cousin Samuel Adams of Boston, to the conservative small-town merchant Roger Sherman of Connecticut, to the Virginia planter-scholar James Madison, all were dismayed by his unorthodox definitions of "republic," "aristocracy," and other central concepts of their political world.

Thus while John Adams's political thought *was* crucial to the movement for America's independence and to the development of the new constitutions of several American states and of the U.S. Constitution itself, Adams was by 1790 speaking a political language that his countrymen could not understand. And no group in America was more remote from his thought than the wealthy urban classes that were beginning to take charge of America's transition from a rural, agricultural society to a more urban and commercial, and ultimately an industrial, nation.

In labeling Adams a bourgeois thinker and actor before the Revolution, I have suggested, Shiriayev has not so much identified the wrong man as the wrong era and the wrong country. In seeing John Adams as a central bourgeois thinker after

---

6. Pocock, *Machiavellian Moment,* 526.

the Revolution, however, Shiriayev does indeed have the wrong man. By the mid-1780s the political history of America and Europe, a historical era that after the American Revolution, and even more strongly after the French Revolution, can with increasing justice be labeled "bourgeois," had taken a decisive turn toward the thought and aspirations of such diverse American leaders as Alexander Hamilton and James Madison, and away from the more austere republican vision of John Adams.

RESPONSE BY B. A. SHIRIAYEV

The author of the review and the author of the article hold two different positions: they evaluate the occurrences and events differently; they even treat and understand the themes differently. Of course many of the positions I took in my article, written now almost twenty years ago, carry the imprint of their times, especially since the article is based on materials from the 1950s and 1960s.

The basis of this divergence of views between my critic and me seems to lie in fundamental differences over the character of American society at the time of the Revolution, the essence of the Revolution itself, and the sociopolitical content of Adams's views. It seems impossible not to admit that the character of the epoch and the role of Adams to no small degree were modernized. At the same time it is impossible to agree with my critic's view that the American Revolution did not bear a bourgeois character. It was bourgeois in spirit, as long as we understand that this spirit involved the negating of feudal institutions and the affirming of individual rights.

My reviewer's remarks are corrective, and they are of course useful for further clarifying the problems brought out by my article.

CHAPTER 4

Jefferson, Franklin, Paine, and the Development of Democratic Sociopolitical Ideas in the United States

by

V. V. Sogrin

Three major figures of the Enlightenment, Benjamin Franklin, Thomas Jefferson, and Thomas Paine, exercised an enormous influence on every facet of contemporary intellectual life in North America. This article will offer an analysis of one of the aspects of their influence—the role of these representatives of the Enlightenment in the evolution of American sociopolitical thought in the age of the American Revolution and the foundation of the United States.

The study of the worldview and political activities of the representatives of the American Enlightenment has long had pride of place in Soviet Americanology.[1] Some aspects of this topic have been fully analyzed, while others still await serious scholarly study. Scholars have been most successful in analyzing the common features and, to a lesser extent, the individual traits in the views of these thinkers. Through a comparative analysis of the sociopolitical ideas of Jefferson, Franklin, and Paine, I will attempt to provide a more comprehensive account of their original contribution to democratic thought in America and to describe their different views on the future course of the socioeconomic and political development of the United States. I will also try to show how the peculiarities of the North American social structure were reflected in the thinking of Jefferson, Franklin, and Paine, and to demonstrate how these thinkers developed the sociopolitical principles of the European Enlightenment.

1. For an analysis of the various aspects of the views and activities of Jefferson, Franklin, and Paine, see the works of M. P. Baskin, I. A. Beliavskaia, N. N. Bolkhovitinov, B. E. Bykhovskii, V. V. Voronov, N. M. Goldberg, L. N. Goncharov, B. S. Gromakov, A. V. Efimov, M. N. Zakharov, R. F. Ivanov, A. M. Karimskii, A. A. Kislova, V. N. Pleshkov, M. I. Radovskii, G. N. Sevostianov, A. I. Utkin, and other Soviet scholars. For a survey of works by Soviet authors that discuss the place and role of the American writers of the Enlightenment in the American Revolution, see G. N. Sevostianov, "Concerning Certain Problems of the History of the American Revolution," *Modern and Contemporary History* 3 (1976), 32–50. This article by V. V. Sogrin was first published in *American Studies Annual for 1979* (Moscow, 1979).

Finally, let us note that Soviet historiography has so far failed to analyze fully the inconsistencies in the economic, social, and political ideas of these writers. A complete demonstration and evaluation of the contradictions in the views of these three figures of the Enlightenment are all the more important since American historiography has done little to clear up the issue.[2]

I believe that in the era of the American Revolution, Jefferson, Franklin, and Paine were interested in four major subjects: the civil rights of man; the prospects for the socioeconomic development of the United States; the theory of the contractual nature of the state and the right to revolution; and the principles underlying the structure of political authority in the United States. This study is devoted to the views of the three men on these subjects.

THE DEVELOPMENT OF THE THEORY OF NATURAL LAW

One of the central themes in the debate between the exponents of feudal and antifeudal ideology in the era of the bourgeois revolutions of the seventeenth and eighteenth centuries was the civil rights of man. Like the representatives of the Enlightenment in Europe, Jefferson, Paine, and Franklin approached this problem from a natural state theory. The American democrats rejected the validity of the dominant legal theory of the day. This theory sanctified the feudal-absolutist institutions in European societies and the vestiges of these institutions in the New World. Paine stated that references to existing written legislation and its interpreters and apologists amounted to scholasticism and merely engendered "the constant clash of authority with authority." In his search for just principles on which a theory of human rights could be based, Paine, like other writers of the Enlightenment, turned to the concept of the state of nature. In such a state, he wrote, "our reason finds sanctuary and discovers the actual truth necessary for the understanding of the rights of man."[3]

The Enlightenment teaching about the state of nature and its just character was rationalistic and speculative. It provided the thinkers of the Enlightenment with a theoretical basis for their criticism of the countless manifestations of inequality among men in feudal societies. Because nothing was reliably known about the original state of mankind, every thinker was able to endow man with qualities and traits that corresponded to the general worldview expressed by this or that current in the Enlightenment.

---

2. American historians have developed two main approaches to this question, which are known as the Progressive and the consensus approaches. The first is characterized by a marked interest in the democratic thought of the American writers of the Enlightenment; the historians adopting this approach contrast the views of these writers and the ideas expressed by moderate and conservative political figures as two different class-based ideologies. The exponents of the second approach, which became dominant among bourgeois historiographers after World War II, aim to emphasize the liberal rather than democratic elements in the thought of the American enlighteners and refuse to recognize any differences of principle between those authors and conservative figures such as Hamilton, Madison, Robert Morris, and others.

3. Thomas Paine, *Selected Writings* (Moscow, 1959), 202.

The writers of the Enlightenment developed several conceptions of the natural state of society. The majority, including Montesquieu and Voltaire, constructed a model that presented society in its natural state as an antithesis of the feudal order. A minority, among them Melier, Mably, and Morelli, endowed it with not only antifeudal but also antibourgeois features. Jefferson, Franklin, and Paine thus had a choice of two European versions of the theory of the natural state. Yet the Enlightenment writers of the United States did not mechanically copy the ideas developed in Europe.

In their interpretation of the theory of the natural state they could not help reflecting the peculiarities of the social structure and historical evolution of North America. It is important to understand that the American Revolution required that they should make their teachings as concrete as possible and transform abstract principles into tangible ideas about the socioeconomic and political freedoms and rights of man—ideas that could be realized in practice. The writers of the American Enlightenment therefore developed the rights and freedoms of man along two different lines: by creating a theory of the natural or ideal social state, and by formulating ideas about the concrete socioeconomic and political rights of the citizens of the United States.

The American thinkers of the Enlightenment imagined the original state of mankind as one in which there had been absolute equality and in which no single individual enjoyed any advantages or privileges in relation to his neighbors. "Man— that was his exalted and only title, and he cannot be given any higher one," was Paine's way of expressing this most humane principle of the Enlightenment.[4] In the Declaration of Independence, which was written by Thomas Jefferson, the first of the "self-evident truths" he stated was that "all men are created equal and are endowed with certain inalienable rights."[5] Remarkably, in their theory of natural equality Paine and Jefferson, unlike many figures of the European Enlightenment, did not believe that private property—the cause of social inequality—had existed when man was in a primordial social state.

On a number of occasions Paine stated very categorically that private property had not existed in the natural state.[6] Moreover, he was the first among the Enlightenment writers in the United States to try to discover the historical roots of private property. He believed that private property appeared as soon as people began to work on the land: "When cultivation began the idea of landed property began with it, from the impossibility of separating the improvement made by cultivation from the earth itself, upon which that improvement was made."[7] At that stage in the development of social science Paine's speculations about the origins of private property were not, and could not be, scientific in character. But in developing his conception of the genesis of private property he certainly produced some insights of a materialist nature.

4. Ibid.
5. *The Papers of Thomas Jefferson,* ed. Julian P. Boyd et al. (Princeton, 1950–), vol. 1, 429.
6. *The Complete Writings of Thomas Paine,* ed. Philip S. Foner, 2 vols. (New York, 1945), vol. 1, 606, 607, 610, 611.
7. Ibid., 611, 612.

Jefferson's opinions about property relations in the state of nature were far less specific than Paine's and, moreover, did not form a cohesive whole. In the Declaration of Independence he did not include ownership of private property among the natural rights of man. There is clear evidence that this omission was deliberate. When at the beginning of the French Revolution Marquis de Lafayette asked Jefferson to correct the draft of the Declaration of the Rights of Man the Frenchman had composed, the only natural right among those the document listed that Jefferson put in parentheses was ownership of private property.[8] Indeed, in a 1785 letter to James Madison, Jefferson had expressed his indignation about the blatant inequality in land ownership in the Old World: "The earth is given as a common stock for man to labour and live on."[9]

Convincing indirect evidence that Jefferson did not view private property as a primordial social institution is provided by the fact that he equated the social structure of the Indian tribes with the natural state.[10] Indeed, the institution of private property did not exist among the Indians. In general, the social relations of the Indian tribes served the American writers of the Enlightenment as concrete material for constructing models of the natural state.

Unlike Jefferson and Paine, Franklin in his speculations concerning the ideal social order very rarely referred to the theory of the natural state. He had very little to say about the original character of property relationships. Nevertheless, Franklin's writings contain the idea that private property was the product of the historical development of society. In 1789, when justifying the right of the state to regulate property differences, he defined private property as the "Creature of Society," which "is subject to the calls of that Society, whenever its Necessities shall require it, even to its last Farthing."[11]

The pronounced manner in which these American writers of the Enlightenment idealized the social structures of the Indian tribes indicates the extent to which they shared the widespread belief of eighteenth-century ideologues about the state of nature as the "golden age" of mankind. Yet this idealization of the natural state was not absolute. Among the American writers of the Enlightenment, Paine was the least inclined to idealize the state of nature. While Paine observed that the transition from the natural state to civilization, which was accompanied by the establishment of the institution of private property, brought about the disappearance of equality, the division of people into rich and poor, and an increase in poverty, at the same time he offered a comprehensive explanation of the benefits resulting from this transition. He pointed to the improvements in land cultivation and to the development of crafts, industry, and science, which were all unknown to the Indians living in a "state of nature."[12] And all three writers of the American Enlightenment shared the belief that

8. Gilbert Chinard, *Thomas Jefferson: The Apostle of Americanism* (Boston, 1946), 84.

9. *Papers of Jefferson,* ed. Boyd et al., vol. 8, 682.

10. Ibid., vol. 11, 49.

11. *The Writings of Benjamin Franklin,* ed. Albert H. Smyth, 10 vols. (New York–London, 1907), vol. 10, 59.

12. *Writings of Paine,* ed. Foner, vol. 1, 610–12.

the disappearance of the natural state and the appearance of private property were irreversible.

Although they accepted a social order based on the private ownership of property, the American writers of the Enlightenment sharply criticized the social contrasts that appeared as that social order evolved. They all optimistically believed in the possibility of fighting such social inequality, but they offered different solutions to the problem. Of their proposals, Jefferson's plans for agricultural reform related most closely to the special character of the socioeconomic situation in the United States. In his view the existence of an enormous fund of undeveloped lands in the western territories represented a superb opportunity for the reestablishment in the United States of a "natural justice" that meant the equal right of every individual to own land. In June 1776 in his draft of the Virginia constitution, Jefferson put forward a program under which all unoccupied land was to be converted into public property and used exclusively to grant each indigent person a free fifty-acre plot of land.[13] Jefferson's draft of the Virginia constitution, with its declaration that all Virginia citizens had the right to a minimum amount of landed property, compared favorably with all those other documents of the Revolutionary era that only dealt with the political structure of the thirteen independent states. Thus Jefferson began to formulate his democratic idea of developing the territories being annexed by the United States into associations of independent small farmers.

In its final form Jefferson's agricultural program included not only the idea of minimum land ownership as the right of every American citizen but also a plan designed to limit land ownership by large landowners. Jefferson did not define maximum land ownership, but he suggested ways of limiting the amount of land persons could own. He proposed a total ban on the sale of unoccupied lands, thus inhibiting the enrichment of land speculators and planters.[14] Other restrictions proposed by him included abolishing the feudal institutions of primogeniture and entail, which were vestiges of the colonial period, and introducing the progressive taxation of land property. While advocating the abolition of inequality in land ownership, Jefferson was extremely skeptical of radical egalitarianism: "I am conscious that an equal distribution of property is impracticable."[15]

Paine rejected the equal redistribution of landed property in even stronger language than Jefferson. During the Great French Bourgeois Revolution he condemned the demands for a law on agriculture that aimed to introduce egalitarian land ownership. Nor did he advocate restoring to each individual the "natural right" to own land. Paine in fact was not one of those who proposed an agrarian path of development for the United States. Besides, he first seriously thought about the way in which the injustices stemming from the unequal distribution of land could be corrected only in the 1790s—after the American Revolution. At that time he was living in his native England, which, unlike the United States, had no unoccupied lands and

13. *Papers of Jefferson,* ed. Boyd et al., vol. 1, 362.
14. Ibid., 492.
15. Ibid., vol. 8, 682.

where any agitation in favor of giving land to the indigent meant directly encroaching upon the estates of the large landowners. Paine regarded such an infringement of the institution of private property as being too radical. But because he nevertheless believed that in the natural state all men enjoyed an equal right to own land, he demanded financial compensation for those individuals who, in the course of social development, had lost that right. The plan he put forward in 1797 in his treatise "Agrarian Justice" envisaged the establishment of a national monetary fund from moneys raised by taxing the large landowners; each landless Englishman over the age of twenty-one would be paid the sum of fifteen pounds and, in addition, every inhabitant of the country over the age of fifty would receive an annual rent of ten pounds.[16]

Franklin's views on the agrarian question were akin to Jefferson's. However, he never did offer a clear-cut program of agricultural reform. He described what he regarded as the ideal type of agricultural relations for the United States in two essays, "Information for Those Who Are Moving to America" (1782) and "The Internal Situation in America" (1786), which were addressed to those Europeans who wished to settle in the New World. These essays depicted the United States as an Arcadia where the prosperous middle class predominated, where "the majority of the people cultivate their own plots of land," where one could meet but "a few large landowners and very few tenant farmers," and where, unlike Europe, there were naturally no rich men and poor people.[17]

It is difficult to imagine that a sober-minded person like Franklin in fact believed that the United States of the Revolutionary period actually embodied that ideal economic system of which Jefferson, for example, could still only dream. Franklin's views were in fact intended to attract to the New World all those Europeans who shared the author's Enlightenment ideas and discourage from settling in America those who wished to make their fortune through land and bank speculation, or those who hoped to live like the aristocracy of the Old World. Franklin's dream was to see America become a "land of labor" and to remain such forever. He believed that a policy of egalitarianism would be unjust toward the most frugal, industrious, and enterprising. Yet at the same time he accepted only those forms of capitalist accumulation sanctified by the Puritan ethic and by his own efforts to gain material prosperity. Franklin, Paine, and Jefferson may be said to have shared the moderately egalitarian current of eighteenth-century social thought.

The limited bourgeois nature of the concept of the rights of man developed by the American writers of the Enlightenment is plain. It may clearly be seen in their attitude toward private property. Although they believed that property had not existed in the state of nature, they recognized the right to private property that had emerged in the course of history and believed that its existence did not prohibit the achievement of social justice. Jefferson, Paine, and Franklin thought that developing private property in the United States would benefit broad segments of the population.

16. Paine, *Selected Writings,* 384.
17. *Writings of Franklin,* ed. Smyth, vol. 8, 604.

These views of the American Enlightenment writers were significantly limited by the remnants of antibourgeois thought in the age of early capitalism. The bourgeois method of production was just emerging, and bourgeois societies faced a long revolutionary process of destroying feudalism before they would become firmly established. Naturally, only later would the contradictions inherent in those societies become apparent and be described.[18] As I have shown, the writers of the Enlightenment were clearly aware of the defects of the feudal forms of land ownership, but the essential character and the consequences of the bourgeois evolution of property remained hidden to them. However, since at that time the historical process essentially entailed the replacement of feudal forms of property by bourgeois forms, the writers of the Enlightenment may be given the credit for providing a theoretical basis for the democratic path of capitalist development in the United States. In this respect Jefferson's agrarian program, which foresaw nothing other than a farm-based path of capitalist development in agriculture, is particularly noteworthy.

Jefferson's agrarian program was not implemented during the American Revolution. In 1777–1778 the Virginia assembly under the leadership of Edmund Pendleton and a group of large planters decisively crippled Jefferson's program by deciding to sell off the fund of western lands. The conditions of the proposed sale reflected the interests of the large landowners. In his drafts of the Virginia constitution of 1783 and of the Continental Congress land ordinance, as well as in his later statements, Jefferson was obliged to make concessions on this issue to the moderately conservative bloc.[19] Here one may speak of Jefferson's pragmatism and his willingness to compromise with his ideological opponents. But it is impossible not to see something else here as well: the genuine drama of one of the great writers of the Enlightenment being unable to realize his democratic ideals in his lifetime because of the particular correlation of class forces in the United States. It was Jefferson's achievement in 1776 to have described the path that American capitalism in agriculture was to follow progressively for the next one hundred years or so, a path that would lead to the adoption of the Homestead Act in 1862.

For the writers of the Enlightenment the most important issue was the political rights of man, not his economic rights. The priority given by Jefferson, Paine, and Franklin to political freedoms was perhaps the most vivid indication of the bourgeois character of their belief that ascribed an absolute value to legal equality at the expense of economic equality. In Part Two of *The Rights of Man*, Thomas Paine refused to see serious property differences remaining in post-Revolutionary America as unjust, for he believed that the most important characteristic of freedom was its guarantee of the political and legal equality of citizens: "There [in the United States] the poor are not oppressed, the rich are not privileged."[20] This idealization by these Enlightenment writers of the results of the American Revolution shows that their definition of equality was a political and legal one.

18. See K.[arl] Marx and F.[riedrich] Engels, *Writings,* vol. 20, 17.
19. *Papers of Jefferson,* ed. Boyd et al., vol. 6, 607; vol. 7, 118, 502; vol. 8, 229, 483, 514, 633, 634.
20. *Writings of Paine,* ed. Foner, vol. 1, 360.

The bourgeois revolutions of the seventeenth and eighteenth centuries were fought under the banner of the political and legal equality of men. However, there were major differences in how this concept was understood. It was the achievement of the American writers of the Enlightenment to offer a consistent and comprehensive bourgeois-democratic interpretation of that concept. They insisted that political, legal, and religious rights should be guaranteed equally to all citizens of the United States regardless of their property holdings, professional occupation, and religious beliefs. In his pamphlet *A Serious Address to the People of Pennsylvania,* published in December 1778, Paine was the first to provide a theoretical basis for this approach. He defended the Pennsylvania constitution of 1776 as the most advanced and democratic constitution of the era of the American Revolution because it provided for the political participation of broad strata of the white male population, including the lower classes of farmers and craftsmen. The affluent citizens of Pennsylvania, who formed the Republican party, opposed the constitution as soon as it was adopted. Paine parried their attacks on the constitution with his usual polemical skill. The pamphlet's underlying theme was that the "inequality of the estates . . . cannot be an argument against rights."[21]

Paine remained faithful to the idea of equal political rights for as long as he lived. In a letter to the members of the French Directory written in 1796, he harshly criticized the Thermidor constitution, which made political rights dependent on the ownership of property. His defense of the opposing point of view exemplified his profound mastery of the theory of the natural state. He argued that all men are by nature endowed with rights that are identical and equal, including the equal right to own property. In the course of historical development many individuals had lost their ownership of land. But no one could take away their natural rights, among which was the birth-given right to equality in land ownership; that was why it was illogical to deprive the poor of the right to vote.[22]

Using arguments and language that were almost identical to Paine's, Jefferson and Franklin upheld the idea of equal political rights. At the Constitutional Convention of 1787 in Philadelphia, Franklin, who was the only one of the three at that gathering, brilliantly defended the rights of the people, who had ensured the victory of the United States in the War of Independence, from the attacks of the moderate and conservative delegates. In 1789, writing in defense of the Pennsylvania constitution of 1776, he firmly rejected the property owners' proposal for replacing the single-chamber legislature with one comprising two chambers, a proposal that was aimed at creating a senate that would separately represent the interests of the rich. Franklin's credo was that civil society should mainly attempt to guarantee "the right to life and liberty in equal measure to all its members, for the poorest among them may lay as much claim to those rights as the richest."[23]

21. Ibid., vol. 2, 282, 283, 285, 286.

22. Ibid., vol. 1, 607.

23. Max Farrand, ed., *The Records of the Federal Convention,* 4 vols. (New Haven–London, 1966), vol. 1, 47, 54, 61, 197–200; vol. 2, 204, 208, 615; *Writings of Franklin,* ed. Smyth, vol. 10,

The legislation that was passed as the result of the American Revolution failed to embody fully the democratic concept of political equality. The promoters of that concept found themselves in a minority among the leaders of the Revolution. Most of the state constitutions promulgated a number of electoral qualifications, including a property qualification. The federal Constitution of 1787 confirmed these restrictions. The legislation produced by the bourgeois revolutions of the seventeenth and eighteenth centuries in general linked political rights to ownership of property. The concept of equal rights developed by the writers of the Enlightenment became a guiding rule for succeeding generations fighting for the democratization of American society.[24]

The doctrine that divided the rights of man into natural and civil was important to the writers of the American Enlightenment. A superficial examination of this doctrine suggests that they considered civil rights to be only natural rights that society had recognized in its laws. In fact, however, these thinkers were saying something else. According to the ideas of the Enlightenment, man in society is not only endowed with civil rights but also retains a number of natural rights. Such natural rights these writers termed imprescriptible or inalienable.

The theory of civil and inalienable natural rights received its fullest development in the works of Paine, for whom natural rights were "all the intellectual rights, or rights of the mind, and also all those rights of acting as an individual for his own comfort and happiness, which are not injurious to the natural rights of others."[25] In other words, the term "inalienable rights" was understood to mean freedom of thought, religion, and speech, as well as the ensuing freedom of the press, assembly, etc. The writers of the Enlightenment argued that civil society did not have the right to restrict or abolish these freedoms, but could only proclaim and defend them. The Declaration of Independence was concerned precisely with inalienable rights, that is, natural rights that are not subject to society's authority.

By civil rights the writers of the Enlightenment meant those natural rights that no single individual could realize or that were capable of endangering others; for this reason these rights were given to society. The individual, explained Paine, has the right to defend his life and liberty and to seek satisfaction if his rights are infringed. But he cannot be the judge in his own cause. Therefore, it is public authority that should be responsible for guaranteeing his rights.[26] Jefferson agreed with Paine on these points.

There were major differences between Jefferson's and Paine's interpretation of the natural and civil rights of man and of the legal doctrine of one of the most important

---

52, 58–59. In their defense of equal political rights, the American writers of the Enlightenment naturally subjected the class divisions in feudal societies and the privileges enjoyed by monarchs and the titled nobility to withering criticism.

24. The limited class-based character of the bourgeois-democratic concept of the rights of man is expressed in its refusal to recognize the important organic causal relationship between political and economic equality.

25. *Writings of Paine,* ed. Foner, vol. 1, 275, 276.

26. Ibid., vol. 1, 275–76; vol. 2, 274.

representatives of the European Enlightenment, Jean-Jacques Rousseau. According to Rousseau, when the individual is in a "social state" all his rights are alienated in favor of society,[27] but, according to the writers of the American Enlightenment, the individual's rights in those circumstances become self-sufficing.

The concept of the rights of man developed by Jefferson and Paine was strongly individualistic. But in the era of the American Revolution it had progressive overtones. This becomes clearer if one bears in mind that during the final stage of the Revolution, moderate and conservative leaders began to show increasing concern for the rights and interests of public authority and tended to ignore more and more the rights of man. Hamilton believed that democratic societies—and he allotted pride of place among these to the United States—were constantly threatened by the possibility that individuals might lose respect for the government, which is why in such societies "the governors require special protection."[28] At the 1787 Convention the moderates and conservatives did their best to demonstrate the need for the maximum strengthening of the authority of government while at the same time deliberately omitting from the draft of the federal Constitution a bill of rights. Yet during the Revolution the writers of the Enlightenment had argued that both the state constitutions and the federal Constitution should list all the civil rights and all the inalienable rights of man.

In the era of the American Revolution the population of the United States was divided into two categories: free people and Negro slaves. The question of slavery preoccupied the writers of the Enlightenment. The formulation and eventual resolution of this question by democratic-minded men was made possible by the development of anticolonialist thought during the ten years prior to the Revolution. The reliance of the anticolonialist thinkers on a theory of natural rights when arguing for the absolute equality between Americans and Englishmen glaringly contrasted with their fellow countrymen's racist views and prejudices. The opponents of the patriots in England did not fail to point out this inconsistency. They asked how men who enslaved their fellow human beings could present themselves as proponents of natural equality. The logic of the doctrine of natural rights tended to deny the existence of any differences among men, and as a result the ideologues of the patriotic movement were obliged to embrace antiracist and antislaveholding views. Criticism of colonial tyranny was incompatible with the sanctification of slavery—a more pernicious form of oppression. Anticolonial thought had to be also antislaveholding in character.

Franklin, who undoubtedly was the most brilliant and prominent of the early critics of colonialism, was one of the first to advance arguments against slaveholding. When doing this he had to overcome some of his own racist views, which he had espoused until the 1760s.[29] In the late 1760s and early 1770s Franklin, assuming the unity of human nature in accord with the theory of natural rights, criticized racial oppression,

27. Jean-Jacques Rousseau, *Treatises* (Moscow, 1969), 161.

28. *The Papers of Alexander Hamilton,* ed. H. G. Syrett et al., 23 vols. (New York–London, 1961–1974), vol. 3, 451–54.

29. Paul W. Conner, *Poor Richard's Politics: Benjamin Franklin and his New American Order* (London, 1969), 28, 29.

condemned the "detestable traffic in the bodies and souls of men," and spoke in favor of the gradual emancipation of the Negroes.[30]

Jefferson expressed his antislaveholding views in his pamphlet *A Summary View of the Rights of British America* (1774). He called racial oppression and the slave trade crimes against human nature. Both in the pamphlet and in the draft of the Declaration of Independence, Jefferson laid the blame for the denial of the Negroes' "sacred rights" to life and liberty solely on the English king ("This piratical war, the opprobrium of *infidel* powers, is the warfare of the CHRISTIAN king of Great Britain," declared the draft). At the same time he expected his countrymen to undertake the kind of obligations that most of them were eventually unwilling to accept. "The abolition of slavery here," Jefferson claimed, "is the greatest ambition of the colonies." Jefferson's positive program included an urgent demand to ban the import of slaves into America.[31]

Paine's speeches in 1775 represented the height of antislaveholding criticism during the pre-Revolutionary period. Unlike Jefferson, he laid the blame for the enslaving of the Negroes not on the English king but on the Americans themselves. Paine did not limit himself to calling for an immediate halt to the import of slaves into North America, but also demanded the simultaneous emancipation of the Negroes in the colonies. On the eve of the Revolution he put forward a program for endowing the freed Negroes with plots of lands for which, however, they would be required to pay a moderate rent. Under Paine's plan the responsibility for caring for sick and old Negroes would belong to their former masters.[32]

Strange as it may seem, 1776 for a time put an end to the development of democratic principles in antislavery writings. This was because after the Declaration of Independence those social groups in the North and South interested in preserving slavery and the slave trade no longer felt the need to propagandize the natural-rights-based equality of all people, and they discarded the mask of being fighters against all forms of oppression. At the Continental Congress in July 1776, Thomas Jefferson became fully aware of the hypocrisy of many of the patriot leaders who professed to believe in natural-rights-based equality. In the Congress not only the representatives of the southern states but even some of the "northern brothers" demanded that the statement condemning the slave trade be deleted from the Declaration of Independence.[33] At the same time the assembly in Jefferson's native state of Virginia in debating a bill of rights strongly attacked the proposition that all men were created equal, a proposition that had become a truism in anticolonial criticism. Somewhat later the Virginia courts declared that the statement in the Declaration of Independence that men are naturally equal did not apply either to free Negroes or to slaves.[34]

30. *Benjamin Franklin's Letters to the Press, 1758–1775*, ed. V. W. Crane (Chapel Hill, 1950), 223.

31. *The American Enlighteners: Selected Works in Two Volumes* (Moscow, 1968–1969), vol. 2, 18–19, 31.

32. Ibid., 18, 19.

33. *Papers of Jefferson*, ed. Boyd et al., vol. 1, 314–15.

34. Dumas Malone, *Jefferson and His Time: Jefferson the Virginian* (Boston, 1948), 228.

Yet under these circumstances Jefferson had the courage to oppose the views of the planter class, to which he himself belonged. His 1776 draft of the Virginia constitution called for a ban on the further importation of slaves into the state. A year later Jefferson introduced in the Virginia assembly a bill containing a similar demand. In 1783, in his draft for a new Virginia constitution he included a provision under which all Negroes born after December 31, 1800, were to be manumitted. His draft of the Continental Congress land ordinance of 1784 contained a proposal for the banning of slavery after 1800 in territories newly joined to the United States.[35] In this way Jefferson hoped to prevent the extension of slavery across the whole country, an extension that southern planters dreamed of day and night. All of these proposals by Jefferson were rejected. More and more often he sounded pessimistic in his statements concerning the prospects for the struggle against slavery in the United States. Eventually he concluded that his generation of antislavery activists was not destined to rid the country of the shameful institution.

There are a number of clearly conservative features in Jefferson's approach to the Negro problem. I am not referring to the gradual method of emancipation he championed—no one at the time envisaged any other method. Jefferson was conservative in his view of what should be the fate of the emancipated Negroes. Unlike Franklin and Paine, he proposed their expatriation from the United States. In his *Notes on the State of Virginia* (1783), Jefferson stated that it was impossible for two races to live together and adduced a number of reasons for this, including some of a "physical and moral nature." He conceded, though in very guarded language, that possibly the Negroes were racially inferior.[36] In a letter to Condorcet in 1791, Jefferson wrote that he would be glad to see any proof that would show these suspicions to be false, but he certainly did not reject them, as his American biographers claim.[37]

Franklin and Paine, who consistently defended the Enlightenment idea of the innately equal abilities of all people irrespective of their racial origin, occupied a progressive position on the racial issue. In 1789, shortly before his death, Franklin, in explaining the program of the Pennsylvania Anti-Slavery Society, firmly rejected the idea of the racial inferiority of Negroes and offered a comprehensive explanation of the true reasons for the downtrodden state of the black Americans. He argued that the inhuman conditions in which white America had earlier placed the Negro slaves had prevented them from developing their physical and intellectual abilities. He ended by calling on the nation to strive for the humane goal of liberating the Negroes so that they could become citizens of the United States with full rights.[38]

The antislavery ideas of the Enlightenment writers represented the first step in the evolution of the democratic tradition that eventually produced the abolitionist doctrine. Yet a great deal of time was to elapse between these two stages in the history

35. *Papers of Jefferson,* ed. Boyd et al., vol. 1, 363; vol. 2, 22; vol. 6, 298, 604.
36. *The American Enlighteners,* vol. 2, 59, 61.
37. Malone, *Jefferson the Virginian,* 268; Bernard Mayo, *Jefferson Himself* (Boston, 1942), 293; Adrienne Koch, *The Philosophy of Thomas Jefferson* (New York, 1943), 118, 119.
38. Benjamin Franklin, *Selected Works,* 412–13.

of democratic criticism of slavery. Thus the democratic leaders of the first American Revolution failed to address a number of questions that occupied an important place in mature abolitionism, such as abolishing slavery, involving the Negro population in the struggle against slavery, and immediately granting to the Negroes civil and political rights equal to those of white people.

CONCERNING THE PATH OF SOCIOPOLITICAL DEVELOPMENT IN THE UNITED STATES

The views of the writers of the Enlightenment on the socioeconomic future of the United States became fully developed in the era of the American Revolution. There were serious disagreements among them on this issue: if Franklin and Jefferson were unreservedly in favor of the country developing in the direction of agrarian capitalism, Paine was increasingly drawn toward the idea of the young bourgeois nation developing along mercantile-industrial lines.

Franklin believed that North America was destined to follow the agrarian path of development, and he had offered arguments in support of this view in his "Canadian Pamphlet" (1760). In his opinion, the development of trade and manufacturing in a given country was linked to the disappearance of unoccupied land and rural overpopulation. Enormous numbers of people, once they had despaired of being able to use their strength in blessed agricultural labor, were forced to hire themselves out to an industrialist or merchant; it was hunger and financial ruin that made them seek a different occupation. Franklin's maxim, "manufactories are established in poverty," clearly expressed his attitude toward the mercantile-industrial path of development.

Franklin was satisfied that North America, which possessed a huge reserve of unoccupied lands, was in no danger of following that particular path.[39] However, on the eve of the Revolution Franklin suggested that the colonies might be able to develop along mercantile-industrial lines. He argued in fact that the severing of economic ties with England would in no way weaken the colonies because in the near future North America would have "its own manufactories."[40] In this case Franklin's retreat from his previous theoretical position was due to propaganda considerations: he wished to convince his countrymen that if North America achieved self-government, she would free herself from the rigid economic control of the mother country, but her own commercial and industrial interests would not be threatened.

During and after the Revolution both Franklin and Jefferson spoke out forcefully and at length about the advantages of agrarian development for the United States. The second half of the 1780s marked the height of their efforts to advance the cause of the agrarian path of development. To a certain degree they found a theoretical justification for their arguments in the views of the physiocrats. But in the main these Enlightenment thinkers based their conclusions on their own comparison between the socioeconomic features of the United States, which remained a largely agrarian country, and the socioeconomic features of western Europe and above all Great Britain

39. Ibid., 237, 246–47.
40. *Franklin's Letters to the Press,* ed. Crane, 275.

and France, where there were many more manufactories. Indeed, Great Britain was undergoing a rapid transition to industrial capitalism. These Enlightenment writers believed that the differences between the relatively underdeveloped and classless society of the United States and the pronounced polarization between rich and poor in western Europe were the result of the different economic paths followed by the New World and the Old World. They regarded the social consequences of economic phenomena as being particularly important. Moreover, Jefferson's and Franklin's evaluations of the two paths of social development had a strong ethical character. In the minds of these thinkers the two paths represented, respectively, good and evil.

The agrarian path of development, Jefferson argued, prevented mass poverty and pauperization; unlike industrial countries, agrarian countries were guaranteed against political corruption, which had become a veritable calamity in England. Only agrarian countries could hope to prevent a moral decline and be able to strengthen their moral foundations and indeed preserve the republican system of government. America, he insisted, should not allow cities to proliferate, for their growth would bring with them all the disasters associated with Europe. Jefferson recognized only the virtues of independent farmers: "Cultivators of the earth are the most valuable of citizens. They are the most vigorous, the most independent, the most virtuous, and they are tied to their country and wedded to its liberty and interests by the most lasting bands."[41]

Franklin emphasized what he regarded as the farmers' moral strengths—their modesty and unpretentiousness, their simple and unassuming ways. In 1787, referring to the growing prosperity of the merchants, traders, and bankers and their increasing desire to lead a life of ease and to consume foreign goods, he sought to comfort himself and those who shared his views by believing that this process would not produce consequences that would be pernicious for the young Republic, for the "large proportion of frugal and industrious farmers inhabiting the interior regions of the American states will act as a firm barrier in the path of the noxious and corrosive influence of the opulence of the maritime cities of the United States."[42]

The existence in the United States of a vast reserve of unoccupied western territories, territories that had been received from the states and that the Continental Congress in 1783 had declared government property, made Jefferson confident that for many decades in the future the country would not experience a problem of agrarian overpopulation; it would fortunately be able to escape the "pernicious" alternative of developing along mercantile-industrial lines. As long as it was still possible to employ people in agriculture, he wrote to John Jay in 1785, it would be undesirable to turn American citizens "into mariners, artisans, or any thing else."[43]

Of course, even in 1785 there existed sailors, merchants, and industrialists in the United States, and Jefferson was far from suggesting that they should engage in agricultural labor. On the contrary, he urged the government to show concern for

41. *Papers of Jefferson,* ed. Boyd et al., vol. 8, 426; vol. 10, 262; vol. 12, 442.
42. Franklin, *Selected Writings,* 582.
43. *Papers of Jefferson,* ed. Boyd et al., vol. 8, 426.

individuals in these occupations as well, demanding, for example, that the United States should insist on equality with other countries in maritime rights. He did not disapprove of seafaring as a profession in the way he did the class of "people engaged in industry," a class that Jefferson believed was the "panders of vice and the instruments by which the liberties of a country are generally overturned." But neither was he enthusiastic at the prospect of growth in U.S. overseas trade, for it promised to lead to rivalry and military conflict with the major European powers. In October 1785 Jefferson expressed his wish that the United States renounce seafaring and involvement in foreign markets. Jefferson also wrote that as long as the population of the United States was engaged in agricultural labor, it should import industrial goods from Europe rather than manufacture them locally. As Jefferson put it, the United States should "keep our workmen in Europe," supplying them with all the necessary raw materials.[44]

During the last ten years of his life Franklin was convinced that the United States was destined to follow the agrarian path for at least another century. He did not believe it possible that a class of workers and craftsmen would emerge in the country, for "cheap land encourages people to leave their trade and begin to farm." Nor did he think that large manufactories would be successful in the United States, as the country lacked a sufficiently large pool of poor people prepared to work for a pittance. Any attempt to establish manufactories under these circumstances would be akin to believing that "one can force nature." As evidence of his prognosis Franklin pointed to cases where attempts to create "large manufactories for the production of linen and woollen goods" in the United States had failed.

On the whole, Franklin was not opposed to the emigration to the United States of European craftsmen, for his country was one where "farmers and even craftsmen" enjoyed respect. But he defined the scope of work for craftsmen in the New World narrowly: they were to "provide the farmers with houses, large furnishings and household utensils, i.e., that which it is not worthwhile to bring from Europe." Franklin liked the fact that the country had a well-developed home and cottage industry that enabled the farmers to clothe and shoe themselves without having to rely on urban manufactories and imported goods. He was pleased that 99 percent of the population was engaged in farming. As for the merchants and shopkeepers who formed a minuscule proportion of the nation, Franklin believed that their number was "much larger than is warranted" by the conditions of the United States.[45]

Jefferson and Franklin did not share the ideas of Robert Morris and Alexander Hamilton about the need to defend national industry through protectionist measures. In a letter to John Adams of November 1785, Jefferson argued that the trade relations between the United States and other countries should be based on the principle of complete freedom. Only England should be denied access to America's markets as punishment for the evil she had caused. Franklin thought that protectionism was absurd because it defended industry that was not viable in the United States anyway

44. Ibid., 633.
45. Franklin, *Selected Writings*, 580–82, 586–90.

and because it would only anger the farmers, who were the only reliable base of support for the government of the Republic. Besides, he believed that protectionist tariffs would not make the craftsmen happier or more prosperous, for higher wages would only make them "drink more and work less."[46]

In addition, Franklin based his arguments in favor of free trade on the theory of economic liberalism. This theory, which was an advanced one for its time, proclaimed free competition to be the only regulator of market relations. Nevertheless, it is difficult to agree with P. W. Conner, who states that Franklin's ideas of economic liberalism were the chief motive for his defense of free trade.[47] Franklin's rejection of protectionism in the United States rested mainly on his conviction that the agrarian path of development would be more advantageous for American capitalism.

Jefferson's and Franklin's agrarianism was highly contradictory. On the one hand, their efforts to defend the democratic, farmer-based course of agricultural development was progressive in character. The social reasoning behind their agrarianism expressed concern for the material needs of ordinary people. On the other hand, their readiness to sacrifice the commercial and industrial interests of the United States on the altar of agriculture did not correspond to the demands posed by the development of an economically viable capitalist system in America. Several years later Jefferson was forced to recognize this. During his presidency (1801–1809) he began encouraging the commercial and industrial development of the United States, which he continued to support after completing his term in office.

During the War of Independence, Paine still shared Jefferson's and Franklin's agrarian dreams.[48] Only in 1786–1787 did he begin defending the commercial-industrial development of American capitalism. During those years Paine fully and vividly expressed his economic views in the treatise "Dissertations on Government, the Affairs of the Bank, and Paper Money," as well as in several "Letters on the Bank." In these letters Paine defended the North American Bank, which had been founded in 1781 by Robert Morris, and spoke out against further issues of paper money. Paine thus stood in opposition to the farmers of Pennsylvania, who hoped that the unlimited printing of paper money and its consequent devaluation would lead to a rise in the price of agrarian products and would make it easier for the farmers to pay their debts.

Paine's position on this question has led several U.S. historians to say that he belonged to Hamilton's camp and to separate him from other democratic figures.[49] This erroneous conclusion was based on the notion, first developed by the Progressive historians Charles Beard and V. L. Parrington, that all democratic thinkers in the era of the American Revolution proposed an agrarian path of development and that all the conservatives reflected the interests of industrial capitalism. In fact, the example of Paine indicates the complex and contradictory way in which democratic thought in the United States developed during this period.

46. *Papers of Jefferson,* ed. Boyd et al., vol. 9, 42; Franklin, *Selected Writings,* 589.
47. Conner, *Poor Richard's Politics,* 74.
48. *Writings of Paine,* ed. Foner, vol. 2, 1142.
49. See Philip Foner's critical commentary in *Writings of Paine,* ed. Foner, vol. 2, 367.

Paine argued that the unlimited printing of paper money hurt all strata of the urban population, from industrialists and financiers to craftsmen and factory hands. For all of them inflation meant that the price of agricultural products and raw materials would grow in proportion to the decrease in the amount of gold and silver backing the bank notes.[50] For the craftsmen and artisans, inflation entailed a sharp rise in the cost of living.

Paine also aimed to show that banks played a useful role in the economic development of the United States. In 1786–1787 he argued that the establishment of the Bank of North America in 1781 contributed significantly to the economic power of the thirteen states waging the struggle against England. Paine showed that banks were able to collect unused monetary assets owned by various strata of the population and to use this hitherto "dead" capital to encourage economic development. He stressed that not only trade and industry but also commercial agriculture were interested in obtaining bank credits.[51]

Paine's arguments in support of the national bank and the use of government incentives for the development of trade and manufactories were similar to Alexander Hamilton's, but there were also major differences in the economic views of these two figures. Paine's economic proposals reflected his obvious and strong concern for the interests of the urban lower classes, which was not true of Hamilton's program. True, Paine would occasionally treat craftsmen, factory workers, and the industrial bourgeoisie as a single whole, emphasizing their supposed community of interests. Views such as these were due to the undeveloped character of capitalist relations and antagonisms in the United States in that period, and to the fact that the determining class characteristics of the bourgeoisie and the workers had not yet become defined.[52] Such views reflected only the objective aspect of the primary stage of capitalist development during which, according to Marx, "the proletariat and those strata of the urban population outside the bourgeoisie either did not yet have any interests separate from those of the bourgeoisie, or did not yet amount to classes, or segments of classes, in their own right."[53]

However, early bourgeois societies were also characterized by another set of objective features—"the general opposition between the exploiters and the exploited, the rich parasites and the toiling poor."[54] Although during the Revolutionary era the formation of antagonistic classes in the bourgeois society of the United States was only beginning, the country was already witnessing social differentiation and social conflicts. Such conflicts were typical not only of the relations among the free and slave populations in the country but also among white Americans. Severe property distinctions between the poor and needy on the one hand and the rich on the other

50. Ibid., 427.
51. Ibid., 386, 394, 397–98, 426–27.
52. Marx observed that until the second half of the nineteenth century the classes in the United States "had not yet acquired their final characteristics" (Marx and Engels, *Writings,* vol. 8, 127).
53. Marx and Engels, *Writings,* vol. 6, 114.
54. Ibid., vol. 19, 190.

existed within the white population. There the two groups were engaged in a constant bitter struggle.

These circumstances were reflected in the views of the ideologues of the conservative wing of the Revolution, namely, in their ideas of factions and the factional struggle. At the Constitutional Convention of 1787 Alexander Hamilton prophetically predicted a further widening of the antagonistic gulf between the factions of poor and rich Americans.[55] Contrary to these kinds of predictions, however, it seems strange that the democratic writers of the American Enlightenment tended to deny the existence of major conflicts within the white population. They saw relations among white Americans as being harmonious, and thus foreshadowed the picture of the "conflict-free" development of the United States in the Revolutionary period painted by modern conservative historians.

Thomas Jefferson did not deny that there were differences between the interests of the country's agrarian and industrial sectors. Yet he declared that conflicts between the rich and the poor and sharp property divisions were more typical of European societies than of the United States. Franklin also wrote that American society had a certain class homogeneity without acute social animosities. It is worth noting that these two thinkers underestimated the scale of Shays's Rebellion and in their analysis of social relations in the United States failed to attach any particular importance to it.

Franklin agreed that "in some states there are parties and disagreements," but then he went on to argue that people differed only over the means for achieving the common goal of "social prosperity"; the partisan conflicts only reflected the struggle of opinions that inevitably occurred in all societies enjoying "the great fortune of political liberty." Franklin was referring to disagreements among the upper classes and closed his eyes to the conflicts between them and the lower classes. Jefferson sought to explain the causes of sociopolitical conflicts in psychological terms, emphasizing the differences in temperament, physique, and morality among individuals. He did not attempt to justify the division of American societies into parties: "If I could not go to heaven but with a party, I would not go there at all."[56]

The reasons for the Enlightenment writers' idyllic depiction of social relations in the United States were many and various. To a certain extent, their depiction manifested their narrow class-based view of society. But, strange as it may seem, their concept of social harmony was also based on a conviction that was clearly democratic. This concept became the cornerstone of the ideas that were so dear to them—popular sovereignty and weak government power. If the white population of the United States had no major differences, all its segments, these writers argued, should therefore enjoy an absolutely equal, identical, and common right to representation within the government. But the doctrine of factions and factional struggle developed by the conservative ideologues and based on a division of the white population into a minority of rich people and a majority of poor people demanded that these two groups should have separate representation in government and that two social contracts—one for

---

55. *Papers of Hamilton,* ed. Syrett, vol. 4, 218, 219.
56. Franklin, *Selected Writings,* 582; Koch, *Philosophy of Jefferson,* 122, 123.

the propertied upper classes, and one for all other citizens—should be established in the United States.

The antidemocratic content of this demand is clear. The concept of factions and the factional struggle was used to favor the creation of a powerful bourgeois-planter government that would be able to keep in check the passions of the poor and needy. Yet the writers of the Enlightenment, who like all democrats assumed that there were no sharp social antagonisms in the United States, considered a dramatic strengthening of the power of the government unnecessary.

SOCIAL CONTRACT AND THE RIGHT TO REVOLUTION

In the period of the war for the independence and formation of the United States the question of government authority was at the center of the social struggle. The writers of the American Enlightenment posed and answered this question on two levels: 1) a theoretical interpretation of the nature, origins, purpose, and ways of changing government authority, and 2) specific projects for its establishment in the United States.

Among these thinkers Paine offered the most profound and exhaustive analysis of the origins of government authority. He was the author of the idea, rich in implications, that the formation of the state is preceded by the formation of society. He argued against those philosophers of the seventeenth and eighteenth centuries who, following Hobbes, had insisted that mankind had left the state of nature only after the creation of the state. Of course, Paine's concept of the nature of society was still naive. He sought to use a psychological approach to explain how society had originated. According to Paine, societies were formed because of the "social attraction" that was innate in every individual. Nature herself "created man for social life," Paine declared in Part Two of the *Rights of Man*.[57]

For Paine, the concepts of "society" and "state" had different moral contents. Society, whose main element, according to Paine, was labor and economic connections among people, "is good, whatever its condition." Only society enabled man to survive in his struggle with nature. Government, on the other hand, amounted to a kind of measure of man's sinfulness. The formation of a government recognized the fact that people were unable to govern themselves according to conscience and were therefore obliged to transfer authority to a political institution specially created for the purpose.[58] Paine's attempt to explain the way the authority of the state was established was idealistic. He believed that of the three ways in which new states were formed— the usurpation of power by a handful of individuals taking advantage of the people's superstition and ignorance, the conquest of one people by another, or a contract concluded by all members of society[59]—only the last was lawful. This belief sounded a progressive note in the era of the bourgeois revolutions of the eighteenth century, which aimed at replacing absolutism with a representative form of government.

---

57. *Writings of Paine,* ed. Foner, vol. 1, 357.
58. Paine, *Selected Writings,* 21, 22.
59. Ibid., 206.

The writers of the American Enlightenment were of course not original in con-cluding that the contractual method of creating state authority was the only just one. The concept of the social contract was central to all schools of bourgeois ideology in the seventeenth and eighteenth centuries. During the war for the independence and formation of the United States this concept was regarded as axiomatic by all Revolutionary forces—that is, by both the democratic and the moderate-conservative wings. The bourgeois ideologues of the United States were preoccupied not with abstract theorizing about the social contract but with trying to decide what its concrete form and sociopolitical content should be.

In fact, in the political vocabulary of the American writers of the Enlightenment the term "social contract" was replaced by the term "constitution," which was seen as its concrete juridical expression. Paine offered the most precise and full definition of the term "constitution." In his treatise *Common Sense* (1776), he criticized the British constitution. By the time of the war for independence and the formation of the United States, he was already reaching the conclusion that Britain lacked a constitution altogether. According to Paine, it was the American Revolution that contributed to the development of constitutional law.

In *The Rights of Man,* Paine concluded that in its form a constitution should differ from the various English charters, acts of Parliament, and court decisions:

> It is a body of elements to which you can refer, and quote article by article; and which contains the principles on which the government shall be established, the manner in which it shall be organized, the powers it shall have, the mode of elections, the duration of parliaments, or by what other name such bodies may be called; the powers which the executive part of the government shall have; and, in fine, every thing that relates to the complete organization of a civil government, and the principles on which it shall act, and by which it shall be bound.[60]

Although the English charters and bills had been based on parliamentary or judicial authority, that, said Paine, could not be the case with constitutional laws. In keeping with the spirit and letter of the theory of the social contract, he recognized the popular will as the only possible source for a constitution. As for the government, Paine argued, it is "merely the child of the constitution" and can neither amend nor abolish it. Jefferson fully shared these views. In his 1776 and 1783 drafts of the Virginia constitution he categorically proclaimed the supremacy and autonomy of constitutional law in relation to legislation. Jefferson believed that the Virginia legislative assembly should have nothing to do with adopting or amending the state constitution.[61]

In the initial stages of the Revolution, Jefferson, like other democratically minded figures, thought the state constitutions should be based on the direct expression of the voters' will. This idea was inspired by the history of the republics of the ancient Greeks—the city-states, whose free citizens would meet in the city assembly to make

---

60. Ibid., 208.
61. *Writings of Paine,* ed. Foner, vol. 1, 376; *Papers of Jefferson,* ed. Boyd et al., vol. 1, 364; vol. 6, 298, 304.

important decisions. Later, however, the proponents of democracy concluded that because the North American states were so much larger and more populous than the Greek city-states, basing the adoption or amendment of a constitution on the direct expression of the will of the free citizens would not be practicable. The task of adopting the fundamental law of the country was entrusted to special constitutional conventions. Jefferson's 1783 draft of the Virginia constitution, unlike his 1776 draft, stipulated that the constitution was to be ratified by a special convention rather than through the expression of the voters' will. The existing Virginia constitution did not satisfy this great democrat because it had only been approved by the state legislature.

Jefferson and Paine were particularly concerned about the relationship of direct democracy to representative democracy in the political system of the United States. Paine warned the Americans against uncritically accepting the views of Montesquieu, who was inclined to equate a republican system with direct popular rule. Paine argued that Montesquieu had developed his theory on the basis of the Greek city-states and that he had been unable to conceive of a republican system of government for states with a large territory. If one were to base one's opinions on the teachings of the French Enlightenment, one would have to conclude that the United States could only exist as a monarchy, at best a constitutional monarchy. Paine could not accept this conclusion. He wrote that a republican system of government could become firmly established in the United States, but only on the basis of representative democracy.[62]

Unlike Paine, Jefferson believed that the political system of the United States should be based on the organic fusion of direct popular rule and representative democracy. His views on this matter became established after the Revolution and acquired their final shape in some of his letters of 1816. Jefferson thought that at the state and federal level only a representative form of government was possible. However, he believed that in villages, districts, and towns, decisions on matters of public concern should be entrusted to meetings of free citizens.[63]

On the question of who should have the right to vote and to conclude the social contract, the American Enlightenment writers subscribed to the most democratic of the interpretations that had been developed by the bourgeois ideologists of the seventeenth and eighteenth centuries. Although almost all the leaders of the Revolutionary camp were strongly in favor of introducing a property qualification for the suffrage, Jefferson, Franklin, and Paine wished to see the franchise extended to the entire free male population of the country.

In his 1776 draft of the Virginia constitution Jefferson formally recognized a property qualification. Under his proposal the right to vote would have been extended to men owning a plot of land of not less than twenty-five acres in rural areas, or one-quarter of an acre in cities. But as his draft provided for granting every indigent person a fifty-acre allotment of land, the principle of universal suffrage for free males in practice remained. Writing to Edmund Pendleton in August 1776, Jefferson went

62. *Writings of Paine,* ed. Foner, vol. 1, 368–70, 372, 376–77.
63. *The American Enlighteners,* vol. 2, 115, 119, 143.

further and spoke against the formal introduction of a property qualification. In his 1783 draft of the Virginia constitution he again linked the right to vote to ownership of a small amount of immovable property. Yet in the *Notes on the State of Virginia,* which provided a more accurate expression of his views, since they were not meant to be submitted to the Virginia legislators for discussion, he stated that the number of voters should not be smaller than the list of members of the militia or state taxpayers. In later years he continued to support the principle of universal male suffrage. For instance, in 1816 he advocated its introduction in Virginia.[64]

Paine offered an ingenious defense of the democratic definition of the right to vote contained in the Pennsylvania constitution of 1776. This is how he parried the arguments of the moderately conservative among the leaders of the Revolution: "Property alone cannot protect the country from an enemy invasion. Houses and land cannot fight; and sheep and oxen cannot to be taught the musket."[65]

It would be no exaggeration to say that the representatives of the American Enlightenment venerated the idea of popular sovereignty. Their attitude to the people and their will was diametrically opposite to that of the moderately conservative leaders of the Revolution. If Hamilton held the cynical view that "the people is a gigantic beast" and another conservative leader, John Adams, called for all power in the country to be transferred to an enlightened political elite, Jefferson never wavered in his belief that, as he stressed in a letter to Washington in 1785, the republican freedoms in the United States could only be preserved if they were "in the hands of the people themselves." This democratic thinker was always ready to sacrifice his opinion to the will of the people: although in 1787 Jefferson criticized the draft of the federal Constitution, he declared that if the democratically elected state conventions would ratify it, he would support their decision.[66]

Jefferson did not deny that the masses could be wrong, that they were capable of being swayed by reactionaries and demagogues. But he thought that the errors of the people could be cured only by educating the masses rather than by limiting their freedoms. Jefferson's political writings are permeated by a belief that educating the masses would have beneficial political consequences. This belief received its fullest expression in Jefferson's letter to George Wythe of 1786, in which he wrote:

> Preach, my dear Sir, a crusade against ignorance; establish and improve the law for educating the common people. Let our countrymen know that the people alone can protect us against these evils, and that the tax which will be paid for this purpose is not more than the thousandth part of what will be paid to kings, priests and nobles, who will rise up among us if we leave the people in ignorance.[67]

Like Jefferson, Paine and Franklin defended the principle of the sovereign will of the people and believed that sovereignty exercised by the enlightened masses would

64. *Papers of Jefferson,* ed. Boyd et al., vol. 1, 344, 345, 352, 358, 489–90, 503–5; vol. 6, 296; *The American Enlighteners,* vol. 2, 51, 119.

65. *Writings of Paine,* ed. Foner, vol. 2, 288.

66. *Papers of Jefferson,* ed. Boyd et al., vol. 9, 151; vol. 10, 244; vol. 12, 442.

67. Ibid., vol. 10, 245.

be ideal. The humanist and progressive views of these American democrats contrasts sharply with the concept of enlightened monarchy expounded by representatives of the conservative wing of the European Enlightenment or with the doctrine of the political supremacy of the bourgeois-planter elite extolled by the conservative leaders of the American Revolution.

Among the progressive concepts developed by the American writers of the Enlightenment was the doctrine of the people's right to carry out a political revolution and overthrow the existing system of government when it began to usurp the natural and inalienable rights of man. This doctrine received its clearest expression in the Declaration of Independence. The author of the Declaration, Thomas Jefferson, rejected the very cautious formulations of John Locke, the originator of the doctrine of the right to revolution, in favor of clear statements about the right and duty of the people to overthrow a despotic government and "to provide new guards for their future security."[68]

Marxist historians have on many occasions offered a detailed analysis of the doctrine of the people's right to political revolution. However, the attitude of the American Enlightenment writers to that doctrine also deserves attention.

In the course of the war for the independence and formation of the United States, the way these thinkers interpreted the right to revolution underwent profound changes. With the republican system of government becoming firmly established in the country, they concluded that in the United States the right to revolution no longer existed and that it continued to exist only in countries where a representative system of government had not yet been introduced. This point of view was given its final theoretical expression in Thomas Paine's 1786 treatise "Dissertations on Government, the Affairs of the Bank, and Paper Money." Paine's arguments were based on his identification of the republican system in general, and the American one in particular, with popular sovereignty. Paine wrote that the preservation of the right to revolt against a republican government based on popular sovereignty in effect means giving the masses the right to overthrow the sovereignty of the people.[69] This was a clear indication of Paine's limited class-based understanding of popular sovereignty; in effect, he was idealizing nominal bourgeois democracy. As the Revolution went on, Paine tended to idealize it more and more. This tendency received its fullest expression in his treatise *The Rights of Man,* where some passages sound like a paean to the young bourgeois Republic.[70]

Jefferson's retreat from the right of revolution first became evident in 1783. In his letter to Edmund Randolph he defended the thesis that the social contract could not be annulled completely and that only specific parts of it could be replaced, and then only upon careful consideration. Jefferson's arguments read like an attempt to compose a charter of immunity for the constitutions of the independent North American states. In 1787, while the federal Constitution was being drawn up, Jefferson declared that

68. Ibid., vol. 1, 430.
69. *Writings of Paine,* ed. Foner, vol. 2, 369.
70. Ibid., vol. 1, 360.

the United States was the only country in the world that had the opportunity to revise and renew its social contract by purely legal means, without recourse to armed force.[71]

Jefferson did not completely rule out the possibility of armed action by the popular masses in the United States. He was, for example, strongly influenced by the rebellion of Daniel Shays. Its impact revived the democratic elements in Jefferson's worldview, which by the end of the Revolution had apparently weakened. In 1786–1787 he developed the doctrine of the necessity of periodic popular uprisings. Contrary to the view of Dumas Malone, his best-known biographer, that Jefferson "never defended the actions of the insurgents in Massachusetts,"[72] Jefferson in some ten letters expressed his sympathy for the rebels and for those farmers who had found themselves in a difficult economic situation.

In analyzing Shays's Rebellion, he concluded that the ability of the people of the United States to defend their rights by force of arms was an indication of the democratic character of the political system rather than of its weakness; that in a conflict between the rulers and the people the people are always right, and their rebellions reveal and correct the abuses of the authorities; and that periodic uprisings are "pleasing to God and nature" and should take place every twenty years to rid the state of abuses.[73] The democratic nature of these ideas is indisputable. And yet they cannot be compared with the truly earth-shattering statement in the Declaration of Independence of the people's right to overthrow a bad government through revolutionary action and replace it with a new one. In Jefferson's view the periodic armed rebellions of the people in the United States should only aim to reveal and correct the mistakes of the government.

Jefferson and Paine did not believe that the constitutions adopted in the period of the war for the independence and formation of the United States would last for all time. On the contrary, for the rest of their days they remained faithful to the democratic idea of the right of each generation to conclude its own social contract. This right was formulated most fully in Paine's *Rights of Man.* "No generation has any right of property where another one is concerned," he wrote. The dead have no rights. Their rights and the contractual expression of these rights—the constitution—should disappear with them. Jefferson expressed similar views. Sometimes their language is almost the same, word for word: "The world belongs to the generation of the living"; "The Creator made the earth for the living, not the dead" (Jefferson); "One must always care for the living, and not the dead" (Paine). In an 1824 letter to Samuel Kercheval, Jefferson wrote that the state constitutions should be revised every nineteen years, in accordance with the frequency with which generations followed each other. Nevertheless, even in these statements Jefferson and Paine did not admit the possibility

71. *Papers of Jefferson,* ed. Boyd et al., vol. 6, 248; vol. 12, 113.

72. Dumas Malone, *Jefferson and His Time: Jefferson and the Rights of Man* (Boston, 1951), xvii, 157, 166.

73. *Papers of Jefferson,* ed. Boyd et al., vol. 10, 621, 629, 631, 633; vol. 11, 49, 92, 93, 174, 526, 527; vol. 12, 356.

that in the United States revolutionary methods could be employed in revising the social contract, changing the constitution, or replacing the government.[74]

The third American writer of the Enlightenment, Benjamin Franklin, did not devote as much attention to the right to revolution as Jefferson and Paine did. In his writings he did not deal at any great length with these issues. Franklin remained opposed in principle to violent political action. He reacted to Shays's Rebellion negatively, as may be seen from his letter to Jefferson of April 19, 1787, where he wrote, "The Insurgents in Massachusetts are quelled: and I believe a great Majority of that People approve the Measures of Government in reducing them."[75] Unfortunately, Franklin's attitude to Shays's Rebellion was in many ways identical to that of the moderate and conservative elements in American society. Yet unlike them, he did not for a moment concede that this action by the masses justified limiting political freedoms in the United States.

PLANS FOR THE REORGANIZATION OF POLITICAL POWER IN THE UNITED STATES

The writers of the Enlightenment played an active part in drawing up, promoting, and defending plans for organizing American governments along democratic lines. During the first stage of the Revolution, when there was a widespread belief within the patriotic camp that the United States would exist as a federation of thirteen sovereign political entities, these writers paid special attention to the state constitutions. When in 1776 Jefferson began work on the draft of the Virginia constitution, he wrote, "It is a word of the most interesting nature and such as every individual would wish to have his voice in. In truth it is the whole object of the present controversy; for should a bad government be instituted for us in future it had been as well to have accepted at first the bad one offered to us from beyond the water without the risk and expence of contest."[76]

In the first year of the war Franklin was elected president of the Pennsylvania convention, which developed the most advanced constitution of the Revolutionary period. The eminent scholar J. P. Selsam, a specialist on this constitution, believes that Franklin's role in formulating a number of its most important passages proved decisive. For a long time historians believed that Paine also took part in drawing up the Pennsylvania constitution. However, while preparing Paine's writings for publication, Philip Foner discovered certain facts that exclude this possibility.[77]

The arguments about the structure of government in the states initially concerned the organization of the three branches—the legislative, executive, and judiciary—and the relationship among them. The contestants in these debates argued over the concepts of separation of powers and "checks and balances," concepts that occupied

74. Paine, *Selected Writings,* 179–80; *The American Enlighteners,* vol. 2, 121–22, 144.

75. *Papers of Jefferson,* ed. Boyd et al., vol. 11, 301.

76. Ibid., vol. 1, 292.

77. J. Paul Selsam, *The Pennsylvania Constitution of 1776* (Philadelphia, 1936), 187; *Writings of Paine,* ed. Foner, vol. 2, 270.

a prominent place in seventeenth- and eighteenth-century bourgeois constitutional thought. But the democrats and moderates differed in their interpretation of these concepts.

The structure of the legislature, the most important branch of the government, was the subject of particularly sharp controversy. The moderates borrowed Montesquieu's idea of a "mixed" or two-chamber legislature, which guaranteed separate representation to the various groups in society. Montesquieu, like Locke, believed that it was advisable to separate the nobility and the bourgeoisie in the legislative body, which could be done by creating two chambers. However, in the United States, where there was no aristocracy, the conservatives hoped that the two chambers could be used to provide separate representation for the affluent and poor sections of the population.

Together with all the other democrats, the writers of the Enlightenment strongly objected to the moderates' plan. Assuming the absolute equality of political rights between the rich and the poor, Franklin and Paine spoke in favor of the joint representation of both and argued for the establishment of a single-chamber legislative authority. Such a unicameral legislature was actually created in Pennsylvania. At once the propertied upper classes in that state, who were afraid that under a democratic franchise they would be unable to dominate the legislature and thus carry out their political agenda, harshly attacked the new legislative body.

Franklin always remained faithful to the idea of a single-chamber legislature. In 1789 he spoke out against the plan devised by the Pennsylvania upper classes to create a senate modeled on those existing in all the other states, a senate that would represent their interests and exercise control over the lower chamber. "Why should the right of control, contrary to the spirit and principles of democracy, be given to the minority, rather than the majority?" wrote Franklin indignantly. It is true that at the Constitutional Convention of 1787 Franklin accepted the idea of a two-chamber national congress. But he believed that the function of the Senate should be only to provide equal representation to the smaller and larger states, and not to protect the upper classes. In his treatise *The Rights of Man*, Paine admitted the possibility of creating a two-chamber legislature, but stressed that the chambers could meet separately only when debating bills and should vote on them together.[78]

In his 1776 draft of the Virginia constitution Jefferson proposed the establishment of a two-chamber legislature. But the two chambers were to be elected by the same voters, and their members were to differ from each other only in age and in the length of their terms: the senators would serve for a year longer than the members of the lower house. In the opinion of the moderates, who argued for the election of senators from the propertied upper classes for life, this amounted to a concession to the "mob." Moreover, contrary to the moderates' desires, Jefferson did not want the lower house subordinate to the upper but the upper house to the lower. Under his plan, the senators

---

78. *Writings of Franklin,* ed. Smyth, vol. 10, 57–58; Conner, *Poor Richard's Politics,* 59; *Writings of Paine,* ed. Foner, vol. 1, 389, 390.

themselves would be elected by the lower chamber. Only the lower chamber could make appointments to official positions, including choosing the governor, and only it had the right to pass financial bills.[79]

The democrats approached the relationship among the branches of government with a desire to strengthen legislative authority at the expense of the executive. The moderates, however, wished to increase the power of the executive, which they assumed would be headed by a single individual. Among the American writers of the Enlightenment the author most concerned with the respective positions of the different branches of the government was Jefferson. Assuming that authorities would mutually limit themselves, he assigned in his constitutional projects of 1776 the task of choosing the executive to the legislature. Moreover, he did not endow the executive with what Locke and Montesquieu, the recognized authorities of bourgeois constitutional thought, regarded as the executive's imprescriptible right to restrict the power of the representative assembly through a legislative veto. Moreover, Jefferson entrusted the legislature with the task of appointing officials—the traditional prerogative of executive power. Finally, to minimize the influence of the governor, Jefferson rejected the formula of a "single and indivisible executive authority," proclaimed by Locke and Montesquieu and every moderate and conservative politician in the era of the American Revolution, and surrounded the governor with a council with wide powers. He provided for annual gubernatorial elections, which the conservatives and moderates regarded as excessively frequent, and refused to allow the reelection of any governor within five years after the end of his first term.[80]

These democratic ideas about the relationship between the legislative and the executive branches, of which Jefferson's drafts were a typical example, were implemented to one degree or another in most of the state constitutions, including that of Virginia. Annual gubernatorial elections were introduced throughout the country, and the governors were deprived of the powers to veto legislation and to make appointments.

In 1783 Jefferson substantially revised his ideas on the relationship between the two branches. The change in his views, however, was due not to conservative or moderate influence but to his own extremely unfortunate experience as governor of Virginia in 1780–1781. When the state was invaded by British troops, Jefferson discovered that he was not able to carry out effectively a single decision as governor: he was hobbled hand and foot by the prerogatives of the legislature.

In his 1783 draft of the Virginia constitution, Jefferson proposed extending the governor's term of office from one to five years to increase the independence of the executive. The governor and the council of revisors were together given the right of a limited legislative veto. The governor was to be the commander-in-chief of the state army and militia and was to be elected by the entire legislative assembly rather than by just the lower house. The governor's salary was fixed by a special article of the constitution and could not be changed by the legislature. Finally, under a state

---

79. *Papers of Jefferson,* ed. Boyd et al., vol. 1, 340–41, 343, 358–59, 489, 504.
80. Ibid, vol. 1, 340–61.

of emergency the governor could dissolve the legislature or move its sessions to another town.[81]

That Jefferson had retreated only to a limited extent from his constitutional principles of 1776 became apparent during the discussions of the federal Constitution of 1787. He was greatly dissatisfied by two of its features: its lack of a bill of rights and its establishment of what he considered an excessively strong office of the presidency based on the formula of a "single and indivisible executive authority." Jefferson demanded that the president's prerogatives should be limited by the collective will of an executive council and proposed that he be restricted to a single term. He argued that if a single individual under the Constitution could be endlessly reelected as president, the government would be turned into an elective monarchy.[82] (Jefferson's fears proved unfounded: George Washington, the president of the United States, refused to seek reelection to a third term, thereby creating an important constitutional precedent that prevented a single individual from holding the most important executive office in the country in perpetuity.)

Jefferson's critique of one aspect of the federal Constitution as undemocratic did not mean that he rejected its other aspect, namely, the dramatic strengthening of the central government at the expense of the rights of the states. Like Franklin, Paine, and many other democrats, Jefferson in the course of the Revolution had become a strong proponent of the centralization of government authority. Nevertheless, the democrats wanted the central government to be founded on the constitutional principles they espoused rather than on the constitutional ideas of the moderate and conservative politicians. This fact is worth emphasizing, since a number of Progressive American historians, led by Merrill Jensen, persist in defending the fundamentally unsound proposition that all democrats were convinced decentralizers supporting the principles enshrined in the Articles of Confederation and that the repeal of the Articles was not inevitable but was rather the result of a clever plot by right-wing forces.

The most determined and outspoken supporter of a strong centralized government in the United States was Paine. In a letter to George Washington written after the adoption of the Constitution of 1787, Paine protested against those who included him among the Antifederalists and expressed his indignation at the claim that Hamilton's party had initiated the revision of the Articles of Confederation. Paine's anger was justified. In December 1780, almost a year before Hamilton had done so, he had called on the state governments to summon a constitutional convention to amend the Articles of Confederation and establish a strong central authority. At the same time he had condemned the claims made by some of the states to a monopoly ownership of the uncolonized territories of the West and had demanded that these lands be declared the property of the Continental Congress. In December 1783 and January 1784 Paine harshly criticized the Rhode Island assembly for refusing to allow the Continental Congress the right to introduce a 5 percent import duty.

81. Ibid., vol. 6, 281, 295, 298–303.
82. Ibid., vol. 12, 350, 351, 356, 357, 425, 439–40, 441, 446, 563.

In August 1783, in one of the pamphlets that he published under the general title "The American Crisis," Paine outlined a program to strengthen the "national sovereignty" of the United States and to restrict the rights of the states. He suggested that the central government should be given the power to conduct foreign policy, establish economic relations with other countries, collect taxes, regulate money circulation, etc. Paine ecstatically praised the abolition in 1787–1788 of the "semi-constitution"—the Articles of Confederation. His critical statements about the federal Constitution of 1787 date to a much later period: in 1795 he criticized the fact that presidential executive authority had been given to a single individual and described the Senate's term of office as too long.[83]

Franklin first outlined his program for a union of the North American provinces in the draft of the Articles of Confederation that he had prepared at the request of the Continental Congress in July 1775. The key difference between Franklin's draft and the text ratified by the states in 1781 was that Franklin envisaged the creation of an executive council, chosen by the Congress and responsible for putting the decisions of the legislature into effect. While serving during the War of Independence as ambassador to France, Franklin urged a broadening of the authority of the Continental Congress, arguing that the states, which so jealously guarded their sovereignty, could never negotiate as equals with the centralized monarchies of Europe. At the sessions of the convention in Philadelphia in 1787 he was a determined proponent of a strong national government; he opposed the particularist tendencies in the smaller states. I have already discussed his critical remarks concerning the intentions of the conservative groups among the Federalists.[84]

Jefferson's attitude toward revising the Articles of Confederation was more complicated and contradictory than Franklin's and Paine's. After the War of Independence, when the chief factor holding the Confederation together—the common struggle against Britain—had lost its importance, he became very anxious about the fate of the North American union. In 1783 Jefferson began to support a proposal to create an executive committee of the Confederation, which would maintain contact among the states when the Congress was in recess. After Virginia agreed to give up its claim to the exclusive ownership of the western territories, Jefferson proposed that the western lands be declared the property of the Continental Congress; this would have strengthened the economic basis for centralizing government authority in the United States. And yet until the draft of the Constitution of 1787 was prepared, his idea for broadening the prerogatives of the central government remained vague. He confined himself to the thesis that the states "should act as a united nation in the international arena and preserve their independence in internal matters." Although he advocated amending and expanding certain sections of the

83. *Writings of Paine,* ed. Foner, vol. 1, 173, 174, 374, 379; vol. 2, 303, 327, 332, 334–66, 692.

84. *Writings of Franklin,* ed. Smyth, vol. 9, 551, 570, 574, 578; Farrand, ed., *Records of the Federal Convention* (New Haven, 1911), vol. 1, 47, 54, 61, 197–200; vol. 2, 208, 209, 615; Conner, *Poor Richard's Politics,* 131–34.

Articles of Confederation, Jefferson was not in favor of replacing them with a constitution.[85]

When in the autumn of 1787 Jefferson received the news in Paris that the draft of a federal constitution had been prepared, he accepted the abolition of the Articles of Confederation without too much regret. He accepted the proposed structure for the federal government; it was to comprise three branches—legislative, executive, and judicial. Jefferson also accepted the broadening of the prerogatives of the central government in both foreign and domestic policy. He objected, however, to the lack of a bill of rights and to the structure envisaged for the executive. His overall attitude to the Constitution is of some interest. Jefferson wanted the draft to be approved by nine of the states, which would ensure its ratification, and rejected by the rest, which would force its authors to make the necessary democratic changes in it.[86] Events developed in a way he had hoped they would. In the course of the process of ratification almost half the states agreed to approve the Constitution only if it were soon supplemented by a bill of rights. In 1791 the Bill of Rights was included in the Constitution.

An analysis of the sociopolitical views of the American writers of the Enlightenment shows them to be remarkably coherent and democratic in spirit, but also to contain many contradictions. The two sides of their views are in a dialectic unity with one another and cannot be discussed in isolation. They were the resulting reflection of the contradictions inherent in the historical development of the United States in the Revolutionary period. The limited class-based nature of the views of these three thinkers may be best seen in the absolute value they attached to formal political democracy and their idealization of the outcome of the American Revolution. But this was largely due to the limited scope for antibourgeois insights during the period of transition from feudalism to capitalism. The achievement of the American writers of the Enlightenment lay in the fact that at the dawn of American history they among all the ideologists of the Revolution set forth the most democratic aims for the socioeconomic and political development of the United States. Their philosophical heritage became an inexhaustible source of ideas for all subsequent democratic movements in the United States.

---

85. *Papers of Jefferson,* ed. Boyd et al., vol. 6, 248–49, 517, 519, 522, 587, 588; vol. 7, 478, 479; vol. 8, 229, 230; vol. 9, 264; vol. 10, 299, 603; vol. 11, 480, 481, 678, 679, 684; vol. 12, 28, 34.
86. Ibid., vol. 12, 350, 351, 356, 357, 425, 439, 440, 441–42, 446, 569, 571.

COMMENT BY PAULINE MAIER

For a historian deeply involved in contemporary American scholarship on the early American Republic, V. V. Sogrin's study of Thomas Jefferson, Benjamin Franklin, and Thomas Paine is literally from another world. Its topic has apparently awakened considerable interest among Soviet scholars, but the roster of previous writers listed in the first footnote—from M. P. Baskin to A. A. Kislova—are unknown to virtually all Americans working in the field. On the other hand, important American contributions to the subject seem equally unknown to Sogrin, who assumes (note 2) that historians in the United States can still be meaningfully categorized under the "Progressive" and "consensus" categories that prevailed thirty or forty years ago, and that even then did injustice to the complexity of many historians' arguments.[1]

The most recent Western secondary work cited seems to be Paul W. Conner's *Poor Richard's Politics: Benjamin Franklin and his New American Order* (New York, 1965). Although Sogrin published his article in 1979, he wrote on the ideology of three Revolutionary Americans without reference to Bernard Bailyn's *Ideological Origins of the American Revolution* (Cambridge, 1967) or the wealth of works on the sources of American thought that both preceded and followed its publication: on Paine without the benefit of Eric Foner's *Tom Paine and Revolutionary America* (New York, 1976); on Americans' conception of the right of revolution without reference to my work on the subject;[2] on constitutional development without Gordon S. Wood's *The Creation of the American Republic, 1776–1787* (Chapel Hill, 1969). He set out to consider "how the peculiarities of the North American social structure" affected his subjects' thought without reference to several important studies in social and labor history that appeared before 1979 and that help identify those peculiarities.

Such limitations were perhaps unavoidable given the difficulty Soviet scholars have faced in getting American publications as well as a language difference that will probably continue to a considerable extent to make Russian and American students of American history separate, self-contained communities. They do, however, affect the end product, even when a study, like Sogrin's, is founded on original sources.

Sogrin's venture to provide a "more comprehensive account" of the "original contribution to democratic thought" of Franklin, Jefferson, and Paine is admirable for its ambition and scope. The effort is one that only a peculiarly intrepid American scholar would undertake, confronted as we are by shelves of books relevant to the subject; and Sogrin's claim is made only within the confines of Soviet scholarship. Still, an individual's "original contribution" by definition can be identified only with reference to a more general evolution of ideas, a subject that has absorbed American

---

1. See, for example, the protest against such labels in Merrill Jensen (who was for many a quintessential "Progressive historian"), *The American Revolution within America* (New York, 1974), 221–24. "All too often," he said, "such labels are used as a substitute for careful reading, research, and intellectual endeavor" (224).

2. Particularly "Popular Uprisings and Civil Authority in Eighteenth-Century America," *William and Mary Quarterly*, 3d ser., vol. 27 (1970), 3–35, and *From Resistance to Revolution: Colonial Radicals and the Development of American Opposition to Britain, 1765–1776* (New York, 1972).

historians of the eighteenth century over the past generations. Their work suggests that "Enlightenment thought" is an extraordinarily inclusive term, encompassing virtually all intellectual contributions of the eighteenth century that emphasized secular over religious sources of truth with an emphasis on reason and scientific observation. Within the Enlightenment there were, however, different schools of thought. Over the previous decades American scholars have drawn careful distinctions between the contributions of eighteenth-century English Commonwealthmen and Scottish writers, "Country" and "Court" spokesmen, "civic humanists" and "liberals," all of whom bore the mark of the Enlightenment. Moreover, in *The Enlightenment in America* (New York, 1976), Henry F. May divided the American Enlightenment into "Moderate," "Skeptical," "Revolutionary," and "Didactic" phases distinguished both by content and chronological development.

This longstanding project in intellectual taxonomy might well have reached (or, more likely, passed) the point of diminishing returns. It has, however, left Western scholars aware of the rich heritage upon which Revolutionary America drew. It has made them resist such statements as Paine was "author of the idea . . . that the formation of the state is preceded by the formation of society," especially since that notion was fully developed by John Locke long before Paine wrote; or such statements as Locke invented the right of revolution. Nor, incidentally, did Thomas Jefferson move beyond what Sogrin characterizes as Locke's "very cautious formulations" of that right: Jefferson—and other Americans as well—drew their conception of the right of revolution from Locke and a series of other English and Scottish writers of the seventeenth and eighteenth centuries, some of whom were even more cautious than Locke. Jefferson acknowledged restrictions on the just exercise of the right of revolution in the Declaration of Independence (governments should not be changed "for light and transient causes," but only "when a long train of abuses and usurpations . . . evinces a design" to reduce the people "under absolute despotism"). These restrictions help explain the opposition to popular insurgency after Independence that Sogrin discusses. In short, the people's right was not denied, only the legitimacy of its exercise under post-1776 circumstances.

The originality of an idea must be measured, moreover, against the contributions of contemporaries as well as predecessors. In a period so fertile in constitutional innovations as that in the United States immediately after Independence, it is extraordinarily dangerous to read individual thinkers apart from the debates of their time and then give them full credit for new concepts. It cannot, for example, be justly asserted that "among the American writers of the Enlightenment"—a category that includes virtually all who contributed to the debates on American government in the 1770s and 1780s—Jefferson was "most concerned with the respective positions of the different branches of the government." The issue absorbed John Adams, James Madison, indeed, everyone concerned with institutional design. The same difficulty dogs Sogrin's discussion of the relationship between popular sovereignty and constitutions. There, it seems, the truly original contributions did not come from conspicuous public figures like Franklin, Jefferson, and Paine—and the study of such "great white men" (which makes good sense where sources are limited, and always rewards the effort) is considered an "elitist" enterprise by many historians in the contemporary United States, where attention has turned toward more humble revolutionaries. Ordinary people in local New England town meetings, and, above all, the thoroughly obscure "Berkshire Constitutionalists" of western Massachusetts, insisted that constitutions were creations of the sovereign people and should be drafted by their representatives in special conventions, then ratified by popular vote. That understanding, realized with and fully articulated in the Massachusetts Constitution of 1780, shaped all subsequent American constitutional development and had a powerful impact in France as well.[3]

When Sogrin asserts that there were essential differences among Franklin, Jefferson, and Paine in their views of the future social and economic development of the United States, he is supported by contemporary American scholarship. The obvious division would seem to pit Franklin and Paine, both former artisans with natural followings among urban mechanics, against the insistent agrarianism of Jefferson. Jefferson was ready to "let our work-shops remain in Europe" and was convinced that those who labored in the earth were "the chosen people of God, if ever he had a chosen people," and that the American Republic would be safe so long as its people were predominantly independent and virtuous farmers. Even as Jefferson composed those often-quoted lines from his *Notes on the State of Virginia* (1785), Paine was arriving at a very different view of farmers in the Pennsylvania backcountry—as men of limited views, concerned with nothing but their immediate affairs, who had no real commitment to the good of the state.[4]

But Franklin—as both Sogrin and Drew McCoy in his book *The Elusive Republic* (1980) affirm—was as intellectually committed to agrarianism as Jefferson. Aware of the new "science of society" developed by eighteenth-century French and Scottish writers, who taught that cultures moved over time from "rude" simplicity to a "civilized" complexity that brought with it a demoralizing inequality and both moral and political decay, Franklin hoped the United States could delay the inevitable. Americans had already passed through the classic progression from hunting through pasturage to agriculture, but if they held off becoming a commercial society—the final state of development—they might also avoid, for a time at least, its poisonous effects. Like Jefferson, Franklin found hope in the vast reserves of land in the West, which would allow the United States to remain for generations a nation of farmers. Not that the country would disdain manufacturing altogether: home manufactures were fine, and also artisanal activities that served, as Sogrin notes, the agricultural population.

3. Gordon S. Wood, *The Creation of the American Republic* (Chapel Hill, 1969), 282–91; Oscar and Mary Handlin, *The Popular Sources of Political Authority: Documents on the Massachusetts Constitution of 1780* (Cambridge, 1966); R. R. Palmer, *The Age of the Democratic Revolution: A Political History of Europe and America, 1760–1800*, vol. 1, *The Challenge* (Princeton, 1959).

4. Thomas Jefferson, Query XIX, *Notes on the State of Virginia* (8th American ed., Boston, 1801), 244–45; Eric Foner, *Tom Paine and Revolutionary America* (New York, 1976), 202.

But Franklin no less than Jefferson wanted to leave the great manufactories of Europe with their impoverished laboring poor in the Old World.[5]

Sogrin does not attempt to understand the political economy of his subjects within the historical model of eighteenth-century Scottish and French writers described by McCoy, but rather judges them according to Marx's model. Jefferson, Franklin, and Paine, he says, shared a limited "bourgeois" perspective apparent in their unwillingness to interfere with property rights and in their denial of conflict—and their persistent vision of American society as conflict-free, which predicted the "consensus" view of "conservative modern historians." They remained blind, he suggests, to what Marx described as "the general opposition between the exploiters and the exploited" of early bourgeois societies, to the conflict between "rich parasites and the toiling poor."

Such conflict existed most egregiously, of course, between white Americans and their black slaves. But 1776 did not "for a time put an end" to the criticisms of slavery: it gave new life to antislavery, as the convictions of Franklin and Paine suggest. The Revolution finally ended the slave trade—which did not, incidentally, go against the interest of the great planters, since the growing demand for slaves in newly opened sections of the South would increase the market value of their slaves once the external supply was cut off. Independence also inaugurated a great age of emancipation that essentially ended slavery in the North, where the incidence of blacks in the population was lower than in the South and slave labor less economically critical.[6] That development made slavery a distinctively Southern institution and increased substantially the number of free blacks whose place in American society became an issue of profound divisiveness. With regard to African-Americans, then, the Revolution fostered at once freedom and also a racism that thereafter persistently sought "scientific" proof of black inferiority because it legitimized "natural" while rejecting "artificial" distinctions among men.[7] Jefferson's "racist" statements in his *Notes on the State of Virginia* are notable not only because they powerfully compromise his image as a champion of equality but also because he openly confronted the issue of racial differences. The tentativeness of his conclusions, moreover, contrasts dramatically with the racist certitude of Southern spokesmen a half-century later.

The conflict that concerns Sogrin was, however, between adult white men—the rich and poor, the alleged exploiters and exploited. Franklin's "Information to those who would remove to America" (1782) seems to him to describe an "Arcadia," a dreamland that did not exist. But note that Franklin wrote explicitly to disparage "wild imaginations" about America. His descriptions of America were more often relative than absolute ("there are in that Country few People so miserable as the Poor of Europe" and "very few that in Europe would be called rich"): he said America was—not that he wished it would become—the "land of labor" where most people cultivated

5. Drew R. McCoy, *The Elusive Republic: Political Economy in Jeffersonian America* (Chapel Hill, 1980), chaps. 1–2.

6. Bernard Bailyn, *Ideological Origins of the American Revolution* (Cambridge, 1967), 232–46; Arthur Zilversmith, *The First Emancipation: The Abolition of Slavery in the North* (Chicago, 1967).

7. Duncan J. MacLeod, *Slavery, Race, and the American Revolution* (London and New York, 1974).

their own lands or practiced a trade and where there were "very few rich enough to live idly upon their Rents or Incomes." Essential elements of his description were repeatedly affirmed by others at the time, including Thomas Jefferson in the famous Query XIX of his *Notes on the State of Virginia,* and they have been reconfirmed by modern scholarship: the free population of British colonial America included an "extraordinarily large number of families of independent middling status, which was proportionately substantially more numerous than in any other contemporary Western society."[8]

That is not to say there was no poverty or wealth in eighteenth-century America or that the disparity between them awoke no conflict or concern. The existence of landless poor and tenants has attracted considerable attention among colonial historians, and economic distress during the commercial depression of the mid-1780s attracted the attention even of Franklin, who tried to make the best of it, and of others, who feared the United States was already falling into the economic patterns of Europe. Overt conflicts of the 1780s were not, however, part of "a constant bitter struggle" between "the rich" and the "poor and needy." The "democratic" debtors who called for paper money in the 1780s, Gordon S. Wood has argued, were proponents of enterprise, expansion, and consumerism; their protests were not the moans of paupers but "the calls of American business." Even supporters of Shays's Rebellion included men of rank and substance within their communities. They fought in part to protect their property and ability to acquire property and were in that sense themselves "bourgeois."[9]

Attitudes toward the genuinely indigent also eloquently testified to the predominance of the middle class and its values. Even in democratic Pennsylvania, only the "industrious poor," who could not work for reasons beyond their control such as illness or age, were considered worthy recipients of charity. More often the impoverished were ranked with the "idle poor," people unwilling to work in a land that respected

8. Franklin's description is in *Writings of Franklin,* ed. Smyth, vol. 8, 603–14, especially 604, 607. For affirmations by his contemporaries, see, for example, Aedanus Burke as "Cassius," *Considerations on the Society or Order of Cincinnati* (Philadelphia, 1783), 5; Charles Pinckney speech of June 25, 1787, in Farrand, ed., *Records of the Federal Convention* (New Haven, 1911), vol. 1, 398, and—for a far more exaggerated statement than that of Franklin—Hector St. Jean de Crevecoeur, *Letters from an American Farmer and Sketches of Eighteenth-Century America* (New York, 1963), especially 61–64. For the views of modern scholars, see Jack P. Greene, *Pursuits of Happiness: The Social Development of Early Modern British Colonies and the Formation of American Culture* (Chapel Hill, 1988), 188, and also, for the seventeenth-century roots of the American quest for independence and freehold land, Stephen Innes, "Introduction: Fulfilling John Smith's Vision: Work and Labor in Early America," in Innes, ed., *Work and Labor in Early America* (Chapel Hill and London, 1988), especially 3–16.

9. The social history literature is cited and evaluated in Greene, *Pursuits of Happiness,* whose conclusions again are not unlike Franklin's: see especially pages 187–88; Franklin, "The Internal State of America," in *Writings of Franklin,* ed. Smyth, vol. 10, 116–22, and McCoy, *Elusive Republic,* 105–6, 115–19. Gordon S. Wood's argument is in Wood, "Interests and Disinterestedness in the Making of the Constitution" in Richard Beeman et. al., *Beyond Confederation: Origins of the Constitution and American National Identity* (Chapel Hill and London, 1987), 69–109, especially 77–91.

and rewarded honest labor, and consigned to often harsh programs designed above all to teach them habits of industriousness.[10] The same obsession with work governed attitudes toward wealth, which evoked suspicion because it allowed the growth of luxury and, with it, of idleness. But to impose a more equal distribution of property by an agrarian law would make all property insecure and, again, undermine the acquisitive impulse that sustained people's willingness to work in the "land of labor." Wealth was, however, gradually denied any claim to political privilege. The federal Constitution of 1787 included no property qualifications for office like those in the first state constitutions of 1776–1780. Rank and office in the Republic were supposed to recognize personal merit, which was not necessarily signaled by wealth. Indeed, as Franklin put it in the Philadelphia convention, "some of the greatest rogues he was ever acquainted with, were the richest rogues."[11]

It is nonetheless true that both contemporary Antifederalists and many modern historians have seen the Constitution as an "aristocratic" document that so structured government that power would rest in the hands of "gentlemen" identified, as Wood put it, by their education, wealth, and leisure.[12] On that there has been no consensus among scholars, most of whom would agree, however, that America's "gentlemen"— many of whom had themselves risen from humble origins—were far more respectful of the aspirations and rights of the people than were their counterparts in contemporary England. There the espousal of radical Paineite doctrines by workingmen led to brutal repression in the 1790s, which, as E. P. Thompson demonstrated, was fundamental to the development of the English working class. The English case became paradigmatic of industrial society for Marx, but American history took a different course. Not only was there no repression of similar severity but the provocative social program in the second part of *The Rights of Man* was considered irrelevant to the United States even by Paine. In America, moreover, Paine's political ideas were commonplace and, in fact, had been largely implemented.[13]

Curiously, the agrarians Franklin and Jefferson have been far more revered in the commercial, industrial United States than Paine, who was at ease with economic

10. See, for example, John K. Alexander, *Render Them Submissive: Responses to Poverty in Philadelphia, 1760–1800* (Amherst, 1980). Alexander concludes that class division was important to the Revolution—although he found virtually no dissenters from the attitudes described here.

11. In Farrand, ed., *Records of the Federal Convention,* vol. 2, 249. Further efforts to dissolve the advantages of wealth include schemes for the broad dissemination of knowledge so the children of rich and poor alike could prepare to take advantage of America's opportunities, and also partible inheritances, dramatized with the abolition of primogeniture and entail, by which estates were divided among all immediate descendents. The legal reforms undertaken after Independence failed to make partible inheritances mandatory except in cases of intestacy. Nonetheless, on into the nineteenth century, knowledgeable people continued to cite the "American law of distributions" as an effective alternative to an agrarian law and a means of preventing the perpetuation of fortunes over time that did not violate the right of property or undercut incentives to work.

12. Wood, *Creation of the American Republic,* and, more recently, "Interests and Disinterestedness," especially pages 81–93.

13. E. P. Thompson, *The Making of the English Working Class* (New York, 1966), and Foner, *Tom Paine and Revolutionary America,* especially 232–33, 261–63.

diversity. The aggressive secularism of Paine's *Age of Reason* had an appeal in Europe, where established churches supported the social order, but alienated large numbers of Americans for whom revivalist Protestantism sustained the causes of democracy and reform. Still, it was less Jefferson's ill-fated proposal for land reform in the 1770s that inspired supporters of the Homestead Act than Paine's *Agrarian Justice* (1796); and, as Eric Foner noted, American labor spokesmen of the nineteenth century remained, in all but a few exceptional cases, within the parameters of Paineite republicanism. They too wanted a world where the poor were not oppressed and the rich had no privileges; they too sought to end poverty, not property.[14]

In fact, the Jeffersonian/Franklinian dream of an enduringly agrarian America was undercut by the demand of ordinary people for "comforts" and "luxuries" that they sometimes experienced for the first time in the 1780s. Jefferson confessed as much in a letter to Washington of March 15, 1784: "all the world is becoming commercial," he observed. The United States could not remain apart from it, especially since "our citizens have had too full a taste of the comforts furnished by the arts and manufactures to be debarred the use of them. We must then in our own defence endeavor to share as large a portion as we can of this modern source of wealth and power." It is difficult to read his statement in the early 1990s without recalling events in Europe over the past few years—especially the masses of East Germans thronging into the West as the Berlin wall came down, returning home with the material "comforts" that consumer-oriented capitalism has so richly provided. They rejected an enforced, austere economic equalitarianism not unlike that of ancient Sparta, which many Americans of the 1780s and 1790s too had explicitly renounced as a model for their future.[15] All this suggests that private property is today, as in the early American Republic, a democratic cause; perhaps also the challenge remains—in Eastern Europe as in the United States—of reconciling private ownership with opportunity, equity, and humanity.

In any case, there remains room enough for Russian contributions to early American history. The fruitful collegiality of contemporary American and European historians of Western Europe shows that barriers of space and language can be overcome. With regard to Russian and American historians of the United States, an information gap is more formidable. The past quarter century saw the publication of an extraordinary number of studies that extended and deepened knowledge of American history in the late eighteenth and early nineteenth centuries. As Russian scholars come to know that work—and we the best of their scholarship—a genuine dialogue can begin.

14. Foner, *Tom Paine and Revolutionary America,* 268, 264–66.
15. In *Papers of Jefferson,* ed. Boyd et al., vol. 7, 26; McCoy, *Elusive Republic,* 72–75, 96–100, 219–20 and passim.

RESPONSE BY V. V. SOGRIN

The first thought that occurred to me upon reading Pauline Maier's comments was, "What a pity that there's no shortage of paper in America!" Maier needed sixteen pages to say what could have been said on a single page. Many of Maier's remarks are of no relevance to the contents of my article. Thus, she expresses at length her views on the ideological processes in Revolutionary America. Several years after my article was published I devoted an entire book to this subject (V. V. Sogrin, *Ideological Currents in the American Revolution of the 18th Century* [Moscow, 1980]). In one of its chapters I discuss at length and in detail the books by Eric Foner, Gordon S. Wood, Bernard Bailyn, and Maier herself of which I was supposedly ignorant because of the existence in the Soviet Union of the so-called Iron Curtain. If Maier had the intellectual courage to learn Russian, she would be in a position to judge Soviet historians less arrogantly and more objectively. As for Maier's criticism that my article contains no references to the book by Bailyn and her own book (neither of which has anything to do with the article's subject), I was reminded of a well-known Russian saying: "No, you're not in danger of dying of modesty."

In her review Maier sounds like an inexperienced historian: while she expresses opinions on a great many subjects, she says little about the concrete goal that I set myself as a scholar when writing the article. My article appeared in 1978. Some of the ideas expressed in it now seem to me outdated. I would be happy to join Maier in her criticism of Marx's thesis about the class limitations of the writers of the Enlightenment, but with this proviso: the thesis in question does not prove that Marx was as limited a thinker as Maier imagines. In particular, he was no less knowledgeable about the principles of historicism than my American colleague.

Finally, I should like to say this. I found Maier's remarks useful in one respect at least. They made me feel grateful that I, together with many other Soviet scholars, no longer have to review the work of my colleagues in the kind of ideologically charged terms with which Maier's comments are replete. I can only wish that Maier will rid herself as soon as possible of the ideological blinders of the Cold War. Then she will not only see that a dialogue between Soviet and American historians is possible but also realize that it started many years before she wrote her review of my article.

CHAPTER 5

Thomas Jefferson's Struggle for Democratic Reforms in Virginia, 1776–1779

by

V. N. Pleshkov

The American bourgeois revolution of the eighteenth century, which led to the creation of a new country—the United States of America—was a major event in modern history. This was "a bourgeois revolution in which the democratic element was very strong."[1] The development of American democratic traditions is inseparably linked with the name of one of the Founding Fathers of the United States, Thomas Jefferson.

Jefferson (1743–1826), a prominent American political figure and statesman, appeared on the political stage of the country at the time of America's War of Independence. During this period he grew from a provincial lawyer into one of the leaders and ideologues of democracy in the American Revolution. Jefferson was the author of the Declaration of Independence—a notable document in American history. Karl Marx described it as "the first declaration of the rights of man."[2]

Jefferson realized that the Declaration of Independence in itself would not lead to the creation of a democratic state. To achieve that goal, it was necessary to root out old customs and usages and to lay the foundation for the democratic development of the country. "I knew," he later wrote in his *Autobiography,* "that our legislation, under the regal government, had many very vicious points which urgently required reformation, and I thought I could be of more use in forwarding that work."[3] Jefferson considered the reform of American society so important and imperative that for its sake he was prepared unhesitatingly to sacrifice his own career interests. He resigned his position as a member of the Continental Congress and declined the flattering offer to travel to Paris with Benjamin Franklin and Silas Deane to take part in the negotiations for the conclusion of a treaty with France.[4]

---

1. William Z. Foster, *An Outline of American Political History* (Moscow, 1953), 177. This article by V. N. Pleshkov was first published in *American Studies Annual for 1975* (Moscow, 1975).
2. K.[arl] Marx and F.[riedrich] Engels, *Writings,* vol. 16, 17.
3. *The Autobiography of Thomas Jefferson,* ed. Dumas Malone (New York, 1959), 50.
4. John Hancock to Thomas Jefferson, September 30, 1776, Jefferson to Hancock, October 11, 1776, in *The Papers of Thomas Jefferson,* ed. Julian P. Boyd et al. (Princeton, 1950–), vol. 1, 523–24.

In September 1776 Jefferson returned from Philadelphia, where the Continental Congress was in session, to his native state of Virginia. It was there that he intended to put his program of democratic reforms into effect.

This aspect of Jefferson's activities has not been fully discussed in Soviet historical literature. An exception is the bill "For Establishing Religious Freedom," which was examined in one of the chapters of the well-known monograph by N. M. Goldberg, who also offered an analysis of Jefferson's views on religion.[5]

Almost nothing had changed in Virginia after the Declaration of Independence. Power in the state still belonged to the big planters who were unwilling to surrender their positions. Almost all pre-Revolutionary offices and institutions continued to function and the laws remained the same. Some planters retained the titles of English baronets. The vast estates and plantations that were passed on from father to son, generation after generation, were not subject to partition or alienation.

True, a republican constitution had been adopted and the famous Patrick Henry had been elected as the first governor of the Commonwealth of Virginia. But this constitution, though it was one of the most radical of the state constitutions, had nevertheless preserved the political power of the planter oligarchy and had left the entire social order almost unchanged. Jefferson was disappointed by this constitution and on several occasions criticized it (his *Notes on the State of Virginia,* the draft of a constitution for the Virginia commonwealth of 1783, the notes on the constitution of 1794, and other writings were devoted to such criticism). He said that it was the inability of the convention to reform Virginia society that had led him to try to achieve such reform by changing the laws. In this connection certain clauses in Jefferson's draft of a Virginia constitution presaged many of the democratic reforms he would propose from 1776 to 1779.[6] Governor Henry had no program of reform, nor even the intention of instituting change. With the exception of its name, the Commonwealth of Virginia remained royalist. It was difficult to build a democratic society on such a foundation, but Jefferson, as he later wrote, decided to try to eradicate every fiber of "ancient and future aristocracy" and to lay the basis "for a government truly republican."[7]

Jefferson's first step in September 1776 was to propose a reform of the state judicial system. The need for this was obvious because from the outset of the Revolution the majority of courts had ceased to function. The Virginia constitution of 1776, having stated the need to establish courts of different instances, granted the legislative assembly the right to constitute them and to define their authority, jurisdiction, procedures, etc. To carry out these tasks the legislature elected a committee, which was headed by Jefferson. The committee divided the bill relating to the organization of the state judicial system into five separate bills, in accordance with Jefferson's wishes.[8]

5. N. M. Goldberg, *Freethinking and Atheism in the U.S.A.: 18th-19th cc.* (Moscow-Leningrad, 1965), 55–91.

6. The Virginia Constitution of 1776, in *Papers of Jefferson,* ed. Boyd et al., vol. 1, 337–45, 347–54, 356–64.

7. *Autobiography of Jefferson,* ed. Malone, 62.

8. *Papers of Jefferson,* ed. Boyd et al., vol. 1, 343, 351–52, 361–62.

In the period from November 25 to December 4, 1776, Jefferson submitted to the committee the texts of all five bills. As early as December 16 a law creating an admiralty court was adopted.[9] Such alacrity and unanimity on the part of the legislators flowed from their realization that a coastal state like Virginia urgently needed a court with maritime jurisdiction.

The other bills created prolonged and bitter debate. Many planters opposed the reopening of the courts. As old debtors who owed money to British merchants, they feared that resuming legal procedures would force them to settle their debts.[10] Only in 1778, when the planters became able to pay their debts with paper money, did the state legislature pass, with major amendments and changes, three of the other bills drawn up by Jefferson.[11] The fifth bill, which pertained to the regulation of judicial procedure in the county courts, was rejected.[12] Those of Jefferson's bills that were adopted began the reorganization of the judicial system in Virginia and served as models for a number of other states.

In October 1776 Jefferson submitted an important draft of a bill to revise the procedure for inheriting property without the right of alienation, that is, a bill abolishing entail.[13] The draft law abolishing the right of primogeniture, which Jefferson later put forward, was closely linked to this bill abolishing entail.[14] Although these bills were introduced and passed at different times, Jefferson justifiably regarded them as forming a single whole.

Entail, primogeniture, fixed rents, and other feudal institutions that England implanted in her American colonies were not prevalent everywhere. As early as the second half of the eighteenth century a number of colonies adopted laws abolishing feudal land relations. In Virginia, however, entail was established by law, and in the opinion of J. Franklin Jameson it was observed even more strictly than in England.[15] Nevertheless, by the beginning of the eighteenth century, planters in Virginia were able to free their estates from entail. Many petitions with such requests were sent to the Virginia legislature.[16] But the Privy Council in England had to approve each act of the local legislature. After 1767 the fee for releasing an estate from entail amounted to twenty pounds plus two pounds for every one hundred pounds of the estate's value under five hundred pounds, and if above that, then an additional pound for each one hundred pounds.[17]

The right of primogeniture was exercised in colonial Virginia only when the owner of the land died intestate, an event that among the wealthy did not often happen.

9. Ibid., 645–49.

10. Dumas Malone, *Jefferson and His Time: Jefferson the Virginian* (Boston, 1948), 250, 259–60.

11. *Papers of Jefferson,* ed. Boyd et al., vol. 1, 607–9, 610–19, 621–41.

12. Ibid., 650–52.

13. Ibid., 560–61.

14. Ibid., vol. 2, 391–93.

15. J. Franklin Jameson, *The American Revolution Considered as a Social Movement* (Boston, 1956), 37.

16. Malone, *Jefferson the Virginian,* 253; Richard Hofstadter, *The American Political Tradition and the Men Who Made It* (New York, 1964), 21.

17. Richard B. Morris, *The American Revolution Reconsidered* (New York, 1967), 90.

Virginians usually endowed all their children, including daughters, with land.[18] Also the practice of allotting a portion of the inheritance to the children upon their attaining their majority, or upon their marriage, limited the law on primogeniture in intestacy. In other cases property was transferred to the children by a deed of property that acquired legal force upon the death of the parents.[19] In 1731 William Gooch, the governor of Virginia, noted that the division of land among all children, including even entailed land, was a common occurrence in the colony.[20]

Thus in Virginia, as in the majority of other colonies, entail and primogeniture, though established in law, were not observed in practice. Nevertheless, Jefferson favored the complete abolition of entail and primogeniture. Even in their limited forms, as was the case in the American colonies, they represented feudal institutions incompatible with democracy and with the Jeffersonian ideal of a republic of free small landholders.

Jefferson's proposals, which were aimed at liquidating the remnants of feudalism in Virginia, were critically discussed in the state legislature. His most formidable opponent during the debate was Edmund Pendleton, the speaker of the lower house. Realizing that Jefferson's proposals enjoyed the support of the majority of delegates, Pendleton resorted to the usual parliamentary tactic—tabling amendments. Jefferson later recalled that during the debate on the bill to abolish entail Pendleton introduced an amendment that gave a landowner the right to decide whether to devise his land in fee simple or in fee tail.[21]

Dumas Malone, the most competent of Jefferson's modern biographers, describes in great detail the process that led to the drafting of the new bill. He shows that Jefferson initially had put forward a more moderate proposal, similar to the one that dozens of years later he ascribed to Pendleton. But realizing there was no serious opposition, Jefferson emended the proposal so as to abolish entail in toto.[22] Malone's arguments appear quite persuasive. Jefferson, in the metaphor used by another biographer, Saul K. Padover, was "adept at widening the cracks he had already made."[23]

Pendleton also stubbornly resisted the bill to abolish primogeniture. He proposed a compromise based on the ancient Judaic principle of allotting the eldest son a double share of the inheritance, as was the practice in Massachusetts and Pennsylvania. Jefferson argued against this proposal, declaring that "if the eldest son could eat twice as much, or do double work, it might be a natural evidence of his right to

18. See, for example, Malone, *Jefferson the Virginian,* 31–32, Appendix 2, 435–39.

19. For more on entail and primogeniture in Virginia, see C. Ray Keim, "Primogeniture and Entail in Colonial Virginia," *William and Mary Quarterly,* 3d ser., vol. 25 (1968); Richard B. Morris, *Studies in the History of American Law, with Special Reference to the Seventeenth and Eighteenth Centuries* (New York, 1930), 73–82.

20. Robert E. Brown and Katherine B. Brown, *Virginia, 1705–1786: Democracy or Aristocracy?* (East Lansing, Mich., 1964), 83.

21. *Autobiography of Jefferson,* ed. Malone, 51.

22. Malone, *Jefferson the Virginian,* 254.

23. Saul K. Padover, *Jefferson* (New York, 1942), 281.

a double portion; but being on a par in his powers and wants, with his brothers and sisters, he should be on a par also in the partition of the patrimony."[24] Jefferson's point of view prevailed. In the autumn of 1785 the bill for the abolition of primogeniture became law.

Jefferson's land reforms, which aimed at turning an aristocratic society into a democratic one, considerably affected economic life in Virginia. And not only in Virginia. They became part and parcel of a movement that spread to other states and led to the abolition of entail and primogeniture in almost all the states within ten years after the signing of the Declaration of Independence.[25]

To carry out his other reforms, Jefferson decided to revise the entire code of existing laws. He introduced a motion to that effect.[26] The motion was approved, and a committee of five "revisors" was elected to implement it. The committee was composed of Jefferson himself as chairman; his old friend and mentor George Wythe;[27] George Mason, the author of Virginia's republican constitution; and Pendleton and Thomas L. Lee. Even at this stage Jefferson had won a rather important victory, for Mason and Wythe were his supporters.

In January 1777 the revisors met in Fredericksburg to discuss their plan of action. Pendleton, supported by Lee, unexpectedly proposed repealing the entire existing code of laws and creating a completely new one, which would have as its model the Justinian Code and the writings of Bracton and Blackstone.[28] Jefferson's proposal preserved the general system of laws, with necessary modifications and simplifications. Creating a completely new code of laws based on untested principles and unfamiliar concepts would have been too time-consuming. Moreover, the interpretation of those laws would have been entrusted to judges who tended to be conservative. Mason and Wythe supported Jefferson's opposition. Pendleton's proposal was rejected.

Mason and Lee refused to take part in revising the code of laws, citing their lack of legal education.[29] The work had to be divided among the three other members. Jefferson was entrusted with revising the common law and statutes dating to before the foundation of Virginia in 1607, Wythe with British law from 1607 until 1776, and Pendleton with the laws of colonial Virginia.[30]

The revisors spent more than two years working on the code of laws. The huge amount of work done by Jefferson, in the opinion of James Madison, "exacted perhaps the most severe of his public labours."[31] Besides writing new laws aimed

---

24. *Autobiography of Jefferson,* ed. Malone, 57.

25. Allan Nevins, *American States during and after the Revolution, 1775–1789* (New York, 1924), 441–45.

26. *Papers of Jefferson,* ed. Boyd et al., vol. 1, 562–63.

27. Wythe considered the task of reviewing the Virginia laws so important that to participate in it he relinquished his position as a deputy in the Continental Congress. George Wythe to Thomas Jefferson, November 18, 1776, in *Papers of Jefferson,* ed. Boyd et al., vol. 1, 603–4.

28. *Autobiography of Jefferson,* ed. Malone, 56.

29. Ibid. Besides, soon thereafter Lee died.

30. Ibid., 57.

31. James Madison to S. H. Smith, November 4, 1826, quoted in *Papers of Jefferson,* ed. Boyd et al., vol. 2, 313.

at democratizing Virginia society, Jefferson significantly simplified the language of the old laws. "I thought it would be useful," he recalled in his *Autobiography,* "to reform the style of the later British statutes, and of our own acts of Assembly; which, from their verbosity, their endless tautologies, their involutions of case within case, parenthesis within parenthesis, . . . are rendered more perplexed and incomprehensible, not only to common readers, but to the lawyers themselves."[32]

In the spring of 1779 Jefferson and Wythe met in Williamsburg and critically compared their work, "weighing and correcting phrase after phrase." When they reached the part of the project completed by Pendleton, they discovered that their colleague, instead of simplifying the complex Virginia laws, had reproduced the language of the laws verbatim, omitting parts he disagreed with. Thus Jefferson and Wythe were obliged to review and correct the laws of colonial Virginia themselves.[33]

The result of this colossal labor was "The Report of the Committee of Revisors"— an example of technical perfection and perspicuous brevity, as Madison called it. Indeed, Jefferson and his colleagues were able to reduce the entire code (including British statutes since Magna Carta, as well as the laws of colonial Virginia) to 126 bills, which were submitted to the General Assembly for consideration.[34]

Many years later Jefferson noted that the assembly beset the entire code with "endless quibbles, chicaneries, perversions, vexations, and delays."[35] On the one hand, it approved as early as 1779 a number of important bills on local government organization, recruitment into the army and the police, relations with the central authority, etc.[36] On the other hand, it initially postponed the debate on the entire "Report of the Committee of Revisors" until the cessation of military operations, and then never debated the report. In 1784 at the insistence of Madison the report was published.[37] It became a "mine of Legislative wealth," from which the Virginia General Assembly would occasionally pluck a nugget of law.[38] Madison, who at the time occupied a leading position in the legislature, led the campaign to extract these "nuggets." By the end of the 1790s, thanks to his efforts, almost half of the 126 bills had become law.[39]

Of all the legislative proposals he introduced, Jefferson attached particular importance to four, namely, those abolishing entail, abolishing primogeniture, establishing

32. *Autobiography of Jefferson,* ed. Malone, 57–58.
33. Jefferson to S. Jones, July 28, 1809, in *The Writings of Thomas Jefferson,* ed. A. A. Lipscomb and A. E. Bergh, 20 vols. (Washington, D.C., 1903–1904), vol. 12, 300. Jefferson was in error when he referred to Pendleton's participation in this meeting (in *Autobiography of Jefferson,* ed. Malone, 58). See for example Edmund Pendleton to Jefferson, May 11, 1779, in *Papers of Jefferson,* ed. Boyd et al., vol. 2, 266–67.
34. *Papers of Jefferson,* ed. Boyd et al., vol. 2, 336–657.
35. *Autobiography of Jefferson,* ed. Malone, 58.
36. *Papers of Jefferson,* ed. Boyd et al., vol. 2, 364–65, 366–67, 367–69, 378–80.
37. Ibid., 310–12, 321.
38. Madison to S. H. Smith, November 4, 1826, quoted in ibid., 313.
39. Adrienne Koch, *Jefferson and Madison: The Great Collaboration* (New York, 1964), 26.

religious freedom, and providing for a universal system of education. These bills were based on the philosophy of bourgeois democracy and were aimed at creating what Jefferson in his writings usually described as a republican society. While the abolition of entail prevented the "accumulation and perpetuation of wealth in select families," the abolition of primogeniture removed "feudal and unnatural distinctions which made one member of every family rich, and all the rest poor." The establishment of religious liberty "relieved the people from taxation for the support of a religion not theirs." The universal education bill made the people "qualified to understand their rights, to maintain them, and to exercise with intelligence their parts in self-government."[40]

The bills abrogating entail and primogeniture were successfully put into effect, since they confirmed the abolition of outdated institutions. However, Jefferson was forced to fight much harder for religious freedom and universal education.

Religious life in the colonies presented a fairly mixed picture, owing to the large number of churches and sects. Congregationalists and Presbyterians predominated in New England, the Baptists prevailed in Rhode Island, and in Maryland there were many Catholics. In Virginia and the two Carolinas the established church was Anglican. In New York almost all religious groups existed.[41]

The numerous sects were hostile to each other, while the established Church of England, being distinguished by a special fanaticism, often subjected the sectarians to every kind of persecution. For example, the first Virginia code of laws—the Dale Code—imposed severe punishments and fines on sect members, as well as on Anglicans who violated canon law.[42]

As the established church, the Anglican Church in Virginia embodied the colonies' ecclesiastical dependence on England. The church, whose presence permeated the entire structure of the colony, had great influence; it exercised control over education, and church parishes played a major political role. The parish vestries, which determined the way of life in each area, were headed by the ruling planters, who often turned these positions into hereditary ones.[43] These same planters were also judges and sat as deputies in the colony's legislature. The political oligarchy that held sway in the colony, the Soviet scholar N. M. Goldberg concludes, directed the activities of the church as well.[44]

In addition, the Anglican Church acted as an instrument of economic oppression. The entire population of Virginia, irrespective of denomination, had to pay church tithes in grain or tobacco to the Anglican clergy. When the price of these products fell, the clergy demanded compensatory payment. The conduct of the priests, which often failed to conform to the norms of conventional morality, could not but provoke the

40. *Autobiography of Jefferson,* ed. Malone, 62–63.
41. Louis B. Wright, *The Cultural Life of the American Colonies* (New York, 1962), 72–97.
42. Claude G. Bowers, *The Young Jefferson, 1743–1789* (Boston, 1945), 193–94.
43. It was no accident that one of the first acts of Bacon's Rebellion was to abolish this rule and make provisions for the regular reelection of vestrymen.
44. Goldberg, *Freethinking and Atheism,* 64.

resentment of the population. The Anglican clergy were not respected by the masses of the people.[45]

By the mid-eighteenth century the Anglican Church in the American colonies had reached a crisis. As N. M. Goldberg stresses, neither its organization nor its actions corresponded any longer to the new prevailing circumstances.[46] The outbreak of the Revolution gave added impetus to the movement to disestablish the Anglican Church and create religious freedom. Jefferson adopted the most progressive position in Virginia on these issues.

Jefferson developed an early interest in religious issues. He had been greatly impressed by a speech Patrick Henry made in 1763 against the church tithe. "Instead of feeding the hungry and clothing the naked," declared Henry, "these religious harpies would, were their powers equal to their will, snatch from the hearth of their honest parishioner his last hoe cake, from the widow and her orphan children their last milch cow, the last bed, nay the last blanket, from the lying-in woman."[47] This stirring speech—one of the first attacks in America on the established church—contributed to the development of Jefferson's views.

Jefferson's journals, published by Gilbert Chinard, shed light on the formation of his worldview. They contain numerous extracts from the writings of ancient authors on questions of religion. Side by side with them we find synopses of the works of the English deists, Bolingbroke and Shaftesbury, and of the treatises of Locke, Milton, Hume, and Montesquieu.

In February 1814 Jefferson sent an extract from his journal to the English materialist philosopher Thomas Cooper. He told Cooper he had written the piece as a student of law, when he "was bold in the pursuit of knowledge, never fearing to follow truth and reason to whatever results they led, and bearding every authority which stood in their way."[48]

In addition to acquainting himself with the works of the English deists, Jefferson studied the literature of the law to prove the illegality of the union of church and state. He concluded that Christianity was not an institution in Anglo-Saxon common law and had been incorporated into it only with the adoption of the Magna Carta, that is, when the "lex non scripta" lapsed and the "lex scripta" began.[49] On this basis, Jefferson concluded that making the Anglican Church the state church in England, as well as introducing Anglicanism into the American colonies as the state religion, was an illegal act that contravened natural law. But according to Chinard,[50] it was not only by studying juridical literature that Jefferson arrived at the idea of the separation of

45. Bowers, *Young Jefferson,* 197; see also James Parton, *The Life of Thomas Jefferson* (New York, 1971; repr. from 1874 ed.), 55–57.

46. Goldberg, *Freethinking and Atheism,* 64.

47. Quoted in Gilbert Chinard, *Thomas Jefferson: The Apostle of Americanism* (Ann Arbor, 1957), 15.

48. Jefferson to Thomas Cooper, February 10, 1814, in *The Complete Jefferson,* ed. Saul K. Padover (New York, 1943), 931.

49. Ibid., 931–37.

50. Chinard, *Apostle of Americanism,* 365.

church and state. As Herbert Aptheker correctly points out, Jefferson's protest against the established religion was also grounded in the "general notion of the freedom of thought, speech and association."[51]

Jefferson considered religion to be the purely private affair of each individual. In his "Notes on Religion," which he compiled in the autumn of 1776, he wrote, "No man has *power* to let another to prescribe his faith. Faith is not faith without believing. No man can conform his faith to the dictates of another."[52] He believed that religion, particularly if made an instrument of state power, represented a danger to a free society. "In any country and at any time," wrote Jefferson, "the priest was the enemy of freedom. He was always in alliance with the despot, encouraging his depredations for the sake of defending the interests of the clergy."[53]

Long before the Revolution, members of the Virginia legislature repeatedly raised the religious question. The sectarians, who protested against persecution by the Anglican Church, flooded the legislature with petitions.[54] A special committee on religious affairs, one of whose members was Jefferson, considered these petitions. The bill "for allowing a free Toleration to His Majesty's Protestant Subjects in this Colony, who dissent from the Church of England" was not accepted.[55] The draft of "Declaration of the Causes and Necessity for Taking Up Arms," submitted by Jefferson to the Continental Congress in June 1775, also failed to gain passage. In this document Jefferson, having recalled in particular that the first colonists had arrived in America in search of civil and religious freedom, called for tolerance and the rejection of domination by any religious sect.[56]

In his drafts of the Virginia constitution, Jefferson stated that "all persons shall have full & free liberty of religious opinion, nor shall any be compelled to frequent or maintain any religious service or institution."[57] As we know, Jefferson's proposed constitution was not adopted.

In 1776 the Virginia convention approved the constitution composed by George Mason. Mason was also the author of the Virginia Declaration of Rights, which had been adopted some time earlier. The last section of this declaration proclaimed the freedom of religion.[58] But there was a great difference between declaring freedom of religious belief and separating church from state.

The Virginia Declaration of Rights aroused a new torrent of petitions from sectarians who demanded the adoption of appropriate laws.[59] These petitions from the

51. Herbert Aptheker, *The American Revolution of 1763–1783* (Moscow, 1962), 302.

52. *Papers of Jefferson,* ed. Boyd et al., vol. 1, 545.

53. Quoted in Adrienne Koch, *The Philosophy of Thomas Jefferson* (Gloucester, Mass., 1957), 136.

54. The texts of some of the petitions are quoted in Charles F. James, *Documentary History of the Struggle for Religious Liberty in Virginia* (New York, 1971; repr. from 1900 ed.), 31–34, 38–47.

55. *Papers of Jefferson,* ed. Boyd et al., vol. 1, 525–26.

56. Ibid., 193–98, 199–203.

57. Ibid., 344, 353, 363.

58. Henry Steele Commager, ed., *Documents of American History,* 2 vols. (New York, 1948), vol. 1, 104.

59. Jameson, *American Revolution Reconsidered,* 68–78.

dissenters, wrote Jefferson in his *Autobiography*, "brought on the severest contests in which I have ever been engaged."[60] Undoubtedly the petitions affected Jefferson, and he used them in the struggle against the church. He introduced several motions in the legislature that called for separation of church and state, for repeal of laws restricting freedom of religion, and also for abolition of both the privileges of Anglican priests and the taxes collected for their church.[61]

Jefferson's proposals created a stir in Virginia. Public opinion in the state became divided. Numerous pamphlets, petitions, and newspaper articles advancing the arguments of one side and attacking the other appeared. Heated debates took place in the streets, in private houses, and in the taverns.[62] A stubborn struggle took place in the assembly. Pendleton and Robert Carter Nicholas, who were supported by the majority of legislators, led the anti-Jefferson opposition. The struggle ended in a compromise: Pendleton and Nicholas were able to preserve the connection between church and state while giving way on the question of religious liberty. "We prevailed so far only, as to repeal the laws which rendered criminal the maintenance of any religious opinions, the forbearance of repairing to church, or the exercise of any mode of worship [other than Anglican];" wrote Jefferson, "and further, to exempt dissenters from contributions to the support of the established church."[63]

But Jefferson did not rest on his accomplishments. An important section of the "Report of the Committee of Revisors" included a bill providing for the establishment of religious freedom.[64] A significant part of this rather brief document was devoted to a philosophical preamble based on the ideas of natural law. In the preamble Jefferson began with the statement that God had created man free and that all endeavors to influence man's conscience "by temporal punishments, or burthens, or by civil incapacitations, tend only to beget habits of hypocrisy and meanness." Jefferson denounced the "impious presumption" of legislators and rulers, who had "assumed dominion over the faith of others, setting up their own opinions and modes of thinking as the only true and infallible" ones. He protested against the established church, which forced a man to "furnish contributions of money for the propagation of opinions which he disbelieves *and abhors.*" Therein, according to Jefferson, lay true sin and tyranny. "Our civil rights," declared Jefferson, "have no dependence on our religious opinions, any more than our opinions in physics or geometry." That is why "the opinions of men are not the object of civil government, nor under its jurisdiction."[65]

The bill's preamble ended with the words that "truth is great and will prevail if left to herself, that she is the proper and sufficient antagonist to error, and has nothing to fear from conflict unless by human interposition disarmed of her natural weapons, free argument and debate; errors ceasing to be dangerous when it is permitted

---

60. *Autobiography of Jefferson,* ed. Malone, 53.
61. *Papers of Jefferson,* ed. Boyd et al., vol. 1, 530–33.
62. Bowers, *Young Jefferson,* 205; Malone, *Jefferson the Virginian,* 274.
63. *Autobiography of Jefferson,* ed. Malone, 53.
64. *Papers of Jefferson,* ed. Boyd et al., vol. 2, 545–47. A Russian translation of the bill is included in N. M. Goldberg's two-volume book *The American Enlighteners* (Moscow, 1969), vol. 2, 47–49.
65. This last phrase was deleted from the text during the debate on the bill in the General Assembly.

freely to contradict them."[66] Following this statement of principle, the bill itself contained this declaration: "no man shall be compelled to frequent or support any religious worship, place, or ministry whatsoever, nor shall be enforced, restrained, molested, or burthened in his body or goods, nor shall otherwise suffer, on account of his religious opinions or belief; but that all men shall be free to profess, and by argument to maintain, their opinions in matters of religion, and that the same shall in no wise diminish, enlarge, or affect their civil capacities."[67] The bill concluded by emphasizing that "the rights hereby asserted are the natural rights of mankind, and that if any act shall be hereafter passed to repeal the present or to narrow its operation, such act will be an infringement of natural right."[68]

This bill establishing religious liberty made Jefferson widely known both in the New and Old Worlds. It not only proclaimed freedom of religion and demanded the severing of the link between church and state but also more broadly implied the importance of full intellectual freedom.

The bill was sharply criticized and widely attacked in the legislature and in the state. This stubborn resistance to the bill indicates that the Anglican Church had many more supporters than Jefferson had suspected.[69] Debate on the bill for the establishment of religious freedom, as well as discussion of most of the other bills contained in the "Report of the Revisors," was postponed.

Nevertheless, Jefferson and his supporters continued their struggle. Through their efforts, in the summer of 1779 a draft law was published as a broadside entitled "A Bill for Establishing Religious Freedom, Printed for the Consideration of the People."[70] Jefferson persisted in disseminating his views on religious freedom. In 1780 and 1781 he wrote, and a few years later anonymously published in Europe, his celebrated *Notes on the State of Virginia*. He devoted one of the chapters in this work to the history of religion in Virginia and the struggle for freedom of religious belief. The appendix to the *Notes* contained the text of the "Statute for the Establishment of Religious Liberty."[71]

---

66. *Papers of Jefferson,* ed. Boyd et al., vol. 2, 546.

67. Ibid.

68. Ibid., 546–47.

69. Jefferson wrote that "by the time of the revolution, a majority of the inhabitants had become dissenters from the established church." *Autobiography of Jefferson,* ed. Malone, 53.

70. *Papers of Jefferson,* ed. Boyd et al., vol. 2, 548. A facsimile of that poster is included in the book (between pp. 304–5). Since the manuscript of the bill has not been found, the text of the poster represents the earliest extant copy of the bill.

71. Thomas Jefferson, *Notes on the State of Virginia* (Philadelphia, 1794), 333–36. Here it should be noted that the text in the appendix differs both from the text of the bill and from the text of the statute as approved by the Virginia legislature. This version of the statute, which Jefferson composed for an unknown reason in 1786, was a variant of both these texts. Owing to the wide circulation of the *Notes on the State of Virginia,* this version became well known in the United States and Europe. It was included in the editions of *The Writings of Jefferson* compiled by Andrew Lipscomb and Albert E. Berg, as well as in the more recent edition brought out by Adrienne Koch and William Peden in *The Life and Writings of Thomas Jefferson* (New York, 1944). *Papers of Jefferson,* ed. Boyd et al., vol. 2, 309–10, 547–52.

In October 1785 James Madison introduced the bill on religion in the state legislature for a second time. The debate on the bill was stormy. The bill's philosophical preamble was especially attacked. Proposals were made to delete the preamble or substitute for it an excerpt from the Virginia Declaration of Rights of 1776.[72] Forced to make concessions, Madison removed a number of the more radical clauses. In January 1786 the bill finally became law.

The "Statute for the Establishment of Religious Liberty" had great significance not only for Virginia but also for the whole of America. Herbert Aptheker rightly describes it as "the pinnacle of the achievements of the revolutionary era in the field of church-state relations as seen from the perspective of civil rights."[73] The Anglican Church in the United States was forced to sever all links with the British church and declare itself an independent Protestant-Episcopalian church. The Dutch and German Reformed churches in the United States were obliged to follow suit. The Catholic Church in America was removed from the jurisdiction of the papal nuncio.[74]

The statute became internationally famous. It was translated into French and Italian and sent to a number of European governments. In France it was included in the *Encyclopédie Méthodique,*[75] and the majority of contemporary works devoted to the United States mentioned or cited it. Jefferson clearly understood the desirability of acquainting the European public with this document. In December 1786 he wrote to Madison from Paris: "It is honorable for us to have produced the first legislature who has had the courage to declare that the reason of man may be trusted with the formation of his own opinions." In the same letter Jefferson reported that the "act for religious freedom has been received with infinite approbation in Europe and propagated with enthusiasm."[76]

But however progressive, the "Statute for the Establishment of Religious Freedom" was still limited. The statute did not guarantee true freedom of conscience, that is, the right not to believe in God. It did not lead to a complete separation of church and state. That measure, as V. I. Lenin wrote, "was promised by bourgeois democracy, but nowhere in the world was it fully implemented."[77]

Passage of the statute did not end Jefferson's struggle for the right to free thought. In 1791 the Anti-Federalist party, of which he was one of the acknowledged leaders, was able to secure the adoption of the Bill of Rights—the first ten amendments to the U.S. Constitution.[78] The first of these proclaimed the freedom of religion, speech, press, and assembly.[79]

---

72. *Papers of Jefferson,* ed. Boyd et al., vol. 2, 548–49; Malone, *Jefferson the Virginian,* 278–79.

73. Aptheker, *American Revolution,* 304.

74. Ibid., 305.

75. *Encyclopédie Méthodique,* Section "Economie Politique et Diplomatique" (1786), vol. 4.

76. Jefferson to Madison, December 16, 1786, in *Papers of Jefferson,* ed. Boyd et al., vol. 10, 602–6.

77. V. I. Lenin, *Collected Works,* vol. 38, 118.

78. See L. N. Goncharov, "On the History of the Political Struggle for the Bill of Rights in the U.S. in 1789–1791," *University Scholarly Papers: The Historical Sciences* 3 (1958), 161–76.

79. Commager, ed., *Documents of American History,* vol. 1, 146.

Jefferson was a deist and as such had materialistic views on nature. And as Marx wrote, "Deism—at least for a materialist—is no more than a convenient and easy way of escaping religion."[80] True, unlike a number of figures of the French Enlightenment, Jefferson criticized not religion as such, but its bearers, and spoke from an anticlerical position.[81] Jefferson acknowledged God as the creator of the universe. He attached particular importance to the moral content of the Christian religion. He was a proponent of pure Christian morality, declaring in one of his letters to John Adams that his aim was to extract the "diamonds in a dunghill."[82] The moral codes he compiled were dedicated to the same end: "The Life and Morality of Jesus of Nazareth," "Syllabus of an Evaluation of the Merits of the Teaching of Christ," etc.[83] Jefferson's views in effect approached atheism. He wrote to his nephew Peter Carr: "Do not be frightened from this enquiry by any fear of its consequences. If it ends in a belief that there is no god, you will find incitements to virtue in the comfort and pleasantness you feel in its exercise."[84] Also Jefferson did much to propagate in America the antireligious and atheistic views of French writers of the Enlightenment, like A. S. Destutt de Tracy, P.S. Du Pont de Nemours, and C. F. Volney.[85] Jefferson's criticism of religion and his struggle for freedom of conscience and free thought had a considerable impact on the democratization of American society at the end of the eighteenth and the beginning of the nineteenth centuries.

Of enormous significance also was the struggle that Jefferson waged for many years to create a system of universal education. He considered the provision of popular education an integral part of the effort to construct a new society founded on the principles of democracy. Jefferson proceeded from the proposition that popular enlightenment was essential to the survival of democracy. Only enlightenment could preserve the state from tyranny, ensure wise and honest government, bring liberty and happiness to all members of society, and create an "aristocracy of talents and virtue," one which he considered the "most precious gift of nature."[86] Jefferson's endeavors to diffuse enlightenment thus flowed from his political principles; he regarded education as a social process. "It is an axiom in my mind," he wrote to George Washington, "that our liberty can never be safe but in the hands of the people themselves, and that too of the people with a certain degree of instruction."[87] Many of Jefferson's contemporaries shared this belief, but Thomas Paine expressed it with particular clarity in his treatise *The Rights of Man.* He wrote, "A nation under a well regulated government should

80. Marx and Engels, *Writings,* vol. 2, 144.

81. M. P. Baskin, *The Philosophy of the American Enlightenment* (Moscow, 1955), 10.

82. Jefferson to John Adams, October 13, 1813, in *The Adams-Jefferson Letters,* ed. Lester J. Cappon, 2 vols. (Chapel Hill, 1959), vol. 2, 384.

83. *The Jefferson Bible* (New York, 1964).

84. Jefferson to Peter Carr, August 10, 1787, in *Complete Jefferson,* ed. Padover, 1057–60.

85. See Goldberg, *Freethinking and Atheism,* 82–84.

86. Jefferson to John Adams, October 28, 1813, in *Adams-Jefferson Letters,* ed. Cappon, vol. 2, 388.

87. Jefferson to George Washington, January 4, 1786, in *Papers of Jefferson,* ed. Boyd et al., vol. 9, 151.

permit none to remain uninstructed. It is monarchical and aristocratical governments, only, that require ignorance for their support."[88]

By the time the Revolution began the American colonists had achieved considerable success in the field of education. But education was still private, expensive, and mainly religious in character. This state of affairs did not reflect the hopes and aspirations of American democrats and above all of Jefferson. Not surprisingly, then, the "Report of the Committee of Revisors" included bills providing plans for universal education. Jefferson regarded educational reforms as the most important of all the reforms drawn up by the committee.[89]

The "Bill for the More General Diffusion of Knowledge" contained a comprehensive description of Jefferson's system of education.[90] The bill began with a preamble of principles stating the necessity of education:

> Experience hath shewn, that . . . those entrusted with power have, in time, . . . perverted it into tyranny; . . . the most effectual means of preventing this would be, to illuminate, as far as practicable, the minds of the people at large. . . . People will be happiest whose laws are best, and are best administered, . . . whence it becomes expedient for promoting the public happiness that those persons, whom nature hath endowed with genius and virtue, should be rendered by liberal education worthy to receive, and able to guard the sacred deposit of the rights and liberties of their fellow citizens, and that they should be called to that charge without regard to wealth, birth or other accidental condition or circumstance; but the indigence of the greater number disabling them from so educating at their own expence, those of their children whom nature hath fitly formed and disposed to become useful instruments for the public, it is better that such be sought for and educated at the common expence of all, than that the happiness of all should be confided to the weak or wicked.[91]

This statement of the state's responsibility to educate the people was followed by a description of the system of education itself. Three stages were envisaged: primary school, secondary school, and university. According to Jefferson's plan, each county in the state was to be divided into districts ("hundreds") in which primary schools would be established. They were to be so situated that all children in a given district could attend them. The schools were to provide free instruction in reading, writing, and arithmetic to all white children of both sexes. Here Jefferson expressed his belief that "instead . . . of putting the Bible and Testament into the hands of the children, at an age when their judgments are not sufficiently matured for religious inquiries, their memories may be stored with the most useful facts from Grecian, Roman, European and American history."[92]

88. *The Complete Writings of Thomas Paine,* ed. Philip S. Foner, 2 vols. (New York, 1945), vol. 1, 428.

89. Jefferson to George Wythe, August 13, 1776, in *Papers of Jefferson,* ed. Boyd et al., vol. 10, 245.

90. Ibid., vol. 2, 526–35.

91. Ibid., 526–27.

92. Jefferson, *Notes,* 214.

The next stage was the six-year grammar school, where Latin and Greek, English Grammar, Mathematics, and Geography would be taught. These schools were private, but the bill provided for the instruction at government expense of a certain number of gifted pupils whose parents were unable to pay for their tuition. Upon completing their studies at the grammar schools, the ablest students would be sent to the College of William and Mary, which would provide free tuition and board to the able children of poor parents.

The bill for "Amending the Constitution of the College of William and Mary" provided for the reorganization of this educational institution. After giving a detailed description of the history of the college, Jefferson sharply criticized the institution in the first part of the bill. Founded in 1693 as a theological seminary, the College of William and Mary was closely linked to the Anglican Church and the colonial administration. As such, it conformed neither to the spirit of the age nor to Jefferson's notion of an institution of higher learning. Jefferson's proposals aimed at secularizing the college, changing its administration and establishing closer links between the college and the republican government of the state. Jefferson suggested abolishing the chair of Theology, as well as the school for Indians that was attached to the college. He believed that missionaries would be quite capable of teaching the Indians to read and write. The missionaries' most important task should be the study of the customs, laws, religious beliefs, and above all languages of the Indians. Jefferson also suggested considerably widening the range of subjects studied at the college by introducing Jurisprudence, Natural Sciences, Medicine, History, Modern Languages, and Fine Arts.[93] Jefferson supplemented his plan for a system of general education with a bill establishing a public library in Richmond, which would receive an annual grant of two thousand pounds for the purchase of books and maps.[94]

Despite certain faults, Jefferson's proposed system of general education formed the basis for the educational system that still exists in the United States today. And although Jefferson's proposals represented a moderate compromise between public and private education, in contemporary Virginia they seemed too radical, fantastic, and socially dangerous. Jefferson's intention to "rake the rubbish" and educate at government expense the gifted children of poor parents provoked particularly sharp objections. Discussion of Jefferson's educational schemes was postponed until the cessation of military operations. And when in 1785 Madison introduced these education bills in the state's General Assembly, they were rejected.[95]

93. *Papers of Jefferson,* ed. Boyd et al., vol. 2, 535–42. In 1779 Jefferson became a member of the Board of Governors of the college. This gave him the opportunity to secure the abolition of the chair of Theology and the establishment of the chairs of Jurisprudence, Medicine, and Modern Languages. *Autobiography of Jefferson,* ed. Malone, 63.

94. *Papers of Jefferson,* ed. Boyd et al., vol. 2, 554. At Jefferson's suggestion the capital of Virginia was to be transferred to Richmond. The transfer of the Virginia capital inaugurated the American tradition of establishing the capitals of the states in small towns located in the geographical center of the state and, if possible, remote from the big cities.

95. James Madison to Jefferson, December 4, 1786, in *Papers of Jefferson,* ed. Boyd et al., vol. 10, 575–76.

In 1796, however, the General Assembly passed an act establishing public schools,[96] an act generally based on the principles of Jefferson's bill. But this act was limited in scope, since it related only to primary schools. The decision whether to have such schools was left entirely to the local authorities. And the latter were not always eager to impose new taxes in order to provide education to the children of the poor. The absurdity of the situation aroused sharp objections on the part of Jefferson. In 1786 he wrote to George Wythe from Paris: "Preach, my dear Sir, a crusade against ignorance. . . . Let our countrymen know that the people alone can protect us against these evils, and that the tax which will be paid for this purpose is not more than the thousandth part of what will be paid to kings, priests and nobles who will rise up among us if we leave the people in ignorance."[97]

Jefferson was not discouraged by the setback he had suffered in his efforts at educational reform. He refined his plans for popular education, took an interest in the organization of education in other countries, and conducted a vast correspondence with eminent European scientists and pedagogues such as Joseph Priestley, Thomas Cooper, Pierre Samuel DuPont de Nemours, and many others.[98]

In Jefferson's lifetime his proposals on education produced but one tangible result—the creation of the University of Virginia. Jefferson dedicated the last years of his life to achieving this goal. He created a new type of university. Unlike the majority of contemporary centers of higher education, this university was completely independent of the church, thus initiating the secularization of academic research and teaching in America. The basis of the university's academic policy was intellectual freedom. The University of Virginia was one of the first to abandon traditional instruction in the three learned professions—theology, law, and medicine—by considerably broadening the number of subjects taught. It was here at Jefferson's initiative[99] that students' right to choose their courses, a right that later became traditional in American universities, was first applied.

The university differed considerably from others in its administration. It abolished corporal punishment and strict control over the students' conduct and way of life and introduced student self-government. The University of Virginia became the first state university in America, thus marking the beginning of the state-supported system of public universities.

It is difficult to exaggerate the impact of Jefferson's university on the development of higher education in the United States. Even before the opening of the university, Jefferson received numerous letters "from almost all the states to the South of the

96. Edgar W. Knight, ed., *A Documentary History of Education in the South before 1880* (Chapel Hill, 1950), vol. 2, 153–56.

97. Jefferson to Wythe, July 13, 1786, in *Papers of Jefferson,* ed. Boyd et al., vol. 10, 245.

98. See for example Richard Hofstadter and Wilson Smith, eds., *American Higher Education: A Documentary History* (Chicago, 1968), vol. 1, 175–76; Knight, ed., *Documentary History of Education,* vol. 2, 263–96.

99. In 1820 Jefferson wrote to his grandson Francis Eppes, "The main rule of our university is that everyone should be free to attend the courses he desires and reject those he does not desire" (quoted in Merrill Peterson, *Thomas Jefferson and the New Nation* [New York, 1970], 975).

Potomac, Ohio and Missouri" whose authors "followed with excitement the activity directed towards the establishment of the university as an event that would free them from the necessity of sending their youth to the universities of the Northern states."[100] But the influence of the University of Virginia was not confined solely to the territory south of the Mason-Dixon line, even though it was at its strongest there. Harvard University and Brown University both used the Virginia experience to modernize their institutions. Thus the University of Virginia played a very important role in the formation and development of American higher education.

Jefferson's system of primary and secondary education was put into practice much later. Not until 1870 did Virginia establish a public school system.[101] And it was then that public schools began to spread throughout the country.

Jefferson's activities in the field of education became known on both sides of the Atlantic. The University of Virginia's curriculum, which broke with traditionally classical university curricula to become significantly more relevant to the practical needs of life, caught the close attention of many European scientists and political figures. Goethe, for example, expressed an interest in it.[102]

Jefferson's indefatigable efforts to diffuse knowledge, and his ideas and projects to that end, had a significant impact on the formation of a system of popular education in the United States.[103] We may confidently state that Jefferson is one of the greatest American pedagogues.

The laws relating to land inheritance, the establishment of religious freedom, and the spreading of education were, in Jefferson's opinion, the most important in the program of democratic reform in Virginia. To conclude discussion of these reforms, it is necessary to mention a number of bills that for various reasons were not passed into law but that, like all of Jefferson's reformist activities during this period, greatly influenced the subsequent development of American society and its institutions: Jefferson's proposals to eradicate Negro slavery and substantially change state criminal law.

Long before the Revolution, slavery and the slave trade had filled many Americans of progressive views with heartfelt indignation. Jefferson was no exception. In 1769, having become a member of the Virginia legislature, he supported Richard Bland's bill to enable slaveowners to free their slaves.[104] The bill was rejected by the votes of slaveholding planters, and Bland was declared an "enemy of the country."[105]

---

100. *Early History of the University of Virginia as Contained in the Letters of Thomas Jefferson and Joseph C. Cabell* (Richmond, Va., 1856), 239–40.

101. James B. Conant, *Thomas Jefferson and the Development of American Public Education* (Berkeley, 1962), 20.

102. Charles Wiltse, *The Jeffersonian Tradition in American Democracy* (New York, 1960), 144.

103. Jefferson's work in the field of education is analyzed in Conant, *Jefferson and the Development of American Public Education.*

104. The text of this bill has not been found in the archives. But Jefferson mentions it in his *Autobiography* and in his letter to E. Coles of April 25, 1814. See *Autobiography of Jefferson,* ed. Malone, 21; *The Writings of Thomas Jefferson,* ed. Paul L. Ford, 10 vols. (New York, 1899), vol. 9, 477.

105. Peterson, *Jefferson and the New Nation,* 44.

American historians have used Jefferson's support of the bill to depict him as one of the first abolitionists in America. But Jefferson was not an abolitionist in the full sense of the word. Despite proposals to abolish slavery and free the slaves contained in many of his writings ("A Summary View of the Rights of British America," the Declaration of Independence of 1776, the draft of the Virginia constitution, etc.), he continued to own slaves. "The leisure that made possible his great writings on human liberty was supported by the labors of three generations of slaves," states Richard Hofstadter, the well-known American historian.[106] Jefferson protested slavery largely for humane reasons, believing that it contravened natural law. Jefferson's position on slavery was passive and often contradictory.

In June 1777 a bill aimed at preventing the further importation of slaves into the state was introduced in the Virginia legislature.[107] It was adopted, with a number of amendments, in October 1778. There is no direct evidence that Jefferson was its author. But as Julian P. Boyd points out, the spirit and language of the bill were very characteristic of Jefferson and reflected his position toward the slave trade.[108]

During this period Jefferson drew up a plan for the gradual emancipation of slaves. The plan provided for the freeing of those slaves who would be born after the adoption of an appropriate law. These children would have to remain with their parents and, depending on their inclinations, would be taught at government expense to till the land, or work as craftsmen, or engage in scientific pursuits. Upon attaining a certain age they would be subject to deportation. The state would be obliged to provide them with weapons, various agricultural implements, utensils, domestic cattle, seeds, etc. They would be declared free and independent, and the United States would have the obligation of ensuring their defense and protection.[109] Jefferson justified deporting the descendants of slaves in this way: "deep rooted prejudices entertained by the whites; ten thousand recollections, by the blacks, of the injuries they have sustained; . . . the real distinctions which Nature has made, and many other circumstances, will divide us into parties, and produce convulsions which will probably never end but in the extermination of one or the other race."[110] Quite a prophetic statement and one that at the same time is far from abolitionist in spirit.

The members of the Committee of Revisors assumed that Jefferson's plan would be rejected by the legislators and would thus create additional difficulties when the other bills were debated. Consequently, a bill was included in the "Report of the Committee" that amounted to the "simple enumeration of existing laws" relating to slaves.[111] In case the discussion of the bill took a favorable turn, the Revisors intended to introduce Jefferson's plan as an amendment. But debate on the bill showed that neither public opinion in the state nor the legislators were prepared at that time to support even a modest scheme for the gradual emancipation of the slaves. As a result

106. Hofstadter, *American Political Tradition,* 19.
107. *Papers of Jefferson,* ed. Boyd et al., vol. 1, 22–23.
108. Ibid., 23–24.
109. Jefferson, *Notes,* 199–200.
110. Ibid., 200.
111. *Autobiography of Jefferson,* ed. Malone, 62.

Jefferson's plan, far removed from reality, remained on paper. To ensure its adoption by a state that largely depended on the labor of Negro slaves would have been difficult. However, Jefferson's proposals to gradually emancipate the slaves partly influenced later development of the idea of deporting Negroes, which in particular led to the foundation of Liberia[112] and other schemes of Negro resettlement.

When reviewing the laws of Virginia, Jefferson attempted to introduce significant changes into the state criminal code. The English colonies had embraced English law, which was divided into common and statute law and in which many ancient statutes adopted as far back as the thirteenth century still remained in force. Engels, referring to the entire body of English criminal law, pointed out that it was the harshest in Europe: "Burning at the stake, breaking on the wheel, quartering, the extraction of intestines from a living body, etc., were the favourite types of punishment."[113] Execution was the penalty for more than 160 crimes.[114] In the course of the eight years he spent practicing law, Jefferson became convinced of the cruelty and senselessness of the laws then in force.

Jefferson approached criminal law reform as an Enlightenment philosopher. The treatise "On Crimes and Punishments" by the well-known Italian jurist Cesare Beccaria was an obvious influence on his views. Beccaria's work, which appeared in 1764, won high praise from the Encyclopedists and was widely known on both sides of the Atlantic. Jefferson, who knew Italian, studied this work closely, and passages from it occupy eighteen pages in his "Commonplace Book."[115] No less important was his familiarity with the "Principles of Penal Law" by William Eden, as well as with the writings of Helvetius, Kames, Montesquieu, and many other thinkers.

Like Beccaria, Jefferson believed that cruel and sanguinary punishments do not achieve their purpose. He sought to mitigate the severity of punishment and make it more humane and rational so that it would conform to the spirit of the age. As early as in the 1776 draft of the Virginia constitution Jefferson proposed the abolition of capital punishment for all crimes except high treason and murder.[116] Like a number of other proposals he put forward in the summer of that year in his correspondence with Edmund Pendleton,[117] he further developed this one while on the Committee of Revisors. At their first meeting in January 1777 the Revisors unanimously supported Jefferson's proposal to preserve the death penalty only in the case of high treason or murder.[118] Based on this fundamental principle, Jefferson drew up a bill on the proportionality of crimes and punishments.[119]

112. M. Iu. Frenkel, *The U.S.A. and Liberia: The Negro Problem in the U.S.A. and the Establishment of the Republic of Liberia* (Moscow, 1964).

113. Marx and Engels, *Writings,* vol. 1, 638.

114. Aptheker, *American Revolution,* 316.

115. Gilbert Chinard, ed., *The Commonplace Book of Thomas Jefferson. A Repertory of His Ideas on Government* (Baltimore, 1926), 298–316.

116. *Papers of Jefferson,* ed. Boyd et al., vol. 1, 349, 359.

117. See Pendleton to Jefferson, August 10, 1776, Jefferson to Pendleton, August 26, 1776., in ibid., 488–91, 503–5.

118. *Autobiography of Jefferson,* ed. Malone, 57.

119. *Papers of Jefferson,* ed. Boyd et al., vol. 2, 492–504.

As always, Jefferson approached the task facing him in a fully responsible manner. In spite of his excellent knowledge of jurisprudence, he carefully perused a great number of juristic treatises and works. It is no accident that the actual text of the bill occupied only part of the manuscript. He filled the other part with a multitude of citations and references to legal sources and with his notes and commentaries.

In the preamble to the bill Jefferson summarized the cardinal principles of penology. They corresponded to his views and principles as stated in the Declaration of Independence. Governments, the preamble said, are created to protect the natural rights of man, and therefore governments must punish those who violate those rights. But since punishment is in itself an evil, it can be justified only insofar as it leads to the reformation of the criminal and the prevention of future crimes. Since the death penalty cannot reform a criminal, it should be only the ultimate, extreme form of punishment. Punishments that are harsher than needed to prevent crime do not achieve their purpose. The clarity of the law can prevent crimes more effectively than the severity of the punishment. Therefore, particular crimes must be clearly linked to particular punishments, thereby rendering justice prompt and immune from error and preventing forensic mistakes.[120]

In accordance with these principles, the Committee of Revisors worked out a scale of the proportionality of punishments to crimes, which provided the basis for the bill drawn up by Jefferson.[121] On this scale all crimes were divided into three categories. The first included treason and murder, which were punishable by death. The second category of crimes, which were punishable by the amputation of a limb, included sexual offenses as well as maiming and disfiguring. The commission of all other crimes entailed hard labor.[122] The bill also abolished the clergy's immunity from secular justice.[123]

Jefferson's bill stipulated that in a number of cases the principle of *lex talionis* would remain in force. Forty years later in his *Autobiography,* Jefferson expressed bewilderment at the way that "revolting principle came to obtain our approbation."[124] Jefferson was opposed to *lex talionis*. In 1778 he sent a copy of the bill to George Wythe to "examine and correct." He noted that "the lex talionis, . . . the simplicity of which we have generally found . . . so advantageous . . . , will be revolting to the humanised feelings of modern times. An eye for an eye, and a hand for a hand will exhibit spectacles in execution whose moral effect would be questionable. . . . This needs reconsideration."[125]

120. Ibid., vol. 1, 492–93.

121. It must be noted that Jefferson himself was not satisfied with this scale (see Jefferson to Wythe, November 1, 1778, in ibid., vol. 2, 230).

122. See "Outline of a Bill on the Proportionality of Crimes and Punishments," in ibid., vol. 2, 663–64. Jefferson proposed employing those sentenced to penal servitude on public work projects: in mines, foundries, shipyards, road construction, etc.

123. Ibid., vol. 2, 503.

124. *Autobiography of Jefferson,* ed. Malone, 57.

125. Jefferson to Wythe, November 1, 1778, in *Papers of Jefferson,* ed. Boyd et al., vol. 2, 230.

There are two possible reasons why the principle of retribution was preserved in the bill. On the one hand, this may have been a compromise concession to Pendleton, who in the course of the work of the Committee of Revisors proved to be someone who was "zealously attached to ancient establishments."[126] On the other hand, Jefferson sometimes excessively idealized the Anglo-Saxon past. *Lex talionis,* being an integral part of Anglo-Saxon law, may have attracted Jefferson by its apparent simplicity.

Madison submitted the bill on the proportionality of crimes and punishments to the Virginia legislative assembly, and after prolonged discussion the assembly rejected it in November 1785 by a majority of one.[127] Thus, as Madison noted, "our old bloody code is by this event fully restored."[128] Rejection of the bill was undoubtedly connected to the fact that some of the bill's provisions, in particular those that reduced the severity of punishments, were considerably ahead of their time. The bill was never passed into law in its entirety, although some of its provisions were later put into effect.

Jefferson soon reached the conclusion that employing prisoners sentenced to hard labor on public work projects was ineffective. The necessity of working in plain view "with shaved heads and mean clothing . . . produced in the criminals such a prostration of character, such an abandonment of self-respect," he noted in his *Autobiography,* "as, instead of reforming, plunged them into the most desperate and hardened depravity of morals and character."[129] As a result Jefferson developed a preference for a prison-based penitentiary system and became one of its most consistent advocates in America.

These were the main democratic reforms conceived by Jefferson and partially put into effect as early as the years of the War of Independence. Jefferson believed it necessary to reorganize society immediately following the Declaration of Independence, without waiting for the conclusion of military operations. Such a reorganization was essential for the creation of a new, independent, and democratic state. Jefferson was well qualified for this immense task. Yet in all his reform efforts he had the active support of only a few kindred spirits. This was the most creative period in Jefferson's legislative activity, for it was inspired by his desire to put into practice the ideas and principles of the Declaration of Independence.

Certainly not all of Jefferson's plans were implemented during that period. He continued to fight until his death for the democratization of American society. Jefferson was correct in believing that the example of his native state would be followed by the rest of the country. This belief was reinforced by his conviction that his ideas about democracy, progress, freedom, and the civil rights of man would become the heritage of the whole of America. He fought and believed. His struggle brought him well-earned fame as one of the first American democrats.

126. *Autobiography of Jefferson,* ed. Malone, 51.
127. James Madison to George Washington, December 24, 1786, in *The Writings of James Madison,* ed. G. Hunt, 9 vols. (New York, 1900), vol. 2, 303.
128. James Madison to Jefferson, January 22, 1786, February 15, 1787, in *Papers of Jefferson,* ed. Boyd et al., vol. 9, 195, vol. 11, 152.
129. *Autobiography of Jefferson,* ed. Malone, 59.

COMMENT BY LINDA K. KERBER

Political upheaval in Eastern Europe and the end of the USSR enable us to read V. N. Pleshkov's essay for what it truly is—not only a thoughtful synthesis of what is known of Thomas Jefferson's struggle for democratic reforms but also moving testimony to the struggle by former Soviet historians to participate in the writing of an international history of democratic thought and action. The American Revolution, R. R. Palmer observed long ago, is best thought of as part of an international democratic revolution, enacted not only in the United States but also in France, Belgium, the Netherlands, Italy, Germany, and England (with varying degrees of success). To write the history of any aspect of that democratic revolution—particularly in the context of academic conditions that prevailed in the former USSR, not least of which have been the lack of free flow of ideas, the virtual exclusion of Soviet historians from participation in international conferences, and the difficulty of access to books and research materials—has been to contribute to the international effort to maintain public memory of a period when the central issues of the relationship between the individual and the state were defined for the modern era.

V. N. Pleshkov's article was published in 1975, and the most recent American publication he cites is from 1970. For American historians, 1970 was near the beginning of a fresh burst of scholarship in social history—a scholarship that has sometimes been called "neo-Progressive" in that it tends to stress the tension between classes and interest groups. More than twenty years later, American historians studying the founding era are highly conscious of the extent to which the conditions for revolution were situated in the international economic changes of the commercial and industrial revolutions, in the social situation of those who supported or opposed the political revolution, and also of the claims of those whose interests were ignored by the Revolution. Although the appearance of the word "bourgeois" in the first paragraph of Pleshkov's essay would have marked it for most American readers in the 1970s as problematic and partisan, using the language of Marxist argumentation awkwardly or inappropriately (few U.S. scholars used the word in 1970), it was unproblematic to focus on class relations during the American Revolution.[1] As I respond to Pleshkov's essay, I find myself giving more space to long-range economic trends than he does. Paradoxically, then, despite the difficulties of transnational conversation, the positions of the two communities of historians may have moved closer together over the decades rather than further apart.

I have little to quarrel with in V. N. Pleshkov's admirable synthesis of Jefferson's agenda for democratic reform. Indeed, the issues that Pleshkov chooses to discuss—

I am deeply grateful for the research assistance of Leslie Taylor of the University of Iowa.

1. I think here particularly of the work of Alfred F. Young, Gary Nash, Edward Countryman, and Sean Wilentz. In recent years, Wilentz writes, American historians have come to "take for granted the inescapable fact that class relations order power and social relationships: they have examined the numerous conflicts and accommodations that give rise to and accompany these relations as a complex series of social encounters, fusing culture and politics as well as economics." Sean Wilentz, *Chants Democratic: New York City and the Rise of the American Working Class, 1788–1850* (New York, 1984), 10.

freedom of religion (and, by implication, of speech), access to education, the transmission of property to the next generation, the vigor with which crime should be punished and the level of cruelty that would be tolerated in doing so, the constraints under which the most vulnerable workers (in Jefferson's time, slaves) should be required to toil— are a sampling of the most significant issues with which every postrevolutionary society has to deal and by which it defines itself in practice.[2] Pleshkov offers us only the beginning of an analysis of post-Revolutionary civic culture in America, but I find myself wondering whether—in his admiration for Jefferson, and in his choice of issues to discuss—we may also read criticism of another revolution that promised democratic reform and failed to deliver. Certainly America in the early Republic was a postrevolutionary society that had to resolve problems of instability and change. The paradoxes of Jefferson's thought mirror the paradoxes of his society, a society committed to maintaining slavery and deferential patterns of relations between the races, yet also a society developing a radically new political system and eroding deferential relations among white men.

It is instructive to contemplate, as Pleshkov does, the influence that a single career can have, the difference that genius can make. But it is important, too, to situate Jefferson's career in the general context of democratic reform in the founding era and to understand civil freedoms in the United States as developing not only from the choices of individuals, but also out of a complex political context. If we wait for another Jefferson we will wait a long time indeed. It is no insult to Jefferson to understand him to be embedded in the discourses of his time, unable to transcend them: it would be counterfactual to expect otherwise.

For example, Pleshkov emphasizes the contrast between Governor Patrick Henry and his successor. Henry had, Pleshkov writes correctly, "no program of reform, nor even the intention of instituting change."[3] But it is unwise, I think, to offer a Jefferson who, in building a more democratic society in contrast to the vacuum that Henry represents, is made to seem virtually original, *sui generis*. The Virginia Declaration of Rights—with its provisions for the free exercise of religion, trial by jury, freedom of the press, and freedom from unlawful search and seizure—was after all drafted not by Jefferson but by George Mason. In virtually every other state there were other men engaged in considering how the basic freedoms of the new polity were to be

2. Some of my comments in this response echo remarks I have made in "The Revolutionary Generation: Ideology, Politics, and Culture in the Early Republic," in Eric Foner, ed., *The New American History* (Philadelphia, 1990), 25–49. Joyce Appleby's work is indispensable to an analysis of Jefferson's ideas and politics: see particularly "The American Heritage: The Heirs and the Disinherited," *Journal of American History* 74 (1987), 798–813; "Commercial Farming and the 'Agrarian Myth' in the Early Republic," *Journal of American History* 68 (1987), 833–49; "What Is Still American in the Political Philosophy of Thomas Jefferson?" *William and Mary Quarterly,* 3d ser., vol. 39 (1982), 287–309.

3. Henry's most recent biographer confirms that "the new state constitution most closely resembled in spirit the old colonial charter, with only the power of the King, Privy Council, and Royal Governor stripped away . . . There is absolutely no indication that Patrick Henry . . . made any effort whatsoever to inject a greater measure of popular participation into the state government." Richard Beeman, *Patrick Henry: A Biography* (New York: 1979), 104, 106.

formulated and in embedding these freedoms both in state constitutions and in state bills of rights. Jefferson's work in Virginia should be credited, I think, not only to his own vision but also to that of his colleagues both in the Virginia legislature and throughout the United States, as royal government was slowly transformed into a newly invented republican political order. Indeed, Virginia was slower than most states to embrace the republican understanding that the people are the constituent power and that a republican constitution requires the convening of a convention of delegates specifically elected for that purpose: Virginia would not call such a convention until 1829.[4]

Studying Jefferson's work in the broad context of social change in the era of the early Republic also serves to caution us against crediting Jefferson with excessively radical intentions. It seems to me an overstatement to claim that Jefferson's land reforms—or indeed any of his reforms—"aimed at turning an aristocratic society into a democratic one." Jefferson himself, after voicing some radical propositions that would give substance to the promise to narrow class distinctions—such as the distribution of seventy-five acres of land to every free man who married—lost interest after he failed to gather substantial legislative support for them.

Perhaps we need to specify what a democratic society means. The law of inheritance, as it stood in 1776, did seem, as Stanley Katz had written, "to symbolize the aristocratic aspects of English government against which the Revolution increasingly directed itself." To change the rhetoric of the law of inheritance was an ideological act that was not without significance: indeed, to abolish primogeniture was to signal that sons were not to be privileged over daughters. But Pleshkov also recognizes, as do virtually all scholars of the subject, that the abolition of primogeniture and entail made little substantive difference. Neither Jefferson nor his colleagues embraced propositions as far-ranging as those developed during the French Revolution, where Jacobins took the position that property is a social creation, and that, as Mirabeau said, "society is . . . entitled to refuse its members . . . the capacity to dispose arbitrarily of their fortune." In Virginia as elsewhere in the early Republic, inheritance patterns when they shifted at all, shifted in response to long-range changes in the economy. As Toby Ditz has written in her careful study of inheritance in New England, it was the commercial revolution that "profoundly" altered families' choices about how property should be passed to the next generation. In the face of new commercial, "bourgeois" relationships, "devices associated with dynastic strategies: primogeniture, entail . . . prototrust arrangements . . . which constrained heirs' powers of alienation and devise" fell out of favor and were replaced by choices that offered each of the children support for their own independent household. It was also increasingly desirable to keep land as a saleable commodity: the commercialization of agriculture put "financial flexibility" at a premium.[5]

4. Beeman, *Henry,* 117.

5. Stanley N. Katz, "Republicanism and the Law of Inheritance in the American Revolutionary Era," *University of Michigan Law Review* 76 (1977), 11. The point about abolishing primogeniture to signal that sons were not to be privileged over daughters is discussed in Marylynn Salmon,

I would also suggest that Pleshkov overestimates the scope and significance of Jefferson's proposals for education. He accurately recognizes that Jefferson's interest in the expansion of access to schooling was widely shared and also that what was fresh and distinctive about Jefferson's plan was envisioning a *system* of state-supported education ranging from the primary to the university level. But Jefferson cannot be credited with putting a system into practice that was a model for schools throughout the country. It would be more accurate, I think, to recognize that Jefferson's interest in education was congruent with that of a wide range of others committed to the republican experiment, who believed that the stability of the Republic rested on the production and reproduction of successive generations of well-informed, judicious citizens. Jefferson was not alone in appreciating the role that schools might play in promoting the diffusion of knowledge and the upward mobility of children. But his own plan for public schooling privileged the gifted and the elite. It made no place for black children, although Quakers had started a free school for Blacks in Philadelphia in 1770. Girls dropped out of his scheme after three years, leaving them only the most marginal schooling while their brothers continued to train their minds, and continuing the severe gender disparity in educational attainment characteristic of contemporary Virginia.[6] Although the University of Virginia did indeed play "a very important role in the formation and development of American higher education," it was not the first state university: it was preceded by the University of North Carolina and others in the South, nor was it the only available model for American universities.

Moreover, just as the laws on primogeniture and entail ratified processes already developing in response to economic change, so too the growth and development of schools *followed,* rather than caused, the sharp rise of literacy characteristic of the late eighteenth century. An increasingly commercial economy relying on written accounts and contracts meant that more people needed to learn to read and write and to use arithmetic. Historians of literacy now tend to argue that the availability of print materials—engendering a felt *need* to read, write, and compute in order to carry out one's work, interact with merchants and traders, and connect with society outside one's own family and immediate community—was the most important force for the spread of literacy both in America and in Europe. The growth of literacy and numeracy seem now to have been due primarily to a commercial revolution that

"Republican Sentiment, Economic Change, and the Property Rights of Women in American Law," in Ronald Hoffman and Peter J. Albert, eds., *Women in the Age of the American Revolution* (Charlottesville, 1989), 449–50. Mirabeau's quote is in Katz, "Republicanism and the Law of Inheritance," 24. Toby L. Ditz, *Property and Kinship: Inheritance in Early Connecticut, 1750–1820* (Princeton: 1986), 63–65, 163–65; Salmon, "Republican Sentiment," in Hoffman and Albert, eds., *Women in the Age of the American Revolution,* 451. See also Ditz, "Ownership and Obligation: Inheritance and Patriarchal Households in Connecticut, 1750–1820," *William and Mary Quarterly,* 3d. ser., vol. 47 (1990), 235–65.

6. Studying the records of orphans courts between 1731 and 1808, Allan Kulikoff finds that while boys learned to read and write, some girls learned only to read; others had no schooling at all. Allan Kulikoff, *Tobacco and Slaves: The Development of Southern Cultures in the Chesapeake, 1680–1800* (Chapel Hill, 1986), 195–99.

rewarded holders of these skills. In the words of the title of one recent book, reading became "a necessity of life."[7]

Pleshkov calls our attention to Jefferson's "Bill for Establishing Religious Freedom" and properly links it—as Julian Boyd did—to claims for "full intellectual freedom." In this statute as elsewhere, the demand for religious toleration and separation of church and state was also a proxy for "the right of the individual to complete intellectual liberty."[8] In the context of the postrevolutionary society, this claim was of enormous significance: it was made perhaps most fluently by Jefferson. It is true, as Pleshkov points out, that it was also made with difficulty: it took seven years and a sharp legislative struggle before the Virginia legislature passed it, and that was a minor matter compared to the length of time and intensity of effort required before Massachusetts and Connecticut disestablished their churches.[9]

Pleshkov overestimates, I think, the extent to which Jefferson stood against his contemporaries and colleagues in other states. Certainly there could be tension among the denominations, but in fact the middle colonies, which were characterized by the widest variety of religious groups, were the regions most tolerant of diversity. Jefferson was not alone in "arriving" at the idea of separation of church and state. A recent commentator has pointed out that "every substantial state constitution written [between] 1776–1800 (and there were nineteen) includes a protection of religious freedom."[10] The cause had long been won in Rhode Island, Pennsylvania, Delaware, and New Jersey, all of which entered the Revolution without established churches; five states disestablished the Anglican Church even before the war broke out.

But Pleshkov is not wrong in his implication—if I read him right—that claiming the right to shape one's own private beliefs was central to the Revolutionary challenge to

7. William J. Gilmore, *Reading Becomes a 'Necessity of Life': Material and Cultural Life in Rural New England, 1780–1830* (Knoxville, 1988); and Richard D. Brown, *Knowledge Is Power: The Diffusion of Information in Early America, 1700–1865* (New York, 1989). Virginia, as Pleshkov mentions, was very late to begin a system of public schools, and then it was established by a Reconstruction legislature. Public schools were well established in the North and West long before 1870.

8. *Papers of Thomas Jefferson,* ed. Boyd et al., vol. 2, 547n.

9. Patricia Bonomi, who has studied the matter in some detail, argues that the poor personal reputation of Virginia (and Maryland) clergy to which Pleshkov alludes was less a matter of their "oppression" than an artifact of the way taxes were raised for their support, encouraging complaint on the local level. "The troubles besetting those two provinces stemmed less, it would appear, from the bad or good quality of their clergy than from one prime circumstance: in Virginia and Maryland alone was the clergy exclusively dependent for its support on a direct colony-wide church tax . . . Only in Virginia and Maryland did clerical salaries and control over the church become perennial issues in local politics . . . There is ample ground to suppose that Anglican ministers in Virginia and Maryland were no less competent, upright, or dedicated than those in other colonies. But . . . they offered all-too convenient targets for anyone who wanted to take a shot at the British state or church." Patricia U. Bonomi, *Under the Cope of Heaven: Religion, Society and Politics in Colonial America* (New York, 1986), 48–49. I would also caution against using Dale's laws of 1611—cruel though they were, they were quickly abandoned—as evidence of practices two centuries later.

10. John K. Wilson, "Religion under the State Constitutions, 1776–1800," *Journal of Church and State* 32 (1990), 753–75.

British practice. That demand may well have been made so clearly in the aftermath of the war because it had been so important in the religious revival known as the Great Awakening that preceded the war. Refusing to take communion in an established church may well have been for many individuals a central psychological experience that made it possible for them to believe there might be other things the state had no right to demand of them. It is *because* the Revolutionary generation was generally a *believing,* not an agnostic, generation that the separation of church and state was so deeply radical.

Those who would, like Pleshkov, celebrate Jefferson's thought are faced with the challenge of dealing with his inconsistencies, particularly the paradoxes of his views and actions on slavery. Some years ago the historian John C. Miller wrote a whole book on the subject, drawing his title from Jefferson's famous observation, "We have the Wolf by the Ears: we can neither hold him nor let him go." Pleshkov recognizes that Jefferson hoped for the abolition of slavery but insisted it be followed by deportation. As president, Miller emphasizes, Jefferson closed the international slave trade but at the same time arranged for the Louisiana Purchase, opening an immense region to the expansion of slavery. "Paradoxically," Miller writes, "some of the accomplishments in which Jefferson took the greatest pride tended to consolidate and perpetuate the institution he abhorred."[11]

It is a paradox that Miller cannot solve, nor can Pleshkov, nor can any other student of Jefferson. The best we can do is face up to it in all its pain and irony. For the paradox of Jefferson's career is the paradox of a Republic that sought to expand freedom—life, liberty, and the pursuit of happiness—to a wider range of people than had heretofore been thought possible and at the same time to rest that freedom on the continuing exploitation of a large portion of its population. It could not be done. If we wish to understand, as Pleshkov writes at the end, "the democratization of American society," we do indeed need to study Jefferson and the Virginia society from which he emerged. But we also need to study the more complex, urban cultures of New York and Pennsylvania, where Jews lived as neighbors of Christians, where substantial communities of free African-Americans lived and worked and even, occasionally, voted. We need to know more about New Jersey, where women were explicitly members of the polity, and more about what was buried in the memories of New Yorkers of the days when Dutch law had recognized capacities among women that English law did not. Jefferson's words rested not only in his often paradoxical behavior but also solidly in a national political community that shared—even if it was not always so eloquent—his hopes and fears, his optimism and his pessimism.

11. John Chester Miller, *The Wolf by the Ears: Thomas Jefferson and Slavery* (New York, 1977), 142. Miller also points out that when Jefferson participated in the revision of the laws of Virginia, "free blacks actually lost ground . . . No effort was made to accord (free blacks) the rights of citizens or equality before the law" (21).

CHAPTER 6

On the Question of the Economic Policies of the First Continental Congress:

The Association

by

Maria O. Troyanovskaya

The First Continental Congress, which met in Philadelphia in September 1774, just two years before the Declaration of Independence, marked an important stage in the development of the Revolutionary movement in the colonies. In a sense, the Congress reviewed the colonists' struggle against the mother country's efforts to consolidate her authority over them by means of taxation and other repressive measures. The Congress was made possible by the rise in the revolutionary consciousness of the inhabitants of the colonies, which had led the thirteen hitherto disunited provinces to join together in common protest. The Congress made the prospect of an armed struggle by the colonists against the mother country more likely. The meetings of the Congress were among the key events in the process that led to the establishment of independence by the colonists.

The Congress decided a number of urgent issues facing the colonies. In the political sphere, it passed the radical Suffolk Resolves, which represented the colonists' response to the "Intolerable Acts";[1] it rejected Joseph Galloway's plan, which envisaged the consolidation of British rule in the colonies; and it drew up the "Declaration of Rights and Grievances," which in many ways presaged the Declaration of Independence.

The main economic problem confronting the First Continental Congress was the boycotting of English goods. After debating this issue, the Congress adopted the Association.

It is worth noting that although many studies dealing with the War of Independence and its origins have been published, there are no monographs exclusively devoted to the First Continental Congress and its economic policies, which are the subject of this article. Nevertheless, several eminent American historians have written about

---

1. These were five repressive acts passed by the British Parliament in the spring of 1774, four of which harmed the interests of the inhabitants of the Massachusetts colony, while the fifth act related to the Province of Quebec. This article by Maria O. Troyanovskaya was first published in *American Studies Annual for 1980* (Moscow, 1980).

the economic policies of the First Congress, and many of their conclusions appear well founded. For example, Carl Becker in his *History of Political Parties in the Province of New York* offered a brief review of the articles of Association,[2] while Arthur Schlesinger in his book *The Colonial Merchants and the American Revolution*[3] concentrated on the circumstances that made the adoption of the Association possible, and Merrill Jensen in his study *The Articles of Confederation* analyzed the way in which the economic policy of the First Continental Congress was carried out.[4]

Among Soviet historians, only V. N. Pleshkov has offered an analysis of the activities of the First Continental Congress, yet in his article Pleshkov has little to say about the Association.[5]

This article aims to treat and analyze the articles of Association as the most important document the First Continental Congress produced, to describe the struggle over matters of economic policy that took place in the Congress, and to retrace the drafting of the text of the Association and discuss the identity of its authors.

The decisions of the First Continental Congress continued the colonists' policy of severing commercial links with the mother country. The American colonists were widely experienced in using economic boycotts as an effective weapon against British policy in America. In the course of the campaign against the Townshend Acts, British imports had been banned in almost all the port cities in the colonies. In the two Carolinas, imports fell from £306,000 in 1769 to £146,273 in 1770; in Pennsylvania from £441,829 in 1768 to £204,978 in 1769 and £134,881 in 1770; etc.[6] Yet even these figures indicate that imports did not cease completely. English merchants tried to find indirect ways of selling their goods in the colonies, frequently using transit trade for this purpose.

The experience of 1768–1770 led many colonists to conclude that future agreements barring imports from the mother country should be drafted in such a way that American merchants would not be tempted to break them. Thus it became necessary to conclude a new agreement that would prohibit the consumption of imported goods. Elbridge Gerry, the Boston patriot, wrote about this to Samuel Adams.[7] In a broader sense the time had come to reorient the colonial merchant class toward serving the needs of the internal market. This was objectively in the interests of developing the country along bourgeois lines; since the old trade relationship that England wished

2. Carl Becker, *The History of Political Parties in the Province of New York, 1760–1776* (Madison, 1960), 151–55.

3. Arthur M. Schlesinger, *The Colonial Merchants and the American Revolution* (New York, 1968), 411–25.

4. Merrill Jensen, *The Articles of Confederation* (Madison, 1960). See also Lynn Montross, *The Reluctant Rebels* (New York, 1950); Pauline Maier, *From Resistance to Revolution* (New York, 1972).

5. V. N. Pleshkov, "The First Continental Congress," *Problems of History* 6 (1976), 213–18. See also *The War of Independence and the Formation of the United States of America,* ed. G. N. Sevost'ianov (Moscow, 1976), 111, 227–29, 271; A. A Fursenko, *The American Revolution and the Formation of the United States of America* (Moscow, 1978), 191.

6. *Annals of Commerce,* 4 vols., ed. D. MacPherson (London, 1804–1805), vol. 3, 563–65, 585.

7. *Writings of Samuel Adams,* ed. Harry Alonzo Cushing, 4 vols. (New York, 1904–1908), vol. 3, 139.

to preserve had begun to hinder this development, it had to take place independently of Great Britain.

Responding to the "Intolerable Acts," in the summer of 1774 many of the colonies concluded associations (agreements) severing relations with the mother country. The Congress was expected to approve these measures and to set a timetable for implementing a similar agreement at the continental level.

When considering the problem of the First Continental Congress's agreeing to economic boycotts, one must bear in mind the economic situation in the colonies immediately prior to and during the Congress. Although the majority of merchants later joined the patriotic camp, they were not prepared to sacrifice their personal interests in the struggle against British domination. They clearly understood that if an agreement providing for the cessation of all trade with the mother country were adopted, it would lead to a shortage of imported goods that, in turn, would produce a dramatic rise in the price of those goods. Accordingly, in the summer and autumn of 1774 the numbers of American orders for English goods to be delivered between September and November were significantly increased. The merchants believed that even if Congress were to ban imports from the mother country after November 1, many of the goods ordered would have already arrived.

It was for these reasons that the conservative merchants of Pennsylvania, New York, and the other colonies refused to support the Bostonians, who that spring had already called for the signing of an agreement prohibiting imports and exports. Instead the merchants, hoping to gain time, suggested that the issue should be debated by the Congress. In Pennsylvania in 1774 the total value of imports rose to £625,500 compared with £426,500 in 1773, while in Virginia and Maryland together it increased from £329,000 to £528,700.[8]

By the time the Congress assembled, no one doubted that an economic boycott of England was likely. But since this issue involved the colonists' vital interests and each delegation had its own views on the cessation of trade, the discussions, particularly over exports, were very heated. Interestingly, during these debates forces in the Congress regrouped; many of the delegates revealed an often exclusive concern with the economic interests of their own colony.

On September 22, 1774, the Congress decided to inform the merchants and all other colonists that orders for goods were no longer to be placed in England and that existing orders were to be canceled.[9] This was the first decision on trade policy toward England the Congress made, and it was the members of the conservative wing in Congress who reacted to it with the least concern.

On September 27, after discussing the possible means of counteracting British policy to reestablish American rights, the Congress decided to impose a ban on the import of all goods from Great Britain and Ireland.[10] This step had been proposed

8. *Annals of Commerce,* ed. MacPherson, vol. 3, 563–65, 585.

9. *Journals of the Continental Congress, 1774–1789,* ed. Worthington Chauncey Ford et al., 34 vols. (Washington, 1904–1937), vol. 1, 41.

10. Ibid., 42.

by Richard Henry Lee of Virginia.[11] He was supported by Thomas Cushing of Massachusetts, who called for an immediate stop to the import of goods. Thomas Mifflin of Pennsylvania and Christopher Gadsden of South Carolina, who were also in favor of this measure, suggested, however, that its implementation should be postponed until November 1 so that the goods already ordered could be delivered. Patrick Henry urged that the ban on imports be postponed until December. With this sort of consensus coming from long experience with nonimportation, even the more conservative delegates did not seriously object to the idea of halting imports from the mother country.

Yet when a few days later the Congress began to consider the question of stopping the export to England of American goods and raw materials, a bitter debate ensued. The problem was that the economies of several of the colonies, particularly those in the South, were almost entirely dependent on exports to European markets. That is why discussion of this vitally important issue led to a regrouping of forces among the colonies. Thomas Cushing and Eliphalet Dyer of Connecticut spoke in favor of an immediate ban on exports; they were supported by John Sullivan of New Hampshire, Thomas Mifflin (of Pennsylvania), and Samuel Chase of Maryland.

On the whole, the delegates from the northern and central provinces were not opposed to the ban on exports, with the exception of Joseph Galloway, a Pennsylvania representative, who believed that this would lead to the impoverishment of tens of thousands of people and adversely affect the landowners.[12] Although originally the delegates from the southern colonies had belonged to the radical faction, they now defended their own interests in the export of rice, tobacco, and indigo. The Virginia delegation, which had been instructed to object to a trade ban until at least September 1775 to ensure that there would be sufficient time to sell the harvest, was against an immediate cessation of trade.[13] Virginia was supported by the two Carolinas, with South Carolina insisting that the export of rice and indigo should not be prohibited at all.[14] As a result, the Congress treated the demands of the southern states sympathetically, decreeing that as of September 10, 1775, the export of all goods to Great Britain, Ireland, and the West Indies would cease, unless the grievances of the American colonists were addressed.[15] Nevertheless, South Carolina's request that rice and indigo be exempt was not granted.

That same day the Congress elected a committee charged with drawing up the decrees to suppress trade. Among its members were four delegates with radical views: Cushing, Mifflin, Lee, and Thomas Johnson of Maryland, as well as the conservative merchant Isaac Low of New York. On October 12, 1774, the committee presented the fruits of its labors—the draft of the Association. Once again the ban on exports became a subject of discussion.

---

11. *Letters of the Members of the Continental Congress,* ed. Edmund C. Burnett, 8 vols. (Washington, 1921–1936), vol. 1, 48.

12. *Journals of the Continental Congress,* ed. Ford et al., vol. 1, 41.

13. Ibid., 42.

14. *Letters of the Continental Congress,* ed. Burnett, vol. 1, 49.

15. Ibid.

The entire South Carolina delegation, with the exception of Christopher Gadsden, refused to sign the Association unless the provisions concerning the suspension of exports were altered. Gadsden, who was prepared to sign the Association as drafted, accused his fellow delegates of deliberately trying to delay its adoption. John Rutledge spoke in defense of the South Carolina representatives. He pointed out that although the total value of exports from Pennsylvania amounted to approximately seven hundred thousand pounds, the value of Pennsylvania exports actually going to England was only fifty thousand pounds; whereas in the case of South Carolina all the colony's rice and indigo exports were destined for the mother country. The ensuing debate left the issue unresolved, and with the exception of Gadsden the South Carolina representatives walked out of the Congress. It took some effort for the other delegates to persuade them to return. The Congress proposed to delete the provision concerning the suspension of rice exports, while for their part the Carolina delegates agreed to withdraw their objections to the provision relating to indigo.

Another problem facing the delegates was the attitude to be adopted toward the Quebec Act. Earlier the Congress had included the act in the list of the colonists' complaints that formed part of the "Declaration of Rights and Grievances" adopted on October 14. However, on October 17 James Duane of New York asked for a reconsideration of the issue. He doubted whether the Association should refer to the Quebec Act along with the four other acts of Parliament. The delegate from New York believed that the Congress would be asking for too much if it were to make the repeal of the Quebec Act a condition for the renewal of trade with England.[16]

R. H. Lee argued with Duane, saying that in his view the Quebec Act amounted to an egregious violation of the colonists' rights. Thomas McKean agreed with Lee, adding that if the act were mentioned in the Association, Protestants in England would support the Americans for religious reasons. When the matter was put to a vote, the majority decided in favor of including the Quebec Act in the list of the colonists' grievances. This action by the Congress revealed the colonists' determination to offer no concessions to England: by voting in this way the delegates expressed their hope, however perfunctorily, that Parliament would repeal the Quebec Act and thus renounce Britain's vast territorial claims in North America. By insisting that the Association should contain a reference to the act, they made the prospects for reconciliation between the two parties even more remote, if not altogether unlikely.

On October 20 the Congress presented the final draft of the Association, signed by all the delegates. The document consisted of a preamble, fourteen articles, and a conclusion.[17]

In the preamble, the colonists, "avowing our allegiance to his majesty, our affection and regard for our fellow-subjects in Great-Britain and elsewhere, . . . and having taken under our most serious deliberation, the state of the whole continent," declared that the cause of all the troubles was the "ruinous system of colonial administration,

16. Ibid., 77–78.
17. For the text of the Association see *Journals of the Continental Congress,* ed. Ford et al., vol. 1, 75–81. Henceforth reference will be made to only its articles, which will be quoted by number.

adopted by the British ministry about the year 1763." The preamble ended with the statement that in the colonists' opinion the most efficacious measures "to obtain redress of these grievances" would be an agreement to halt the import and consumption of goods produced in the mother country and the export of goods to the mother country.

Article 1 confirmed the decision to stop the import of goods from Great Britain and Ireland. Article 2 specified that the ban on imports included slaves (who were chattel), and that the colonists undertook not only to refrain from participating in the slave trade but also to refuse to hire out their vessels for that purpose. December 1, 1774, was the date when the agreement to ban imports from the mother country was to come into effect.

The radical character of this provision of the Association is worth noting. As we know, even the final draft of the Declaration of Independence failed to address the question of slavery, although Jefferson had originally composed a paragraph condemning slavery. We also know that the Constitution of 1787 did not provide for the suppression of the slave trade. The practice of importing slaves was not to end until twenty years after the adoption of the Constitution. So on the problem of slavery the Continental Association went further than all the documents subsequently produced by the American Revolution.

Article 4 provided in detail for a ban on the export, whether direct or indirect, of "any merchandise or commodity whatsoever to Great-Britain, Ireland and the West Indies." Rice was to be the only exception. The fact that this article not only forbade direct exports but also the export of goods through third parties or via the transit trade went a long way toward ensuring compliance with the agreement; it certainly made it more difficult to break it. The export of goods was to cease as of September 10, 1775. The Association justified this delay in the implementation of the export ban by "the earnest desire . . . not to injure our fellow-subjects in Great-Britain, Ireland, or the West Indies," though, as we saw, the colonists were merely trying to ensure that they would be able to sell their 1774 harvest.

According to Articles 5 and 6, merchants trading with England were to inform their agents that henceforth no goods were to be sent to America; shipowners were advised to "give positive orders to their captains, or masters, not to receive [prohibited goods] on board." The names of those violating these instructions were to be publicized. These two articles amounted to a partial guarantee that the laws passed by Congress would be observed.

But the main guarantee that the agreement would be honored was the refusal to use goods manufactured in the mother country—the subject of Article 3. Unlike the guarantees described above, this one was economic in nature. Under Article 3 the colonists undertook "from this day" not to use goods that had been imported from or were suspected of having been imported from England. This provision not only created additional difficulties for potential violators of the law but also in effect deprived such persons of any real incentive to break it. Even if it would have been possible to import banned goods, it would have been very hard to sell them; and to import them without selling them would have made no sense.

The provisions of Article 3 could be contravened only in exceptional circumstances, which were the subject of Article 10. This article was of great importance for those merchants whose goods would not have arrived by December 1. If the goods were delivered between December 1, 1774, and February 1, 1775, the owner could return them, store them in a warehouse, or sell them under the supervision of the local committee. If the merchant chose to sell them, he was to be reimbursed in the amount of the original value of the goods, while "the profit, if any," should be "applied toward relieving and employing such poor inhabitants of the town of Boston, as are immediate sufferers by the Boston port-bill." Goods that arrived in the colonies after February 1, 1775, were to be "immediately sent back without being unpacked." Article 10 shows that the Association endowed the various local committees with considerable power.

In addition to these measures, the Association listed prohibitions aimed at decreasing the colonies' dependence on England. Articles 7, 8, and 9 outlined the internal policies of the Congress. The colonists were to use their "utmost endeavors" to stimulate "agriculture, arts and the manufactures of this country." Article 9 stipulated that merchants should not take advantage of the shortage of goods caused by the Association; they should sell goods at prices that were customary during the previous twelve months.

One article called on Americans to cultivate "frugality, economy, and industry" and to "discourage every species of extravagance and dissipation." This was a reference to horse racing, cockfighting, and other diversions. When a death in the family occurred, none of its members would "go into any further mourning dress, than a black crape or ribbon on the arm or hat for gentlemen and a black ribbon and necklace for ladies."

Such details, however insignificant they may appear today, were of major importance to the American colonists and helped to strengthen their resolve and determination. The demand that funerals be conducted in a modest fashion was obeyed, and soon it became a matter of pride in a given county that even rich people were being buried with much less pomp than before. The *South Carolina Gazette* of December 19, 1774, reporting the death of a wealthy woman, noted that "few had more friends than this most amiable and excellent lady, yet [Paragraph 2] of the 8th Article of the Continental Association was strictly adhered to at her Funeral."[18]

Articles 11 and 12, as well as certain provisions of Articles 5, 6, and 10, were devoted to implementing Congress's decision to subject England to an economic boycott. The Association declared that when a merchant was detected violating the agreement, "we will not, from thenceforth, have any commercial connexion with such merchant" (Articles 5 and 6). Indeed, the authors of the Association went further: Article 11 stressed that in each county, small town, and city, those enjoying the right to vote in elections to the assemblies should elect a special committee. The main task of these committees would be "attentively to observe the conduct of all persons" toward the Association and to discover and investigate violations of its provisions. If the committee concluded that violations had indeed taken place, it was to inform

18. Quoted from David L. Ammerman, "The Continental Congress" (Ph.D. diss., Cornell University, 1966), 141.

the local newspaper immediately of the names of the perpetrators, who would be publicly condemned "as the enemies of American liberty." Everyone was to sever all contacts with such persons. Moreover, entire cities and provinces, when they failed to comply with the provisions of the Association, were to be subjected to the same kind of ostracism.

The Congress did not issue specific instructions for implementing the articles of the Association, except for the guidelines contained in Article 10. As a result, the elected local committees were in a position to determine their own course of action. In most cases the committees wielded broad powers, and their activities were only partly under the control of the local authorities. In fact, the Association specified that the existing committees of correspondence were to maintain contact with the elected committees, supervise their activities, and exchange with them any information pertaining to the implementation of the Association's provisions. Moreover, each colony had the right to adopt any measure necessary for the enactment of the Continental Association.[19]

In the final paragraph of the Association, the delegates promised on behalf of their electors to obey its provisions until Parliament repealed all the acts listed in the text. It is worth noting that the entire list of the grievances contained in the Association was included without any changes in the Declaration of Independence.[20]

The economic program adopted by the First Continental Congress was a significant and striking development in the anticolonial movement of the American provinces. Although many of the colonies had already undertaken measures such as the severing of commercial ties, what distinguished the Association was the scale on which the decisions of the Congress to suspend trade with England were to be carried out. Carl Becker, the noted historian of the American Revolution, called this the "nationalization" of the principle of nonimportation that had hitherto been purely local.[21]

Some American historians have argued that there is a certain similarity between the decisions of the colonial assemblies and the Association. Such a view appears valid. First, the very term "association" in the sense of "agreement" was mainly used in the southern colonies.[22] A comparison of the text of the Continental Association with that of the resolutions of the colonial assembly in Virginia shows a clear connection between the two. In turn, the Virginia Association duplicated the plan that had earlier been drawn up in Fairfax County.

The resolutions adopted by the voters of Fairfax County at a meeting on July 10, 1774, had been drafted by George Mason.[23] The most prominent figure present at this meeting was George Washington, who took an active part in the discussions of these resolutions both in Fairfax and later at the provincial congress. Washington's interest

19. *Journals of the Continental Congress,* ed. Ford et al., vol. 1, 79–80.

20. John Adams, *Works,* ed. Charles F. Adams, 10 vols. (Boston, 1850), vol. 2, 377.

21. Becker, *Political Parties,* 152.

22. *Journals of the Continental Congress,* ed. Ford et al., vol. 1, 75. For an etymology of the term "association" in the sense of "agreement," see J. F. Jameson, "The Association," *Annual Report of the American Historical Association* (Washington, 1920), 303–13.

23. Douglas S. Freeman, *George Washington: A Biography,* 7 vols. (New York, 1948–1957), vol. 3, 366.

in the matter and his direct involvement in the publication of these resolutions are confirmed by the fact that an original copy of one of the resolutions was found among his personal papers. Moreover, before the meeting Washington and Mason spent a long time in conversation,[24] probably discussing the resolutions. It would be reasonable to suppose that Washington subsequently brought a copy of the Fairfax Association to the Virginia provincial assembly, where the Virginia Association was adopted. The Virginia delegates to the Continental Congress then took it to Philadelphia.

It is significant that the author of the Fairfax resolutions, when outlining the steps to be undertaken by the colonists at the county and provincial level, was in fact putting forward a comprehensive plan of action for the entire continent. Like the Continental Association, the resolutions adopted by the county meeting began by stating that for constitutional reasons the colonists refused to obey the acts of the British Parliament and then listed the acts in question. Next, the citizens of Fairfax approved the idea of a colonial union and called for the summoning of a special Continental Congress that would implement the Fairfax Association throughout the continent.[25]

The measures to be employed in the struggle against the laws passed by Parliament and the plans for putting those measures into effect were almost identical to the ones proposed in the Continental Association: nonimportation of goods was to begin soon, while nonexportation was to be suspended until the fall of 1775.[26] Moreover, both the Fairfax and the Virginia associations banned the buying and selling of slaves during the time imports were forbidden. This provision was also included in the Continental Association.[27]

As for halting all trade with the mother country, the Fairfax resolutions stated that goods imported into the colonies in contravention of the agreement were either to be returned or were to be stored in a warehouse by the local committees. Merchants were to swear a public oath that they would not use these goods, and if a merchant refused to take such an oath, the committees had the right to inform the public so that his neighbors would know that he was an enemy of his country.[28]

None of the articles in the Fairfax resolutions provided for a ban on the use of goods imported from the mother country, and the resolutions did not contain any instructions concerning the election of a special committee in each locality. Apparently it was expected that the existing Committees of Correspondence would discharge these new functions. The Virginia Association stated, however, that the signatories to the agreement were to elect special committees in each county.[29]

The Fairfax resolutions foreshadowed the decisions of the Continental Congress on two other points. The first of these concerned the establishment of incentives for making the economy more independent of the mother country: the county meeting

24. Ibid.
25. *American Archives,* ed. Peter Force, 4th ser., 6 vols. (Washington, 1837–1858), vol. 1, 597–602.
26. Ibid., 600–601.
27. Ibid., 600, 687, 914.
28. Ibid., 600.
29. Ibid., 915.

decided to encourage local manufacturing and sheep breeding. The colonists were urged to follow the principles of "temperance, fortitude, frugality, and industry."[30] Second, the citizens of Fairfax County were to "sever all trade, intercourse, and dealings with any colony, province or city that evade or refuse to accept the plan adopted by the General Congress."[31] Although this provision was not included in the Virginia Association, it was to form part of the program adopted at Philadelphia.

There is such close similarity between the Virginia Association and the Continental Association that the texts are in places literally identical. Let us, for instance, take Article 6 of the Virginia Association and Article 7 of the Continental Association. The Virginia Association says:

> We will endeavor to improve our breed of sheep, and increase their number to the utmost extent; and to this end we will be as sparing as we conveniently can, in killing of sheep, especially those of the most profitable kind, and if we should at any time be overstocked, or can conveniently spare any, we will dispose of them to our neighbours, especially the poorer sort of people, upon moderate terms.[32]

The Continental Association says:

> We will use our utmost endeavors to improve the breed of sheep, and increase their number to the greatest extent; and to that end, we will kill them as seldom as may be, especially those of the most profitable kind; nor will we export any to the West-Indies or elsewhere; and those of us, who are or may become overstocked with, or can conveniently spare any sheep, will dispose of them to our neighbours, especially of the poorer sort, on moderate terms.

Further evidence of the similarity between the texts of the Virginia Association and the Continental Association is provided by the article that forbade merchants to raise their prices. Here it would be instructive to compare the texts of three different Associations.

The Fairfax Association reads

> and that merchants and venders of goods and merchandise within this colony ought not to take advantage of our present distress, but to continue to sell the goods and merchandise which they now have, or which may be shipped to them before the first day of September next, at the same rates and prices they have been accustomed to do within one year last past; and if any person shall sell such goods on any other terms than above expressed, that no inhabitant of this colony should, at any time forever thereafter, deal with him, his agent, factor or storekeeper for any commodity whatsoever. [33]

The Virginia Association reads

> merchants and other venders of goods and merchandise within this Colony ought not to take advantage of the scarcity of goods that may be occasioned by this

30. Ibid., 600.
31. Ibid., 601.
32. Ibid., 687–88.
33. Ibid., 600.

association. . . . They ought to sell the same at the rates they have been accustomed to for twelve months last past; and if they shall sell any such goods on higher terms, or shall in any manner, or by any devise whatever, violate or depart from this resolution, we will not, and are of opinion that no inhabitant of this Colony ought, at any time thereafter, to deal with any such person, their factors or agents, for any commodity whatever.[34]

The Continental Association reads:

Such as are venders of goods or merchandise will not take advantage of the scarcity of goods, that may be occasioned by this association, but will sell the same at the rates we have been respectively accustomed to do, for twelve months last past.—And if any vender of goods or merchandise shall sell any such goods on higher terms, or shall, in any manner, or by any devise whatsoever violate or depart from this agreement, no person ought, nor will any of us deal with any such person, or his or her factor or agent, at any time thereafter, for any commodity whatsoever.[35]

Although many provincial and local meetings proposed measures resembling the ones that were approved by the Continental Congress, it probably would be difficult to find other examples of such striking textual similarity. Indeed, almost every provision of the Continental Association was already contained in the Fairfax resolutions or the Virginia Association. The only provision in the two Virginia documents absent from the Continental Association was the resolve decreeing that merchants should swear an oath that they would obey the terms of the agreement. Nevertheless, after the Congress completed its work, the inhabitants of every county in Virginia were obliged publicly to place their signatures under the text of the Continental Association, even though it contained no such requirement: this was an example of revolutionary improvisation on the part of the Virginians.

Everything that has been said here can lead only to this conclusion: George Mason and George Washington were in all probability the joint authors of the Continental Association.

On October 22, after the delegates to the Congress signed the Association, they decided to reassemble in Congress on May 10, 1775. The Congress finished its work on October 26, 1774.[36] The reaction of the majority of Americans to the Association was enthusiastic, and its provisions were implemented quickly and efficiently. The Association gained the approval of all the colonies except Georgia. In accordance with Article 14, South Carolina then declared a boycott of Georgia. Its example was followed by Pennsylvania and Maryland, and then by New York, Virginia, and New Jersey.

In summing up the results of the successful operation of the Continental Association, one should note the following figures (in thousands of pounds sterling):

34. Ibid., 683.
35. *Journals of the Continental Congress,* ed. Ford et al., vol. 1, 78.
36. Ibid., 85.

Imports

	1774	**1775**
New England	563	72
Virginia & Maryland	529	6
New York	438	1
The Carolinas	378	6
Pennsylvania	626	1
Georgia	57	113

The total level of imports to the colonies thus fell by 97 percent.[37]

The reaction in England to the Association adopted by the First Continental Congress was violent. George III described it as an attempt to destroy the trade of the empire.[38]

After the resolves forbidding the import of goods from the mother country had been in effect for four and a half months, several developments resulted in the Association becoming more than just a protest measure; it assumed the force of martial law. The events at Lexington and Concord showed that the Association no longer made sense as a device aimed at forcing Parliament to repeal its acts and that its efficacy could be restored only if it were amended. Upon the outbreak of hostilities the Committees of Correspondence in the colonies began to introduce the necessary changes into the Association. First of all, the ban on exports, which was originally planned for the beginning of September 1775, was advanced to a much earlier date.[39] Moreover, throughout the colonies defense associations (that is, agreements) were concluded. To achieve their now paramount military goals, the colonists changed the purpose of the Continental Association; by the middle of 1775 the Association had in many ways changed out of all recognition. The Second Continental Congress approved all the changes in the Association that had been dictated by the new reality.[40]

The First Continental Congress's adoption of the Association marked a new departure in the growing Revolutionary movement of the colonists. First, by giving the Association the force of law the Congress approved the policy of economic resistance to England by all the American provinces; the Congress can be said to have "nationalized" this policy. Second, the provisions of the Association not only provided for a boycott of England but also described the measures for putting it into effect.

37. *Annals of Commerce,* ed. MacPherson, vol. 3, 563–65, 585.

38. *The Correspondence of King George the Third,* ed. G. Fortesque, 6 vols. (London, 1927–1928), vol. 3, 154. For a more detailed account of the reaction in England to the adoption of the Association, see Paul Ford, "The Association of the First Congress," *Political Science Quarterly* 6 (1891), 615–24.

39. Schlesinger, *Colonial Merchants,* 599.

40. Ibid., 559–63.

After the Congress concluded its deliberations, committees of inspection charged with watching over the implementation of its decisions appeared throughout the length and breadth of the colonies. Third, the Association provided for the development of manufacturing in the colonies, which was in the objective interests of American society.

By adopting the Association, the First Continental Congress declared itself in favor of radical means for carrying out the struggle against the policy of the mother country and thus brought the events of Lexington and Concord and the ultimate secession of the colonies closer.

COMMENT BY RONALD HOFFMAN

In 1813 John Adams reminisced to Thomas Jefferson about the character of the First Continental Congress. "America," observed Adams, "is in total ignorance, or under infinite deception concerning that assembly. To draw the characters of them would require a volume, and would be considered as a caricature print; one third Tories, another Whigs and the rest mongrels." Adams's point, however humorous, cannot be missed: the First Congress contained differences of opinion that were wide and deep. While M. O. Troyanovskaya understands this reality, she needs to give greater emphasis to the divided context that informed the Congress's policies and actions. Essentially, the author must address two points if her account, originally published in 1980, is to achieve greater meaning. First, the pattern of sharp social and political conflict that preceded the meeting of the First Congress and that influenced its decisions requires more extended attention. The climate of rancor and passion that swept through the colonies constitutes an indispensable perspective from which to interpret and assess the significance of the first gathering of their representatives in Philadelphia. Second, the author's value-free descriptive treatment of the Congress must be joined with a more analytical approach if historians are to derive any real benefit from her work.

Troyanovskaya begins her account of the First Congress by noting that its meeting was the product of "the rise in the revolutionary consciousness of the inhabitants of the colonies, which had led the thirteen hitherto disunited provinces to join together in common protest." Presumably, the author is using the term "disunited" to describe what Adams intended when he referred to the colonies as "thirteen clocks." But if the colonies were divided externally in 1774, they were also beset by internal divisions as well. No one can gainsay that by 1774 a revolutionary consciousness had swept through the colonies in the wake of Great Britain's passage of the Coercive Acts—indeed, it was a movement similar to the *"rage militaire"* that would erupt in the aftermath of the fighting at Lexington and Concord. Nonetheless, neither the revolutionary consciousness of 1774 nor the *rage militaire* of 1775 embraced all segments of the population—the social reality of Revolutionary colonial society was far more complex than such terms suggest.

Take Virginia first. As Troyanovskaya argues, Virginia—uncharacteristically, I might note—took the lead in opposing British policy in 1774. There local committees called for the support of Boston and the adoption of a program of nonimportation and nonexportation to eliminate all commercial ties with Great Britain. The call for nonimportation was traditional since the tactic had been applied during the Stamp Act and Townshend Acts confrontations, and it met with little opposition. But the bolder concept of nonexportation encountered stiff resistance from the beginning, as did another grassroots suggestion—a moratorium on all debt payments to British merchants and the closure of the colony's courts. When the Virginia convention commenced its deliberations on August 1, 1774, the divisions among the delegates were compromised by the adoption of a plan that scheduled the start of nonimportation for November 1, 1774, and nonexportation before August 10,

1775. The call for nonpayment of debts and the dissolution of the courts was rejected.

Elsewhere the forces advocating militant resistance fared less well. In New York and Philadelphia and even to some degree in Boston, the merchants and their conservative allies fought the radical Whigs to a near draw during the first round of reaction to the Boston Port Act. Ultimately in these cities a series of compromise resolutions and positions was passed, none of them as specific as those of Virginia. In the northern colonies, memories of the property destruction that had occurred during the opposition to the Stamp Act and the fragmented and ineffectual boycotts that had been undertaken in resistance to the Townshend Acts persuaded mercantile men of wealth and their political colleagues to act vigorously in opposing any precipitous action that might result in renewed violence and disorder. Although they failed in their goal of preventing the Congress from convening, two of the major delegations to it, New York and Pennsylvania, were dominated by conservatives. In Massachusetts, Samuel Adams and his supporters fared better, but only after intense maneuvering and through the use of irregular tactics. Both Samuel and John Adams knew they had been in a fight and that the opposition to their policies in Boston and throughout the province had been formidable. Many in Massachusetts, throughout New England, and in other regions of British North America remained skeptical of the program advanced by the radical Whigs and resented enduring the economic sacrifices called for by the policies of nonimportation and especially nonexportation.

This concern with context leads to my second point, and here I want to draw M. O. Troyanovskaya out somewhat further on her interpretation of the causal factors that were central to the coming of the American Revolution. Nearly two decades ago, Michael Kammen referred to a "kind of cold war" that had been going on between the political economy–minded partisans of Merrill Jensen and the ideologically committed disciples of Bernard Bailyn. While Kammen's description was relatively accurate then, the range of important scholarship has expanded considerably, and the interpretative thrusts that presently define the coming of the Revolution can no longer be neatly placed into two discrete schools. Nevertheless, if the terms Whig and neo-Whig and Progressive and neo-Progressive have lost some of their antediluvian specificity, it is still possible to draw two broadly different approaches to the motivational forces and sequence of activity that preceded the War of Independence.

In an influential essay published in 1976, Bailyn argues that the coming of the Revolution can best be understood in "ideological terms." Other dimensions, he contends, were relatively insignificant: "The outbreak of the Revolution was not the result of social discontent, or of economic disturbances, or of rising misery, or one of those mysterious social strains that seem to beguile the imaginations of historians straining to find peculiar predispositions to upheaval." Instead, Bailyn locates the central explanation for the Revolution in a crude, incomplete, and unformalized constellation of values and perceptions that had evolved among the American colonists for a century and a half. This cluster of beliefs, Bailyn maintains, lay at the heart of the Revolutionary movement and shaped its outcome and consequences. Defined by historians as "republican ideology" for more than twenty years—though not explicitly formulated as such by Bailyn in his acclaimed *The Ideological Origins of the American Revolution* (1967)—these ideas are credited with providing a common framework for Revolutionary America—an ideological context that habituated the colonists to perceive British policy as a conspiracy against their liberty that demanded a vigorous reaction. Of classical origin, this ideology opposed concentrated wealth and power, standing armies, and bureaucracies, and as resurrected by Florentine writers during the Renaissance, it was used to explain why republics, the most sublime form of political governance, had invariably proven to be such fragile entities. Carried forward again by seventeenth-century English opposition writers and mixed by them with the property-centered traditions of medieval English common law, such ideas provided a similarly compelling explanation of the forces that had corrupted the English state. And even though Parliament's expanding sphere of influence partially muted their effect in England during the first half of the eighteenth century, these ideals flourished in the faction-ridden environment of British North America.

Gordon Wood extends and elaborates Bailyn's analysis in his enormously influential book *The Creation of the American Republic, 1776–1787* (1969), the first section of which examines the ideological rhetoric that motivated the colonies to revolution. Wood accepts at face value the Whigs' explanations for their opposition to British policy in the 1760s and 1770s. Although maddening at times in his ambivalence— he flirts continually with social aspirations and economic tensions as motivating influences—Wood ultimately argues that the Whigs were pursuing justice rather than power. Equally important, he contends that the Revolutionaries were absolutely sincere when they professed as their motivation the creation of a just and virtuous society, a complex of sentiments that he more recently has argued drew inspiration from the enlightened and benevolent ideas of eighteenth-century Masonic thought. Central to Wood's analysis of republicanism is the concept of virtue—that a successful republic required its leaders and citizens to sacrifice their personal interest willingly for the greater good of the whole. The salient problem for the Revolutionary leaders of the 1770s, Wood maintains, was that they recognized that their society was not virtuous. These men—these "disinterested patriots"—pushed the colonies into the crucible of rebellion out of the conviction that a virtuous society would emerge. They believed that through the morally regenerative experience of revolution and especially the creation of republican governments, a restructured relationship of the citizen to the state would be established. Hence, Wood interprets the Whigs' decision for revolution as a purifying and redemptive transition to the creation of a virtuous republic: "What ultimately convinced the Americans that they must revolt in 1776 was not that they were naturally and inevitably republican, for if that were truly the case, evolution not revolution, would have been the eventual solution. Rather it was the pervasive fear that they were not destined to be a virtuous and egalitarian people that in the last analysis drove them into revolution in 1776."

Subsequent to the work of Bailyn and Wood, other scholars have extended and deepened our understanding not only of the language of republicanism but also of the languages of discourse that informed the world of England and her North American colonies. The most notable of these, the corpus of sentiments and beliefs associated with liberalism that Joyce O. Appleby and others have so powerfully reconstructed has constituted a major challenge to the dominance of republican ideology. The liberal values posited by these scholars have particularly influenced interpretations of the constitution and the post-1790 social and economic development of the United States. The relevance of liberal convictions for the coming of the American Revolution has also been suggested, although less concretely demonstrated.

The elaboration of ideology that characterizes the writings of the republican or civic humanist and liberal schools has also contributed significantly to the efforts of scholars to reconstruct the context of perception for other classes besides elites. Inspired and encouraged by the work of Jesse Lemisch and Alfred F. Young, these historians have recovered the political, ideological, and religious experiences and visions of persons that traditional narratives of the Revolution either treated too narrowly or entirely left out. The new range of vantage points is as broad as human society and includes enslaved men and women, artisans, seamen, ordinary farmers, middle-class women, indentured servants, and Indian nations.

While no one can gainsay the enormous advances made possible by the historians of political and cultural language, the comprehensive applicability of their argument regarding the coming of the American Revolution is still severely tested by another tradition of interpretation, the Progressive or neo-Progressive school. The best of this work includes and is an extension of the scholarship of Carl Becker, Arthur Schlesinger Sr., and Merrill Jensen, all of whom M. O. Troyanovskaya cites in her essay. This scholarship incorporates several essential elements. First—and this needs to be emphasized for the record—the most able of these writers never eschew the power of ideas. But they strongly contend that all of an individual's experiences and circumstances must be weighed when accounting for behavior. Second, the best of these scholars clearly reject any form of economic determinism. As Carl Becker wrote in 1909, "the motives of individuals are rarely so simple as that, the motives of classes, never." The core of the Progressive argument is not fixated on political economy but maintains instead that opportunism, the quest for power, and an individual's position in society account for the pattern of struggle that developed between Great Britain and her mainland North American colonies. This emphasis does not vitiate ideological commitments as a motivational factor, but it does contend that the driving force actuating pre-Revolutionary politicians was the acquisition of power.

Stated explicitly, the Progressive tradition and the most astute of the neo-Progressive writers assume that people respond to a given situation by trying to determine its implications for individuals. The people's conclusions—which are mediated by their interests—shape their actions and reactions. In contending that the Revolution's leaders and followers were "interested," the Progressives and their contemporary fellow travelers reason that the motives of all the actors in the imperial drama were influenced by a variety of considerations that included a desire for power, a commitment to principle, and the pursuit of social and economic advancement. Moreover, to be "interested" is not equated in Progressive scholarship with being evil, manipulative, or hypocritical—though any or all were possible—but rather with being influenced by the range of circumstances built into the environment. One of the most decisive of these realities is a subject central to M. O. Troyanovskaya's discussion of the First Continental Congress—specifically, the vast array of experiences and interests that existed within the colonies and that made the creation of unity exceedingly difficult. To mold from this diversity a viable constituency constituted the single greatest challenge that the opponents of Great Britain faced, and in this process the use of an ideological rhetoric that reflected the fears and interests of both the authors and the people was essential. Certainly the content of that rhetoric was important, but so too were the uses to which it was put. And sometimes—how frequently no one can say—that rhetoric may have masked the real motives of the Revolutionaries, even from themselves. For the Progressive and neo-Progressive historians, ideological discourse can be properly understood and its causal impact assessed only within the context of the events actually taking place and with reference to the particular circumstances of the individual participants. And it is only through this process of historical analysis that a comprehensive interpretation can be advanced to explain why human beings are willing—or can be induced—to take grave risks at times of disorder, confusion, and danger.

As an example of the differing approaches of these two historical schools of interpretation, let us take the enormously complicated period from Britain's repeal of the Stamp Act in 1766 to its passage of the Tea Tax in 1772. The Progressive tradition reconstructs these years within a format that takes into account a diversity of social and economic realities—ideology, religion, commodity prices, currency regulations, occupational structures, and the varied experiences of elites and ordinary people. The conclusion is that all of these conditions shaped and tempered anti-British sentiment and action. What this perspective illuminates is the welter of confusion generated as the filter of individual circumstances produced contradictory patterns of behavior. Within the colonies and especially the cities—the centers of resistance—a patchwork of shifting alliances formed and disintegrated. In the absence of any clear direction, various groups—impassioned Whigs, merchants, conservative elites, and laboring classes—sought to position themselves for maximum advantage.

In contrast to the Progressive perspective, the neo-Whig or republican school posits an entirely different vision for those years. Rather than diversity and conflict, the historians of this interpretive persuasion stress uniformity and purposefulness as colonies cohered by the traditions of shared ideology moved inexorably toward independence. Within this framework of analysis, the Progressive emphasis on the differences of pre-Revolutionary America in terms of class, popular aspirations, and intensely competing interests is dismissed or relegated to a theme of secondary significance.

Similarly, the two schools present sharply different portrayals of the years 1774–1776. Again, while neo-Whig scholars emphasize how ideology provided a bedrock consensus for independence, the Progressives stress two desperate struggles—one within the empire, the other within the colonies. From the initial stirrings of local activity through the elaborate extralegal organizations mandated by the First Continental Congress's adoption of the Continental Association, militant Whigs and moderate men, according to the Progressives, fought each other for positions of power that would give to the victor the opportunity to direct the future course of events. In general, the conservatives more than held their own. For men whose souls were, according to neo-Whig scholars, allegedly on fire with the "contagion of liberty," the leaders in many colonies behaved with remarkable restraint, a posture that was approved by some of the substantial elements of the citizenry and disapproved by others. Well aware of the extent to which other social realities constrained his passion for independence, John Adams provided a typically cogent metaphor for those years. "America," he wrote to his wife, "is a great unwieldy body. Its progress must be slow. It is like a large fleet sailing under convoy. The fleetest sailors must wait for the dullest and slowest."

My asking M. O. Troyanovskaya to set her essay within the context of the historiography of the coming of the American Revolution may seem somewhat uncharitable since she does not address the Revolution's causal linkage. However, the topics with which she is concerned—the economic policies of the First Continental Congress and that body's divisions over economic forms of retaliation—cannot be properly understood without a consideration of the circumstances and variety of motives that brought the delegates to Philadelphia in September 1774. Troyanovskaya's views in this regard would be especially interesting in terms of the revolutionary tradition within which she wrote her essay in 1980 and the demands for rethinking and reinterpretation inherent in that ideological system's subsequent demise. A far less cosmic but nevertheless visible process of reconceptualization is currently underway in Western scholarship as historians attempt to contextualize and reinterpret the American Revolution within new cultural, geographic, and epistemological landscapes. In both cases it will be interesting to see whether these mutual shifts in revolutionary perspectives yield new knowledge and fresh and imaginative insights.

RESPONSE BY MARIA O. TROYANOVSKAYA

I cannot but express my gratitude with the very thorough analysis of Ronald Hoffman's commentary on my essay regarding the economic policies of the First Continental Congress and—in particular—its adoption of the Association. However, the main point that he makes is that I have not clarified sufficiently "the context that formed the Congress's policies and actions" and "the political conflict that preceded the meeting of the First Congress," and—in still more general terms—"the social reality of Revolutionary colonial society." Presumably, in order to fill that gap Hoffman himself goes on to describe the state of Revolutionary sentiments in the colonies beginning with Virginia and including New York, Philadelphia, and Boston. This very valuable information could, in my view, form part of a more comprehensive study of the Continental Congress, which is known to have been undertaken by Jack N. Rakove, *The Beginnings of National Politics* (1979) and J. C. Marsden, *King and the Congress* (1987) as well as by a number of publications by H. James Henderson.

The purpose of my essay, which was written in 1978 and happened to be my first publication, was to examine the economic policies of the First Continental Congress, the genesis of the ideas that formed the basis of the final text of the Association and of the political realities in the context of which it was discussed and subsequently adopted. The other important decisions by the Congress—such as the adoption of the radical Suffolk Resolves and of the Declaration of the Rights and Grievances, which in a certain sense was the forerunner of Jefferson's Declaration of Independence, etc.—I found possible to mention only in passing.

As for the period preceding the First Continental Congress, there, too, I dwelt only on the economic aspects of the life of the colonies and on the cases where trade with Britain was restricted. I also consciously left aside such important and interesting topics as the causal factors that are essential to the coming of the American Revolution. It was the changing interpretation of these factors that influenced America's historiography ("Progressive" or "neo-Progressive" school versus the so-called ideological school) throughout the twentieth century. What Ronald Hoffman has to say about this is very interesting and valuable. Especially thought-provoking was Hoffman's assertion that very often ideological rhetoric might have masked the genuine incentives (*including* the economic ones) that determined the conduct of the American Revolutionaries, bearing in mind the wide specter of long- and short-term interests that were characteristic of Britain's American colonies before—and even after—the Declaration of Independence. This diversity of opinion can partially explain the conflict among the Revolutionaries over not only the problem of the legal and philosophical basis of the relationship between the colonies and Britain but also the internal consequences for the colonies—should independence be declared.

Since the publication of my article in 1980, no further research in the Soviet Union has been devoted to the activities of the First Continental Congress. That being so, the very interesting and imaginative ideas put forth by Ronald Hoffman could in the future provide guidelines for me if I were to decide to deal once again with the problems prior to the War of Independence.

CHAPTER 7

The Financial Legislation of the Continental Congress, 1775–1783

by

O. V. Kriuchkova

Even today American scholars still engage in heated debate over the financial activities of the Second Continental Congress. The polemic was begun at the end of the last century by the appearance of the works of the historians Albert S. Bolles and Charles J. Bullock.[1] These authors severely criticized the financial policies of Congress in the period prior to 1780, that is, during the time when the Congress was most susceptible to pressure from the democratic camp of the Revolution—the popular masses. Measures adopted by Congress such as its campaign against profiteers and hoarders of goods and its declaration that paper money was legal tender for the payment of private debts, etc., undoubtedly met the demands of the working people of America and aroused the hatred and anger of the property-owning sections of the country. It was the position of the latter that was reflected in the works of the American historians of the late nineteenth century. Moreover, late-nineteenth-century events apparently influenced these authors. For example, in the 1870s the country was shaken by the movement of the Greenbackers, whose main demand was the issuance of "cheap" paper money and silver coins. The farmers believed that this would make it easier for them to pay their debts. In the 1880s and 1890s numerous populist organizations repeated these demands. Hoping to prove the senselessness of this movement, the above-mentioned historians decided to treat similar events of the eighteenth century as an instructive example.

In the 1940s analogous judgments were made in two studies, John C. Miller's *Triumph of Freedom, 1775–1783* and Homer C. Hockett's *Political and Social Growth of the American People, 1492–1865.*[2] These historians reproached Congress for subjecting the country to terrible inflation with its policy and for inflicting irreparable

---

1. Albert S. Bolles, *Financial History of the United States from 1774 to 1789, Embracing the Period of the American Revolution* (New York, 1879); Charles J. Bullock, *Essays on the Monetary History of the United States* (New York, 1900). This article by O. V. Kriuchkova was first published in *American Studies Annual for 1975* (Moscow, 1975).

2. John C. Miller, *Triumph of Freedom, 1775–1783* (Boston, 1948); Homer C. Hockett, *Political and Social Growth of the American People, 1492–1865* (New York, 1944).

harm upon the moral qualities of Americans (in their opinion the financial activities of the Congress had crushed the naive idealism of their compatriots and engendered in them the insatiable desire to make money). The sympathies of these authors are wholly on the side of Robert Morris (the head of the financial department of the Confederation during the last period of the war), with his demonstration of respect for property, and his anticipation of certain aspects of Hamilton's policy.

In recent years the historian E. James Ferguson has reappraised the Bolles-Bullock conception.[3] In a study rich in factual material this author, developing the promising features of Charles A. Beard's economic ideas, attempts to discover the social roots of the financial policy of the Congress. Ferguson concludes that the demand for the issuance of paper money came from the agrarian sections of the population, whereas the measures undertaken by Robert Morris reflected the interests of the mercantile bourgeoisie and the landowners of the middle states. Of course Ferguson has a far-from-Marxist understanding of the class struggle during the period of the Revolution; his term "agrarian sections" of the population includes such heterogeneous forces as planters, the rural bourgeoisie, and farmers, but his desire to uncover the social pressures and interests lying behind the actions of Congress certainly deserves attention.

Don Higginbotham, a professor at the University of North Carolina, agrees with Ferguson's conclusions on a number of points.[4] In his study he sets out to prove that the issuance of paper money was the only measure to which Congress had recourse, and an unavoidable one; and inflation was caused by a number of objective factors relating to wartime conditions. His views of Morris's financial policy differ markedly from those of Ferguson. Ferguson regards Morris's policy as a reflection of the interests of the upper bourgeoisie and the creditors, while Higginbotham speaks of such abstractions as the desire to establish a more effective system of government, etc. Higginbotham's views, of course, represent a step back in comparison with Ferguson's conception.

This article attempts to analyze the financial policy of the Second Continental Congress, on whose activities the success of the American army on the field of battle and the very cause of American independence in many ways depended. Studying this subject is also important because until now, no Soviet historian has analyzed it.

When investigating the financial policy of the Congress it is necessary to consider these questions: what were its features at different stages of the war, in whose interests was it conducted, and what effect did it have on different sections of the population?

Three stages may be distinguished in the financial activities of the Congress. The first lasted from 1775 until 1779. During this period, Congress bore the entire burden of military expenditure, using paper money for this purpose. The excessive issuance of printed money led to inflation and price increases. Under pressure from the masses of the people and the congressional radical wing, the Congress was forced to declare war on the speculators and recommend maximum prices on goods.

3. E. J. Ferguson, *The Power of the Purse: A History of American Public Finance, 1776–1790* (Chapel Hill, 1961).

4. Don Higginbotham, *The War of American Independence: Military Attitudes, Policies, and Practice, 1763–1789* (New York-London, 1971).

During the second period (the end of 1779 to the beginning of 1781) Congress transferred some of the responsibility for supplying the army to the states, thus attempting to put its spending and revenue into a certain balance. In March 1780 Congress devalued the old paper money and issued new paper money, measures that turned out to be ineffective.

During the third period (1781–1783) the advocates of a strong central authority represented by Robert Morris, the head of the financial department, were in control of financial policy. Their policy included the establishment of a bank, the issuance of banknotes exchangeable for gold, a balanced budget, the introduction of federal taxes, and other measures whose ultimate aim was to strengthen the power of Congress.

The activities of Congress during the first period coincided with the most difficult stage of the war. In 1776 the English captured New York and in September 1777 the Americans evacuated Philadelphia. Although the American victory at Saratoga in October 1777 marked the turning point in the course of the war, the prospects of the young Republic still remained grave. From the first days of its existence the Continental Congress confronted a serious problem: how to finance the army? Congress lacked its own resources, it did not have the right to impose taxes on the population, the prospects for an internal loan seemed unpromising (the propertied classes would not lend money without a reliable guarantee of repayment of capital), and foreign loans were not to be hoped for. In order to pay for its spending, Congress then resorted to issuing paper money, which it declared equivalent to specie, and backed the convertibility of it by a public guarantee. On June 22, 1775, the Congress decided to issue $2 million (one paper dollar was declared equivalent to a silver Spanish dollar).[5] As military operations widened, the need for money increased. In 1777, the year that was the turning point of the entire war, Congress was obliged to issue currency every month and at times every two weeks. The total amount of paper money issued by Congress in 1775–1779 totaled $226 million; in addition the states issued the sum of $209 million in paper money.[6]

Members of the Continental Congress were aware that excessive issuance of paper money could have a deleterious effect on its rate of exchange. John Adams repeatedly declared that taxation by the states to remove the excessive amount of money represented the only means of preventing a devaluation of the dollar.[7] On July 29, 1775, Congress requested the state assemblies to collect taxes in order to withdraw the first $3 million from circulation. Congress proposed that the number of inhabitants of all ages in each state, including blacks and mulattoes, should determine the sum to be contributed in taxes by each assembly. The sums were to be paid in four annual installments from November 1779 to November 1782 inclusively (it was

5. *Journals of the Continental Congress, 1774–1789,* ed. Worthington Chauncey Ford et al., 34 vols. (Washington, D.C., 1904–1937), vol. 2, 103, 105.

6. Ferguson, *Power of the Purse,* 30.

7. *Letters of Members of the Continental Congress,* ed. Edmund C. Burnett, 8 vols. (Washington, D.C., 1921–1936), vol. 2, 455.

anticipated that by 1779 military operations would have ceased).[8] The money thus collected was to be deposited in the Continental treasury, where it was to be destroyed. If the states proved unable to collect these sums in paper money, the shortage could be covered in specie.

The local authorities, however, were unable to adopt a policy of taxation for a number of reasons. First, it was an increase in taxation that had led to an explosion of anger by the colonists, and in the opinion of many Americans the continuation of such a policy by Congress would have been insane.[9] Second, the local governments themselves were just forming; they were weak and at times lacked real authority. The war had severed normal commercial links, so such sources of revenue as import and export duties had been temporarily cut off. Also because English military operations had brought chaos and disorder, the states had refrained from introducing taxation at the beginning of the war. The excessive issuance of paper money by Congress led in the autumn of 1777 to its depreciation.

The reverses suffered by the American army on the field of battle also contributed to the drop in the value of paper money. Monetary inflation spelled danger for Congress. To reestablish confidence in the currency, Congress published a report on December 28, 1778, stating that rumors that Congress would not redeem paper money with specie were false and confirming Congress's intention to make such an exchange when the war was over.[10]

Inflation meant a relentless rise in prices. In the autumn of 1779 in Philadelphia, one hundred pounds of flour cost $95, a hat, $400, a pair of shoes, $125, and a suit of clothes, $1,600.[11] But even at these prices many necessary items were unavailable.

Under these conditions of unprecedented price increases, persons receiving a fixed wage and, above all, the workers and the lower ranks in the army found themselves in a particularly difficult position. Under pressure first from these sections of the population, as well as from the radical group in Congress (Samuel Adams, Richard Henry Lee, and others), the state governments and Congress began to adopt measures aimed at reestablishing the value of paper money and combating speculation.

The actions taken by Congress included the following: a declaration that paper money was legal tender, recommendations to the states to control both prices and the cost of labor and services, the introduction of an embargo on the export of food products, a campaign against speculation, and a policy of confiscating hoarded goods. Starting in the spring of 1775, local governments began to declare paper money to be legal tender, and Congress in its turn requested that the assemblies legalize the status of the Continental currency.[12] On January 14, 1777, Congress recommended that the states adopt laws providing for the confiscation of goods that were sold for paper money at inflated prices.[13]

8. *Journals of the Continental Congress,* ed. Ford et al., vol. 2, 221–23.
9. Ibid., vol. 12, 1049.
10. Ibid., 1261.
11. George Stimpson, *A Book About American History* (Greenwich, Conn., 1962), 126.
12. Ralph Volney Harlow, "Aspects of Revolutionary Finance, 1775–1783," *American Historical Review* 35 (1929), 55.
13. *Journals of the Continental Congress,* ed. Ford et al., vol. 7, 35.

In addition to legislative efforts to keep the exchange value of the currency at the level of its nominal value, in 1776–1779 various steps were taken to control prices. In Congress Richard Henry Lee, a planter from Virginia; Samuel Chase from Maryland; and John Armstrong spoke passionately in defense of this policy. The policy was opposed by John Witherspoon, the president of Princeton College; Dr. Benjamin Rush from Pennsylvania; and the Pennsylvania lawyer James Wilson. First to adopt a policy of price control were the New England states. In December 1776 representatives from four states met in Providence, Rhode Island, and passed "an Act to prevent Monopoly and Oppression." The act set maximum prices for essential goods (clothing and food), regulated the wages of hired workers, established prices for imported goods, and set rates for interstate transportation of goods.[14]

In February 1777, after the local authorities had ratified this act, they referred it to Congress for discussion. In Congress the proponents of price control prevailed and they approved the act of the states of New England. Moreover, Congress suggested that the other states hold similar conventions. Representatives from New York, New Jersey, Pennsylvania, Delaware, Maryland, and Virginia were to meet in York, Pennsylvania, in March 1777, and delegates from North and South Carolina and Georgia were expected to assemble at Charleston.[15]

In the opinion of the American historian Ralph Harlow, the policy of price control represented the culmination of the Americans' naive belief in the power of law.[16] Such an interpretation of price control appears to be incorrect. Congress was aware that by themselves these legislative efforts to control prices could not produce the desired results unless they were conducted on a broad scale in all places and were accompanied by the withdrawing of surplus paper money from circulation and the discontinuing of new issues.[17] For a number of reasons (the weakness of central and local government, the lack of coordination between the actions of the radical wing in Congress, and those of the democratic elements in the country) the policy of price control was indeed unsuccessful, but it was a legitimate policy and it met the demands of the broad masses of working people. It is appropriate to mention here that the Jacobin government in 1793 also found the establishment of a maximum price for essential goods to be important.

The convention of the southern states failed to take place in May 1777, and the meeting at York collapsed after representatives from Maryland, Pennsylvania, and Delaware rejected the plan approved by Virginia, New Jersey, and New York.[18] In August 1777 the delegates of the regular meeting of New England in Springfield decided to abandon the policy of price control because of the discontent of well-to-do farmers who had been forced to sell their products at fixed prices.

14. Harlow, "Revolutionary Finance," 57.

15. *Journals of the Continental Congress,* ed. Ford et al., vol. 12, 124–25.

16. Harlow, "Revolutionary Finance," 54.

17. *Journals of the Continental Congress,* ed. Ford et al., vol. 12, 124; vol. 15, 1054; vol. 14, 649–50.

18. Curtis P. Nettels, *The Emergence of a National Economy, 1775–1815* (New York, 1962), 28.

In November 1777 Congress again recommended to the states that they should hold regional conventions. In response, in January 1778 in New Haven, Connecticut, delegates from the New England states and from New York, New Jersey, Pennsylvania, and Delaware met and discussed the question of price control, which, it was proposed, would be enforced in all states. But the interests of the various states clashed, making it impossible for them to reach a decision.[19] Seeing that the policy it had recommended had failed, Congress proposed in June 1778 the repeal of all acts relating to the fixing of prices.[20]

A new attempt to resurrect price controls was made in the middle of 1779 by a number of towns in New England and the western counties of the middle colonies (where vacant land had been settled mainly by poor farmers with an interest in purchasing goods at regulated prices). In October 1779 delegates from New York and from several towns in the northern states (Eastham, Boston, Plymouth, and others) met in Hartford. They drew up a plan, later recommended to the other states as the Hartford Plan, but growing inflation hampered its implementation.[21] As a result, the policy of price control was not conducted on a confederation-wide scale. Only in a few towns in New England, where workers and craftsmen were particularly strong, was the policy of price control put into effect.

Simultaneously with this policy, Congress developed methods for a campaign against speculators and persons hoarding food and essential goods. The congressional resolution of October 31, 1776, already contained a recommendation to the assemblies and committees of safety to adopt suitable measures against hoarders of goods. In such cases it was suggested that the goods be confiscated, with the owners being paid at low prices.[22] Congress enthusiastically greeted the initiative of the committee of safety of Pennsylvania, which in the winter of 1776 assumed the obligation of distributing the salt imported into the state, bypassing the merchant profiteers who were getting rich from the salt trade.[23] To regulate trade, Congress in December 1777 proposed that the states limit the number of individuals engaged in retail trade. According to Congress's plan, importers would have the right to sell goods only to those few who had been granted licenses to engage in retail trade. Those lacking such licenses would be forbidden to buy more goods than were necessary for personal consumption. Violating these regulations would result in a term of imprisonment.[24]

By the summer of 1778 Congress was confronted with a new problem. Since limits on price rises had not been introduced everywhere, merchants tended to transport goods to areas that did not have fixed prices and from these areas often sent them to other countries. Therefore, on June 4, 1778, Congress recommended that the states

19. Ibid.
20. *Journals of the Continental Congress,* ed. Ford et al., vol. 11, 569.
21. Nettels, *National Economy,* 29.
22. *Journals of the Continental Congress,* ed. Ford et al., vol. 6, 915–16.
23. Ibid., 1014–15.
24. Ibid., vol. 9, 1045.

stop the export of flour, wheat, rye, rice, beef, pork, and cattle beyond the borders of the country.[25] On June 8 Congress extended the embargo on these goods until November 15, 1778.[26] Commerce between the states was subject to strict regulations: Pennsylvania and other agricultural states to the south were allowed to export flour, grain, and rice only to the northern states and to sell them there at prices established by the authorities. In October 1778 the embargo on the export of food was extended until January 30, 1779, and in December 1779 extended further until April 1, 1780.[27] Congress extended the embargo because the profiteers had continued to purchase wheat in large quantities in the hope of resuming its sale at inflated prices upon the expiration of the embargo.

The actions of Congress directed at fighting the profiteers and hoarders of food stirred the broad masses of the people who, putting the proposals of Congress into practice, often went significantly beyond its recommendations. The congressional resolution of November 19, 1779, advised the states to establish prices for goods and charges for services that could exceed the prices existing in 1774 not more than twentyfold.[28] The Revolutionary masses vigilantly watched over the implementation of Congress's decisions, harshly punishing transgressors.[29] Thus in 1779 in Boston the case of Sarson Belcher, accused of selling beaver hats for a sum that exceeded by thirteen pounds the one fixed by the authorities, was tried in court.[30] Also in Boston in 1777, some people were banished for profiteering.[31] Simultaneously in New York, two soldiers of the Continental Army and a mob of neighboring women invaded the house of a tea merchant. Outraged by the speculative prices, they vandalized the merchant's warehouse and took away as much tea as they could carry.[32] Such incidents were far from isolated.

Thus the congressional policy of regulating prices and combating speculation objectively reflected the interests of the broad masses of farmers, workers, and craftsmen. It represented one of the radical thrusts of the Congress.

Clearly realizing that an important reason for depreciating the currency was the enormous quantity issued, Congress developed a series of measures aimed at withdrawing some of the paper money from circulation. One such measure was the requirement that the states should deposit a certain sum in banknotes with the Continental treasury by a particular date. On November 22, 1777, Congress demanded that the states pay $5 million into the treasury.[33] In order to deposit this sum, the

---

25. Ibid., vol. 11, 569.

26. Ibid., 578.

27. Ibid., vol. 12, 976; vol. 15, 1383.

28. Ibid., 1290.

29. For more on the struggle against the speculators see Richard B. Morris, "Labor and Mercantilism in the Revolutionary Era," in *The Era of the American Revolution: Studies Inscribed to Evarts Boutell Greene,* ed. Morris (New York, 1939), 129–30.

30. Ibid.

31. Ibid., 131.

32. Ibid.

33. *Journals of the Continental Congress,* ed. Ford et al., vol. 9, 955.

states were obliged to introduce taxation. But the withdrawal of such a small sum from circulation could not resolve the problem confronting Congress. That is why the resolution of January 2, 1779, provided for the payment into the treasury of another $15 million in 1779. The same resolution obligated the states to pay a further $6 million per annum in the next eighteen years.[34]

But all the efforts of Congress in the period before 1780 to reduce the amount of paper money in circulation and to find the sums needed to cover federal spending without resorting to new issues (both, however, at the expense of the states) turned out to be ineffective. The states resorted to taxation only reluctantly, and consequently money was deposited in the treasury very slowly.

Another measure of Congress that was designed to pay for its spending was the internal loan. Compared with the sums received from the payments made by the states, this measure brought more tangible results. The policy of internal loans began on October 3, 1776, with the issue of a loan of $5 million.[35] The holders of bonds were guaranteed a 4 percent interest per annum, and the principal was to be repaid after three years. The bonds were issued in values from three hundred dollars to one thousand dollars and were sold in all federal loan offices, which were created for this purpose in the states. At first subscription to the loan proceeded slowly, because the central government lacked authority and was unstable. Besides, the amount of the interest did not make purchase of the bonds particularly attractive. To stimulate business at the loan offices, a proposal was made in Congress to raise the interest to 6 percent. This proposal led in February 1777 to stormy debate in Congress, resulting in its approval.

The increase in the interest heightened the demand for bonds. By September 1, 1777, the total sum of paper money deposited with the loan offices amounted to approximately $3,787,000.[36] The receipt in the beginning of September 1777 of a secret subsidy of 2 million livres from France introduced yet another change in the policy of loans. A proposal was made in Congress to pay out the interest on all loans issued before March 1, 1778, in promissory notes drawn on that subsidy.[37] This measure was designed to increase significantly the number of bond holders. And indeed, subscription to the loans became a profitable affair. The loan offices accepted paper money at face value, whereas owing to inflation, its real value was significantly lower.

The total amount of money deposited with the treasury from the moment the policy of loans began equaled $67,077,000. The bonds were largely held by the affluent strata (merchants, the northern bourgeoisie, planters) and represented a lucrative way of investing capital. Particularly profitable were bonds bought with depreciating money before March 1, 1778. They were valued above other kinds of papers and remained largely in the hands of their first owners until the time the loans were

---

34. Ibid., vol. 13, 21–22.
35. Ibid., vol. 5, 845–46.
36. Davis R. Dewey, *Financial History of the United States* (New York, 1903), 46.
37. *Journals of the Continental Congress,* ed. Ford et al., vol. 8, 724.

repaid. Bonds purchased after March 1, 1778, guaranteed receipt of the interest in paper money, which represented only a small profit. But despite this, they became popular, mainly because merchants accepted them from the federal authorities in lieu of paper money. Such bonds were valued significantly more highly than paper money. When in September 1780 the depreciation of paper dollars reached the level of seventy-five to one, bonds issued in 1779 were sold at the exchange rate of twenty-four to one (in relation to specie).[38]

So as a result of the issuance of internal loans, Congress was able to collect certain sums, which were used to cover federal expenditures. But the pursuit of the loan policy meant in the first place the enrichment of the affluent strata, who converted their depreciated paper money into income-producing securities.

Foreign loans were an important source of congressional revenue. The advisability of resorting to them was the subject of passionate debate in Congress. The opponents of loans pointed out that the size of these subsidies would be strictly limited and that the loan provisions implied reliable guarantees of repayment, which Congress was not in a position to offer.[39] Despite these objections the views of the proponents of foreign aid prevailed, and by 1780 Congress had received a number of loans from France, Spain, and Holland. Their size during this period was not very large, but the most important thing was that these loans made possible the purchase of military equipment that was so urgently needed by the Continental Army.

The entire amount of foreign aid before 1780 consisted of the following sums:

1) Funds received from the French government: a subsidy in 1777 of 2 million livres, a loan in 1778 of 3 million livres, and a loan in 1779 of 1 million livres, amounting to a total of 6 million livres; funds received from the Beaumarchais's firm "Roderique Hortales and Co." amounting to 4.5 million livres; funds received from the company "Farmers General of France" amounting to 846,000 livres. The total amount of French assistance was in excess of 11 million livres (approximately $2.1 million).
2) Funds received from the Spanish government totaling 375,000 livres (approximately $70,000).
3) Funds received from Holland in the form of private loans totaling 80,000 florins ($32,000).[40]

Within the total sum of federal revenue, foreign assistance before 1780 amounted to the modest figure of $2,202,000 (or 4 percent). Therefore, the greater part of military spending was covered by internal funds, and in the final count the main burden of the war was borne by the working masses.

Spending by the Continental Congress in the period before 1780 amounted to the enormous sum of $263 million. Americans had known nothing like this in their entire previous history. It is quite understandable that fighting a war with such a powerful state as Great Britain required enormous sums of money. But at the same time one of the reasons for such large outlays was embezzlement within the machinery of federal

38. Ferguson, *Power of the Purse,* 40.
39. *Journals of the Continental Congress,* ed. Ford et al., vol. 12, 160.
40. Ferguson, *Power of the Purse,* 40–42.

government and the supply services of the army. In 1778–1779 a series of scandals involving profiteering in federal departments erupted in the country.

It is important to point out the clearly expressed contradictory character of Congress's financial policy in the period from 1775 to 1779. This was due both to pressure from the different social strata in American society as well as to the outcome of the struggle between opposing groups within the Congress itself.

Under pressure from the radical wing of the Revolution, Congress adopted a number of measures (such as the fixing of prices and the drive against speculators) that objectively reflected the interests of working America and that should have improved the situation of the broad masses of farmers, craftsmen, and the petty bourgeoisie. At the same time the entire complex of measures that developed and implemented the policy of internal loans testified to the victory of the bourgeois-planter bloc in solving financial problems.

On the whole the financial policy of Congress before 1779 reflected the bitter struggle between the democratic and the bourgeois-planter camps of the Revolution, a struggle in which, even with certain concessions on the part of the democratic forces, the conservative group was able to prevail. It was the working masses of America that carried the burden of the debilitating and protracted war with Great Britain.

By the end of 1779 the financial system of the Confederation was in a state of crisis. The outlays of Congress were enormous, and it was forced to resort to new issues, which led to the complete depreciation of the paper dollar. Also particularly large sums were spent on the quartermaster service and the army's food purchasing service. Their combined expenditure for the first three years of the war amounted to more than $51 million. In the spring of 1779 the financial department of Congress reported that, allowing for inflation, the outlays of these services would soon lead to catastrophic consequences for the Confederation. Moreover, the military situation was alarming. In 1780 military operations shifted to the southern states. In May the English captured Charleston, and in July the American General Horatio Gates was defeated at Camden.

At the end of 1779 Congress was feverishly searching for ways out of the crisis. During this time several plans involving the receipt of foreign financial assistance were considered. In August 1779 Henry Laurens, the former president of the Continental Congress, left for Holland to try to obtain a loan.

Because the procurement of loans from overseas entailed many difficulties and consumed much time, Congress stopped further issues early in September 1779. By September 1, 1779, the total amount of money in circulation had reached approximately $160 million; Congress then decided that the total amount of money issued would not exceed $200 million.[41]

A few days later, on September 13, Congress in an address to the states announced the reform of the army supply service. Under the new plan the provision of food to the army was entrusted entirely to the states in specific quotas. By this measure

41. *Journals of the Continental Congress,* ed. Ford et al., vol. 15, 1019.

Congress sought to free itself of the most onerous item of expenditure—provisioning the army.

In this way Congress initiated a new relationship with the states in which spending by the central authority began to be more in line with its revenues. Purchases previously made by federal agents now had to be made by local authorities. Since in 1779 the states had not in fact paid money into the treasury, the form of payment now took a different form—that of deliveries in kind. Objectively the new system had a number of advantages for Congress. First, at the prices existing at the end of 1779 and beginning of 1780, all Congress's money would still have been insufficient to make the purchases for the next campaign; second, it was expected that the absence of competition between the federal agents and the agents of the states would somewhat reduce the prices of goods; third, it was assumed that the implementation of the new policy would allow the states finally to fulfill congressional demands for the depositing of paper money, which would decrease its quantity and reestablish its value; and fourth, the need for the food purchasing service, the most ruinous of all for Congress, was obviated.

Congress issued its first demand for the supply of provisions on December 14, 1779.[42] The states were charged with supplying a certain amount of flour and wheat, with the value of the goods supplied automatically reducing the sums that the states had been obliged to deposit under the resolutions of 1777–1779. The congressional resolution of February 25, 1780, required the states to contribute large quantities of provisions and forage for the maintenance of the army. The purchases were to be made at fixed prices. Those states that had laid in the necessary supplies were freed of paying two-thirds of the money they were obliged to deposit with the treasury under the resolution of October 6, 1779.[43]

The new system of army supply was not totally free of shortcomings. It entailed some decentralization and implied a greater degree of dependence on the individual states. Often the required quantity of goods did not arrive by a specified date, the quantity was insufficient for the needs of the army, and the quality was sometimes inadequate. As a result Congress was unable to discontinue entirely the purchases made by its own agents.

In 1780 Congress embarked on another attempt to transfer part of military spending onto the shoulders of the states. It requested the states themselves to pay the wages of their army units, as well as the bonus due the troops as a result of inflation. Congress confirmed disbursement of pay by the states to the period ending on August 1, 1780. Some states—Massachusetts, Connecticut, Rhode Island, New Jersey, New York, Maryland, Virginia, and North and South Carolina—made payments to their troops in subsequent years as well, specifically in 1781 and 1782. To compensate for inflation-related losses in pay, soldiers were issued "military certificates," which later came to represent a significant part of the debt of the states.

42. Ibid., 1377.
43. Ibid., vol. 16, 196–97.

The attempt to make the states the guarantors of the new federal money was the logical conclusion of the new congressional policy. By the resolution of March 18, 1780, a new system of monetary circulation was introduced in the United States. Henceforth paper money was to be jointly guaranteed by the federal government and the states but issued and replaced only by the states themselves. The old paper money was tied to gold in the ratio of forty-to-one. The states were obligated to pay $15 million in old money or specie into the treasury every month.[44] The proposed reform was meant to provide Congress and the states with a significant income and a stable currency. But this measure was also unsuccessful.

At the beginning of 1780, Congress's financial problems remained. By the spring of 1780 the federal treasury was almost empty. On March 8, 1780, the treasury board reported that not more than a ten-day supply of bread remained in the warehouses.[45] During this period Congress began to resort on a large scale to paying merchants for their deliveries with bonds. From September 1779 until the end of 1781, Congress issued bonds in the enormous sum of $30 million. These bonds reflected not the sums deposited with the loan offices, but payments to merchants who had made deliveries.

Soon Congress embarked on the path of using certificates. These were used by the various auxiliary services of the army, particularly the quartermaster service and the food purchasing service. The certificates acted as a substitute for money and the value of the goods received was indicated on them. The certificate-based system of payment was closely linked to requisitions. When prices rose sharply in 1779, requisitions, which were made either by state commissioners or those appointed by Congress, became the main means of providing food and material supplies to the troops. It is difficult to estimate the total number of certificates issued. According to congressional data, by the beginning of 1781 the food purchasing service and the quartermaster's service had issued certificates in the sum of $95 million.[46]

The majority of certificates issued before 1780 were pieces of paper of no value that were often incorrectly filled out and issued by persons lacking the proper authority to do so. To put a stop to such practices, on August 23, 1780, Congress established a standard form for the certificates that stated the type of goods and services, the value in specie, the price, and the name of the service receiving the goods. The new certificates guaranteed an interest of 6 percent. This reform was meant to assuage the farmers who were refusing to produce more than they needed for personal consumption and to put an end to the clashes that took place between the population and the army commissioners during requisitions.

Wishing to strengthen confidence in the certificates, Congress on May 26, 1780, required the states to accept them as tax payments and to count the sums thus gathered toward the quotas the states were obliged to pay into the Continental treasury.[47] In this

44. Ibid., 262–67.
45. Ibid., 244.
46. Ibid., vol. 19, 165.
47. Ibid., vol. 17, 463.

way the problem of paper money came to be linked to the problem of the certificate-based debt.

Thus the beginning of 1781 signified the end of the second period in the financial policy of the Continental Congress. The huge deficit in the congressional budget during these years had finally led to a collapse of the system of paper money. The question arises: How did inflation affect the various sectors of the population?

First, inflation enormously enriched the propertied classes. During this period both the merchants, who, foreseeing the further depreciation of money, had raised the prices of goods, and the industrial bourgeoisie of the North, who became rich from the uncontrollable rise in the prices of goods outstripping the modest increases in workers' wages, were able to build up their fortunes significantly. Inflation afforded boundless scope for the activities of dealers and speculators of various types who followed price movements and were able to turn a depreciating currency into a source of guaranteed income by buying land, securities, and goods.

Second, inflation seriously affected those sections of the population that received a fixed wage. These were above all the workers and the soldiers and sailors of the Continental Army, which largely consisted of the poorest farmers and craftsmen who had been attracted by the prospect of receiving a wage, a piece of land, and an incentive bonus from the government. Calculations show that the total amount of money spent on the war equaled approximately $135 million in specie and that the postwar debt equaled approximately $66 million; that is, during the course of the war more than half of total spending had been largely at the expense of the broad masses of the working people.[48]

In the postwar period the ruling classes of America sought to redeem both the promissory notes that were in the hands of the poorer sections of the population (certificates), as well as the paper money; yet neither was redeemed at its face value but rather at its depreciated value, amounting to further plundering of the masses.

At the same time the bonds that were in the hands of the bourgeoisie and the merchant class of the northeast were the only type of security for which holders received compensation on favorable terms. In 1780 Congress recalculated the value of bonds in specie, as a result of which the value was substantially raised. In this way bonds purchased with depreciating money became a source of permanent income for their owners, since during the war Congress had guaranteed the receipt of regular interest payments, and upon the conclusion of military operations the bonds were declared to be equivalent to gold and silver specie in a manner advantageous to their holders. During the next period the holders of bonds—the creditors of the state—became one of the most active forces in the conservative grouping that campaigned for the establishment of a strong central authority capable of curbing the democratic elements in the country and transferring the payment of debts onto the shoulders of the broad masses of the people.

Thus the financial legislation of Congress in the period before 1781 led to the significant enrichment of the mercantile-industrial bourgeoisie of the northeast and

48. Ibid., vol. 19, 432–33; vol. 20, 455–56, 499.

the central states (and also the largest planters in the South), as a result of which their position converged with that of the conservative camp (the landowners of the middle states and the financial circles in the northeast). The struggle for a strong, conservative central authority became the common program of this bloc.

The period from 1781 to 1783 represents a new stage in the financial policy of Congress. The situation of the United States was perilous. The English had captured a number of important positions in the South. The Continental Army, maintained through requisitions that provoked the resentment of the population, at times was threatened by disbandment because of the shortage of stores and provisions. The bankrupt policy of issuing paper money and the parlous state of the finances of the Confederation raised the question: Would the rebellious provinces be able to prosecute the war further?

Dissatisfaction with the halfhearted activity of Congress, which was characteristic of the first six years of the war, resulted from pressure from both conservative and radical forces in the country and led to turmoil within the various classes.

On the one hand, the working masses demanded a more decisive struggle against the speculators and the embezzlers of public funds and expressed their outrage over Congress's cruel reprisals against soldiers, sailors, and the urban poor, who had been driven to despair. This democratic camp demanded an intensification of the Revolution.

On the other hand, the propertied classes (merchants, bourgeoisie, planters) were displeased with such congressional policies as price-fixing, trade embargoes, and the campaign against hoarders of food. The landowners of the central states condemned Congress's Revolutionary activity, the owners of securities wanted congressional guarantees of debt redemption, and both groups were interested in strong government authority as an instrument of coercion over the working masses. As a result, in 1780–1781 those with conservative views prevailed in a number of states. The composition of forces in Congress also changed to the conservatives' advantage.

In February 1781 these defenders of a strong central authority fundamentally reorganized the financial department, and Robert Morris, a Philadelphia merchant who expressed the interests of the rich merchants of Pennsylvania, was appointed its head. He was the co-owner of the large company Willing and Morris, and also had close business links with other trading companies. Morris demanded two conditions before accepting the position of head of the financial department: first, that he be allowed to continue his private commercial activities while on government service, and second, that he be granted the right to appoint and dismiss personnel not only in his own department but also in other departments involved in financial affairs. After a month-long discussion, these conditions were accepted.

Morris, having assumed his post, was soon able to broaden his initial powers. He established control over the naval department. The board of the admiralty and a number of other naval boards were abolished and their functions were transferred to Morris. Moreover, he came to control such important aspects of foreign policy as communication with American envoys abroad as well as questions relating to foreign loans. He was in charge of the import and export of goods belonging to the federal government, army supply, and the awarding of contracts to merchants.[49] His influence was strengthened by the fact that one of those who shared his views, Robert R. Livingston, became the head of the department of foreign affairs.

In Morris's wide-ranging plan for the reorganization of the country's finances, he gave highest priority to the creation of a stable paper currency guaranteed by gold and silver reserves. He proposed the establishment of a Bank of North America for this purpose. The total capital of the bank was to amount to $400,000 in silver or gold. He envisaged a board of seven directors to manage the activities of the bank. The bank would issue banknotes, exchangeable for silver or gold at the bearer's request; these notes could be used for the payment of debts and taxes. The creation of other banks of issue was to be prohibited.[50] The bank was to grant loans to the state, keep government financial funds, discount promissory notes, etc. It was assumed that this would be a mixed joint-stock bank with the participation of private and state capital. Morris's business partner Thomas Willing became the bank's president. The initial private capital of the bank amounted to $70,000, and Congress added $254,000. In the period between 1782 and 1784, the bank granted Congress short-term loans in the sum of $1,272,000.

Morris devoted particular attention to achieving a balanced budget. His activity was directed toward the maximum reduction of federal spending. The main source of revenue for Congress during this period was foreign loans, which had grown considerably in comparison with previous years. Besides foreign assistance, Morris was able to obtain substantial contributions from the states. In 1781 these contributions consisted in food deliveries, in repayment of part of the federal debt, and in payments into the federal treasury. The contributions from the states were all the more important since they brought specie into the treasury.

A characteristic feature of Morris's policy was strict economy. In 1781 certain army boards and departments were abolished and the hospital service was reorganized. The army's uniform-purchasing service was put under the supervision of Morris himself. By June 17, 1783, 250 men, whose combined salaries totaled $126,000 per year, had been dismissed in the purchasing service alone.[51]

Thus the main features of Morris's financial policy were a balanced budget, revenue from the states received in specie, large foreign loans, the use of banknotes guaranteed by silver or gold as a medium of circulation, a regimen of economy, and rigorous centralization of the financial service.

But the question remained: who would pay the federal debts already in existence and how would they be paid? The proponents of a strong central authority assigned a special place in their program to the federal debt. First, its existence turned the large army of creditors into a source of support and a bulwark for the central government. Second, the regularity with which the interest was paid out strengthened confidence

49. Ibid., vol. 20, 721; vol. 21, 943, 1070.
50. Ibid., vol. 20, 545–46.
51. Ibid., vol. 24, 398.

in the government and thus guaranteed the success of future internal loans. Morris's policy toward the federal debt was to a considerable degree determined by these considerations. Prior to 1782 the debt of Congress was represented solely by bonds, which it undertook to repay in specie. At the insistence of Morris, Congress in February 1782 took stock of and verified the other debt obligations of the federal government, such as the certificates issued by the quartermaster service and the food purchasing service. In addition, it checked the army accounts. They were all included in the federal debt, and as a result by the spring of 1783 the debt had grown from $11 million to $34 million.

Having obligated the government to repay this increased federal debt, Morris and his supporters wanted Congress to recognize the necessity of the central authority's having the right of introducing and levying taxes, since without that stable source of revenue the debt could not be paid off. Morris's supporters launched a campaign to give Congress the right to introduce a federal tax in the very beginning of 1781. On February 3, 1781, the committee chaired by John Mathews recommended that Congress introduce a 5 percent tax on all goods imported to the United States, with the exception of those goods that were bought by the central government or the governments of the states.[52]

Morris meant the import tax to be only a first step. In addition, he proposed the introduction of a land tax, a poll tax, and a tax on alcoholic beverages. The sums thus raised would be spent on paying the interest on the federal debt. Since the proposed plan contravened the provisions of the U.S. Articles of Confederation, the agreement of all the states was necessary for it to be adopted.

To exert pressure on Congress and the states, Morris ordered that the payment of interest on bonds be suspended. This order created much consternation among the mass of creditors, as Morris intended. A congressional committee consisting of representatives from all the states was formed to discuss the situation. On September 4, 1782, the committee issued a report demanding that the states deposit the sum of $12 million for the payment of the interest due on government loans. For this purpose the following taxes were proposed: a land tax in the amount of one dollar per every one hundred acres; a poll tax in the amount of 50 cents on males aged 16–21, one dollar on males aged 21–60, and 50 cents on slaves aged 16–60; and an excise duty on alcoholic beverages in the amount of 12 1/2 cents per gallon. Use of the reserve of western land was stipulated as an important means of repaying the federal debt.[53]

However, in the course of the congressional debate on the report, substantial disagreements among the states emerged, and as a result the committee's proposals were not accepted. The land tax caused tension between the small states of New England and the large states of the South. The delegates from New England, where land was expensive, suggested that taxes should be based on acreage, whereas the southern states, where land was cheap, wished to base taxation on land value. The poll tax was extremely unpopular in a number of states. Moreover, it raised the possibility

52. Ibid., vol. 19, 112–13.
53. Ibid., vol. 23, 545.

that taxation would be based on the number of blacks, a possibility which southern planters vehemently opposed. An excise tax would have caused widespread anger among the agricultural population. The discussion of specific types of taxes also revealed powerful tensions between the eastern and western states. As an alternative to taxation the eastern states proposed using the reserve of unoccupied western lands upon their transfer to the jurisdiction of Congress.[54]

Sharp disagreements in Congress among the states made it impossible for a joint decision to be reached on any single question, with the exception of the tax on imports. In the spring of 1782 all the states, except Rhode Island, approved the introduction of this tax. As a result of Rhode Island's refusal to approve this proposal, an import tax was never introduced in the United States during the period of Confederation.

An analysis of the financial policy of Congress during the years of the War of Independence allows us to draw certain conclusions. Throughout the War of Independence the financial activities of the Continental Congress concentrated on the needs of the war. This policy underwent considerable changes that correlated with the changes in class forces in the country. The financing of military operations during the first years of the war was carried out with paper money. The essence of this system consisted in the following: lacking silver and gold specie, Congress paid for expenditures with paper money, which at the end of the war was to be withdrawn from circulation by the imposition of taxes. In this way the war brought riches to the merchants, industrialists, and planters—the suppliers of goods to the army— and all the costs fell on the shoulders of the ordinary taxpayer. Such a system of financing certainly suited large sections of the merchant class, the nation's industrial bourgeoisie, and the planters, who formed the moderate camp of the Revolution.

Before the appearance of inflation this system met the demands of the radical camp of the Revolution. This camp included the most revolutionary-minded circles of the bourgeoisie, the bourgeois intelligentsia, and the planters, as well as the broad masses of the people. The shortage of a sufficient quantity of money in circulation hindered the economic development of the colonies and hampered the payment of taxes by the poorest sections of the people. That is why during the pre-Revolutionary period a main demand of the farmers was the issuance of "cheap" money, which would have enabled them to settle their debts and thus escape from financial bondage. In the 1760s–1780s, the demand for cheap money was a kind of indicator of the farmers' movements in the country. The democratic elements envisaged further financing of the war by means of confiscating land and other property belonging to the Loyalists. In the early years the broad masses of the people supported the policies of Congress, and in the newly prevailing conditions of inflation, pressure from the radical wing led to such congressional actions as the campaign against speculation, the policy of regulating the price of goods, a trade embargo on the export of food stuffs, etc.

The financial legislation of Congress during the years of the War of Independence led to the significant enrichment of the industrial bourgeoisie of the northeast, the

54. Ibid., vol. 25, 866–962.

merchants, and a proportion of the planters who made up the moderate camp of the Revolution. As a result, their position increasingly came to resemble the platform of the conservative elements represented by the landowners of the middle states and the financial and commercial circles of the northeast.

The approaching end of the war raised the question of the nature of political authority in the postwar period. The conservative camp of the Revolution, represented by Morris, Hamilton, and Madison, put forward its program for the future political system in the United States. The main demand of this camp was for a strong central authority capable of curbing the forces of democracy and resolving the problem of government debts in a manner advantageous to the propertied strata, which would have meant the further enrichment of the ruling classes.

The exclusion of the masses of the people from participation in the political life of the country by means of a high property qualification, the existence of a regular army as a force for the suppression of democratic actions, a strong currency in the form of silver and gold money, direct taxation of the population, the establishment of a bank that would contribute to the centralization of free financial capital—these were some of the features of the system that conservatives supported.

The consolidation of the conservative forces in the country led to a regrouping of the factions in the Congress itself. Supporters of a strong central authority were able to secure important positions in the machinery of the state. Under the pretext of finding resources for the payment of federal debts, Morris, who headed the financial department, put forward the idea of creating financial reserves belonging to Congress itself. Using the disturbances in the army and the pressure from creditors, the Morris faction attempted to get Congress and the states to agree to implement a set of measures that ultimately would create a government that protected unconditionally the interests of the powers that be. However, during the years of the War of Independence the combined conservative-moderate camp was unable to put its program into effect. The positions of the radical camp of the Revolution were still strong in both the Congress and in the country, and the radicals prevented the revision of the Articles of Confederation during this period. Events in later years led to a further divergence of forces and the final victory of the bourgeois-planter bloc on a nationwide scale.

The analysis of the financial activities of Congress demonstrates a certain contradictory nature in its policy as a result of pressure from both radical and conservative forces within the Revolutionary camp. Moreover, the consolidation of forces, which eventually led to the adoption of the Constitution of 1787, began much earlier—in the last years of the War of Independence. The chief conclusion to be drawn is that it was the working masses of America that carried the main burden of military spending and brought victory to the young Republic.

COMMENT BY JOHN M. MURRIN

The financing of the Revolutionary War and the hyperinflation that accompanied that effort used to occupy a prominent place in general histories of the era.[1] Writing just after World War II with the Great Depression and, no doubt, the Weimar Republic's encounter with runaway prices both very much in mind, John C. Miller devoted a lengthy chapter, nearly 8 percent of his book, to "Inflation and Its Consequences" prior to the appointment of Robert Morris as minister of finance. John Richard Alden in his widely disseminated New American Nation Series volume on the war gave the subject half a chapter in 1954. Seven years later E. James Ferguson provided the fullest analysis of Revolutionary finance that has ever been written.[2]

Then something happened. Ferguson was so thorough that perhaps subsequent historians thought his subject could now be taken for granted and summarized quite briefly. Another possibility seems just as plausible. A long generation of prosperity after 1940 had erected a barrier between historians and the economic crisis of the Revolution. It no longer interested them. At any rate, accounts of the subject became brief, even perfunctory. In a book more than twice as long as his 1954 history, Alden covered the topic in two and one-half pages out of 524. Don Higginbotham gave it something more than three pages out of 467, and Marshall Smelser set aside five out of 376. In Robert Middlekauff's comprehensive history of the period, the subject gets less than two pages out of 665 and is treated almost literally as an afterthought. It comes into the narrative after the war has ended and is discussed as part of the background to the Constitutional Convention of 1787.[3]

O. V. Kriuchkova is, in short, quite correct to alert us to the significance of a topic that we seem in danger of forgetting. She is kinder to us than we deserve in describing our interest in the subject as the "heated debate" it used to be but no longer is. Paper money and the problem of inflation engrossed far more of Congress's attention than drafting the Articles of Confederation and probably generated a deeper level of public concern than anything else except the war itself and, for more limited periods of time in some places, the transformation of constitutional systems. Although Miller wrote many years before a coherent ideological school developed its distinctive interpretation of the Revolution, he understood that the debate over finance and inflation was a continuing dialogue about public virtue and private

1. The author wishes to thank Eugene R. Sheridan for his comments and suggestions. Sheridan is associate editor of the *Papers of Thomas Jefferson* at Princeton University and before that appointment was associate editor of the *Letters of Delegates of the Continental Congress* in Washington, D.C.

2. Miller, *Triumph of Freedom,* 425–77; John Richard Alden, *The American Revolution, 1775–1783* (New York, 1954), chap. 14, especially pp. 214–21; Ferguson, *Power of the Purse.*

3. John Richard Alden, *History of the American Revolution: Britain and the Loss of the Thirteen Colonies* (London, 1969), 448–50; Higginbotham, *War of American Independence,* 289–96 (although pp. 292–96 are more about other matters); Marshall Smelser, *The Winning of Independence* (Chicago, 1972), 101–4, 289–91; Robert Middlekauff, *The Glorious Cause: The American Revolution, 1763–1789* (New York, 1982), 593–95.

interest, about whether Americans were any more patriotic than Britons, about—in a word—the viability of the principles of 1776. Political economy evolved, after all, out of moral philosophy. The eighteenth century had difficulty thinking about wealth except in moral terms. Yet apart from some of Wayne Carp's observations in his fine monograph on the supply officers of the Continental army, this protracted and absorbing controversy has yet to find a historian willing to explore its fuller significance.[4]

Kriuchkova approaches the subject from a different angle, of course. She sees the paper money emissions before 1780 and the scattered attempts to dampen inflation by controlling prices as an expression of the most democratic phase of the Revolution. By contrast, the triumph of Robert Morris and more conventional methods of governmental finance gave power to men who demanded "a strong central authority capable of curbing the forces of democracy and resolving the problem of government debts in a manner advantageous to the propertied strata, which would have meant the further enrichment of the ruling classes." Morris and his associates made sure that someone else finally paid for the war. In Kriuchkova's judgment, "the working masses of America . . . carried the main burden of military spending and brought victory to the young Republic."

Many historians trained in the United States would accept much of this analysis. Most agree that the mid-1770s did generate a radical ferment that brought new men to power and inspired unprecedented dreams of liberation in many spheres of human activity. The old elite, to the extent that it remained in power, had to run hard even to appear to lead. Many also see the triumph of Robert Morris as something close to a counterrevolution and certainly as a prelude to the more successful nationalist movement that produced the federal Constitution in 1787. Two economic historians have recently calculated that the war reduced per capita gross national product in the United States by about 46 percent between 1774 and 1790. In this sense ordinary householders certainly did pay the heaviest costs of achieving independence.[5]

4. See Istvan Hont and Michael Ignatieff, eds., *Wealth and Virtue: The Shaping of Political Economy in the Scottish Enlightenment* (Cambridge, England, 1983); E. Wayne Carp, *To Starve the Army at Pleasure: Continental Army Administration and American Political Culture, 1775–1783* (Chapel Hill, 1984).

5. See in general Gary J. Kornblith and John M. Murrin, "The Making and Unmaking of an American Ruling Class," in Alfred F. Young, ed., *Beyond the American Revolution: Explorations in the History of American Radicalism* (DeKalb, Ill.: Northern Illinois University Press, 1993), 27–29. Important local studies include Ronald Hoffman, *A Spirit of Dissension: Economics, Politics, and the Revolution in Maryland* (Baltimore, 1973); Richard A. Ryerson, *The Revolution Is Now Begun: The Radical Committees of Philadelphia, 1765–1776* (Philadelphia, 1978); Steven Rosswurm, *Arms, Country, and Class: The Philadelphia Militia and the "Lower Sort" during the American Revolution* (New Brunswick, N.J., 1987); and Edward Countryman, *A People in Revolution: The American Revolution and Political Society in New York, 1760–1790* (Baltimore, 1981). For Robert Morris, see especially E. James Ferguson, "The Nationalists of 1781–1783 and the Economic Interpretation of the Constitution," *Journal of American History* 56 (1969–1970), 241–61; and Richard H. Kohn, "The Inside History of the Newburgh Conspiracy: America and the Coup d'Etat," *William and Mary Quarterly,* 3rd ser., vol. 27 (1970), 187–220. For the decline of household income by the 1780s, see

The difficulty lies more in the way that Kriuchkova brings this story together. Much of her analysis presupposes a more sophisticated society and economy than North America possessed in 1775. Her language would be far more appropriate to the Civil War era or even later.

For example, she asserts at the outset that paper money "met the demands of the working people of America and aroused the hatred and anger of the property-owning sections." Robert Morris "reflected the interests of the mercantile bourgeoisie and the landowners of the middle states." Slaves aside—and they are an exception of enormous importance—most of the physical work done by males in British North America was performed by people who owned their own farms or shops or had reasonable expectations of acquiring that status in the normal course of the life cycle. Most farmers' sons could still expect to own land or, as in the Chesapeake and the Hudson Valley where leasehold systems were becoming quite important, they could still hope to acquire leases for fairly long terms, although such opportunities were declining as the growth of population gave new advantages to landlords. Also, most journeymen could still expect to become master craftsmen some day. Even many indentured servants arriving from abroad shared these ambitions and often fulfilled them. No sharp demarcation had yet appeared between "working people" and those who owned property, except in areas of plantation agriculture and in New York's manorial society, although anxieties about such a division did exist and grew more acute in the Revolutionary era. Under these conditions, Kriuchkova ought to be more specific about who constituted "the ruling classes of America," especially during a decade when membership in the economic and political elite was changing drastically.[6]

Kriuchkova also speaks of "the mercantile-industrial bourgeoisie of the northeast and the central states (and also the largest planters in the South)," whose "position converged with that of the conservative camp (the landowners of the middle states and the financial circles in the northeast.)" Here again the language suggests a society with organized banks and investment houses, major industries, and a sharp cleavage between these men of wealth and everyone else. No doubt such individuals as Robert Morris looked forward to a day when they could take such distinctions for granted, but they did not yet exist in 1780, not even in Philadelphia, the Republic's largest

---

John J. McCusker and Russell R. Menard, *The Economy of British America, 1607–1789* (Chapel Hill, 1985), chap. 17, especially pp. 373–74. The authors caution against taking these rough estimates too literally, but they also point out that during the Great Depression of 1929 the comparable drop was 48 percent.

6. For the argument for widespread opportunity across the normal life cycle, see Jackson Turner Main, *Society and Economy in Colonial Connecticut* (Princeton, 1988). See also Sung Bok Kim, *Landlord and Tenant in Colonial New York: Manorial Society, 1664–1775* (Chapel Hill, 1978); Countryman, *A People in Revolution*, 13–25; Gregory A. Stiverson, *Poverty in a Land of Plenty: Tenancy in Eighteenth-Century Maryland* (Baltimore, 1977); Willard F. Bliss, "The Rise of Tenancy in Virginia," *Virginia Magazine of History and Biography* 58 (1950), 427–41; Allan Kulikoff, *Tobacco and Slaves: The Development of Southern Cultures in the Chesapeake, 1680–1800* (Chapel Hill, 1986), 132–34, 296–97.

city. When Morris and his associates created the Bank of North America as one of their major financial reforms, they capitalized it at $400,000, a very modest sum by comparison with the federal debt, which Congress had recently reduced by a ratio of forty-to-one from $200 million to $5 million, or by contrast with the Bank of the United States, which was capitalized at $10 million in 1791. After six years of debilitating war, the country simply lacked large concentrations of fluid capital, even though some individuals—probably not very many—had grown rich during the conflict.

I do not mean to deny that artisans frequently resented the social and political pretensions of merchants and looked for and often found effective ways to combat them. In many states, western farmers certainly distrusted the financial power of their merchant creditors, who in turn either resided in port cities or were tied to other merchants who lived there. As the economic crisis that accompanied the war reached its most acute phase between 1779 and 1781, fissures opened even between journeymen and master craftsmen. But the world of 1780 was still far short of the social tensions we associate with nineteenth-century industrialization, and the language that Kriuchkova uses to describe economic cleavages sometimes has the unfortunate effect of obscuring rather than clarifying who resisted whom and why. Who, for instance, were "the landowners of the middle states"? Were they the Hudson Valley manor lords with their gigantic estates, or the ordinary farmers of Pennsylvania who typically held at most a few hundred acres?

Let us look briefly at the politics of paper money to suggest some of these difficulties. Kriuchkova associates the congressional emissions of 1775–1776 with a response to radical pressures. At one level, she is undeniably correct. Most of what the Second Continental Congress did—take on a war, create an army, open negotiations with foreign powers, determine the legitimacy of the governments of individual colonies, and finally repudiate the British crown after fifteen months of fighting— acquired a cumulative, radical momentum that led to American independence.[7] On the other hand, it does not follow that delegates who voted for paper money saw the issue in these terms or believed that they were appeasing radical sentiment. Outside of New England and the Carolinas, colonial experience with paper money before 1775 had been quite successful and generally had not produced strong class antagonisms. Delegates who knew the history of the specific colonies they represented understood this pattern and accepted fiat money as a proven and convenient way to raise revenue quickly and effectively for military purposes.[8]

Inflation gradually destroyed a consensus that everyone but overt Loyalists at first agreed to share. Among radicals, for example, Thomas Paine had strong reservations about the desirability of fiat money but accepted what he could not change. And through 1776, at least compared with what happened later, the value of the Continental dollar held up well. After emissions in 1775 and 1776 of $25 million by Congress

7. Jerrilyn Greene Marston, *King and Congress: The Transfer of Political Legitimacy, 1774–1776* (Princeton, 1987).

8. Leslie V. Brock, *The Currency of the American Colonies, 1700–1764* (New York, 1975).

(plus £5.4 million and $2.1 million by the states), the dollar still retained 80 percent of its original specie value. But in the last quarter of 1776, George Washington's army very nearly collapsed, the British seemed on the verge of an overwhelming victory, then Washington counterattacked at Trenton and Princeton, and the British finally withdrew most of their outposts from New Jersey.

What both sides had hoped would be a short war was obviously becoming a long one. In subsequent emissions of paper, Congress no longer gave dates for redemption, and the value of the Continental dollar began to sink dramatically. Its value had always depended on its eventual redemption in taxes, which would now have to be levied by governments that had achieved independence. Doubts about whether and when the great day would arrive weakened the currency, and its depreciation forced Congress to issue ever more to keep paying its bills.

A significant fact about the great inflation that neither the existing American literature nor Kriuchkova's essay adequately grasps is how relentless, steady, and almost unchanging this process was. Contemporaries believed that things did not get truly out of hand until 1779. They simply were not accustomed to thinking exponentially. We can sympathize with this failing, especially when a person finally needed a cart rather than a wallet to carry his cash to a transaction. Nevertheless, plotted on a logarithmic graph to capture the *rate* of decline, the depreciation of the dollar was almost a straight-line process, never a sudden collapse. The French alliance provided a respite (and for a few months even a slight reversal) for most of 1778, no doubt sustained by hopes that Britain would have to quit and the war would soon be over. Congress, which had met the initial inflation of 1777 by cutting back its emissions to $13 million from $19 million in 1776, issued the enormous sum of $63.5 million in 1778 and succeeded in keeping more men under arms than during any other year of the struggle.[9] But the French presence at first brought only more soldiers and sailors to feed, and as 1778 turned into 1779, the decline of the dollar resumed and took only about half a year to compensate for the 1778 pause and then again became almost a straight line from the second quarter of 1779 into 1781.[10]

By the beginning of 1781 Congress had difficulty maintaining five thousand Continentals under Washington's command, probably only a fraction of the number of armed Loyalists serving with the British army. Congress had also ceased to print money and had transferred the burden of sustaining the army to the states, as Kriuchkova shows. But depreciation continued if only because the states in 1780–1781 issued more than £57.4 million and another $3.4 million. All efforts to halt it, whatever their source, failed.

9. Charles H. Lesser, *The Sinews of Independence: Monthly Strength Reports of the Continental Army* (Chicago, 1976), xxx–xxxi.

10. For the rate of depreciation, see Ferguson, *Power of the Purse*, 32. For a table of annual emissions by the states and Congress, see Ralph V. Harlow, "Aspects of Revolutionary Finance," *American Historical Review* 35 (1929–1930), 46–68, after p. 50. For the impact of the French alliance on the American economy, see Richard Buel Jr., *Dear Liberty: Connecticut's Mobilization for the Revolutionary War* (Middletown, Conn., 1980), 152–59 and passim.

GRAPH A
PRICE OF $1 SPECIE IN CONTINENTAL DOLLARS

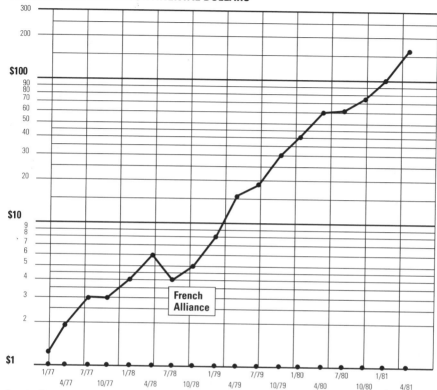

Source: E. James Ferguson, *The Power of the Purse: A History of American Public Finance, 1776–1790* (Chapel Hill: University of North Carolina Press, 1961), p. 32.

Internally the fiscal and military crisis of 1780–1781 was the most severe trial of the war because it revealed a society that had almost lost the ability to defend itself. As British soldiers ravaged the Virginia countryside, the government of the largest state of the union was seldom able to muster any effective militia response against them despite enormous emissions of money, even when it asked most militiamen to serve only for very short periods. The main difference between the crisis of 1781 and that of the winter of 1776–1777 was that the British were also nearing exhaustion. The field army of Charles, Earl Cornwallis was much smaller than General William Howe's had been in 1776. It could maraud and destroy. It could not occupy or pacify effectively. Even so, it took a French fleet and army to give Washington the resources to win at Yorktown.[11]

11. See Allan Kulikoff, "The Political Economy of Military Service in Revolutionary Service in Revolutionary Virginia," in his *The Agrarian Origins of American Capitalism* (Charlottesville: University Press of Virginia, 1992), 152–80.

Kriuchkova is probably correct to see radical Revolutionaries struggling fiercely to sustain the value of Continental paper through price controls and other regulations, while conservative patriots began to challenge the whole system. But she exaggerates the degree to which wealthy people had been able to profit from inflation. If most of them found it beneficial, why did nearly all of them turn against the paper money that made their gains possible? She is also too ready to dismiss the noneconomic argument that hyperinflation demoralized American society. Above all it eventually demoralized many of the radical patriots she is eager to defend. It permitted many of the elite of the land to return to Congress by 1781 and push through Morris's program of fiscal reform.[12]

The politics of inflation were grimmer and more complex than Kriuchkova ever concedes. She never gives adequate attention to *wage* controls as part of the regulatory effort, nor does she ask whether ordinary working Americans greeted that prospect favorably. From her own evidence, not everyone who resisted price controls was wealthy or uncommitted to the Revolution. For example, she cites the case of Sarson Belcher, denounced in Boston in 1779 for selling beaver hats above the allowed price. Twenty other hatters came to Belcher's defense, and even when pressured, only four backed down. On this occasion price controls threatened to alienate all of the master craftsmen in a particular trade.[13]

Philadelphia is the best-studied case of this process in which efforts to control prices divided the artisanal community against itself and eventually created a popular majority against paper money. Radicals did hope that they could uphold the value of paper, first through concerted interstate legislative regulation, and then in 1779 through sustained extralegal crowd action. But nothing stopped the slide, and in the Fort Wilson clash of late 1779 some radicals, mostly master craftsmen, joined conservatives in suppressing another group of armed radicals, mostly journeymen organized as militia privates. A year later the opposition (Republican) party, including Robert Morris, won the Philadelphia city elections for the first time. Radicals could no longer agree on an economic policy that would hold all of them together. By the 1780s, Thomas Paine would even be defending Morris and the Bank of North America.[14]

In 1775 paper money divided conservatives and united radicals. By the 1780s hostility to it united conservatives and divided radicals. Demands for new emissions came from the countryside, not the cities. From Boston to Baltimore artisans rallied overwhelmingly behind the Constitution of 1787, one clause of which prohibited further state emissions.[15] For that matter, a very large majority of the men who signed

12. E. Wayne Carp, "The Origins of the Nationalist Movement of 1781–1783: Congressional Administration and the Continental Army," *Pennsylvania Magazine of History and Biography* 107 (1983), 363–92.

13. Richard B. Morris, "Labor and Mercantilism in the Revolutionary Era," 76–139, at 129–30.

14. See Eric Foner, *Tom Paine and Revolutionary America* (New York, 1976), especially chaps. 5–6; John K. Alexander, "The Fort Wilson Incident of 1779: A Case Study of the Revolutionary Crowd," *William and Mary Quarterly*, 3rd ser., vol. 31 (1974), 589–612.

15. Compare John P. Kaminski, *Paper Politics: The Northern State Loan-Offices during the Confederation, 1783–1790* (New York, 1989) with Sean Wilentz, *Chants Democratic: New York*

either the Declaration of Independence or the Articles of Confederation had reached similar conclusions. For signers of the Declaration, support for ratification of the Constitution grew from an initial ratio of three to one, to become six to one when the process was complete. Among signers of the Articles, the comparable shift went from four to one to become fifteen to one.[16] Clearly, many radicals changed their minds and their political positions over time, and the way that they experienced hyperinflation and reacted to it probably accounts for much of this transformation.

By 1781 most men, radical and conservative, shared the conviction that a central government ought to exist and ought at a minimum to have the power to collect import duties. Only the need for unanimous ratification by all thirteen states prevented the impost amendments of 1781 and 1783 from winning approval. Ironically, had either been adopted, there may well have been no constitutional convention in 1787 and certainly no proposed new government that utterly discarded the procedure for amendment prescribed by the Articles. In that limited but important sense, the Constitution of 1787 was a revolutionary, though nonviolent, act. The decision to put the new Constitution into effect after only nine states had ratified it marked an illegal overthrow of the existing legal order. If resistance to all federal taxes was still a radical position in 1781, it had become a self-destructive conviction. It permitted Federalists to argue, in a manner that even many veteran radicals eventually found convincing, that they had to risk destroying the union in order to save it.

City and the Rise of the American Working Class, 1788–1850 (New York, 1984), chap. 2, especially p. 67.

16. Jackson Turner Main, *The Antifederalists, Critics of the Constitution, 1781–1788* (Chapel Hill, 1961), 259–60.

RESPONSE BY O. V. KRIUCHKOVA

I am very grateful to John M. Murrin for his interesting and informative comments. I agree with his view that the presentation and treatment of the material require a somewhat more up-to-date approach, that a description of the dynamics of the inflationary processes would have been desirable, and that the topic in question should be analyzed in a more detailed and comprehensive manner. In this way we may better account for the contradictory and changing interests of the different strata in American society in the period of the War of Independence.

CHAPTER 8

The Articles of Confederation and the Union Forever:

On the History of the Creation of the First American Constitution

by

V. L. Ushakov

In March 1781 a long-awaited celebration took place in the United States. Americans greeted the news of the completion of the ratification of the Articles of Confederation and Perpetual Union—America's first constitution—with the pealing of church bells, fireworks, official receptions, and other festivities.[1] This is what one Pennsylvania newspaper said about the newly established constitutional union of the thirteen states: "Thus has the union, begun by necessity, been indissolubly cemented. Thus America, like a well constructed arch, whose parts, harmonizing and mutually supporting each other, are the more closely united the greater the pressure upon them, is growing up in war into greatness and consequence among the nations."[2]

But eight years passed, and the "perfect arch" of the Articles of Confederation and Perpetual Union lay in ruins. On March 4, 1789, the first American constitution, which had been adopted by the Second Continental Congress in November 1777 and had come into force after being ratified as required by all the states in March 1781, was replaced by a new U.S. constitution, which is still in effect today.[3]

---

1. *Journals of the Continental Congress, 1774–1789,* ed. Worthington C. Ford, 34 vols. (Washington, D.C., 1904–1937), vol. 19, 138–39, 186, 208–14. This article by V. L. Ushakov was first published in *Problems of General History* (Moscow, 1973).
2. Merrill Jensen, *The New Nation* (New York, 1950), 26–27.
3. A number of Soviet historians have studied the history of the American Revolution of the eighteenth century, the class struggle during this period, and the process whereby the American Republic was formed. For examples, see A. V. Efimov, *The U.S.A. Paths of Capitalist Development* (Moscow, 1969); A. A. Fursenko, *The American Bourgeois Revolution of the 18th Century* (Moscow-Leningrad, 1960); A. A. Fursenko and N. N. Bolkhovitinov, chap. 2 in *Essays on Modern and Contemporary U.S. History,* ed. G. N. Sevostianov, 2 vols. (Moscow 1960); A. A. Fursenko, "The American and French Revolutions of the 18th Century," *Problems of History* 11 (1972).

For more than two hundred years American scholars and politicians have studied the history of the creation of the U.S. Constitution, as well as other issues in the era of the struggle for independence.[4] They have differed in their opinions about the course, character, and outcome of the first American Revolution; they have also held differing views about the adoption and brief existence of the first American constitution—the Articles of Confederation—as well as about how and why this constitution was replaced by another. A number of authors, including such eminent scholars as Charles Beard, Merrill Jensen, and others, believe that the adoption in 1787 of the second constitution in place of the Articles of Confederation was a conservative step. In their view, the new constitution reflected the victory in American society of the forces that had abandoned the democratic ideas of the Revolutionary period. With the aid of the second U.S. constitution and the establishment of a new system of government, these forces secured their victory on a national scale. These scholars, particularly Jensen and his followers, have on occasion successfully argued that the struggle for independence was a largely "democratic movement" and that its importance lay in the "raising of the political and economic status" of the colonies' population. "The Articles of Confederation," writes Jensen, "were the constitutional expression of this movement and embodiment in government form of the philosophy of the Declaration of Independence."[5] However, it would appear that the historians who hold such views, including Jensen, tend to overrate the Articles of Confederation as an embodiment of the democratic ideals of the period. Moreover, Jensen and the other scholars of this school have trouble analyzing and evaluating the objective causes that led to the creation of the Constitution of 1787 and are not always able to offer a comprehensive and satisfactory explanation of these causes.

Other bourgeois scholars deny that the War of Independence was revolutionary in character. These historians are guilty of partially or even completely ignoring the democratic changes that took place in American society during that period. When considering the history of the Articles of Confederation—their adoption and role in the political life of the country—these authors (John Fiske before World War II, and Robert E. Brown, Clinton Rossiter, and Forrest McDonald in the postwar period) downplay the important successes achieved by the democratic Revolutionary forces in the course of the anti-British struggle, and at the same time, by stressing the mistakes and failures of the patriots, exaggerate the difficulties they experienced. They describe the Articles of Confederation as flawed, and yet do not explain why such a document

4. Several studies by Soviet scholars offer a historiography of the American Revolution of the eighteenth century. See N. N. Bolkhovitinov, "Contemporary American Historiography," in *New and Contemporary History* 6 (1969); Bolkhovitinov, "The U.S. War of Independence and Contemporary Soviet Historiography," *Problems of History* 12 (1969); I. P. Dementiev with V. L. Malkov and S. M. Askoldova in *Essays on New and Recent U.S. History,* ed. G. N. Sevostianov (Moscow, 1960), vol. 1, chap. 12 and vol. 2, chap. 12; Dementiev, in *Historiography of the Modern Period of the Countries of Europe and America,* ed. I. S. Galkin (Moscow, 1967), part 1, chap. 5 and part 2, chap. 6; Dementiev with V. L. Malkov and G. G. Nadgafov in *Historiography of the Modern Period,* part 1, chap. 5 and part 2, chap. 10; P. B. Umanskii, "Problems of the First American Revolution," in *The Central Problems in U.S. History in American Historiography,* ed. G. N. Sevostianov (Moscow, 1971).

5. Merrill Jensen, *The Articles of Confederation* (Madison, 1940), 15, 239.

was created. By painting an idealized picture of the adoption in 1787 of the second U.S. constitution as an event that won the approval of the majority of the American people and led to the triumph of democratic traditions and institutions in the country, the historians of this school are in fact guilty of distorting the history of the United States.

In this article I will discuss the history of the creation of the Articles of Confederation, the character of this first constitution, and the factors and circumstances affecting the process that led to its adoption—one of the central documents of the American bourgeois revolution of the eighteenth century. If we are to understand the significance of the American Revolution, we must analyze and understand the Articles of Confederation.

The history of the establishment of the American Republic and in particular the history of the creation, adoption, and replacement of the first U.S. constitution very clearly reflected the struggle of the classes and various strata in American society; it was a struggle that decided the question of political power in the country and fundamentally determined the direction that the American bourgeois revolution took.[6] This struggle began long before the colonies gained their independence. The worsening crisis in the relations between the British colonies and the mother country was accompanied by an aggravation of the antagonisms within American society. As the heterogeneous anti-British movement grew and was transformed into a mass phenomenon embracing all the colonies, the divisions and stratification within it increased. The American patriots' slogans and demands reflected the positions of the various social groups in colonial society. The aims of these groups were often provincial and even parochial. Each group had its own views on what ought to be done in reorganizing American society. This fact determined not only the nature and extent of economic and sociopolitical change that these groups and strata in American society found acceptable but also the degree to which they were able and prepared to fight to bring these changes about. These groupings acquired a clear identity and became differentiated from each other during the 1760s and the first half of the 1770s; this process continued in the years the colonies struggled with the mother country, ran through the proclamation of independence by the various states and the sessions of the two Continental Congresses, and ended with the war against England.

The liberation movement in America became interwoven with the struggle for power waged by the ruling classes. The representatives of large segments of the upper and middle bourgeoisie, which in the majority of American provinces, towns, and counties was fighting for the right to participate in government, attacked the narrow circle of Loyalists that controlled local administration in the colonies and enjoyed a position of privilege.[7]

6. A number of theoretical works by K. Marx, F. Engels, and V. I. Lenin discuss the problem of the class struggle waged to decide the fundamental issue of a social revolution—the issue of power. See, for example, K. Marx and F. Engels, *Writings,* vol. 3, 32–33 and vol. 8, 6; V. I. Lenin, *Collected Works,* vol. 31, 133, 145; vol. 34, 200.

7. Merrill Jensen, *The Founding of a Nation* (New York, 1968), especially chap. 3.

The masses of farmers and townspeople were also being drawn into political activity, strengthening the radicalism of the patriotic camp and contributing to a rise in anti-British feeling. The programs put forward by the petty bourgeoisie and the masses of the exploited expressed not only the task facing all American society, that is, resistance to England's colonial policy, but also the political and economic aims of these groups. They demanded the democratization of the country and the right to take an active part in its political life. In particular, they called for the equality of all members of society, the broadening of civil and political rights and freedoms, the destruction of the power and influence of the ruling clique, and the democratic reform of government everywhere in accordance with the needs and interests of all the people in North America. They wanted to destroy the hierarchy of officials, to simplify the structure and procedures of government, to make officials subordinate to the control of the people, etc., thereby weakening the governmental institutions of repression in the hands of the ruling classes. These demands were reflected in the movement to decentralize and simplify government, which occasionally led to outbursts of separatist sentiment.[8]

In the conditions then prevailing in America, fulfilling these political demands would have solved some of the country's economic problems. Democratizing and broadening popular control over government would have gained the people access to the land and led to a popular solution of important economic problems involving taxation, credit, cheap money, and economic activity in the towns, counties, and states.[9]

The masses also made various economic demands. For example, the farmers in the state of New York tried to improve conditions for renting and purchasing plots of land. They wanted to reduce rent payments, to abolish the various obligations of the tenant farmers, and to break up and sell the estates of the large landowners. In the coastal towns the sailors and port workers demanded an improvement in pay and labor conditions, etc. Other strata of both the urban and rural population also took part in mass political actions that were often directed against not only British domination but also the ruling classes in American society.[10]

8. The suspicion with which broad sections of the population and even the ruling classes in America viewed the state—the Leviathan—arose during their struggle against the attempt by a strong, centralized British government to subordinate the colonies economically, politically, and ideologically, and to establish in them a strong local administration with powerful institutions of repression at its command. Such an administration would be independent of the population of the colonies and would dominate it. The sympathy for decentralization was due to the economic, political, and ideological differences among the colonies, which hindered the development of vitally important ties among them. All this affected the emergence of the liberation movement and the formation of the independent American state. These factors influenced the system of government established in the United States and the two American constitutions. Jensen, *The Articles of Confederation,* 243–44, ff.; Sydney G. Fisher: *The Evolution of the Constitution of the United States* (Philadelphia, 1910), especially chaps. 5–7; *The Papers of Thomas Jefferson,* ed. Julian P. Boyd et al. (Princeton, 1950–), vol. 1, 323–27; *Diary and Autobiography of John Adams,* ed. Lyman H. Butterfield, 4 vols. (Cambridge, Mass., 1961), vol. 2, 245–48.

9. Elisha P. Douglass, *Rebels and Democrats* (Chapel Hill, 1955), chap. 11, etc.

10. Staughton Lynd, *Class Conflict, Slavery, and the United States Constitution: Ten Essays* (Indianapolis-New York, 1967); Jesse Lemisch, "Jack Tar in the Streets: Merchant Seamen in the Politics of Revolutionary America," *William and Mary Quarterly,* 3rd ser., vol. 25 (1968).

The slogans and pamphlets of those years clearly reflect the way in which the revolutionary situation in America developed. The demands of the masses found expression in the programs put forward by the local and national leaders belonging to the left wing of the Revolution. Thomas Paine, Thomas Jefferson, and other political and government figures responded to these demands.

Thus Thomas Paine declared that the main aim of the American Revolution was to bring about democratic changes in society and government. Many of his writings, including his most important work, *Common Sense*, contained plans for reforming the social and political life of America. Paine's proposals reflected the demands of the masses: he favored abolishing the monarchy and all political, religious, and racial privileges and restrictions in society. Paine was among the first to equate the Revolutionary struggle for independence with a democratic reorganization of American society in which the equality of all its members would be affirmed.[11] He outlined the main paths the American Revolution should follow. He proposed simplifying government by making it democratic. He wanted to bridge the gulf between political institutions and the people and to bring government under the control of the people. Yet Thomas Paine also spoke in favor of creating a strong and united centralized state that would be based on democratic principles. In this respect his proposals differed from those put forward by democratic leaders such as Thomas Burke. A delegate to the Second Continental Congress, Burke was one of the most influential politicians both in the Congress and in North Carolina, which he represented. Burke strongly defended those democratic figures that advocated a weak government. During the drafting of the Articles of Confederation he became one of the spokesmen for a powerful body of opinion demanding a decentralized state. In his defense of democratic principles Burke used the separatist attitudes of the moderate and conservative delegates from the South and from other states, and with their support was able to implement several of his ideas. Burke was particularly successful in decentralizing the system of government.[12]

The colonial administration weakened rapidly in 1773–1776. During those years the masses increased their political activity against the old institutions of government. In most of the colonies the royal administrations were either neutralized or liquidated. A number of decisions of the Second Continental Congress, particularly its resolution of May 10–15, 1776,[13] effectively destroyed the old state machinery. Towns, counties, and provinces in America now governed themselves through local bodies and various patriotic organizations. Finding themselves in control in many localities, the masses fought against the influence and power of the upper bourgeoisie and attempted to bring about social and economic changes in the interests of the people.[14]

11. *The Complete Writings of Thomas Paine,* ed. Philip S. Foner, 2 vols. (New York, 1945), vol. 1, 31, 45, 370; vol. 2, 269–302, 915, 1180, 1490, 1498–501.

12. *Dictionary of American Biography,* ed. Allen Johnson, 20 vols. (London, New York, 1928–1937), vol. 3, 282–83.

13. *Journals of the Continental Congress,* ed. Ford, vol. 4, 357–58.

14. Richard Frothingham, *Life and Times of Joseph Warren* (Boston, 1865), 376, etc.; *American Archives,* 4th and 5th ser., ed. Peter Force, 9 vols. (Washington, D.C., 1837–1854), 4th ser., vol. 2, 177, etc.; vol. 4, 834, etc.

The rise in popular revolutionary activity seriously alarmed the upper classes. In 1776 General Gage warned the Americans that resisting the policy of Great Britain might bring about an internal revolution.[15] In 1774 Gouverneur Morris, a political figure from New York, expressed similar ideas.[16] He believed that the only way to preserve "order" in the country was to reconcile immediately with the mother country. The dread of revolution, the frightening and uncertain prospect of independence, the weakening of the authority of government and the upper classes in the colonies—all forced the moderate leaders of the liberation movement to pay more and more attention to the system of central government the country would form. In 1768 John Dickinson, the author of the *Letters of a Pennsylvania Farmer* and later one of the chief authors of the first constitution of the independent American Republic, anxiously asked his readers, "If one day we secede, what kind of new government will be established?" And in May 1774 Morris wrote that his fellow citizens were concerned about whether a future government would be aristocratic or democratic and that they were making every effort not to allow any radical changes in society.[17]

The views on government of these conservative leaders of the opposition move-ment, who formed a sizable proportion of the delegates to the two Continental Congresses, as well as those of the representatives of the ruling classes who belonged to the "neutral" groups in society, coincided to a certain extent with the views of the Loyalists. Like the Loyalists, conservative leaders in the patriotic camp condemned the economic and democratic demands of the broad masses of the people. They claimed that the masses were irrational and that their lack of knowledge and experience would be catastrophic for society. Therefore, they argued, it was imperative during this critical period for the ruling classes to guide the broad masses of the people. These leaders sought to promote moderation and to keep the revolutionary energy and aims of the masses within "reasonable limits."[18] The conservatives and the Loyalists were united by the class basis of their political and social views, though they differed in their actual plans for reorganizing society. If the proposals of the most reactionary of the Loyalist groups had been implemented, the liberation movement would have been suppressed and the colonies would have been further subordinated to the British government. The more moderate Loyalists wished to unite Great Britain and its North American colonies in a single state and to ensure the colonies' dependence on England for a long time to come. If their plans had been put into effect, the power and influence of their leaders in the colonies would have been strengthened. The aims and interests of most of the patriotic leaders, who wished to achieve economic and political independence and were competing with the British administration and the Loyalist groups for power in American society, were the opposite. The positions of

15. *The Correspondence of General Thomas Gage with Secretaries of State, 1763–1775,* ed. Clarence E. Carter, 2 vols. (New Haven, 1931), vol. 1, 95.

16. *American Archives,* ed. Force, 4th ser., vol. 1, 343.

17. *Writings of John Dickinson,* ed. Paul L. Ford (Philadelphia, 1895), 277–406; *American Archives,* ed. Force, 4th ser., vol. 1, 342.

18. *The Papers of Alexander Hamilton,* ed. Harold C. Syrett et al., 15 vols. (New York, 1961–1969), vol. 1, 175; vol. 2, 650.

the two parties became clear during the debate over the plan for a new system of colonial government and for the settlement of the conflict with Britain presented to the First Continental Congress by the Pennsylvania delegate Joseph Galloway.

Galloway, fearing that a continuation of the conflict with the mother country would lead to undesirable political changes for the ruling classes, proposed to reconcile the two sides on terms that he believed were advantageous to both the Americans and the British. His plan envisaged the creation of a strong central administration in America to be controlled by representatives of the local aristocracy. The British government would have to agree to a partial loss of power and to share rule over the colonies with this central American administration. Galloway's reform was intended to ward off major sociopolitical and economic changes in American society and to preserve the power of the existing conservative groups. Some of the moderate political figures (John Jay and others) were inclined to support this plan. But the radical leaders of the Revolution and even many moderates who represented the interests of broader sections of the ruling classes (Richard Henry Lee, Patrick Henry, John Adams, and others) would not agree to Galloway's plan. Thanks to their efforts, Galloway's plan and similar other proposals were rejected.[19]

The failure of this plan and the subsequent decision by Galloway and his supporters to become Loyalists compromised the ideas of the centralizers and weakened the conservative wing of the patriotic movement. But at the Second Continental Congress, which met in May 1775, conservatives and moderates made up the majority of delegates. It took the left wing of the Congress (Samuel Adams and others) and a faction of moderate delegates (John Adams and others) almost a year before they were able to gain the support of the undecided delegates and overcome the resistance of the most adamant opponents of independence, led by John Dickinson. Once this was achieved, however, a resolution to draft a declaration of independence, to conclude alliances with foreign powers, and to plan a confederation of the states was introduced in Congress. This happened on June 7, 1776.[20]

The Second Continental Congress functioned in an atmosphere of controversy. No doubt the tendency to unify the states was based on 150 years of common colonial development and the actual experience of the war against England. Yet the states were seriously divided economically, politically, and ideologically. These divisions were revealed among the delegates to the Congress. In many of the debates over the various issues in the Congress, the different factions and groupings repeatedly came together, combined into blocs, and then again split from each other. But in the debates over the central government for an independent America, certain fundamental social antagonisms became apparent.

---

19. *Journals of the Continental Congress,* ed. Ford, vol. 1, 44–51; *Letters of Members of the Continental Congress, 1774–1789,* ed. Edmund C. Burnett, 8 vols. (Washington, D.C., 1921–1937), vol. 1, 51, 87–88.

20. Richard Frothingham, *The Rise of the Republic of the United States* (Boston, 1910), appendix 11; *Journals of the Continental Congress,* ed. Ford, vol. 5, 424; *Letters of the Continental Congress,* ed. Burnett, vol. 1, 476.

The Congress included both delegates who continued to entertain hopes of re-joining the British Empire as well as those who secretly and even openly supported the restoration of the monarchy. Among the latter was a group of delegates from the slave-owning states of the South and New York, who were particularly opposed to any democratic changes in social and governmental institutions. These men wanted to make only the most superficial changes. They were prepared to accept a decla-ration of independence and the introduction of a republican system of government. However, they believed that all top positions in the executive and judicial branches of government and all the seats in the upper chambers of the legislatures should be held for life and should be filled by members of the upper strata of the bourgeoisie and the planter class. In the spring of 1776 Carter Braxton of Virginia presented a plan that was a compendium of such proposals.[21]

John Adams expressed the views of the moderate leaders of the Revolution. He realized that any restoration of the monarchy in America was no longer realistic and that the same was true of the plans developed by the conservative leaders of the patriotic camp. He criticized these plans (for example, the one presented by Braxton) and repeatedly warned that the aristocratic and oligarchic regimes in the South and in the middle states would inevitably be democratized. Adams and several other moderate leaders in the Congress realized that political changes were necessary to reflect the development of a bourgeois society. He believed that without such changes, victory in the war of liberation was impossible. Yet although Adams supported the establishment of a republican system of government in America and a certain democratization of the social life of the country, he spoke out strongly against the theories and activities of the democrats, particularly those of Thomas Paine. John Adams was one of the most active of those who tried to slow down democratization at the state and national level and to direct it into channels that would make it acceptable to the bourgeoisie.[22]

21. *American Archives,* ed. Force, 4th ser., vol. 6, 748–54; *The Works of John Adams,* ed. C. F. Adams, 10 vols. (Boston, 1865), vol. 4; *Letters of Richard Henry Lee,* ed. James Curtis Ballagh, 2 vols. (New York, 1970), vol. 1, 150.

22. In his treatise *Thoughts on Government,* John Adams stated that the new system of government must have a two-chamber legislative body in which the upper and the lower chambers would balance each other. The chief magistrate of the state should enjoy wide prerogatives, including the right to appoint officials to government positions and to control the activities of the legislative bodies through his right of veto. The judiciary would exercise control over the legislative and executive branches. Under this plan all these elements in the government controlling one another would in fact fulfill a single function—that of protecting the political and economic domination of the bourgeoisie, despite the author's insistence that the countervailing factors in the machinery of government would help to preserve a constant balance of power among the different groups in society. In his political activities, however, Adams did not remain faithful to his ideal of a complicated system of government. His concrete proposals frequently contradicted the theoretical model of the state he had developed. Thus Adams, who had claimed that under his plan the people would have the opportunity of exercising power in society, opposed a broadening of the franchise in Massachusetts. He found the contents of the Massachusetts charter of 1691, which limited the voting rights of the population and guaranteed that a few rich families would control the political machinery in the province, quite satisfactory. See

From the beginning of 1774 until the middle of 1776 the structure of central political authority did not appear to be at the center of attention. The issue of the colonies' independence was far more urgent. In fact, however, the two problems were closely linked. Declaring independence entailed politically reorganizing American society, which in turn shaped the question of independence. The conservative and some of the moderate leaders of the ruling classes associated the independence of the colonies with a revolutionary upheaval in society.[23] A desire to prevent such an upheaval determined their policy in the Congress and in the country at large.[24] In an attempt to postpone a declaration of independence, the most conservative among the delegates suggested that first a strong central government should be established and an alliance with France and other countries concluded.[25] They hoped that if these plans were carried out, they would be able to keep the Revolution developing in a moderate direction.

Liquidating the royal administration in 1776 undermined the influence of the conservative politicians. In some states (Pennsylvania, New York, and others) the radicals replaced the conservatives in positions of power. This led the group of conservative Pennsylvania and New York politicians headed by John Dickinson, James Wilson, and others to campaign even more actively for a central government, which they hoped would act as a counterbalance to the democratic tendencies at the local level.[26] The conservatives participated more vigorously in the affairs of the Congress. The moderate delegates also altered their policies in the Congress. On May 10–15 they together with the left wing secured the acceptance of a resolution[27] that undermined the conservatives' influence and helped radicals come to power in the states, which in turn helped in adopting the Declaration of Independence. As the Revolution continued to unfold, the moderates began to cooperate with the conservatives in shaping national policy and in attempting to stop the development of democratic

---

Vernon L. Parrington, *The Main Currents of American Thought,* 3 vols. (Moscow, 1963), vol. 1, 382–97; John Adams, *Works,* vol. 4, 193–200; Adams, *Diary and Autobiography,* ed. Butterfield, vol. 2, 57–58.

23. Paine referred to this belief in his *Common Sense:* "I have heard some men say . . . that they dreaded an independence, fearing it would produce civil wars." The subject was also discussed by a Maryland delegate to the Continental Congress, who was afraid that "new men" would occupy "the seat of power." Paine, *Writings,* ed. Foner, vol. 1, 27; *Letters of the Continental Congress,* ed. Burnett, vol. 1, 431–32.

24. The Galloway plan of 1774 served this purpose. This was one of the reasons why the conservatives (Dickinson), who feared that any attempt to unite the colonies would strengthen the position of the proponents of independence and would bring it closer, in 1775–1776 spoke out against the draft of the Articles of Confederation that Benjamin Franklin presented to the Second Continental Congress in 1775. *English Historical Documents,* ed. Merrill Jensen (London–New York, 1955), vol. 9, 802; *Journals of the Continental Congress,* ed. Ford, vol. 2, 195–99.

25. *Life and Correspondence of Joseph Reed,* ed. William B. Reed, 2 vols. (Philadelphia, 1847), vol. 1, 153.

26. Jensen, *Articles of Confederation,* chap. 4.

27. *Journals of the Continental Congress,* ed. Ford, vol. 4, 342, 357–58; *Letters of the Continental Congress,* ed. Burnett, vol. 1, 353–55.

tendencies that they themselves had contributed to in May.[28] This cooperation enabled the moderate and conservative delegates to overcome the resistance of the left wing in the Congress, whose members were disunited and inconsistent on a number of issues. Reactionary Loyalists as well as the leaders of the conservative-moderate patriotic bloc concentrated their criticism on those figures in the Congress and in the states who espoused democratic views. Firm democrats such as Thomas Paine, who was in a minority even among the democratic leaders of the Revolution, had to face the united front of all the patriots.[29] Those Revolutionary leaders (Matlock, Franklin, Paine, and others), who had contributed in 1776 and after to a number of democratic provisions in the Pennsylvania constitution, were subjected to withering criticism. In the midst of the armed struggle with Great Britain the proponents of independence aimed to unite all the patriots. They even tried to recruit allies from the right-wing camp. Without give-and-take and the making of concessions, the many groupings and factions could never have come together in the fight for the independence of the states. Political maneuvering and compromise were characteristic of the Congress throughout its history, but these were particularly important in the spring and summer of 1776. The conservative delegates took advantage of the distractions of the patriotic camp. The preoccupation of many of the congressional leaders with the struggle for independence allowed some conservative and moderate delegates, led by Dickinson, to become members of the Congressional committee charged with producing the draft of a constitution for a union of the American colonies, which were on the verge of proclaiming their independence. In this committee they hoped to decide upon an appropriate political system.[30]

The predominance of conservative and moderate forces on the committee charged with composing the first draft of the first American constitution—the Articles of Confederation—affected the character of that document. The draft drawn up by Dickinson and approved by the committee described a federation of "colonies," even though the states had already gained their independence. The Dickinson draft naturally embodied the conservatives' belief in a strong central government. The draft contained numerous provisos and exceptions that allowed for broad interpretation of the central government's authority and that granted the "colonies" in the federation only limited power. In many cases it gave the Congress what was in effect unlimited authority. Among the articles in the Dickinson draft were several that provided for a permanent executive that would have effectively functioned as a central government. Had the draft been approved without any changes, the Articles of Confederation would have limited the states' authority and freedom to carry out internal policies and reforms; it would have subjected American society to a centralized power that was not answerable to the will of the people.[31]

28. J. Paul Selsam, *The Pennsylvania Constitution of 1776* (New York, 1971), chaps. 4–5.

29. Paine, *Writings,* ed. Foner, vol. 2, 915, 1180, 1946.

30. *Journals of the Continental Congress,* ed. Ford, vol. 5, 428–29, 431, 432; *Papers of Jefferson,* ed. Boyd et al., vol. 1, 314–15.

31. *Journals of the Continental Congress,* ed. Ford, vol. 5, 545–46; *Letters of the Continental Congress,* ed. Burnett, vol. 1, 517.

The Dickinson draft was supported by the conservatives who had been defeated in their states by more democratic leaders. During the debate over the Articles of Confederation and the long wait for their ratification, Hamilton (who had monarchist views), the more moderate Washington, and their supporters strenuously sought to achieve the aims outlined in the Dickinson draft. However, some conservatives and a group of southerners (Edmund Rutledge and others) who felt secure in their states were reluctant to surrender the power of the states to a strong central government. They refused to support Dickinson. The southern conservative delegates had their own political agenda that was different from that of the conservative centralizers from the middle and northern states. Moreover, the Dickinson draft did not envisage any greatly expanded role by these same ruling classes in the government of the country. Thus politicians who were connected with the broader sections of the planters and bourgeoisie and wished to assume power were not very enthusiastic about the Dickinson draft. For these reasons alone the delegates constituting the right wing and the center in the Congress did not act in unison; although constituting a majority, they lacked organizational and ideological cohesion at the most critical moments in the unfolding drama of the Revolution.[32]

Yet the left wing in the Congress was not united in its attitude to the Dickinson draft either. Many delegates with democratic views understood the essence of Dickinson's proposals and opposed them. At sessions of the Congress they cooperated with some of the more moderate delegates (Thomas Burke and others frequently enjoyed the support of conservative representatives from the South). Some democratically minded representatives, as well as several moderate and conservative delegates, saw their own interests strongly linked to the policies and interests of their states rather than to the interests of the Union; this was true, for instance, of the Virginia delegates during the debate on the western territories. Lacking national political experience, they had a localist perspective and were critical of Dickinson's excessive centralizing tendencies. To a certain degree they had been influenced by those European thinkers who believed that a democracy could not exist in states with large territories. The fact that Dickinson's plan implied the restoration of the strong central government and the oligarchic power that had been the colonists' twin enemies for so many years also provoked opposition. Reflecting the demands of the masses to democratize government and strengthen the political influence of ordinary citizens, the radical leaders in the Congress, who had links with local leaders in the towns, counties, and states, could only conceive of decentralizing the system of government. But in the course of the Revolution some of them became less radical. For example, representatives from Virginia (Patrick Henry and others) and Massachusetts (Samuel Adams and others) abandoned their original plans for democratic change and proposed reforms that were more moderate in character (a limited extension of the right

32. *Hamilton, Papers,* ed. Syrett, vol. 1, 176; *The Writings of George Washington,* ed. John C. Fitzpatrick, 34 vols. (Washington, D.C., 1931–1944), vol. 5, 92; Reed, *Correspondence,* ed. Reed, vol. 1, 193; *Journals of the Continental Congress,* ed. Ford, vol. 4, 353; *Letters of the Continental Congress,* ed. Burnett, vol. 1, 256, etc.

to vote, etc.) There were disagreements among those political figures who held democratic views and who saw America's future in a strong but democratic state. Some of them supported not the essence of the Dickinson plan but its principle of centralism: during the debates in the Congress and in the states and towns, they tried to make this plan more democratic. Others were undecided or rejected the idea of centralism.[33]

These and other factors influenced the debates over the Articles of Confederation in the Congress and the subsequent ratification campaign in the states. In the course of sharp and prolonged debates in the Congress the initial draft was rewritten and expanded. The arguments between James Wilson and Thomas Burke, which reflected the antagonisms between the conservatives and the radicals, the centralists and the separatists, greatly affected the text of the Articles. Burke insisted that the articles substantially strengthening the power of the Congress should be changed. He was able to thwart almost all the attempts by the conservative centralists to establish a strong government apparatus.[34] The Articles of Confederation that eventually emerged from the struggle over the draft of the constitution differed in major ways from the conservatives' initial version.

If the most significant feature of the Dickinson plan was the creation of a central government endowed with broad and unlimited power over the most important areas of the country's political life, the final version of the Articles of Confederation[35] was characterized by a clear division of political authority: the states were to have certain powers, while the Continental Congress was given its own prerogatives. These prerogatives were clearly stated and defined. The Congress did not have the right to violate or intervene in state legislation. It had no blanket supremacy over the state authorities. But the final version of the Articles of Confederation did make the Continental Congress the only body wielding power throughout the country. The Congress was to consist of a single chamber, in which each state would have one vote. The Congress was to be headed by an elected president. Every year each state was to appoint a delegation according to rules determined by the state legislature. The delegations comprised from two to seven delegates, who were to be maintained by their state. A state had the right to recall its delegates. A delegate

33. Jensen, *Articles of Confederation,* chaps. iv–xii; Douglass, *Rebels and Democrats,* chap. 11, etc.

34. Thomas Burke was an opponent of the conservative centralist James Wilson and attacked the measures aimed at strengthening the central administration. He believed that these measures limited both the independence of the states in conducting internal policy as well as the rights of individuals. Burke's actions were, on the one hand, intended to preserve states' rights and the popular right to liberty, contributing to the development of the democratic movement in America opposed by the conservative centralists. Yet on the other hand, Burke's defense of the states' freedom to carry out their own internal policy helped not only the radicals who were in power in Pennsylvania but also the separatist conservatives in the southern states, who as a result of Burke's success were now free to act to preserve the aristocratic regimes and the institution of slavery in their states. *Journals of the Continental Congress,* ed. Ford, vol. 7, 95; vol. 9, 908; *Letters of the Continental Congress,* ed. Burnett, vol. 1, 234; vol. 2, 243.

35. *Journals of the Continental Congress,* ed. Ford, vol. 5, 546–54; vol. 9, 907–25.

could sit in the Congress for not more than three years out of every six years; he was not allowed to occupy any paid position in the government of the United States. In the Congress the delegates enjoyed freedom of speech and personal immunity. When the Congress was in recess, authority would be exercised by a "Committee of States," to which each state could appoint one representative. The business of government would be conducted by commissions and officials appointed by the committee. Under the constitution, a decision on important matters required the agreement of nine states. Like the revolutionary committees that had existed during the War of Independence until new state constitutions were adopted, the Congress had many functions. The Confederation constitution provided neither for the formation of an administration nor for a chief executive. The Congress combined legislative and executive authority. Executive authority was exercised by the Congress largely through the authorities in the states. The Congress was in charge of national defense and supervised the army. The Congress and its committees composed of members of the state delegations collectively performed some of the functions of a central government. The Congress had the authority to declare war, conduct foreign policy, and regulate trade with the Indians. It could regulate weights and measures and was in charge of the mails. It supervised the minting of coins by the Confederation and by the states but could not regulate the states' issuing of paper money. The Congress did not have the power to regulate foreign trade directly. Under the constitution the states were allowed to raise their own militia—their own armies; they also enjoyed other important rights, such as the power to introduce tariffs and to collect taxes. The federal budget was to be made up by contributions from the states. Thus the Congress described in the Articles could not regulate the national economy or reliably defend the economic and diplomatic interests of the American bourgeoisie in the world.[36]

One of the major problems facing the American bourgeois revolution was the regulation of national commercial and industrial activities. The rapidly developing and potentially enormous U.S. economy certainly demanded continental actions that would reflect the desires of the American bourgeoisie. Because this first American constitution—the Articles of Confederation—did not fulfill these demands, the American bourgeoisie subsequently tried to have it changed.

The Articles of Confederation failed to address another issue that democratic leaders of the Revolution like Jefferson and Paine had discussed—slavery. The problem of slavery affected the character of this first national constitution. The concern of conservative southerners over the fate of the "peculiar institution" strengthened their localist attitudes and helped prevent them from granting the Congress significant political power to regulate economic activity. For their part, the conservative elements in the middle and northern states were also reluctant to solve this problem democratically at the national level. The solution of the problem of slavery was left to the states.[37]

36. Ibid., vol. 9, 907–25.
37. Ibid., vol. 5, 548, etc.; vol. 9, 785, etc.; vol. 2, 48, etc.

The final version of the Articles of Confederation submitted to the states for debate and ratification on November 17, 1777, came into effect only on March 1, 1781. The principal cause of the delay in ratification was the disagreement over one of the main issues of the Revolution—the disposition of the western territories. Two groups of states, headed respectively by Maryland and Virginia, contested the right to control the western lands. In the course of this controversy Maryland, which could make no formal claim to the western territories, appealed to the Congress. This state advocated the creation of a strong central government that could control the administration of the western lands. Virginia, which claimed these lands on the basis of its charter, wanted a weak central government. Since the Articles of Confederation did not provide for a strong central authority, Maryland tried to sabotage ratification of the Confederation in order to get Virginia to cede its lands to the central government. Virginia finally made some concessions, making it possible for the Articles of Confederation to come into effect.[38] The disposition of the western lands was left for the Congress to work out.

The long delay in ratification meant that the Articles of Confederation came into effect when forces in the country had gradually started to change in favor of the moderate and conservative groups. This fact helped these groups in their move to amend the first national constitution. The aim of this movement was once again to fight for a strengthening of the central government against the "mistakes" and "extremes" of the democratic leaders who, having clearly defined and strictly limited the powers of the Congress, had given the states wide latitude in the conduct of internal policy. In 1775–1778 having power in the states firmly in the hands of the democratic leaders meant that reforms and democratic changes in the life of the country could be carried out.

The Articles of Confederation expressed much of what the American people had gained. This constitution proclaimed the country's independence and rejected monarchy. It helped to consolidate republican institutions, traditions, and attitudes in American society. The constitution of the Confederation sealed the union of the states that had been created by the resistance and the war against Britain. It reflected the demands of the masses and in particular their calls for a strengthening of popular control over government, for democratization, and for the weakening of the power of the bureaucrats.

The drafting and adoption of the Articles should have contributed to the process of democratic change. However, the Articles did not express democratic ideas and demands clearly and fully enough. This first national constitution did not become a comprehensive program for major social reform. The Articles of Confederation failed to develop the democrats' demands for "life, liberty and the pursuit of happiness" expressed in the Declaration of Independence. It did not meet the needs of those who supported a centralized democratic state—a progressive form of government. The first constitution established a Confederation or Union of States, every member of which enjoyed considerable independence, rather than a centralized democratic

---

38. Ibid., vol. 2, 196; vol. 5, 549; vol. 9, 843; vol. 15, 1063; *Letters of the Continental Congress,* ed. Burnett, vol. 2, 140, 257.

state. The special features of the Articles of Confederation resulted from various factors, the most important being the complicated distribution of forces in American society during the Revolutionary period. There was no unity within the different social strata of the Revolutionary patriotic camp. In the course of the Revolution no single group among the patriots was able to establish its superiority. In the complex conditions of a constantly developing revolutionary process aggravated by the need to wage a war of liberation, the patriots had to unite rather than fragment their forces. They were therefore obliged to compromise in order to solve the important internal problems facing the country. In these circumstances the Confederation reflected the difficulty Americans had in overcoming their disunity and their lack of mutual understanding—the heritage of more than 150 years of colonial history. In 1787–1789, having strengthened their position as a result of the successes of a rapidly developing capitalism and the defeat of the democratic forces, the ruling classes were able to create a centralized state.

COMMENT BY JACK N. RAKOVE

Immodest though it may seem, my first reaction to V. A. Ushakov's essay is to wonder whether or how its arguments set forth back in 1973 would have been affected had its author been able to read more recent works, including my own work on the Articles of Confederation, Peter S. Onuf's brilliant treatment of jurisdictional controversies and the development of American federalism, and Jack P. Greene's partly synthetic, partly monographic survey of continuities between the problems of dividing power within the British empire and the new American Republic.[1] Each of these works discards key assumptions that Ushakov shares with Progressive historiography; in distinct yet complementary ways, each locates the first phase of American federalism in a context that attributes little importance to the internal politics of the thirteen original states or the aspirations of different classes. My writings stress how the exigencies of revolutionary politics led the framers of the Articles of Confederation to settle on a reasonably pragmatic division of authority between Congress and the states. Onuf uses the territorial controversies that accompanied independence to illuminate a number of conceptual problems, from the meaning of citizenship to the definition of statehood to the logic of federalism as a solution to the political debilities of the states. Greene draws substantially on our two works in his concluding chapters, but adds a great deal more by showing that notions of customary provincial autonomy were deeply rooted in both the theory and practice of the British empire prior to the Revolutionary agitation that began in 1765.

Since Ushakov's article was published in Russia in 1973, it would be unfair to fault him for not responding to or incorporating these approaches in his essay. Taking his work on its own, however, I still find much to criticize. The basic problem is not so much that its guiding assumptions seem dated but rather that too much of its argument relies on abstractions that do not accurately describe the realities of Revolutionary politics.

The first difficulty that all scholars face in assessing the Articles of Confederation is to avoid viewing the first federal constitution from the natural vantage point of 1787. There is, of course, good reason to interpret the federal constitution as the Federalists originally treated it—that is, as a combined remedy for both the "imbecility" of Congress under the Articles and the vices of republican government within the states. But the obvious fact that the constitutional politics of the late 1780s had this dual character does not prove that the same matrix of concerns had operated in similar fashion a decade earlier when the Continental Congress drafted the Confederation during one of the most difficult phases of the military conflict. The great error of Merrill Jensen's approach (or more broadly, the Progressive historians' approach) to the framing of the Articles, I believe, was to establish a false symmetry between

---

1. Jack N. Rakove, *The Beginnings of National Politics: An Interpretive History of the Continental Congress* (New York, 1979); Peter S. Onuf, *The Origins of the Federal Republic: Jurisdictional Controversies in the United States, 1775–1787* (Philadelphia, 1983); and Jack P. Greene, *Peripheries and Center: Constitutional Development in the Extended Polities of the British Empire and the United States, 1607–1788* (Athens, Ga., 1986).

the two constitutions. In Jensen's familiar formulation, the Articles of Confederation represented the democratic impulses that came to the fore of American politics at independence, while the Constitution marked a victory for conservatives seeking protection and retrenchment from the radical excesses of republican politics in the states.

Ushakov seems to dissent from this position in the opening paragraphs of his essay, noting that Jensen and others tend "to overrate the Articles of Confederation as an embodiment of the democratic ideals of the period," and that they also "have trouble analyzing and evaluating the objective causes that led to the creation of the Constitution." Yet I am puzzled to detect where, in the body of the essay, Ushakov departs from the familiar contours of the Progressive approach. As I read his essay, it still seems to suggest that the drafting of the Articles of Confederation should be viewed within a framework that sets the democratic aspirations of the "masses" within the states against the centralizing desires of conservative "ruling classes." Perhaps more than Jensen, Ushakov reveals an awareness of the difficulty of explaining all facets of congressional politics as a function of maneuvers among rigidly defined blocs of delegates. After a rather puzzling reference to the "tendency to unify the states . . . based on 150 years of common colonial development," Ushakov notes that the states were seriously divided "economically, politically, and ideologically" and these divisions produced divisions in Congress, where "different factions and groupings repeatedly came together, combined into blocs, and then again split from each other." Yet by persistently invoking such labels as "conservative," "radical," and "moderate," and by suggesting that these descriptions correspond to very different notions of structures of political authority as well as positions on strategies of resistance, Ushakov follows a well-trod path. It is noteworthy, for example, that he links conservative patriots with outright Loyalists in their mutual dread of the consequences of revolution, in part by according more importance to Joseph Galloway's plan of Anglo-American union than it deserves, in greater measure by suggesting that "the conservatives and Loyalists were united by the class basis of their political and social views, though they differed in their actual plans for the reorganization of society." One can only wonder what the concept of class unity means when Loyalists and conservatives differed on both the issue of resistance and social reorganization.

But the most important basis for assessing this article is, of course, its treatment of the Articles of Confederation. And here is exactly where Ushakov's approach is most problematic.

The central issue centers on the question of whether the initial movement for drafting articles of confederation was the product of a conservative campaign to establish a strong "central government" to act "as a counterbalance to the democratic tendencies at the local level." As Ushakov sees it, the draft prepared by John Dickinson in June 1776 could have sustained the development of a "strong central government." The Dickinson plan "contained numerous provisos and exceptions that allowed for broad interpretation of the central government's authority and granted the colonies in the federation only limited power," while simultaneously granting "Congress what was in effect unlimited authority." This draft, Ushakov adds, was supported by conservatives who "had lost their power to more democratic leaders" in the states.

A claim as broad as this needs two sources of support to be compelling. It would be useful, first, to identify exactly which clauses in the Articles would have had the far-reaching implications Ushakov ascribes to them and how they would have worked to protect the interests of their "conservative" authors and advocates. In the second place, such an interpretation of the *constitutional* thrust of the Articles also requires a credible *political* explanation of how a Congress representing states with different interests, and elected by legislatures presumably responsive to democratic forces within the individual states, would actually muster the consensus required to exercise its powers vigorously. (This second reservation is, of course, essentially Madisonian.)

As to the first of these points, it is true that Dickinson did envision a form of confederation that would limit the autonomy of the states in certain ways. Article XVIII of the draft reported by the committee Dickinson chaired contained a pregnant clause stating that Congress could not "interfere in the internal Policy of any Colony [state], any further than such Policy may be affected by the Articles of this Confederation." Yet susceptible to expansive interpretation as this clause might theoretically have been, in operation it was almost certainly intended to refer to areas of governance tied to the conduct of war and its logistical support. Whether it would also have been understood to allow Congress to interfere with "internal Police" for other reasons—in the sense, say, that Madison later proposed giving the national government a veto over all state laws—is much to be doubted. The most notable inroad on state autonomy that Dickinson considered lay in the realm of religious belief: his first draft included a provision affirming that individuals should suffer no "abridgement of their civil Rights for or on Account of their religious Persuasion, profession or practice." This proposal, however, did not survive the scrutiny of the larger committee; nor does the evidence suggest that Dickinson or anyone else contemplated any analogous reduction in the other residual legislative powers of the states. In short, it is difficult to see how the Dickinson plan would have worked to retrench the political power of the "ruling classes" even if it had been adopted in its entirety.[2]

Ushakov pays little attention to the one issue that proved most controversial during the debates of July and August 1776: the question of control over western lands. Here, indeed, the Dickinson plan would have eroded the powers of the states—or rather, of those states that had plausible claims to the "waste lands" of the interior—while endowing Congress with a crucial responsibility for the future development of the country. But after heated debate, a majority of the states in Congress rejected the proposed powers over the West. Again, it is not easy to see how this issue can buttress the interpretation that Ushakov advances, largely because it divided the states into two competing blocs based not on issues of class or social structure but on the accidents of their colonial charters.

In arguing that the course of democratic politics in the states was *not* a factor in the framing of the Articles of Confederation, I do not mean to suggest that members of Congress were oblivious to the possibility that revolution would disrupt traditional social relations or bring unwanted challenges to existing structures of authority. Such

2. I discuss the evolution of the Dickinson plan in *Beginnings of National Politics,* 151–62.

fears obviously preyed deeply on the minds of men like Robert Morris, Gouverneur Morris, James Wilson, John Jay, and others. But remarkable or puzzling as it may seem to us, these concerns did not affect their thinking about the problem of confederation in the mid-1770s—or even, for that matter, in the early 1780s. There is, quite simply, little if any evidence to indicate that the framers of the Articles approached their task with anything remotely resembling the convictions that a decade later persuaded Madison that the solution to the distinct problems of the confederation *and* of republican government within the states were closely and necessarily linked. Neither time nor experience allowed the authors of the first federal constitution to think much beyond the immediate problems they faced in managing the war effort. On the whole, they moved quickly to establish a fairly pragmatic division of authority between Congress and the states and found their deliberations imperiled only when they had to resolve three issues—western lands, representation, and the apportionment of expenses— that divided the states into blocs formed on the basis of palpable interests. Far from worrying that an excess of democracy in the states would disrupt the war effort, the framers assumed—naively, it turned out—that republican virtue would be the animating principle leading the states to carry out their federal duties. As Madison observed in 1787, the framers of the Articles had overlooked the need to find some method to compel the state governments to obey congressional decisions because they acted "from a mistaken confidence that the justice, the good faith, the honor, the sound policy, of the several legislative assemblies" would secure the requisite compliance.[3]

Suppose, however, that "centralizing" tendencies did have greater weight in 1776– 1777 and that Congress was vested with at least as much authority as conservatives ideally might have wanted. How easily would Congress have mustered the political consensus required to impose its will on recalcitrant states or social groups, and how would this authority have been exercised? The short answer to these implicitly skeptical questions is that Congress would have found it enormously difficult to do either. An assembly composed of representatives from avowedly provincial societies, subject to annual elections by the state legislatures, and whose members' private interests were linked to those of their states, would hardly have been in a position to set its course in defiance of the complex and diverse interests of its constituents. Neither in the Dickinson plan nor any other draft of the Confederation do we encounter the idea that Congress should legislate directly. The entire notion that some serious form of "centralization" was a viable option in 1776 is hard to accept. In my view, then, Ushakov goes much too far when he argues acceptance of the Dickinson plan would have "subjected American society to a centralized power that was not answerable to the will of the people."

This speculation is, in any case, undermined by the ensuing explanation that Ushakov immediately offers for the revisions of the draft Articles of 1776. Though I am not wholly comfortable with his description of the divisions within Congress,

---

3. James Madison, "Vices of the Political System of the United States," in *The Papers of James Madison,* Robert Rutland et al., eds. (Chicago and Charlottesville, 1962–), vol. 9, 351.

he nevertheless is correct to explain why excessive centralization would have been politically unacceptable in this early phase of the Revolution. So, too, I agree with Ushakov that "the final version of the Articles of Confederation was characterized by a clear division of political authority" between the states and Congress. But the central question remains: was this division a function of an explicitly and self-consciously democratic, state-oriented ideology, designed to further "reforms and democratic changes in the life of the country," or was it more the consequence of the framers' pragmatic attempt to allow Congress to direct the war effort while recognizing that a host of administrative decisions about the support of the war could be intelligently taken only at the level of the states?

To persuade me that the former position was correct would require more evidence than Ushakov has been able to provide here, or for that matter, than Merrill Jensen offered for a similar thesis half a century ago.

RESPONSE BY V. A. USHAKOV

I should like to thank my American colleagues for their interest in my work and particularly Mr. Jack N. Rakove for his careful analysis and detailed review of my article.

Rakove discusses in some detail recent publications on the subject of my article. He shows their role in undermining the positions of the Progressive historians (particularly Merrill Jensen), the influence of whose principal ideas, he believes, my article reveals. I am not authorized to offer a defense of the positions of Progressive historiography—a task which, I think, could be better performed by Jensen's followers. I should only like to make two points. First, the names of Beard, Jensen, and the other eminent representatives of this school are known outside the United States. The considerable amount of research they carried out has on the whole helped rather than hindered the work of subsequent generations of historians. In this sense it may be said that the members of the Progressive school have written some of the more illustrious pages in the annals of historical knowledge. Their books, whatever their strengths and weaknesses, continue to enjoy a wide readership. And if some scholars still take the writings and conclusions of the Progressive historians into account, surely this does not amount to some terrible professional *faux pas*. Indeed, we have the example of Rakove himself, whose review contains concessions to the Progressives' commonsense approach as well as to certain facts and propositions that they discussed with special rigor. I refer to Rakove's acknowledgment in principle that the events of the Revolution had a profound impact on the minds of men like Robert Morris, Gouverneur Morris, James Wilson, John Jay, and others, who as a result became apprehensive about the consequences of the Revolution. Also my reviewer does not openly, or as a matter of principle, reject the Progressive interpretation, which states that the struggle for the adoption of the Constitution of the United States took place in conditions of heightened tension when some of the Constitution's supporters, striving to protect their interests, resisted the pressure of the democratic forces. My second point, therefore, is that to attempt to debunk this older generation of historians without trying to understand the logic of their development as scholars and without examining not only their mistakes but also their achievements would be to proceed in an unscientific manner.

The issue may also be formulated thus: which weapons from the armory of modern scholars, including Rakove, are worth adopting and even perfecting; and which ideas and insights in the works of other historians, including representatives of the Progressive school, appear preferable? Here it is necessary to compare the views of the Progressive historians with those of my reviewer. To justify his approach, Rakove examines the premises which, in his opinion, influenced the Progressives' conclusions. As Rakove puts it, "the great error of Merrill Jensen's approach (or more broadly, the Progressive historians' approach) to the framing of the Articles . . . was to establish a false symmetry between the two constitutions." This error, Rakove says, is evident in the Progressives' evaluation of the conditions, character, and goals of the constitutional policies pursued by American leaders in the late 1770s and late 1780s.

237

They almost automatically applied criteria appropriate for analyzing the creation of the Constitution of 1787 to the study of the processes that led to the writing of the Articles of Confederation. Rakove believes that the authors of the Articles had yet to confront the problem of correcting the "vices of republican government within the states"; in addition, they had yet to decide how to remedy the weaknesses of Congress under the Articles of Confederation. Having expressed his belief that there were significant differences in the goals pursued by the respective authors of the two American constitutions, Rakove suggests that in spite of the patriot leaders' fears of undesirable social developments, "the course of democratic politics in the states was *not* a factor in the framing of the Articles of Confederation."

Let us consider who is right here, and in what way. If we are to assume that the Progressive historians failed fully to take into account the particular features of the two stages in the constitutional development of the United States and were guilty of applying to the Articles of Confederation the same complex of analytical techniques and approaches they applied to the Constitution of 1787, Rakove's criticisms would appear to be generally well founded and justified. Indeed, it can be said that when writing their books the Progressive historians did not consider the investigation of the respective characters of the two periods of constitutional development to be their chief task. Thus, Jensen was anxious to show the continuity in the policies of the leaders of the patriotic camp and stressed the significance of the presence in the 1770s and 1780s of similar factors determining the course they followed. Yet Rakove's approach, although it has its advantages, suffers from what are potentially considerable shortcomings. That is to say, implicit in this approach is the danger of treating as absolute the differences in the two stages of the constitutional development of the United States and of overlooking the similarities in the situations that existed in the late 1770s and the late 1780s; his approach also entails the risk that the patterns of causality likely to have determined the strategies of the political forces then active would escape scholarly scrutiny. Certainly, in tackling the question Rakove raises—that of determining the specific character of the two periods of constitutional development and of ascertaining the influence of that character on the constitutional documents that were adopted at the time—the scholar should not be biased in favor of either one of these interpretations. What is called for here is a more profound scientific investigation of the history of these two periods so that we may identify not only the major, minor, and ostensible differences between them but also the factors and characteristics they had in common; after all, all these elements together influenced the fate of the constitutional documents.

These considerations are also relevant when one evaluates another important difference between Rakove and the Progressive historians. In Rakove's opinion the Progressives (and therefore to some extent this scholar, since I, says Rakove, "share" Jensen's "key assumptions") are guilty of ignoring or underestimating the many and varied realities of "revolutionary politics" and, in trying to explain all the events of the period within the framework of sociopolitical antagonisms, are guided by artificial models and "abstractions." Yet while accusing me and the Progressives of one-sidedness and oversimplification, Rakove in his review reveals how rigid his own approach is. In effect, he refuses to admit even the possibility that socioeconomic antagonisms generated by the social realities of the period may have influenced the constitutional development of the United States in the 1770s. We are faced with a rigid model of a different kind and a bias toward another extreme, which together create the danger that elucidating and analyzing the complex and varied factors of "revolutionary politics" will find its expression in the substitution of first causes by less important ones.

The historical record contains vivid enough testimony by the leaders and members of the various political factions about their intentions, aims, and methods during the successive stages of the Revolution. In the light of this testimony Rakove's thesis—which states that the movement advocating the drafting of the Articles of Confederation was not "the product of a conservative campaign to establish a strong 'central government' to act 'as a counterbalance to the democratic tendencies at the local level' "—may be corrected or even termed questionable. The same is true of his contention that the fears of conservatives like Gouverneur Morris or James Wilson of what they regarded as the undesirable sociopolitical consequences of the Revolution "did not affect their thinking about the problem of confederation in the mid-1770s—or even . . . the early 1780s." Rakove's statement that "the course of democratic politics in the states was *not* a factor in the framing of the Articles of Confederation" is equally questionable.

Within the scope of my response I can only cite some, albeit interesting and revealing, historical evidence. At the start of the Revolution some politicians, like Gouverneur Morris, believed that only the strong arm of the mother country was capable of suppressing chaos in America; only Great Britain could keep American society within the framework of legality and prevent radical changes that threatened to deprive the upper strata of their power and positions.[1] Today his remarks are quoted by many historians. Less well known are the statements in a similar vein by James Duane made during sessions of the First Continental Congress about the need for a supreme controlling authority in America.[2] Likewise in the spring of 1774 Thomas Wharton stated that a "supreme legislature" was the power that should "adopt laws relating to general policy" and also "restrain the spirit of anxiety in any of the colonies and provide England, as well as the colonies, with greater security."[3] This is what Thomas Paine said about Americans like Duane and Wharton in his treatise *Common Sense:* "They dreaded an independence, fearing that it would produce civil wars."[4]

1. *American Archives,* ed. Peter Force, 4th ser., 6 vols. (Washington, D.C., 1837–1848), vol. 1, 342–43; *The Diary and Letters of Governeur Morris,* ed. A. C. Morris, 2 vols. (London, 1889, 1980), vol. 1, 4–7, etc.

2. *Letters of Members of the Continental Congress,* ed. Edmund C. Burnett, 8 vols. (Gloucester, Mass., 1963), vol. 1, 24–25, 38–44, especially 42.

3. Quoted in Merrill Jensen, "The Idea of a National Government during the American Revolution," *Political Science Quarterly* 58 (1943), 359–60.

4. *The Complete Writings of Thomas Paine,* ed. Philip S. Foner, 2 vols. (New York, 1945), vol. 1, 27; Thomas Paine, *Selected Writings* (Moscow, 1969), 44.

The positions of the various political factions became clearly defined in 1774–1776 as the process of political reform and the creation of new power structures in the colonies unfolded. The revolutionary events in Massachusetts—the masses' demands for the democratization of sociopolitical life, for the removal from power of some moderate politicians, and for the implementation of measures that even many of the patriot leaders considered "leveler"-like—forced the leaders on at least two occasions in 1775 to approach the Continental Congress for advice in creating new organs of authority capable of controlling the situation. The journals of the Continental Congress and the writings of John Adams, who was also alarmed by the leveler-like mood of the masses, show that for the time being the Congress confined itself to offering moderate advice, which, according to Adams, satisfied only the conservative delegates from Pennsylvania and New York (John Dickinson and James Duane). However, beginning in the summer of 1775 the other colonies also experienced increased political ferment and the establishment of more and more new institutions of authority. In the autumn of 1775 Dickinson, wishing to halt these developments, managed to get the Pennsylvania legislature to instruct its delegates to the Continental Congress to oppose measures changing the governments of the colonies or declaring them independent.[5]

By the summer of 1776 the situation in America had changed. Although a number of politicians still feared that "new men will occupy the seat of power" in the states,[6] some of them, finding themselves pushed to the threshold of inevitable change, sought to strengthen their positions. Carter Braxton's behavior was revealing. He continued to denounce the northerners for what he considered their intolerable predilection for "democracy" and to claim that the leaders of New England "were presented with the best opportunity . . . to rid themselves of dependence and avail themselves of their beloved democracy." But at the same time he demanded that all the tensions in the country be diffused, that a union of the states be created, and that a central authority be established; these, he believed, were the indispensable conditions for the United States to declare independence.[7] Braxton put forward his own plan for the organization of government in the states. On behalf of change and American independence, John Adams advocated a somewhat different program. In March of 1776 he wrote:

> All our misfortunes stem from a single cause—the reluctance of the southern colonies [to establish] a republican government. . . . The difficulty lies in the drafting of constitutions for the individual colonies and of a continental constitution. Each colony should establish its own government, and then . . . a union must be brought into being. This can be done only by proceeding on the basis of popular principles and rules which so [conflict] with the inclinations of the barons of the South and the propertied interests in the middle colonies . . . that I sometimes fear the consequences. Nevertheless, patience and perseverance will in time overcome all these obstacles.[8]

5. *Journals of the Continental Congress, 1774–1789,* ed. W. C. Ford et al., 34 vols. (Washington, D.C., 1904–1937), vol. 2, 76–78, 83–84, etc.; *Diary and Autobiography of John Adams,* ed. Lyman Butterfield, 5 vols. (Cambridge, Mass., 1964), vol. 3, 326, 351–53, etc.
6. *Letters of Continental Congress,* ed. Burnett, vol. 1, 431.
7. Ibid., 420–21.
8. Ibid., 406.

The left wing of the Congress was largely able to carry out its program. In spite of resistance from the conservatives, particularly Dickinson's ally James Wilson, the Congress on May 10–15, 1776, passed a resolution, with a preamble, that dissolved the old colonial administration and cleared the way for the establishment in the colonies of new power structures independent of the British crown.[9] As a result the reform of the state governments gathered momentum in the succeeding months; in Pennsylvania, for example, political figures such as Wilson and Dickinson were forced to retreat before leaders who held more radical views. Adams had declared: "The grandees, patricians, . . . nabobs, call them what you will, sigh and moan . . . but in vain. . . . The arrogance that is born of the offensive dominance of the few, the so very few rich family monopolies will be destroyed." His prophetic words were now coming to pass.[10]

In these circumstances Dickinson, Wilson, and their followers refused to support independence and continued to focus their attention on organizing the central government of the United States. In his speech in Congress of July 1, 1776, Dickinson repeated many of Braxton's earlier arguments against independence and in favor of the preliminary establishment of a union and the adoption of a national constitution. The speech showed the importance the conservative forces attached to such a constitution for the Confederation. Under the impact of Revolutionary events these conservative leaders drew up their plans, resulting in the draft of the Articles of Confederation that Dickinson composed in the summer of 1776. Thus, Article III of the draft read: "Each colony shall preserve and apply its currently existing laws, rights and customs to the extent it deems necessary." Thus, having failed to prevent the adoption by the Congress of the resolution of May 10–15, the conservatives now intended to protect their positions with the help of the Articles of Confederation. Wilson's ally Dickinson inserted into the text of the future national constitution a kind of statutory antidote. Its purpose was to avoid the automatic and total abolition of the old institutions of state government and to prevent the states from introducing into their constitutions and laws changes that threatened the conservatives with the loss of their power and influence. There were major differences between Dickinson's draft version of Article III of the Articles of Confederation and the text of Article III in Benjamin Franklin's draft of 1775. Franklin's version of Article III in effect directed the patriots to carry out democratic reforms in the colonies, but Dickinson's version was meant to hinder as much as possible the implementation of such reforms.

An examination of the main points in Dickinson's draft reveals his desire to establish a strong central government in the United States. This government would be capable of guaranteeing certain political interests if they should be confronted by undesirable (that is, democratic) developments at the local level. The centralizing

9. *Journals of the Continental Congress,* ed. Ford, vol. 4, 342, 351, 357–58. See also V. A. Ushakov, "Aspects of the History of the Political Struggle in the American Colonies on the Eve of the Proclamation of the Declaration of Independence," *The American Annual, 1978* (Moscow, 1978), 262–73.

10. Quoted in Merrill Jensen, *The Founding of a Nation* (New York, 1968), 665. See also Ibid., 24–25.

tendencies of Dickinson's draft were discussed extensively and sometimes even paradoxically in the debates. The text that emerged as a result of these debates, including the so-called Burke-Wilson confrontation, differed considerably from the one Dickinson had drafted. As James Wilson regretfully observed, the authority of the central government was weakened in the final version.[11]

Rakove declares that "the most important basis for assessing" my article is its "treatment of the Articles of Confederation. And here is exactly where Ushakov's approach is most problematic." Rakove criticizes my view that Dickinson's draft "contained numerous provisos and exceptions that allowed for broad interpretation of the central government's authority and granted the 'colonies' in the federation only limited power," and that at the same time gave the "Congress what was in effect unlimited authority." The reviewer believes this statement is so "broad" that additional evidence must be adduced in its "support." He accuses me of mistakenly approaching and treating the Articles of Confederation, and asks, first, "which clauses in the Articles would have had the far-reaching implications Ushakov ascribes to them" and "how they would have worked to protect the interests of their 'conservative' authors and advocates." Second, he says that, if my interpretation is to be substantiated, "a credible *political* explanation" must be offered to show "how a Congress representing states with different interests, and elected by legislatures presumably responsive to democratic forces within the individual states, would actually muster the consensus required to exercise its powers vigorously."

These then are Rakove's conclusions. Let us now examine the true state of affairs. First I should like to explain the role and significance of Article XVIII in Dickinson's draft. His draft consisted of twenty articles, of which Article XVIII was the longest. It was somewhat shorter than the preceding seventeen articles (Article XVIII is almost as long as the first thirteen articles put together). Article XVIII defined the status and sphere of activity of the "Assembly of the United States" (the Congress), listed its powers and prerogatives, and described the sequence in which they should be exercised. Article XVIII and Article XIX, which contained many provisions and determined the position, role, sphere of activity, and method of governance of the "Council of State"—the supreme executive and administrative body—together take up half of Dickinson's draft. I stress again that these articles were entirely devoted to describing the powers and prerogatives of the central organs of the government of the United States.

So what were these powers and prerogatives? Article XVIII gave the Congress the right to decide questions of war and peace; to formulate the rules governing the capture of prizes and trophies; to issue letters of marque and to establish tribunals for the adjudication of disputes about prizes and trophies and for trying cases of piracy and crimes on the high seas; to conduct the foreign policy of the United States and conclude treaties and alliances with foreign princes and powers; to conduct relations and to regulate trade with the Indian tribes and purchase land from them; to settle

---

11. *Letters of Continental Congress,* ed. Burnett, vol. 1, 517–18; Merrill Jensen, *The Articles of Confederation* (Madison, 1940, 1970), 242.

disputes among the "colonies" over questions of jurisdiction, borders, etc., and also to limit the territory of the old "colonies" and determine the territory and the borders of new ones; to control the military policy of the country and decide a number of questions relating to the upkeep and development of the army and navy and the conduct of military operations; to control defense spending and other expenditures; to regulate the country's financial affairs, including the minting of coins, the emission of banknotes, and the contracting of loans; to appoint the members of the council of state and the various committees, and to choose civil and military officials and commanders to conduct the affairs of the United States; to establish standards for weights and measures; to control and supervise the postal service; and to decide other matters in accordance with the interests of the United States. Article XIX also gave the council of state broad executive and administrative powers. Therefore, under Dickinson's plan the central government would have possessed effective levers for exercising strong influence on the "colonies"—the subjects of the Confederation—and for controlling the most important aspects of the life of the country. For instance, just the power to appoint civil and military officials responsible for implementing national policy and settling disputes among the "colonies" made it possible for the central government to exert strong pressure on any "colony" that might prove refractory. In the light of what has been said it becomes clear that my reviewer mistakenly attempts to reduce the central government's possible influence over the states merely to "areas of governance tied to the conduct of war and its logistical support." Yet even this sphere of activity was rather broad and provided the central government with ample scope for influencing policy, administration, and economics.

As the example of Article XVIII shows, Rakove's treatment of the Articles of Confederation is not completely faultless or beyond question. Indeed, the caveat in Article XVIII he cites not only prohibited the Congress from intervening "in the internal Police of any Colony, any further than such Police may be affected by the Articles of this Confederation" but also forever forbade it "to impose or levy any Taxes or Duties" other than postal ones. It is true that this caveat deprived the central government of important powers: the Congress could decide only the size of the sums to be spent and the method of their expenditure to carry out national policy or implement measures that served the interests of the individual "colonies"; and, in accordance with the procedure for calculating the financial quotas for each colony, it could require them to make appropriate payments or deliveries of goods to the central government. However, in all other cases—which represented a wide spectrum of issues—Article XVIII permitted the Congress to intervene in the internal policies of any colony. Such intervention was authorized if seven or nine out of the thirteen colonies agreed to it—a barrier that could be surmounted quite easily.

Other articles in Dickinson's draft imposed restrictions on the activities of the governments of the "colonies" and, if interpreted in a certain way, could be used against any member of the Union that pursued independent policies, let alone unsanctioned radical reforms. In addition to Articles XVIII and XIX, these were Articles II, III, IV, V, VIII, IX, X, XI, XII, XIII, and XIV. What were the constraints imposed by these articles and how would they have operated? Let us consider at least some of these restrictions. We have already discussed the significance of part one of Article III. The second part of this article was a kind of replica of the provision in Article XVIII; that is, it confirmed the prerogatives of the central government and the state authorities. Article II proclaimed the eternal indissolubility of the Union, into which the "Colonies" entered to ensure "their common Defence, the Security of their Liberties, and their mutual and general Welfare," and obligated the "Colonies" to render assistance to one another "against all Force offered to or attacks made upon them or any of them, on Account of Religion, Sovereignity, Trade, or any other Pretence whatever." The wording of Article II was broad and comprehensive. The article could be used not only against external enemies but also against violators of the peace inside the country—for example, against a state that was undermining the Union and damaging its members in one or all of the areas listed, or against a state that encroached upon the members' interests on "any other Pretence whatever." In any case, Article II placed no restrictions on the central government in this respect. Since soon thereafter the United States invented the doctrine of broadly interpreting the provisions of the Constitution, the possibility of such a scenario eventually occurring could hardly be excluded.

All that has been said here does not mean that such a course of events was preordained or inevitable; however, it shows the possibilities implicit in the wording of some of the articles of Dickinson's draft. The main aim of the authors of Articles IV and V was to forestall possible divisions among the members of the Union and hinder the development of separatist tendencies within it, as well as to prevent the states from conducting separate negotiations with the governments of Great Britain and other countries. At the same time Articles IV and V were worded so as to place in limbo the leaders of any state who violated the peace by undertaking radical reforms that lacked congressional sanction. Without the permission of Congress the states were categorically forbidden to request assistance from and negotiate and sign treaties with other states or foreign princes and powers. Other articles in the Dickinson draft also contained provisions that, if the need arose, could be used against those state governments that displeased the majority in Congress. The answers to the questions posed by my reviewer who finds it "difficult to see how the Dickinson plan would have worked to retrench the political power of the 'ruling classes' even if it had been adopted in its entirety" are partly to be found here as well.

I will now address the question of how the mechanism of collective sanctions would have been set into motion in the Congress. Rakove believes that the Congress was incapable of reaching the consensus that was so necessary for the decisive exercise of its prerogatives since the members of Congress were strongly committed to the interests of their home states and hardly would have been able to ignore completely the complex and varied interests of their electors. For these reasons Rakove finds the possibility that Congress might have undertaken such coercive policies hard to accept.

Although I am not sure that the mechanism for the adopting sanctions would have worked perfectly, without delays, hitches, or other difficulties, and above all, without intrigues and struggles among the political factions in the Congress and in the states, I can point to a fairly large number of instances where such actions by the Congress were successful. Let us recall the case of the adoption of the resolution and preamble of May 10–15, 1776, which doomed the old colonial administration and some conservative politicians to the loss of their power and influence. One could also mention the numerous cases where the Congress passed resolutions relating to the particular localities and adopted measures directed against the Loyalists— decisions that allowed for suppressing forces in disagreement with the majority of patriots. Many of these documents began with lengthy preambles about the threats to the Americans' rights and freedoms and the need to defend America against external dangers and the machinations of internal enemies. So we see that the Congress had the necessary experience, although in life no one is guaranteed freedom from difficulties and surprises.

My respected opponent appears to agree with some of my conclusions, particularly my evaluation of the final version of the Articles of Confederation and my explanation of the reasons why "excessive centralization would have been politically unacceptable in this early phase of the Revolution." Among the major factors that slowed down the process of rapprochement among the states and hindered the drafting and ratification of the Articles of Confederation were border disputes and the complicated claims of the states to the western territories. Rakove is probably right to say that in my study I did not analyze these subjects in sufficient depth. But in an article of limited length it is impossible to discuss every aspect of the history of the drafting and adoption of the first national constitution.

To sum up, although my article and Rakove's response show that we frequently differ in our opinions and conclusions over the Articles of Confederation, there are a number of points of agreement between us. The attempt my American colleague has made to establish the particular character of the process that produced the Articles of Confederation and the Constitution of 1787 and to study the many factors that shaped the realities of "revolutionary politics" deserves attention. However, if the evidence collected by historians has failed to convince Rakove of the importance of studying the sociopolitical dimension of the Articles of Confederation and of determining the role played by the various political forces in the creation of the structures of government in the United States, the propositions and arguments in his review have in turn failed to convince me of the absolute correctness of the views he and his colleagues espouse. As a representative of the East (in geographical relation to the United States), I am tempted to quote the parable about the elephant and the blind men who were asked to describe that animal. One of them touched the elephant's leg, another his trunk, and so forth, whereupon they all refused to believe each other and started to argue about who was right. The Articles of Confederation present such a large subject for study that it would appear that scholars have not yet analyzed their every aspect. But instead of comparing what they know and putting that knowledge together, at present they all defend their own individual interpretations. In the field of scholarship, no less than in that of politics, it may take time for new thinking to emerge. Nevertheless, my hope is that the two sides—the American and Soviet—have opportunities to succeed. It is now a question of realizing those opportunities.

CHAPTER 9

The American Farmers' Uprising under the Leadership of Daniel Shays, 1786–1787

by

Boris M. Shpotov

On August 29, 1786, there was unusual excitement on the roads leading to Northampton (a small town in the western part of the state of Massachusetts). Since early morning armed groups of farmers from the neighboring settlements of Hampshire County had been hurrying to the square where the courthouse stood and occupying all the approaches to the building. That day a session of the court of common pleas, which had jurisdiction over the cases of insolvent debtors, was to begin. When the judges entered the square in a solemn procession, they were met by the angry shouts of a crowd of fifteen hundred people, and the guards posted at the door to the court stood barring the way with arms at the ready. Thus began the 1786–1787 Massachusetts uprising, which came to be known as "Shays's Rebellion," after its best-known leader. This was the largest popular movement of the American Revolution in the eighteenth century and one of the most important political actions by farmers in the entire history of the United States. It reflected the depth of anger that a large segment of the small farmers and craftsmen felt at the socioeconomic results of the first American Revolution. The revolts of the poor were a response by the working masses to the new social order that the bourgeoisie and the planters had established in their own class interests.

Modern historians in the United States frequently disparage the role and significance of Shays's Rebellion and other popular movements in the American Revolution, as can be seen in the works of the "neoconservative" school—Robert Brown, Daniel Boorstin, Louis Hartz, Benjamin F. Wright, and others.[1] Brown sees the "middle class" exercising complete sway in American society at the time of the Revolution, making

1. For a detailed analysis of contemporary currents and schools in the American historiography of the Revolution of the eighteenth century, see N. N. Bolkhovitinov, "The U.S. War of Independence and Contemporary American Historiography," *Problems of History* 12 (1969), 73–88; and Bolkhovitinov, "Some Problems of the Historiography of the American Revolution of the Eighteenth Century," *Modern and Contemporary History* 6 (1973), 146–66. This article by Boris M. Shpotov was first published in *Modern and Contemporary History* 4 (1975).

any social tensions or conflicts impossible. In the opinion of Wright and especially Hartz, political actions by the working masses, and in particular the Massachusetts uprising, were moderate and "liberal," rather than revolutionary. Edmund Morgan's monograph on the formation of the American Republic says almost nothing about Shays's Rebellion, while in another work he completely denies the possibility of class antagonisms in eighteenth-century America, arguing that all Americans supposedly strove to acquire property, which served to unite rather than separate them. Boorstin, on the other hand, ignores altogether the issue of class struggle during the period of the Revolution. In his article "Reflections on Violence in the United States," Richard Hofstadter also speaks of the absence of a revolutionary tradition in America. He replaces the class struggle with various forms of "violence" that may have been of an economic, political, racial, religious, or other character. He alleges that this violence never disturbed "political stability" and lacked any social tenor. And the ruling circles supposedly always believed in the apolitical character and innocuousness of "acts of violence" such as Shays's Rebellion. Robert A. Feer, a new scholar in the field, completely denies a causal link between Shays's Rebellion and the adoption of the federal Constitution, in effect subscribing to the conclusions drawn by the conservative historians.[2]

This thesis about the peaceful and painless resolution of social tensions during the period of the American Revolution and about the "unrevolutionary mood" of the popular masses largely flows from a deliberate failure to mention well-known facts in the history of the class struggle in 1786–1787. But the "Progressive" historians and some other authors approach these popular movements from a different perspective. In his controversial article, Merrill Jensen regards the process that led to the formation of the United States as the struggle between two tendencies: the desire of the "lower classes" to develop the Revolution further and the attempts by the "upper classes" to stop the growth of the democratic movement.[3] The historians of the New Left— Jesse Lemisch, Staughton Lynd, and Alfred Young[4]—in studying the revolutionary tradition of the American people have not uncovered any new sources on the popular movements of 1786–1787. Historians such as Bernard Bailyn, Jensen, Lemisch, Pauline Maier, Ronald Hoffman, and others have concentrated on the political struggle

2. See Robert E. Brown, *Middle-Class Democracy and the Revolution in Massachusetts, 1691–1780* (Ithaca, 1955); Benjamin F. Wright, *Consensus and Continuity, 1776–1787* (Boston, 1958); Louis Hartz, *The Liberal Tradition in America* (New York, 1955); Edmund S. Morgan, *The Birth of the Republic, 1776–1789* (Chicago, 1956); Edmund S. Morgan, "The American Revolution: Revisions in Need of Revising," *William and Mary Quarterly,* 3d Ser., vol. 14 (1957), 3–15; Daniel Boorstin, *The Genius of American Politics* (Chicago, 1953) (it is revealing that by the early 1970s ten editions of this book had appeared); Richard Hofstadter, "Reflections on Violence in the United States," *American Violence: A Documentary History* (New York, 1970); Robert A. Feer, "Shays's Rebellion and the Constitution: A Study in Causation," *The New England Quarterly* 42 (1969), 388–410, and others.

3. Merrill Jensen, "The American People and the American Revolution," *Journal of American History* 57 (1970), 3–35.

4. For a detailed account of this see B. M. Shpotov, "The Historians of the New Left on the Class Struggle during the Period of the War of Independence," *Problems of History* 2 (1974), 177–85.

in the 1760s and 1770s; consequently, in the last decade American historians have almost completely lost interest in the events that took place in Massachusetts. Owing to the bicentenary of the formation of the United States, it is the authors of the definitive biographies of the Founding Fathers and the editors of their writings who now enjoy the greatest prestige.[5]

Shays's Rebellion has not yet been the subject of special study by Marxist historians, but its role and place in the American Revolution have already been established: the rebellion was an attempt by the "lower classes" to achieve its goals by "plebeian methods." The War of Independence was distinguished by the fact that although "the democratic element was very strong," the haute bourgeoisie was able to preserve its power until the end.[6]

In every bourgeois revolution, one sees not only antagonistic supporters and opponents of the ancien régime but also "a general opposition between exploiters and the exploited, rich spongers and poor toilers."[7] Waging war on the mother country united the efforts of the opposing classes for a while, but when the war ended, the situation radically changed. Having acquired power, the bourgeoisie and planters decided that their goals had been achieved and thus concluded the Revolution. The mood of the masses was different. Unlike the ruling clique, the masses were interested in developing the Revolution further.

The farmers, craftsmen, and workers who had shouldered the main burden of the War of Independence expected a decisive democratization of the social order and an improvement in living conditions. Meanwhile the working people had to carry the weight of the postwar financial and economic burdens. The huge government debt, which was being paid almost entirely by means of taxes levied on the population, and the saturation of the market with the products of English factories after the signing of peace led to specie flowing overseas or into the pockets of creditors. The acute shortage of money in circulation forced ordinary Americans to resort either to barter or to the services of usurers. Under such conditions the recovery of debts and the levying of taxes in specie impoverished the population and reduced its least affluent segment to complete penury. Insolvent debtors were put in jail, where prisoners were kept in inhuman conditions. This was frequently the lot of the poor farmers because most taxes fell precisely on immovable property such as houses, barns, and allotments. The profits of farmers were extremely low. In the 1780s the number of

5. See N. N. Bolkhovitinov, "Some Problems," 146–48; A. N. Shlepakov, "The U.S.A. on the Threshold of the Bicentenary of Independence," *Problems of History* (1973), 198. Shays's Rebellion had earlier been described in detail in a number of works that were largely objectivist in character. See for instance the monograph by Marion L. Starkey, *A Little Rebellion* (New York, 1955). The book by George R. Minot, a contemporary who was the clerk of the state house of representatives, is a valuable source on the history of the Massachusetts uprising. George R. Minot, *History of the Insurrections in Massachusetts in 1786 and the Rebellion Consequent Thereon* (Worcester, 1788; 3d ed., New York, 1971).

6. *Studies in Modern and Recent U.S. History* (Moscow, 1960), vol. 1, 104; A. V. Efimov, *U.S.A. Paths of Capitalist Development* (Moscow, 1969), 407, 411; William Z. Foster, *An Outline of American Political History* (Moscow, 1955), 177.

7. K.[arl] Marx and F.[riedrich] Engels, *Works,* vol. 19, 190.

farmers forced to sell their property for a song to pay creditors and tax collectors grew rapidly.

A court investigation, an auction, and the debtors' prison were frequently the lot of the poor, who were defenseless before the tyranny of the authorities; thus forceful attempts to stop court sessions and thwart the carrying out of court sentences spread throughout the colonies. During the Revolution popular conventions and assemblies at the local level met spontaneously, and their resolutions were printed in the newspapers and conveyed to the state legislatures. Those who took part in these gatherings believed that legislative initiative should come directly from the voters. This idea won great popularity with the masses. The lower classes saw their actions against judges and officials as defending freedom, property, and democracy. The chief economic demand of the majority of the rural population was the cheapening of money by issuing paper currency, which would have made it easier to pay debts and taxes. In addition, people proposed that accounts should be calculated not in money but in kind. The movement for debtor-relief legislation, which was joined by a number of merchants and planters who had been ruined by the war, was so strong throughout the country that in 1785–1787 paper money was officially adopted in the states of Rhode Island, New York, New Jersey, Pennsylvania, Georgia, and the two Carolinas. A partial moratorium on the recovery of debts was imposed and sometimes permission was granted to pay them in kind. These measures amounted to a significant concession to the working masses and in a number of cases prevented major uprisings of the poor, particularly in the South.[8]

Circumstances in the New England states developed differently. The rural population consisted largely of poor farmers who were burdened by debts and taxes. The payment of taxes and the usurious interest on mortgages consumed the lion's share of their income, and all their attempts to protest were to no avail. Only in Rhode Island, where the assembly was controlled by the small farmers, were the laws for the protection of debtors operating with full force. In neighboring Massachusetts, on the other hand, taxes were higher than anywhere else, and the inhabitants were taken to court for the nonpayment of the smallest debt. During just the first half of April 1782 the Hampshire County court received 221 petitions, almost all of them suits brought by creditors. It was this situation that provoked the first eruption of the people's anger: a crowd of poor people attempted to stop by force a session of the state supreme court and of the court of common pleas. The ringleaders were retired soldiers of the Continental Army whom the state government had not yet paid but was nevertheless taxing on an equal basis with all other citizens. The militia dispersed the mob, and its leader, the former Connecticut minister Samuel Ely, fell into the hands of the authorities. At his interrogation Ely sharply and fearlessly criticized the state constitution, declaring that the governor and the judges were waxing rich at the people's expense and that the legislative assembly was a useless and unnecessary institution.[9] On July 15, 1782, the people released Ely from jail. To prevent the

8. *The Papers of Thomas Jefferson,* ed. Julian P. Boyd et al. (Princeton, 1955), vol. 11, 279.

9. Lee N. Newcomer, *The Embattled Farmers: A Massachusetts Countryside in the American Revolution* (New York, 1953), 136.

release of other figures in the movement, the state authorities mobilized a detachment of almost fifteen hundred militia. To escape persecution Ely fled to Vermont, but was soon arrested there.

Fearing the growth of popular discontent, the government of Massachusetts agreed to certain concessions; on July 3, 1782, it allowed debtors to pay their creditors not in money but in agricultural produce during a one-year period. This measure, however, did not save the situation, and upon the expiration of the law's period of validity, debt recovery was resumed with new and greater vigor. The events of 1782 were, in the words of George R. Minot, "the first signal for hostilities between creditors and debtors, between the rich and the poor, between the few and the many."[10] Frequently a debtor was someone else's creditor, and bringing a lawsuit against one person was enough to produce a whole avalanche of court cases. In 1784–1785 in Worcester County in western Massachusetts, four thousand court actions were brought, that is, almost every single family was sued; in Groton in 1784–1785 every third or fourth resident was tried between one and twelve times. In February 1786 alone the Hampshire County court received 333 petitions for the recovery of debts. In 1786 the jail in the small town of Concord held three times as many persons imprisoned for the nonpayment of debts as other criminals, and in Worcester there were twenty times as many! The costs of trying the cases were high, and a whole army of lawyers, clerks, and attorneys lived at the expense of the litigants. It is no surprise that the people regarded judges and lawyers as their sworn enemies.

The Massachusetts legislature (the General Court) received numerous petitions demanding an improvement in the position of the poor. Farmers from the settlement of Greenwich wrote in January 1786 that the total sum of their taxes equaled the income from their farms, that the property of debtors was auctioned off daily at very low prices, and that court costs were excessively high:

> Many of our good inhabitants are now confined in gole for det and for taxes: maney have fled. . . . Honoured Sirs, are not these imprisonments and fleeing away of our good inhabitants very injurious to the credit or honour of the Commonwealth? Will not the people in the neighbouring States say of this State: altho' the Massachusets bost of their fine constitution, their government is such that itt devours their inhabitents? . . . We therefore most humbly pray your honours to admitt a paper currancy and make itt a tender in all payments whatsoever, or some other way to releave your petitioners as your honours in your grate wisdom shall think most proper.[11]

Poor farmers were outraged by the large salary the governor of Massachusetts received (eleven hundred Massachusetts pounds per annum) and the financial extortions inflicted upon them for the purpose of raising money to pay the interest on the national debt. Declining wealth affected the people's political participation: those who

10. Minot, *History of the Insurrections,* 15.
11. A. A. Guber and A. V. Efimov, eds., *A Reading-Book on Modern History* (Moscow, 1963), vol. 1; for the full English text see Samuel E. Morison, ed., *Sources and Documents Illustrating the American Revolution 1764–1788 and the Formation of the Federal Constitution* (Oxford, 1929), 208–10.

received a yearly income of less than three pounds or who owned property in the value of less than sixty pounds were deprived of the right to vote. The western counties were often unable to send the requisite number of representatives to the General Court, for to travel to Boston and live there was expensive; therefore inhabitants of those areas demanded that the seat of the legislative assembly be moved to the interior of the state. The situation in the western and central counties was gradually becoming more tense. The refusal of the General Court to pass a bill authorizing the issue of paper money and the introduction of new taxes in the summer of 1786 triggered an armed uprising.

Once again, as at the time of military operations against the English colonists in 1775, loud calls to defend the rights and privileges of the people from malicious encroachments were heard in the taverns and other sites of mass meetings and gatherings. The most active citizens, who had formerly served with the Continental Army or the state militia, donned their old uniforms and retrieved the weapons they had laid away. The distinguishing mark of the Regulators, as the rebels occasionally called themselves, were the green sprigs they wore on their hats. In the summer of 1786 people's conventions met in western Massachusetts. Their collective demands were: the transfer of the General Court from Boston to the interior of the state, the issue of paper money, the lowering of attorneys' fees, the reduction of the salaries of government officials, and the suspension of court proceedings against debtors until the position of the people had improved. In addition the delegates to the conventions put forward important political demands: the abolition of the state senate, which was controlled by the rich, and a revision of the Massachusetts constitution. At the same time the citizens of the state were advised to refrain from any "illegal acts" and to seek redress of their grievances in a purely constitutional manner.[12]

The common people, however, decided to act, and on August 29, fifteen hundred armed men forced the judges to leave Northampton. A week later three hundred men led by a retired officer, Adam Wheeler, surrounded the courthouse in the town of Worcester. The judges managed to make their way to the door of the court but were met by bayonets leveled at their chests. The judges tried to hold a session of the court in a neighboring house, but the people expelled them from there as well. As a result the court of common pleas gave a written promise to disband for an indefinite period, while the magistrates' court promised to disband until November 21, 1786.

Court sessions were disrupted in a number of other places as well, and the rebels from Middlesex were joined by men from Hampshire County. "They took possession of the Court House and paraded with great insolence before the court who had assembled at a small distance"; then the leader of the rebels, Captain Job Shattuck, ordered the judges to disperse in the name of the people. In Bristol County three hundred militiamen led by Major-General David Cobb attempted to defend the judges, but the judges left voluntarily. Eight hundred rebels armed with clubs and muskets broke into the debtors' jail in Great Barrington (Berkshire County) and released the prisoners. In September 1786 rebels prevented court sessions in the western and

---

12. Morison, ed., *Sources and Documents,* 221; Minot, *History of the Insurrections,* 34–37.

central counties from being held.[13] The Regulators were successful without having to use weapons; as soon as the intimidated judges agreed to postpone the court session, the Regulators went home peacefully. There was no looting, violence, or loss of life on either side. But in spite of this the authorities charged the rebels with forming "unlawful assemblies" and alleged that the rebels had armed themselves with muskets, sabres, clubs, and other weapons to commit "acts of violence." The authorities held that where such acts occurred, the sheriff had the right "to disperse it [the gathering] and to apprehend the persons who compose it." And in the case of his orders being disobeyed, he was authorized to order the militia to open fire.[14] But the militia, which was staffed by ordinary citizens, frequently went over to the rebellious people. The rebels were in great need of a respected and experienced leader; Captain Shays of Pelham, Hampshire County, eventually came to be that man.

The biographical information about the man whose name was given to the uprising of the Massachusetts farmers is fairly scant.[15] Daniel Shays was born in 1747 into a poor family. It is not known whether he attended a school of any kind, but he learned to write, as may be seen from certain documents that survive. At the age of twenty-three Shays became employed as a laborer on one of the farms in Brookfield and earned what in those days was a respectable wage—fifty-three dollars per month. Contemporaries recalled that he had "pleasant manners and was a good worker." In 1772 Shays married the daughter of a wealthy citizen of Brookfield and three years later acquired a farm in Pelham. However, he was unable to devote himself to farming: the War of Independence broke out and Shays was called up for military service. He spent several months serving with a detachment of Minutemen (volunteers ready to take the field fully equipped at the first summons) and having distinguished himself in the fighting at Bunker Hill was promoted to sergeant. Shays took part in the Ticonderoga expedition of 1775, after which, as a lieutenant, he was charged with the military training of recruits. He fought at Saratoga in 1777 and in 1779 was already promoted to captain. A year later Shays, having served for five years, was discharged. He was one of the few to be awarded a sword engraved with the bearer's name, which was presented by the Marquis de Lafayette, George Washington's comrade-in-arms, but soon thereafter Shays was forced to sell it because he was in need of money.

In 1780 Shays returned to Pelham, where he was elected to the local government a number of times. He also served as a delegate to one of the popular conventions in Hampshire County. His military service, however, did not save him from poverty, and his family shared the fate of hundreds of other farmers' families that were burdened by debts and taxes. In 1784 Shays was prosecuted for failure to pay a twelve-dollar debt, and in September 1786 he signed a promissory note for 18 1/2 shillings. This, then, is a brief sketch of the man who at the outbreak of events in no way stood

13. Ibid., 39, 43–44, 47; Morison, ed., *Sources and Documents,* 222.

14. "Powers of a Sheriff," The Bowdoin and Temple Papers (henceforth referred to as BTP), *Collections,* Massachusetts Historical Society, 7th ser., vol. 6 (1909), 109–10.

15. Walter A. Dyer, "Embattled Farmers," *New England Quarterly* 4 (July 1931), 464–66.

out from among the ordinary American people of his day, but whose name in a few months became known all over the country.

In August and September 1786, Shays had not yet joined the rebels. But soon the citizens of Pelham elected him to direct the military training of the Regulators, thus promoting him to the ranks of the movement's leaders. Men obeyed Shays and followed him willingly, as can be seen in the events that took place in Springfield on September 26.

That day the rebels decided to disrupt a session of the state supreme court. A dense cordon of armed men was to surround the place where the court was to meet and refuse admittance to anyone. Attacking the supreme judicial authority in the state in this way represented a new stage in the uprising and alarmed not only the Massachusetts government but also the Continental Congress. The U.S. military department, headed by Henry Knox, was particularly anxious because Springfield happened to be the site of a federal armory that contained some seven thousand rifles with bayonets, thirteen hundred barrels of gunpowder, and two hundred tons of cannonballs and grapeshot. These stocks, sufficient to supply an entire army, could easily be captured by the rebels. Major-General William Shepard faced the difficult task of defending the armory and the supreme court from an attack by numerically superior rebel forces. Taking four hundred rifles from the arsenal and rolling out a field gun, Shepard stationed his troops on the approaches to the courthouse.

General Knox, who arrived at the scene of the incident a few days later, described the events of September 26 as follows. Shepard commanded nine hundred men, many of whom were former officers of the Continental Army. The rebels numbered some twelve hundred men, of whom three hundred were armed with rifles with bayonets attached, six hundred with ordinary militia muskets, and three hundred with clubs and sticks. The majority of the rebels were from Berkshire and Worcester counties. The aim of the insurgents was to prevent a meeting of the supreme court. The session opened on Wednesday, but on Thursday the justices postponed it indefinitely; being surrounded, they deemed it impossible to conduct business. On the same day, adds Knox, the militia and the rebels returned to their homes. According to the information Knox had received, the rebels were in an aggressive mood and were about to engage in battle, but "the prudence of their leader [Daniel Shays] prevented an attack on the government troops. The disaffection to the government which exists in this county and Berkshire, is risen to an alarming height, and will probably terminate most seriously." The supreme court decided against holding a session in Berkshire County where the atmosphere was also extremely tense.[16]

In Boston and its environs the situation was relatively calm. On September 27 Governor James Bowdoin summoned an extraordinary session; at the same time popular conventions assembled in Middlesex, Bristol, and Worcester counties and addressed a number of petitions and complaints to the General Court. Delegates from forty-one towns in Worcester County protested about the location of the General

---

16. *Journals of the Continental Congress,* ed. W. C. Ford, (Washington, D.C., 1904–1937), vol. 31, 739, 752; Minot, *History of the Insurrections,* 50–51.

Court in Boston, the shortage of currency in circulation, the impossibility of paying debts and taxes, and the existence of common pleas and general session courts:

> The feelings of the people are deeply wounded when they see the officers of these courts living in the elegance of eastern magnificence. . . . It is with indignation that the good people of this county have seen more money lavished by a single grant of the General Court on one officer of government who has rendered himself generally disagreeable to the people . . . and the fees of those office we apprehend are fully adequate to his services.

The petition requested the legislature to alleviate the situation of the debtors and to conduct a referendum on the question of amending the state constitution.[17]

Many petitions from other towns and villages were also received. In Worcester a committee of correspondence was formed to coordinate the actions being carried out in the various counties—a device that earlier had been used in overthrowing the English colonial yoke. But the Worcester convention called upon the population of the county to be calm, not even suspecting that the state legislature had shelved the people's petitions, deeming them illegal.

How to put down the disorders was the most important issue discussed at the session of the General Court. The Massachusetts house of representatives, more democratic in composition than the senate, advocated reducing the governor's salary, suspending prosecutions for nonpayment of debts, and permitting payment of debts in kind. Several members spoke out in favor of abolishing or reforming the courts of common pleas and general-session courts. The senate, however, rejected these proposals, and while arguments and discussions between the two houses continued, the supreme court held sessions in Taunton and Cambridge (Middlesex County). While in Taunton the court met under a strengthened guard; the governor ordered a detachment of almost two thousand militiamen and volunteers and several guns to Cambridge, which the rebels did not dare to attack.

Meanwhile the Continental Congress was receiving Knox's letters and reports on the situation in Massachusetts and neighboring states. These reports were passed on to a "secret commission," which after studying the reports recommended that the U.S. government should intervene in the events taking place. "Unless speedy and effectual measures shall be taken to defeat their [rebels'] designs, they will possess themselves of the arsenal at Springfield, subvert the government [of the state] and not only reduce that commonwealth to a state of anarchy and confusion, but probably involve the United States in the calamities of a civil war."[18] Consequently the Congress decided on October 21, 1786, to increase the forces under its control from 700 to 2,040 men by means of recruitment. In addition Knox asked the governor of Connecticut to send a militia detachment of 1,200 to 1,500 men to Massachusetts in case the armory was threatened.[19] In Massachusetts it was feared that the General Court would not allow federal intervention in the affairs of the state, so the order to recruit soldiers was

17. Morison, ed., *Sources and Documents,* 210–13.

18. *Secret Journals of the Acts and Proceedings in Congress,* 2 vols. (Boston, 1821), vol. 1, 268–70.

19. October 18, 1786, *Journals of the Continental Congress,* ed. Ford, vol. 31, 886–87.

given under the pretext of subduing the Indians. Even so, because of a shortage of money in the treasury, the merchants of Boston assumed responsibility for financing the struggle against the rebels.

General Shepard's agents intercepted and brought to Boston a circular signed by Shays. It read: "Gentlemen: By information from the General Court they are determined to call all those who appeared to stop the Court to condign punishment. Therefore I request you to assemble your men together, to see that they are all armed and equipped with sixty rounds, each man to be ready to turn out at a minute's warning."[20] The order was addressed to the local authorities in Hampshire County, who had sided with the rebels. Having received this document, the members of the General Court agreed to give the sheriffs and constables the right to arrest without investigation or trial. The General Court promised to pardon only those who by January 1, 1787, would swear an oath of loyalty to the government, but the pardon did not extend to the movement's leaders. The legislation also permitted those taxes that were introduced before 1784 to be paid in kind.[21] The main demands of the rebels thus remained unfulfilled. Five days after the General Court was dissolved, a people's committee assembled in Worcester and adopted a declaration proclaiming the people's right to control the actions of the authorities. The government was incapable of understanding the interests of the poor, the declaration stated, and as a result was pursuing a "mistaken policy."[22] And when on November 21 members of the court of general sessions arrived in Worcester, 150 armed insurgents prevented them from entering the building.

Upon learning of this insurgence Governor Bowdoin ordered the mobilization of the state militia. The rebels in turn attempted to assemble their forces from Middlesex, Bristol, Worcester, and Hampshire counties to prevent the militia from entering Middlesex. But the operation was poorly prepared and the various rebel detachments failed to join up. Meanwhile, the sheriff of Middlesex County, riding at the head of one hundred mounted men, tracked down several leaders of the rebellion, namely Shattuck, Parker, and Page. The last two were arrested on the spot, while Shattuck managed to escape. Bad weather, including a blizzard, hindered the posse; only after a lengthy search was Colonel Henry Wood able to discover Shattuck's trail. Surrounded by a ring of horsemen, Shattuck resisted desperately until felled by a saber blow, after which he was tied up and taken to the Boston jail. At the same time a reconnaissance force of cavalry was sent to Worcester County to ascertain the rebels' intentions. Soon, however, this unit had to withdraw.

> The seeds of war are now sown; two of our men are now bleeding. . . . I request you to let this letter be read and for you and every man to supply men and provision to relieve us with a reinforcement. . . . We are determined here to carry out point. Our case is yours. Don't give yourself a rest and let us die here, for we are all brethren. Shays.[23]

20. Quoted in Starkey, *Little Rebellion,* 91.
21. Minot, *History of the Insurrections,* 68–70.
22. Ibid., 72–73.
23. Quoted in Starkey, *Little Rebellion,* 101.

This was the proclamation that Shays addressed to his fellow citizens, and soon rebels began to stream to Worcester, where another court session was scheduled for the beginning of December. The governor ordered the court session in Worcester postponed until January 23, 1787, hoping that during the intervening period the government would succeed in crushing the rebellion. In obedience to the governor's order the judges went away, but the rebels kept moving into the city. Shays himself brought a 350-strong detachment from Rutland; volunteers from other localities were also arriving, and soon his forces numbered up to one thousand men. The governor and his advisers were greatly alarmed by the concentration of such large rebel forces only a few dozen miles from the state capital and ordered sentries posted in Boston, the prison guard strengthened, and all available troops assembled. It is difficult to say whether Shays and his comrades intended to storm the state capital or whether they wanted merely to intimidate the government by a demonstration of strength and force it to make concessions. In any case, having occupied Worcester, they were at a loss as to what to do next. The early winter, with its severe cold and snowfalls, brought military operations on both sides to a standstill. The rebels, although freezing and starving, conducted themselves with fortitude and discipline. Several men in Shays's detachment froze to death; the roads leading to the rear were cut off by snow drifts. In the end the detachment was forced to withdraw.

The leaders of the rebels, understanding the need for coordinated action, created the Committee of Seventeen in the beginning of December 1786 to give the movement a more organized character. The committee, which was formed in Hampshire County under the chairmanship of Captain Daniel Gray, comprised the most respected leaders of the uprising, including Shays. Another member was Moses Sash, a thirty-two-year-old black who during the War of Independence had served as a private in the Massachusetts army. Shays promoted him to the rank of captain.[24] The Committee of Seventeen was responsible for the conscription and training of recruits and the procurement of food and ammunition, as well as the circulation of proclamations and declarations addressed to the population. In performing these tasks the leaders of the uprising used the experience and practical knowledge they had acquired during the first months of the War of Independence when the creative revolutionary genius of the people had formed liaison committees and detachments of Minutemen. The rebels' committee issued a number of proclamations listing the demands and grievances of those who had taken up arms.

Thus the proclamation to the people of Hampshire County stated that

> the present expensive mode of collecting debts, which by reason of the great scarcity of cash, will of necessity fill our gaols with unhappy debtors; and thereby a reputable body of people rendered incapable of being serviceable either to themselves or the community. . . . A suspension of the writ of Habeas Corpus, by which these persons who have stepped forth to assert and maintain the rights of the people, are liable to be taken and conveyed even to the most distant part of the commonwealth, and thereby

24. Sidney Kaplan, "A Negro Veteran in Shays's Rebellion," *Journal of Negro History* 33 (April 1948), 123–29.

subjected to an unjust punishment. The unlimited power granted to Justices of the Peace and Sheriffs, Deputy Sheriffs, and Constables, by the Riot Act, indemnifying them to the prosecution thereof; when perhaps, wholly actuated from a principle of revenge, hatred, and envy.

The leaders of the rebellion firmly rejected the allegation that they were acting under the orders of British emissaries. Thomas Grover, a member of the Committee of Seventeen, sent a letter that was similar to the proclamation to the owner of the newspaper, the *Hampshire Herald*. The letter noted that the state authorities were inflicting upon the common people, particularly farmers, "more damage than the savage beast of prey."[25]

Despite the unsuccessful expedition to Worcester the rebels' strength remained undiminished. On December 14 General Shepard reported to the governor that in Hampshire County Shays had 970 men available to him and that the total number of rebel troops in the three western counties was as many as 1,500.[26] On December 26 the Regulators stopped a court session in Springfield. Three hundred armed men drew up in front of the courthouse, and the committee they elected presented to the judges a petition stating: "We request the Honourable Judges of this Court not to open said Court at this Term, nor do any Kind of business whatever, but all kinds of business to remain as tho no such Court have been Appointed. Luke Day, Daniel Shays, Thomas Grover." The judges, having no protection, decided to leave. The rebels behaved in a peaceful manner and did not insult the members of the court in any way.[27] According to eyewitness reports, this expedition was conducted in an orderly manner and with such thorough precautions that the sheriff of Springfield had suspected nothing. A number of letters reported that Daniel Shays was the main initiator and leader of the operation; without an order from him the men would not have left their homes. It was also noted that the leaders of the rebels had been discouraged by their unsuccessful march on Worcester and now feared arrest. Shays, it was said, was "very thoughtfull, and appears like a man crowded with embarrassements."[28]

At the end of 1786 the rebellion reached its climax, and the uncoordinated attempts to disrupt court sessions began to turn into organized and systematic resistance. But there was no clear-cut plan for further action, and things went no further than the closing of the courts. Shays displayed indecisiveness, vacillating but not yielding to suggestions that he surrender to the authorities.[29]

The governor used a generous loan of five thousand pounds from a merchant of Boston to form and arm a militia corps of forty-four hundred men and twenty guns, not including volunteers. Command of these troops was given to General

---

25. For the full English text of the letters of Grey and Grover, see Minot, *History of the Insurrections,* 83–87.

26. BTP, *Collections,* vol. 6 (1909), 117, 118.

27. Ibid., 121–22.

28. Ibid., 122–24, 125–26.

29. Richard B. Morris, "Insurrection in Massachusetts," in *America in Crisis: Fourteen Crucial Episodes in American History,* ed. Daniel Aaron (New York, 1952), 41–43.

Benjamin Lincoln, a veteran of the War of Independence. And although Bowdoin's orders to Lincoln described the general's main tasks as protecting the civil courts and assisting the authorities in apprehending the rebels, the governor granted him the widest powers.[30]

Upon learning of these military preparations the leaders of the rebels dispatched orders to the chief officers of the units under their command. An order sent on January 16, 1787, to Captain John Brown, a member of the Committee of Seventeen stated:

> According to undoubted intelligence received from various parts of this Commonwealth, it is determined by the Governor and his adherents not only to support the Court of Common Pleas and General Sessions of the Peace, to be holden at Worcester next week, by point of sword, but to crush the power of the people at one bold stroke, and render them incapable of ever opposing the cruel power, Tyranny, hereafter, by bringing those who have stepped forth to ward off the evil that threatens the people with immediate ruin, to an unconditional submission, and their leaders with an infamous punishment. Notwithstanding it is thought prudent, by a number of officers and others, convened at Pelham on the 15th of Jan. inst. . . . that the people of the county of Hampshire immediately assemble in arms to support and maintain, not only the rights and liberties of the people, since our opponents . . . refuse to give opportunity to wait the effect of their prayers and petitions. This is therefore to desire you to assemble the company under your command, well armed and equipped, with ten days provisions, and march there . . . by Friday, the 19th instant, there to receive further orders.
> —Daniel Shays, John Powers, Reuben Dickinson, John Bardwell, Joel Billings[31]

On January 22 Lincoln's army entered Worcester, its very appearance forcing the scattered groups of rebels to withdraw, and the following day the judges began their session unimpeded.

Two days later a series of events occurred in Springfield that were described by one contemporary as a declaration of war on the United States by the rebels.[32] Given the clear superiority in numbers, training, and weapons enjoyed by the government troops, Shays's decision to capture the federal armory in Springfield and thus to engage in a trial of strength with Lincoln's army was audacious. Having significantly outdistanced Lincoln, Shays left Rutland on January 22 with a contingent of twelve hundred men and set off on a fast march to Springfield, thereby cutting off the armory and the troops guarding it from the main body of government forces. En route he initiated talks with other rebel commanders and sent a messenger to Captain Luke Day with a proposal for a joint attack on the armory on January 25, 1787. But General Shepard's men intercepted Day's reply in which he reported that he would be able to join Shays with four hundred men but only on the following day. Shepard's detachment thus received timely warning of the rebels' plans and almost one thousand infantry and four guns, muskets loaded and fuses burning, were drawn up at the foot of the hill on which the numerous warehouses containing weapons and ammunition stood. Not having received Day's reply and apparently assuming that his silence indicated a

30. Minot, *History of the Insurrections,* 99–101.
31. Quoted in Kaplan, "Negro Veteran," 127.
32. *American Historical Review* 2 (1897), 693.

readiness to participate in joint operations, Shays ordered his troops to advance on the armory. At around 4 P.M. the rebels were observed marching up the road to Boston. General Shepard later reported to the governor that Shays led his men by platoons in an extended column. His men halted within 250 yards of the armory. Officers sent by General Shepard offered a "final warning" to the rebels, but Wheeler, Shays's adjutant, declared that Shays's men had no intention of dispersing. Shays ordered his troops to advance and the rebels marched forward on the double. Then the guns spoke. The first two salvos were aimed overhead to frighten the rebels, but then grapeshot cut into the very middle of the attacking column. Another two shots from a 5 1/2 inch howitzer and the rebels fell back in confusion, ignoring the orders of Shays, who tried to stop them but to no avail. Without artillery it was impossible to breach Shepard's defenses, for the general with great foresight had taken care to construct redoubts.[33] The attack was not renewed; the rebels were demoralized by their failure.

On January 27 Lincoln's troops entered Springfield. Four infantry regiments and a force of cavalry, the latter accompanied by four guns, crossed over the ice to the other bank of the Connecticut River. At the same time Shepard's militia advanced upstream, driving a wedge between the detachments of Shays and Day which held positions on the two banks of the river. Day's detachment scattered as soon as Lincoln's cavalry approached the hamlet it occupied and Shays, fearing a flanking movement, hastened to the northeastern part of the state. Here his forces were considerably augmented at the expense of the local population and, by Minot's calculation, came to number some two thousand men.[34] On January 30 the rebels moved into fortified positions in the village of Pelham, but they were hungry, half-frozen, and starving. Lincoln sent Shays an ultimatum demanding immediate and unconditional surrender, promising in this case to ask the General Court for a pardon.[35] Shays replied that only a guarantee of immunity could put an end to the struggle, "but," he added, "we do not wish to tarnish the soil we acquired at such high cost in the last war with the blood of our brothers and neighbors."[36] The rebels' committee sent to Boston a petition that was similar in content, but the General Court refused to consider it. The inhabitants of the local villages, who sympathized with Shays, asked Lincoln and Bowdoin to cease their military operations, which they feared might provoke a civil war.[37]

33. *Documents Relating to the Shays's Rebellion,* 694–95. Important information about the defeat of Shays's forces at Springfield is also to be found in the Papers of the Continental Congress, 1774–1789, which are kept in the National Archives of the United States. A full set of this series of documents on microfilm was recently received by the State Public Historical Library, Moscow: Papers of the Continental Congress, 1774–1789, National Archives Microfilm Publications (further referred to as NAMP), #247, roll 164 (Letters from Maj. Gen. Henry Knox), pt. 2, 177–80, 187, 193–95, 197–98, 201, 211–15. In his recently published monograph Van Beck Hall erroneously states that Shays attacked Shepard's troops only to advance and effect a joining of his forces with Day's detachment. Van Beck Hall, *Politics without Parties: Massachusetts, 1780–1791* (Pittsburgh, 1972), 225. The same mistake may be found in Anna Rochester's book, which states that the insurgents were able to capture the arsenal. Anna Rochester, *American Capitalism: 1607–1800* (Moscow, 1950), 114.

34. Minot, *History of the Insurrections,* 128.

35. Ibid., 118–19.

36. Ibid., 120–21.

37. *Documents Relating to Shays's Rebellion,* 696–99.

In an effort to win time Shays drew out the negotiations and then unexpectedly withdrew to the town of Petersham. Learning of his withdrawal, Lincoln flew into a rage and decided to catch up with him and immediately destroy his detachment. The thirty-mile march to Pelham began on February 3 at 8 P.M. The troops, accompanied by guns and supply trains, had to battle icy winds and a heavy snowfall and spent the entire night crossing the mountainous terrain, bogging down in the deep snow. Some of the men suffered frostbite, but the corps of volunteers marched steadily forward and surprised the rebels. The advanced units entered the town unhindered and were followed by the artillery battery. While the rest of the troops were arriving, 150 rebels surrendered and their main forces dispersed without offering resistance.[38] Nevertheless, according to an eyewitness the volunteers "felt sympathy for Shays's party" and to avoid firing at his men, discharged their rifles into the ice-coated snow. The affair thus ended without bloodshed.[39]

On February 13, 1787, Bowdoin was informed by the governor of New Hampshire that the remnants of Shays's detachment had crossed the border of his state and were heading for Vermont. According to the governor's information, Shays had called upon his men to head for the town of Putney, but only three of them had chosen to follow him. The rest had thrown away their weapons and had hired themselves out as laborers on the farms in the vicinity of Westmoreland.[40] The defeat at Petersham put an end to the uprising as an organized movement, although rebels who refused to surrender to the authorities continued for a long time to trouble the inhabitants of Massachusetts with daring raids launched from the border areas of Connecticut, Vermont, and New York. Nor did the fighting in Berkshire County end immediately. In West Stockbridge two hundred rebels opened fire on a unit of volunteers that had been sent to clear them from the town. In the ensuing exchange of fire two of the rebels were wounded and eighty-four taken prisoner. A considerable number of them gathered in the village of Adams, but when the militia appeared, they retreated to Williamstown; soon, however, they were forced to withdraw from there as well. Yet, as Minot points out, the rebels' desire to join forces to halt the sessions of the courts was so strong and so many of them set off under the command of a Major Whiley for the town of Washington (Berkshire County) that Lincoln and Shepard decided to move the main body of their troops there. Before their arrival 250 farmers attempted to disrupt court proceedings in the village of Lee, but the militia forced them to disperse. Whiley's band was also scattered. In the town of New Braintree (Worcester County) rebels hid behind stone walls and fired at the enemy. A few men from this band, who were guarding "friends of the government" they had arrested, fell into the hands of the authorities.[41] Finally, on February 26 several dozen rebels led by Captain Hamlin

---

38. Albert B. Hart, ed., *American History Told by Contemporaries,* 5 vols. (Washington, D.C., 1898–1903), vol. 3, 193–94; Minot, *History of the Insurrections,* 132–34; NAMP, #247, roll 164, pt. 2, 223–26.

39. Massachusetts Historical Society, *Proceedings,* 2d ser., vol. 15 (Boston, 1902), 372.

40. BTP, *Collections,* vol. 6 (1909), 134.

41. NAMP, #217 (see note 38); Minot, *History of the Insurrections,* 144–46.

conducted a daring operation. Discovering that General Lincoln was accompanied by only a small escort, they decided to take him prisoner and to this end launched a sudden raid into Hampshire County from the territory of New York state. But the moment was lost: their force of mounted men arrived too late. Bursting into Stockbridge, the rebels, according to Minot, "made prisoners of a great number of the most reputable inhabitants." A detachment of government troops arrived from Sheffield and Great Barrington; the ensuing fire fight was the most violent of any that occurred during the entire period of the Massachusetts uprising. The rebels began to fire from long range. Two men in the government detachment were killed and one wounded; two rebels were killed and thirty wounded, among whom was Hamlin himself.[42] During this time one of the rebel leaders, Ely Parsons, issued the most radical proclamation composed during the period of the rebellion. It differs greatly from the brief and terse messages written by Shays:

> Friends and Fellow Sufferers, Will you now tamely suffer your arms to be taken from you, your estates to be confiscated, and even swear to support a constitution and form of government, and likewise a code of laws, which common sense and your consciences declare to be iniquitous and cruel? And can you bear to see and hear of the yeomanry of this Commonwealth being parched, and cut to pieces by the cruel and merciless tools of tyrannical power, and not resent it even unto relentless bloodshed? Would to God, I had the tongue of a ready writer, that I might impress on your minds the idea of the obligation you, as citizens of a republican government, are under to support those rights and privileges that the God of nature hath entitled you to. Let me now persuade you, by all the sacred ties of friendship, which natural affection inspires the human heart with, immediately to turn out and assert your rights.

Further in the letter came a call to encircle and annihilate Shepard's army and then inflict on Lincoln's army a second Saratoga.[43]

But by this time the leadership of the movement had been destroyed. Lincoln's men in the western counties were arresting all those under suspicion, and Bowdoin had reached agreement with the governors of the neighboring states on the apprehension of fugitive rebels. Cavalry patrols were sent out to the border areas, but they were not always able to catch the fugitives. Thus one of Lincoln's emissaries managed to arrest Shays's comrade Wheeler in the state of New York, but a crowd of New Yorkers freed him and "triumphantly bore him back."[44] Captain Jason Parmenter, who during the uprising had "exerted himself very much to annoy the government," fled on horseback to Vermont where he was captured after a long chase. And the citizens of Brattleboro, Vermont, gave shelter to Day and told the officer and his small force of cavalry that had been sent to apprehend Day that they were pursuing "the most virtuous of our citizens." In response to the threat of force, the townsmen of Brattleboro took up arms and as a result the detachment had to withdraw.[45] Writing

---

42. Minot, *History of the Insurrections,* 149–50.
43. Ibid., 146–47. In 1777 at Saratoga an English army under General Burgoyne surrendered to the Americans.
44. BTP, *Collections,* vol. 6 (1909), 143.
45. Ibid., 147, 153–55.

at the beginning of March to the Massachusetts congressional delegation, Governor Bowdoin stated that the only reason the rebellion had not been completely suppressed was the aid and support rendered to the rebels by the areas of New York and Vermont adjoining northwestern Massachusetts.[46] Rebel military action on the Massachusetts border continued until the middle of May.

The instigators of the movement and its active participants faced the death penalty. Large numbers were "convicted of seditious words and practices," among them prominent citizens and officials of the state government. One member of the Massachusetts house of representatives was subjected to humiliating punishment: he was placed under a gibbet with a rope around his neck and upon paying a large fine had to sign a written statement promising to "keep the peace, and to be of good behaviour, for five years."[47] Ordinary "Shaysites," as the rebels were known at the time, were forced to swear an oath and then released.

Meanwhile, the rebellious spirit that still prevailed among the population finally found its expression in a major political victory: in the spring elections of 1787 the people radically changed the composition of the General Court by electing as members a large number of Shays's sympathizers. John Hancock, who was known for his liberal views, was elected the new governor. As a result the people were able to realize some of the aims of the rebellion, in particular, the abolition of imprisonment for the nonpayment of debts and a reduction in the governor's salary. Eventually all fourteen death sentences were commuted, although two of the prisoners were granted this only at the very last minute. In 1788 Shays, for whose head $750 had been promised, and his comrades Day, Wheeler, and Parsons were also granted amnesty. Shays briefly returned to his hometown of Pelham, but there was no longer a place for the former rebel leader. He moved to New York state, to the small town of Sparta in Ontario County, where he lived to a ripe old age. Shays spent his final years in poverty and oblivion; only when he was seventy did he manage to obtain a modest pension of $20 per month as a veteran of the War of Independence. Occasionally travelers and the merely curious, who remembered the events in Massachusetts, would come to see the former leader of the rebels.[48] The exact date of his death is unknown; it is believed that he died on September 29, 1825, having lived to the age of 78.[49]

Like many other of the American poor's political actions, Shays's Rebellion was a spontaneous outburst against the arbitrary rule of judges and officials. Although the uprising was not accompanied by a division of the property of the rich, those who took part in it sought to undermine the power of the ruling elite, to democratize the state constitution, and to improve the situation of the needy. The rebels attempted to organize and to use their Revolutionary wartime experience. The uprising shook the whole of Massachusetts and led to a sharp demarcation of the political forces in the state. The government was supported by the big landowners, creditors, a majority of the officials, and senior army officers. The rebels apparently numbered not more than

46. Ibid., 167.
47. Minot, *History of the Insurrections,* 172.
48. Starkey, *Little Rebellion,* 251.
49. Dyer, "Embattled Farmers," 480.

two thousand to three thousand men, but the uprising and its declared aims helped to consolidate broad opposition to the government's policies, an opposition that came to include approximately one-third of the inhabitants of the state.[50] The leaders of the movement, however, lacked the political experience necessary to bring together all the discontented elements, and the radical wing of the bourgeoisie failed to join the movement and assume its leadership.

The class struggle during the American Revolution had its peculiarities. The main goal of that Revolution—the winning of independence—had been successfully achieved prior to 1786. The political actions by the lower classes in America began to gather strength after the national bourgeoisie and planters had come to power. Although the popular movements of the postwar period aimed to develop further the social gains already won, they were connected neither with the struggle for independence nor with the destruction of the feudal relations of production. That is why Shays's Rebellion did not equal in scale and intensity the antifeudal struggles of the peasants during the English bourgeois revolution in the seventeenth century and the French bourgeois revolution in the late eighteenth century. In the American Revolution the indigent classes did not demand real equality in as strong a voice. The proletarization of the rural population had not yet advanced as far as in England, where the primary accumulation of capital was proceeding at a terrific pace, farmers were being driven off the land, and estates were being enclosed; nor had it gone as far as it had in France, where class differentiation among the peasants was much more pronounced than in America.[51]

Nevertheless, the class struggle of the working masses during the final stage of the American bourgeois revolution was active and militant in character, and the Massachusetts uprising was not the only example of political action by the lower classes. Similar events, though somewhat smaller in scale, took place in other states. On September 20, 1786, a rebel detachment of three hundred to four hundred men surrounded the building of the legislature in the capital of the state of New Hampshire and attempted to force the government to make concessions to the working people. The rebels were dispersed by the authorities and their leaders arrested. In 1786–1787 a tense situation also arose in Rhode Island. The lot of working people there remained hard because the merchants and shopkeepers had refused to trade as a sign of protest, and in retaliation the farmers had stopped bringing food to the cities. A famine began in the state and unemployment grew, leading to spontaneous disturbances.[52]

The inhabitants of the adjoining state of Vermont suffered from the financial policies of the authorities—high taxes and judicial prosecutions for the nonpayment of debts. In August 1786 poor farmers, craftsmen, and farm laborers gathered at a meeting in Rutland where they submitted a petition in defense of those who had "fought for their rights and the liberty of mankind." Two months later several dozen insurgents tried to stop a session of the court of common pleas in Windsor. The most

---

50. Minot, *History of the Insurrections,* 104–5.

51. Efimov, *U.S.A.,* 407–8.

52. John B. McMaster, *A History of the People of the United States from the Revolution to the Civil War,* 8 vols. (New York-London, 1920), vol. 1, 345–47, 355.

important attempt to disband a court occurred in Rutland at the end of November 1786. The sudden appearance of a large crowd took the judges by surprise, but the court rejected a demand to disband. Thereupon some one hundred armed rebels led by Thomas Lee, a veteran of the War of Independence, burst into the courtroom. Despite his martial exploits and his colonel's rank, Lee was a poor man who had spent time in a debtors' prison. The following morning troops summoned by the sheriff dispersed the assembled crowd and arrested several dozen people. Some of them, led by a Captain Cooley, resisted and were forced to surrender after an exchange of fire.[53]

Scattered attempts "to abolish taxes and disband the courts" took place in Connecticut, New York, Pennsylvania, New Jersey, and the two Carolinas. "So great and general are the obstructions to the recovery of debts," stated the *Journals* of the Continental Congress, "that in several districts remote from Charleston, the Courts have been prevented by tumultuous and riotous proceedings from determining Actions for debt."[54]

In 1785–1787 some actions directed against the financial policies of the authorities and against unjust taxation took place also in the west of Virginia. In Washington County popular conventions and local committees called upon the population to refuse to pay taxes, to boycott elections to the assembly, and to secede and establish their own state. This movement was headed by Colonel Arthur Campbell. According to incomplete information, cases of armed resistance to the government were recorded in 1784–1788 in the three western counties of Virginia. In 1787 Blake Mathews, a poor farmer, formed a band of rebels numbering 150 men (some reports suggest there were twice as many) to prevent the confiscation of the debtors' property. In his proclamations Mathews called on the people to take up arms, but his band was defeated and he was imprisoned.[55]

In 1786–1787 major disturbances occurred in Maryland. In one county the number of poor people brought to ruin and unable to pay their debts and taxes was so large that, according to the sheriff, the jails could not hold even one-fifteenth of them. The population boycotted the auctioning off of property and in some cases even confronted the authorities. Thus, for example, in June 1786 crowds stopped a court session in Charles County by force, whereupon the governor declared a statewide state of emergency.[56]

Although the authorities in the various states suppressed these actions of working people with relative ease, the situation remained tense and highly explosive. In response to Shays's uprising and other political actions by the poor, the ruling classes, wishing to consolidate the system of exploitation, sought to create a strong centralized authority. "I never saw so great change in the public mind, on any occasion, as has

53. Ibid., 350–54.
54. *Journals of the Continental Congress,* ed. Ford, vol. 31, 786, 788.
55. Francis H. Hart, *The Valley of Virginia in the American Revolution, 1763–1789* (New York, 1942), 125.
56. Philip A. Crowl, *Maryland during and after the Revolution: A Political and Economic Study* (Baltimore, 1943), 92–94, 106–7.

lately appeared in this state as to the expediency of increasing the powers of Congress, not merely as to Commercial Objects, but generally," wrote Stephan Higginson, a Boston merchant, to Knox. "You will endeavour no doubt to draw strong Arguments from the insurrection in this State in favour of an efficient General Government for the Union."[57]

Shays's Rebellion provoked a strong political response in the country, and in this sense it became an event of national importance. As was conceded by one political figure, Congress considered the events in Massachusetts to be of major significance; every individual had a personal stake in resolving these events, for on this seemed to depend his life, liberty, and property.[58] George Washington expressed the general opinion of the ruling elite when he declared that the Massachusetts rebellion was the best proof of the weakness of the Confederation.[59] In the opinion of James Madison, who was one of the most important figures at the Constitutional Convention in Philadelphia, the rebellion was the factor that significantly speeded up the adoption of the new Constitution.[60] It is revealing that the Antifederalists, who were against the Constitution, were just as opposed to the rebellion as the Federalists.

Among the prominent U.S. political figures of the day only Thomas Jefferson regarded the rebellion as an expression of patriotism and civic virtue. "God forbid we should ever be 20 years without such a rebellion," he wrote. "What country can preserve its liberties if their rulers are not warned from time to time that their people preserve the spirit of resistance? Let them take arms. . . . The tree of liberty must be refreshed from time to time with the blood of patriots and tyrants. It is its natural manure."[61]

In the words of William Foster, the American Communist historian, Shays's uprising showed the ruling class how the people can wage a struggle for democratic freedoms.[62] Thorough Marxist-Leninist analysis of the class struggle in America in the years following the War of Independence convincingly disproves the arguments of the neoconservatives and those bourgeois historians who speak of a "middle-class democracy" and the consensus of fundamental class interests during the period of the formation of the United States. "The American people," wrote V. I. Lenin, "possess a revolutionary tradition,"[63] and the uprising of the Massachusetts farmers represents one of the pages in its annals.

57. *Annual Report of the American Historical Association for the Year 1896* (Washington, D.C., 1897), vol. 1, 743, 751.

58. *Letters of Members of the Continental Congress,* ed. Edmund C. Burnett, 8 vols. (Washington, D.C., 1928–1936), vol. 7, 480.

59. *The Writings of George Washington,* ed. John C. Fitzpatrick, 29 vols. (Washington, D.C., 1934–1944), vol. 29, 51–52.

60. *The Records of the Federal Convention,* ed. Max Farrand, 4 vols. (New Haven, 1927), vol. 1, 318, vol. 3, 547.

61. *Papers of Jefferson,* ed. Boyd et al., vol. 12, 356.

62. William Z. Foster, *The Negro People in the History of America* (Moscow, 1955), 70.

63. V. I. Lenin, *Collected Works,* vol. 37, 58.

COMMENT BY RICHARD BUEL JR.

Because Soviet historians view the American Revolution as ushering in the triumph of a bourgeois order, they cannot but see it as fundamentally flawed. Of all its major developments, one would expect them to identify most with Shays's Rebellion. Nothing appears to underline our Revolution's limitations more than the insurrection of 1786, in which a debtor, proletarian element turned against the conservative, creditor leadership. As Boris Shpotov observes, "The revolts of the poor were a response by the working masses to the new social order that the bourgeoisie and the planters had established in their own class interests." Accordingly, his account of Shays's Rebellion focuses on those details of the story that seem to confirm the narrow class character of post-Revolutionary American politics.

Though his sources are not entirely clear from his references, his account obviously owes something to the New Left historiography about which he published an article in 1974. His article on Shays's Rebellion was written at the same time and is based exclusively on literature published before 1972. Much New Left history has been published since then, and one would very much like to know Shpotov's present response to that work, especially to the work of two representatives of the New Left school who published at the end of the 1970s. I am referring to Barbara Karsky's article "Agrarian Radicalism in the Late Revolutionary Period" and David Szatmary's book, *Shays's Rebellion.*[1] Inspired by the work of Eric Hobsbawm and E. P. Thompson, both see the insurrection in Massachusetts more as a clash between cultures, in this case a more traditional agrarian culture and an innovative commercial culture, than as a clash between opposing classes.[2]

Yet even if Shpotov had had an opportunity to rewrite his 1975 article in light of new and more recent scholarship, he would have had difficulty getting access to it, for it has only recently begun to appear in print. I am thinking particularly of the work produced for two scholarly conferences held in 1986, one sponsored by the Colonial Society of Massachusetts and the other by Historic Deerfield in conjunction with Amherst College. A selection of papers from these two conferences, entitled *In Debt to Shays,* was edited by Robert A. Gross and published in 1993. This volume places under one cover, making it conveniently available to Soviet scholars, more innovative scholarship about Shays's Rebellion than has been produced in the past half-century. This volume includes, in the best tradition of Western scholarship, essays representing all ideological persuasions, and I suspect Shpotov will be happy to learn

1. In Erich Angermann, Marie-Luise Frings, and Hermann Wellenreuther, eds., *New Wine in Old Skins: A Comparative View of Socio-Political Structure and Values Affecting the American Revolution* (Stuttgart, West Germany, 1976), 87–114; David P. Szatmary, *Shays's Rebellion: The Making of an Agrarian Insurrection* (Amherst, Mass., 1980).

2. See Richard D. Brown, "Shays's Rebellion and the Ratification of the Federal Constitution in Massachusetts," in Richard Beeman, Stephen Botein, and Edward C. Carter II, eds., *Beyond Confederation: Origins of the Constitution and American National Identity* (Chapel Hill, 1987), 113–27. See also John L. Brooke, "To the Quiet of the People: Revolutionary Settlements and Civil Unrest in Western Massachusetts," *William and Mary Quarterly,* 3d. ser., vol. 46 (1989), 425–61.

that among them is one that speaks the same idiom as that used by the New Left in the 1960s.[3]

But the voice of the old New Left is distinctly a minority one in this volume. The majority of the authors represented in *In Debt to Shays* embarked on scholarly careers at a time when the New Left was at the apogee of its influence, and many of the authors show this influence in their concern for understanding the rebellion in the Shaysites' rather than the elite's terms. Nevertheless, the traditional Marxist categories associated with class struggle have been largely abandoned in the new scholarship. This is because from a microperspective—and most of the papers focus on particularities rather than generalities—the concept of class defined by one's relationship to the means of production does not bear up under close scrutiny in eighteenth-century America. Or, to put it another way, it does not seem to explain what one most wants explained, namely what it was that separated the Regulators from their pro-government adversaries.

Although class seems to occupy a diminishing role in the new historical discourse about Shays's Rebellion, its place is being taken by community and religion. Of the two, community seems to have attracted the widest attention. It is the focus, for instance, of Gregory H. Nobles's analysis of Shays's own town of Pelham. Communal characteristics are also invoked by John L. Brooke, in perhaps the most innovative analysis in this volume, to explain why individuals in some Worcester County towns behaved in ways that seem inconsistent with their class identity. Brooke argues that the corporate character of one's town was often more important than one's personal economic interest. Thus the population of the largest town in the sample of six he chose to study in detail, comparatively cosmopolitan and commercial Brookfield, disproportionately supported the government and numbered many debtors among the ranks of its militia marching against the Regulators. On the other hand, people in some of the smaller backwater towns of the region disproportionately supported the Regulation, numbering among the ranks of those challenging the government half the local creditors.[4] In Brooke's analysis the towns that responded as homogeneous, corporate societies, either in opposition to or in support of the Regulation, in turn have to be distinguished from towns that responded more pluralistically.

Brooke's analysis does not discard economic considerations entirely. Thus he finds a correlation between rich creditors who supported the government and poor debtors who supported the insurgents in the towns that lacked corporate character. But the significant thing about these pluralistic towns is that proportionately fewer people

---

3. Robert A. Gross, ed., *In Debt to Shays: The Bicentennial of an Agrarian Rebellion* (Charlottesville, 1993). A New Left viewpoint within this volume is Joseph A. Ernst, "Shays's Rebellion in Long Perspective: The Merchants and the Money Question," 57–80.

4. Gregory H. Nobles, "Shays's Neighbors: The Context of Rebellion in Pelham, Massachusetts," in Gross, ed., *In Debt to Shays*, 185–204, and John L. Brooke, "A Deacon's Orthodoxy: Religion, Class, and the Moral Economy of Shays's Rebellion," ibid., 205–38. Massachusetts militia law allowed dissidents to escape service in expeditions by paying a nominal fine, so it cannot be argued that the Brookfield men were coerced into marching. Nobles uses Shays's own town to make the point about participation in the Regulation by people in smaller towns.

in them responded either one way or the other to the insurgency. The vast majority remained neutral. Economic considerations also figure in his analysis of the towns that responded in a corporate manner, but they lead to unexpected conclusions. He notes, for instance, that the creditors in pro-government Brookfield were also debtors to creditors outside the community, whereas the creditor element that supported the insurgents in predominately Shaysite towns did not owe money to distant creditors. A class analysis might have led one to expect something different, with creditors who were simultaneously debtors being under more pressure to side with the rebels than creditors who weren't simultaneously debtors.

Brooke sees religion rather than economic interest as the most significant factor in determining the character of a community and thus whether it would support or resist the Regulation. He argues that the towns that responded in a corporate manner to the rebellion, either for or against, tended to be orthodox communities, though ones with significantly different characteristics. Those that supported the government were most likely to have established churches whose pulpits were filled by conservative ministers. Those that supported the insurgency tended to have churches where the pulpit either was not filled or where there had been recent controversy about the minister. These churches were often under the supervision of lay deacons. Finally, the pluralistic towns tended to be those that had lost their religious homogeneity to the inroads of the dissenters.

Brooke's emphasis on religion is seconded in a provocative essay by Stephen A. Marini.[5] But Marini, though acknowledging the originality and cogency of Brooke's microanalysis, feels that the notion of a "deacon's orthodoxy" fails to do justice to the profound religious disorders that plagued the Massachusetts landscape at the time of the insurgency. Marini acknowledges that the rate of pulpit vacancy was unusually high in areas that strongly supported the rebellion, but he also argues that on a town-by-town basis throughout interior Massachusetts as many Shaysite communities had settled ministers as lacked them. For Marini, other religious variables are more important in accounting for the insurgency at the micro level, such as the minister's length of tenure and the resources available to areas in economic crisis to support a settled minister.

Marini is also interested in why Congregationalism as the established state religion proved so ineffective in stemming the tide of the insurgency. He attributes its impotence to the collapse of orthodoxy's authority after the Revolutionary War. The Congregational establishment was weakened by the doctrinal tensions between the advocates of the New Divinity and Arminianism and by the massive inroads made by dissenting sects like the Universalists, Free Will Baptists, and Shakers in the "New Light Stir" of the early 1780s.[6] For Marini, Shays's Rebellion is simply one dimension

5. Stephen A. Marini, "The Religious World of Daniel Shays," in Gross, ed., *In Debt to Shays,* 239–80.

6. Marini has published an excellent monograph on this subject entitled *Radical Sects of Revolutionary New England* (Cambridge, Mass., 1982).

of the profoundly disordering changes affecting all levels of life that accompanied the Revolution in Massachusetts.

In focusing on the social and religious tensions endemic to New England society, the analyses of this new generation of historians transcend the limitations of the "neoconservative," consensus school, which Shpotov so roundly condemns. These historians also conceptualize the insurrection in subtler hues than the crude opposition of rich against poor, which seems to satisfy Shpotov. Massachusetts experienced economic crisis in the mid-1780s, but it came apart along more complex seams than anyone, including the New Left, has hitherto imagined. The picture that emerges is one of a society responding to severe pressures with less homogeneity than has until now been assumed. The new scholarship, in short, paints a picture of Massachusetts in which the various social components defy easy categorization.

So far I have confined my comments largely to the insurgents. But the new scholarship also has some interesting things to say about the pro-government forces who are usually held responsible for provoking the uprising. Shpotov, quoting Marx and Engels, sees this element as "rich spongers" relentlessly exploiting the mass of "poor toilers" who had "shouldered the main burden of the War of Independence." The new scholarship paints the protagonists in a very different way.

For one thing, it questions whether the Federalists that opposed the insurrection were quite the minority that the phrase "rich spongers" suggests. Instead it sees them as a much more heterogeneous coalition of people, though predominately from the eastern part of the state, than Marx's and Engels' terminology would suggest.[7] It also contests the idea that the courts acted as a special instrument of the creditor interests in oppressing the poor debtors.[8] Finally it challenges the idea that the Shaysites had borne a disproportionate burden of the fighting during the war: it argues instead that at best the majority of insurgents had participated only peripherally in the war effort and had come late to the cause.[9] If anyone could be said to have borne the burden of the war, it was the pro-government forces. Lincoln's army drew much more heavily both in its officers and in its ranks on veterans of the Continental Army than did Shays's force, which, William Pencak believes, helps explain why the insurgents were no match militarily for the government's forces.[10]

There was another factor besides military skill involved in the successful suppression of the rebellion. Lincoln could get his troops to perform heroic feats under extreme conditions of hardship that the rebels were not prepared to emulate; this suggests that

---

7. See Stephen E. Patterson, "The Federalist Reaction to Shays's Rebellion," in Gross, ed., *In Debt to Shays,* 101–20.

8. See Jonathan M. Chu, "Debt Litigation and Shays's Rebellion," in Gross, ed., *In Debt to Shays,* 81–100.

9. See Nobles, "Shays's Neighbors."

10. William Pencak, "The Fine Theoretic Government of Massachusetts is Prostrated to Earth," in Gross, ed., *In Debt to Shays,* 121–44. The role of veteran officers in repressing the rebellion has been previously canvassed in Sidney Kaplan, "Veteran Officers and Politics in Massachusetts, 1783–1787," *William and Mary Quarterly,* 3d. ser., vol. 9 (1952), 29–57.

the government's troops were committed to their enterprise to a degree in excess of anything their adversaries possessed. Shpotov carefully suppresses this aspect of the story.[11] The forced march of February 3 over difficult terrain in a blizzard and at night is attributed to Lincoln's rage rather than his troops' willingness to respond. He ignores the fact that the rebels could have eluded their pursuers had they taken proper precautions. For Shpotov the most significant aspect of this heroic exertion is that the government troops were reluctant to shed rebel blood when they finally surprised and overpowered them, implicitly distancing themselves from their commander's anger. But the new scholarship suggests that the leniency displayed to the rebels by the government forces was part of a shared commitment between officers and men to uphold the humane standards of Revolutionary republicanism rather than evidence of a latent class division within their ranks. Once the government forces had won the upper hand, leniency was a self-consciously pursued policy, necessary for reintegrating the rebels into the consensual framework of the Republic as well as for demonstrating to the world the superiority of the republican to all other forms of government.[12] The picture that emerges from the new scholarship, then, is one in which the pro-government forces assumed the role of vindicators of the Revolution against those who would have sacrificed its achievements to their personal interests and convenience.

Shpotov and his Soviet colleagues will undoubtedly regard such sympathy for pro-government attitudes as examples of "false consciousness." Viewed from the perspective of world historical processes, the bourgeoisie simply deluded themselves. But judgments about false consciousness in turn depend on knowing how the story is going to come out, something that the theorists of "scientific socialism" of the early industrial era were convinced they knew on unquestionable authority. Scholars in the late twentieth century have reason enough to doubt such claims and consequently to eschew such judgments. In the absence of certain knowledge about where the historical process is going or should go, we have no alternative but to try to understand historical periods in the terms in which the historical actors understood them. And when we do this, it becomes gradually clearer that contemporaries had reason to view the Shaysites as part of the problem rather than as part of its solution.

Shpotov concludes his paper by arguing that Shays's Rebellion was only the most visible sign of a generalized discontent among the backcountry poor of the American continent. He canvasses carefully, as others have done before him, the manifestations of debtor discontent outside of Massachusetts. The argument seems designed to show that the Massachusetts insurgents were responding to "objective" conditions rather than behaving as ne'er-do-wells or malcontents. Though it would be hard to deny that the Shaysites had their sympathizers in other states, there is a problem with Shpotov's attempt to portray the rebels as part of an emerging class deeply at odds with the new bourgeois order. If this had indeed been the case, should not their sense

11. Shpotov makes much of the Shaysites outdistancing Lincoln's government forces in the race for the Springfield arsenal, ignoring the fact that the insurgents had less distance to cover.

12. See Alan Taylor, "Regulators and White Indians," in Gross, ed., *In Debt to Shays,* 145–60.

of alienation have increased in subsequent years? Shays's Rebellion was not to be the last tax rebellion of the early national period; indeed it was quickly followed by the Whiskey Rebellion and Fries's Rebellion in Pennsylvania during the 1790s.[13] Nor did tension between urban creditors and proprietors and backcountry debtors quickly vanish. But insurgencies of the backcountry poor like Shays's Rebellion declined in subsequent years and were replaced—or so the new scholarship suggests—by more fruitful action aimed at achieving a reasonable compromise between eastern creditors and local interests.[14]

The success of the American political and legal system in defusing potentially explosive conflicts arising out of tensions associated with expansion during the first half-century of the Republic is more remarkable than its occasional failures. The Shaysite movement was a passing phenomenon, particular to the economic problems associated with the immediate post-Revolutionary era, not the beginning of an escalating conflict between a triumphant bourgeoisie and an increasingly alienated rural poor. This is a facet of the American experience that Soviet historians may have difficulty accepting. They will be tempted to dismiss the above claim along with much of the new scholarship as American exceptionalism, reflecting our imprisonment in bourgeois "subjectivism."[15] But if they want what they say about our Revolutionary and early national eras to be taken seriously by American scholars of the late twentieth century, they are going to have to transcend the limitations of the New Left historiography of the 1960s and address themselves to the questions that the scholarship is raising today. If they are unable to make this adjustment, they will be read in the United States only as curiosities, revealing more about the state of Soviet historiography than contributing to the common scholarly project of understanding Shays's Rebellion and the American Revolution.

13. The most reliable account of the Whiskey Rebellion is Leland D. Baldwin, *Whiskey Rebels: The Story of a Frontier Uprising,* rev. ed. (Pittsburgh, 1968). A more recent account, Thomas P. Slaughter, *The Whiskey Rebellion: Frontier Epilogue to the American Revolution* (New York, 1986) fails to establish a coherent perspective on the Whiskey Rebellion. For Fries's Rebellion, see Harry M. Tinkom, *The Republicans and Federalists in Pennsylvania, 1790–1801* (Harrisburg, Pa., 1950) and Russell J. Ferguson, *Early Western Pennsylvania Politics* (Pittsburgh, 1983).

14. Taylor, "Regulators and White Indians."

15. Asia E. Kunina, "V plenu sub" ektivizmu: O metodologicheskikh tendentsiiakh v sovremennoi burzhuaznoi istoriografii SShA," (Imprisoned by Subjectivism: Methodological Tendencies in Contemporary American Bourgeois Historiography), *Novaia i Noveishaia Istoriia* 3 (1986), 60–75.

RESPONSE BY BORIS M. SHPOTOV

I am grateful to Professor Buel for informing me of the more recent work on Shays's Rebellion. Some of it I am aware of. I was, for example, able to use the materials in David P. Szatmary's book (1980) in my monograph *The Farmers' Movement in the United States in the 1780s and 1790s* (Moscow, 1982).[1] I also took into account the results of Szatmary's research in an article I wrote on the occasion of the two hundredth anniversary of the Massachusetts rebellion.[2] My review of Szatmary's book was published in 1982.[3]

The article that Professor Buel reviewed was written many years ago, in 1973–1974, and was indeed one of my first works on U.S. history; nevertheless, I feel that Buel's harsh criticism is justified and to the point. Buel bases his critical remarks on the very recent publications by American historians to which he refers. These works, so far as I can judge from what he says about them, lead me to believe that the conclusions in my own article, and also in the earlier works by American scholars I used, should be modified or revised. Yet Professor Buel does not criticize me on the grounds that with the passage of time my article has become outdated, but rather reproaches me for following the methodological procedures that were dominant in our historiography at the time and that mandated a class-based, Marxist interpretation of all popular movements and revolutions.

I will not try to justify myself by declaring, "That was then," or by pointing to the pluralism existing in my country today. There is a Russian proverb that says, "What the pen writes the axe cannot erase." I should like to tackle this issue from a different angle.

Let us imagine that the unfortunate article was written not by me but by someone else. Let us further imagine that it is a solid and respectable piece of work containing no Marxist incrustation or New Left jargon. And let us say that the author of the article reaches the following conclusion:

> Shays's Rebellion was above all else an expression of the struggle between debtors and creditors for their property rights in the conditions of economic chaos and deflation prevailing after the War of Independence. The former demanded the adoption of laws that would protect their property according to the value system of a noncommercial agricultural society and advocated the printing of paper money, the introduction of the right to repay one's debts or pay one's taxes in kind, and the temporary suspension of judicial prosecutions for the nonpayment of debt. The latter (the representatives of commercial society), who held the reins of power, were categorically opposed to such a solution. Because the debtors (who were largely small farmers in the western counties of Massachusetts) were unable to achieve victory by lawful means, they began to band together and interrupt court sessions by force.

1. See the review by Professor Norman E. Saul, *Journal of American History* 70 (December 1983), 657–58.

2. "The Farmers' Rebellion of Daniel Shays (1786–1787)" in *USA: Economics, Politics, Ideology* 2 (1987), 46–54.

3. *Modern and Contemporary History* 3 (1982), 190–93.

And I could go on. But Professor Buel, having read this, would reach for the tome entitled *In Debt to Shays* on his shelf and again say, "I'm sorry, sir, but this still won't do."

Could this happen if the article were free of all Marxist clichés and the discussion promised to be serious? Yes, indeed, and for the same reason—the fact that different degrees of inference from the historical material are possible. A given piece of research generates conclusions only on a predetermined level—whether that of the system, that of its components or, lastly, that of its elements. Professor Buel has provided examples that show how meticulous research conducted at the micro level (particularly with reference to communal and religious criteria) failed to uncover among the Regulators or the rest of the population anything resembling class divisions in the Marxist sense.

Everyone understands that individual elements do not possess all the attributes of the system, and vice versa. The "non-Marxist conclusion" I quoted above may appear to be a balanced one. But when one examines it under a microscope, one sees that it is totally wrong. There were indigent debtors everywhere, even in Boston. This would not have been unusual even in a prosperous center of commerce. Nor was the extension of credits to farmers something uncommon. And yet hired laborers and all other wage-earners, despite their relative poverty, had no desire to be paid for their labor in paper money that was losing its value. Moreover, Szatmary's system-level conclusions about the existence in Massachusetts of two opposing "cultures"—a commercial one in the east and an agrarian one in the west—fail to explain local factors, such as the influence of corporatism and organized religion on the correlation of social forces. So it is not the "iron postulates" of Marxism but the peculiarities of the system-based approach that are responsible for the discrepancies to which Professor Buel refers.

Structural microanalysis has opened dramatic new possibilities for research. It has made it possible to discover the patterns of social behavior in the incorporated towns; this behavior was very interesting, especially in light of the traditional individualism of Americans. But as I understand it, the question of whether the insights thus gained apply only to the objects of study or whether they offer the opportunity to reach new conclusions at the level of the system remains open. This means that all generalizations must remain at the level of Brookfield, Pelham, and the others.

At the micro level, we must either concede that a considerable degree of similarity among the structures being compared existed, with the pro-Shays community in no way differing externally from the anti-Shays community and the neutral community, or be reduced to dealing with individual phenomena of various kinds that, it would seem, cannot be understood with the help of any general laws and that merely reflect the diversity of human behavior. One can understand the reluctance of a well-to-do citizen to take part in the anti-Shays campaign when for a modest payment he could gain exemption from military service, or the willingness of a poor debtor, who lacked the money to obtain an exemption, to join the expedition and unexpectedly earn some money. But is it possible to make all these "examples from life" fit a particular system when other examples of an entirely different kind can be immediately adduced? For the time being one must confine oneself to the trivial conclusion that the poor did not always side with Shays and the rich were not always his enemies. But is there really anything in Marxism that would contradict such a conclusion? Does the equally banal truth that there is a "general opposition" between the poor and the rich imply that the struggle between the two groups involved every one of their members?

"Pure" structuralism would only allow us to reach the following logical conclusions. First, that some among the poor supported Shays, some opposed him, and some remained neutral. Plus and minus together amount to zero; therefore Shays's Rebellion did not reflect the interests of the poor masses. Second, one cannot speak of a struggle between rich and poor, for some of the poor were on the side of the rich. Third, the western counties of Massachusetts cannot be regarded as the fulcrum of the rebellion because some of the towns were neutral and some were even opposed to Shays.

Or one may refrain from drawing any conclusions at all and limit oneself to presenting the data gathered from the microanalysis of the historical material.

But then one day the question will arise; what happened to the rebellion? Where did it disappear to? What were its causes, aims, and motive forces? Taken as a whole, what kind of phenomenon was this? The answers one must look for would be hidden among the mass of micro-objects that were studied in isolation. The structural analysis of the two opposing sides does not reveal any major differences between them, nor can it determine the "general line" followed by either group. And it becomes clear that this rebellion, which had to be fought by government troops, which caused alarm in the state capital and in the Continental Congress, which was even the subject of discussion abroad,[4] was an event whose significance went beyond the village or the parish, extending to the level of the state and indeed the whole nation.

If Robert A. Gross and his colleagues do not stop halfway but continue the research they began so successfully and carry it through to its logical conclusion by looking at the "upper floor" of the system, they will have a major scholarly achievement. Historians then will be able to devise a radically new model of social conflicts that will supersede the old economic, class-based interpretations.

Without extolling or defending the principles of the class-based approach,[5] I will try to explain what I meant when I described Shays's Rebellion *in general terms* as a class conflict. A class is not the same as a *community*, a conglomeration of people that possesses all those material, social, cultural, religious, and other attributes that, taken together, characterize a given civilization, but it is an abstract sociological category. This category is linked to the Marxist concept of the "means of production," the meaning of which has evolved over time. A class not only stands in a particular

4. Nikolai N. Bolkhovitinov, *Russia and the U.S. War of Independence, 1775–1783* (Moscow, 1976), 161.

5. I do not believe that this approach has universal application, nor do I think that it will be used by historians indefinitely. In my view, it is historically limited, for it is an organic part of the Marxist theory of the socioeconomic formation. If in Ancient Greece and Rome or during the period of "classical" capitalism in the Middle Ages the interests and antagonisms of the various classes, estates, and corporations were the decisive factor, it is the universal values of humanity and civilization that are the most powerful historical force in the world today.

relation to the means of production, as Professor Buel points out, but also has a well-defined "class interest," that is, its own set of social demands. This class interest does not appear spontaneously but is the result of the interaction of that particular class with other classes. However, I do not propose to give a detailed exposition of this somewhat arid nineteenth-century theory. Instead I will offer a few examples that will illustrate the way in which it is used, and then I will return to a discussion of Shays's Rebellion.

During the French Revolution some of the rural "communities" were engaged in a revolutionary antifeudal struggle, while others (in the Vendee) were persistently and violently counterrevolutionary. If one were to confine oneself to the study of the "community," one would only be able to verify and analyze these facts at the same level—the level of the community. However, then one would be ignoring the main historical reality of the period—the objectively revolutionary role of the peasantry *as a class* in the bourgeois revolution. The peasant wars of the seventeenth and eighteenth centuries in Russia all had the same class goal—the abolition of serfdom and the transfer of ownership of the land to the peasants. That is why these rebellions are called peasant wars. Yet these movements and the groups that fought against them were markedly heterogeneous in composition. Here an analysis of the "communities" would not reveal the fundamental, system-generating factor, which does not depend on "accidental deviations," such as the presence of nonpeasant elements in the ranks of the rebels, the prevalence of a utopian belief in the possibility of social reconstruction through the enthronement of a "peasant" or "good" tsar, etc.

I say all this to illustrate my point that the terms "class" and "community" do not describe the same object but two social realities of a different order. Moreover, the two terms belong to different levels of historical discourse: one is abstract, the other is concrete. If Professor Buel believes that it was my intention to lump these terms together, he is mistaken. In fact, the goals that I and the authors of the most recent works on Shays's Rebellion have pursued were very different.

In analyzing Shays's Rebellion, I proceeded from the assumption that the aims of the Regulators on the whole reflected the interests of the small landholders and the village poor, whether they served in the militia, occupied a neutral position, or belonged to a given church (of course, I refer to material interests). Once people's material interests were affected, it turned out that the mostly poor, though not homogeneous, masses in the western counties were opposed by the large landowners, rich merchants, and financiers of the eastern counties. This second group had been chiefly responsible for shaping the social politics that the Regulators tried to resist. The reaction of the ruling elite to Shays's Rebellion was uniform both within the state and beyond its borders (Thomas Jefferson was the sole exception.)[6] Irrespective of their political attitude toward the issue of the reform of the central government (that is, their division into Federalists and Antifederalists), the members of the ruling elite collectively concluded that Shays's Rebellion was directed against property, law, and

6. Boris M. Shpotov, *The Farmers' Movement in the United States in the 1780s and 1790s* (Moscow, 1982), 93–119.

order. In fact, this was not the case, for the Regulators were not levelers, but this is how the elite, because of its "class thinking," viewed the Regulators' movement. This type of class thinking—legitimistic and strongly hostile to any threat to the "achievements of the Revolution" and "popular sovereignty"—has been characteristic of all revolutionaries who have won political power in all periods and all countries with a few rare exceptions. Concerning the events in Massachusetts, the delegates to the Continental Congress in Philadelphia were also of one mind (only Benjamin Franklin's statements deviated somewhat from the consensus).

The picture of the conflict is complicated by the plethora of nuances and halftones that accompanied this fundamental opposition to the rebellion. A class-based analysis would aim only to "establish the trend." Since in real life a given trend will typically produce accidental deviations (which also characterize the process), I should like to say that the argument about the nature of Shays's Rebellion is to a significant degree an argument about terminology, rather than specifics.

A few words about one characteristic example and the differences in its interpretation. I refer to the armed clashes that took place during the insurrection, or more precisely, to Professor Buel's belief that the events of February 4, 1787, reflected the completely classless nature of the conflict. It is not among the Regulators that he finds evidence of this classlessness but among the government troops commanded by General Lincoln. Basing his conclusions on the new school of history, Buel states that the reason for the minute number of casualties and the generally brilliant outcome of the campaign was the restraint of the troops. Because the officers and soldiers of the militia were keenly aware of the interests of the Republic and the desirability of a future consensus between Shays's supporters and the other citizens, they decided to avoid bloodshed. Had "class divisions" among the troops, or between the troops and the rebels, existed, nothing like this would have happened, says Buel. This is another interesting example of analysis at the micro level.

The explanation Professor Buel offers for the restrained behavior of Lincoln's soldiers is logical. I also agree that in general the government troops were inclined to treat the enemy charitably. And if he has found documentary evidence indicating that prior to battle the officers and soldiers actually resolved to conduct themselves in this noble fashion, this would amount to proof of an important historical fact.

Nevertheless, I am not sure that the search for an explanation of the absence of bloodshed and casualties should be confined to only one of the two opposing sides. Because of the superiority of Lincoln's forces, the suddenness of his attack in the morning darkness, the unpreparedness of Shays's men, and perhaps their reluctance to fight, the Regulators immediately scattered. Some of them surrendered, and some of them led by Shays fled the field of battle. No resistance was offered, and in the end this is what determined the outcome. But Lincoln's troops could not have foreseen that there would be no resistance. In the end, no battle actually took place and, in my opinion, events unfolded in the way they did because of an accidental concurrence of circumstances. It is difficult to say what would have happened had the insurgents opened fire. One can only speculate as to how Lincoln's detachment would have reacted then.

I find it difficult to agree with Buel's high opinion of the results of the operation. These were in every way inconclusive—the ringleaders of the movement and some of the Regulators were able to escape. And yet, as I see it, Lincoln could have first encircled the rebels, who were camped for the night in a small town, or, using some of his forces, could have severed their line of retreat and then demanded their capitulation. Because of the position of Shays's men, it would have been possible to carry out such a plan without any interference. Indeed, if Lincoln's soldiers' heroic nighttime forced march, covering thirty miles over snow-covered ground, was a reflection of their discipline and fortitude, then the indecisive outcome of the operation was due largely to their commander's poor generalship. I do not believe that Shays and a number of his men were able to escape because of some "agreement" to exercise restraint. Their escape was probably also due to chance.

One may interpret these events as a unique example of mutual forbearance on the part of the government and the insurgents. Or one may try to put these events in historical context by examining the aims of the rebels and the courses of action open to them. The civil courts were the main object of their attacks. Their interruption of court sessions was peaceful in nature because the judges were afraid to argue with armed mobs. The attempt to capture the armory represented a departure from the methods the rebels had previously employed in the struggle. As for the "republican restraint" of the government's troops supposedly designed to reintegrate the rebels into the system of consensus, it must be said that the civil authorities did not display the same pacific inclinations. Fourteen death sentences were handed down; even a popular Revolutionary democrat such as Samuel Adams demanded capital punishment for the insurgents. Eventually, however, all were commuted. Shays's Rebellion was radically different from a peasant war, the aim of which is always to seize power from the state (hence the need to storm cities and besiege fortresses and to use terror and violence).

In offering a moral evaluation of Shays's Rebellion, the representatives of the new historical school say that the veterans of the Continental Army, who made up the militia detachments that fought Shays, were the true "vindicators" of the Revolution, whereas Shays's men were willing to sacrifice its achievements for their "personal interest and conveniences." But there is another side to the story. To understand it one must recall the well-known statement by Thomas Jefferson, who said that he preferred the "turbulence" of democracy to the "calm of despotism." As for the "personal" material interests of Shays's supporters, it must be said that all they wanted was to defend the hard-earned property of their families, rather than to take what belonged to others. One must not forget that these were propertied farmers, who were industrious, not greedy.

Of course, Shays's Rebellion did not amount to a continuation of the American Revolution. Nor did it have a lasting effect on the historical development of the country. Yet after the suppression of the rebellion the composition of the state legislature became more democratic, a more liberal governor was elected, the number of court sessions in the counties was reduced, and most important, delinquent debtors were no longer subject to mandatory imprisonment. Were not all these developments progressive in character? Did they really undermine the achievements and victories of the Revolution?

From the point of view of universal human values it is difficult to sympathize always with revolutions or other manifestations of violence and extremism; and it is difficult, as was the case with Soviet historians, always to side with those who are on the "Left" (of course, their attitude to developments within the Soviet system was different). The class-based approach has its own ideological and emotional coloration, its own bias, and in this sense lacks objectivity. We all now realize this. Nevertheless, it is still true that the American Revolution and Shays's Rebellion are among the most humane examples of such actions.

I thank Professor Richard Buel for his expert and meticulous review of my article. I have tried to offer my best defense. He concludes his remarks by saying that the time has come for Russian historians to assimilate the ideas born in the great debate that forms part of the civilized discourse of mankind and to join that debate, which has been going on for many years without them and which they have ignored for too long.

I am happy to say that here Professor Buel and I are in total agreement.

CONTRIBUTORS

RUSSIAN CONTRIBUTORS

Nikolai N. Bolkhovitinov is Head, Center for North American Studies, Institute of General History, Russian Academy of Sciences, Moscow.

Olga Vladimirno Kriuchkova is associated with the Institute of U.S. and Canadian Studies, Russian Academy of Sciences.

Gennadi P. Kuropiatnik is chief researcher of the Institute of General History, Russian Academy of Sciences.

V. N. Pleshkov is deputy director of the St. Petersburg branch of the Institute of Russian History of the Russian Academy of Sciences.

B. A. Shiriayev is chair of the History Department and Professor of History at St. Petersburg State University.

Boris M. Shpotov is the leading researcher in the Institute of General History, Russian Academy of Sciences.

V. V. Sogrin is the head of the Department of the Institute of General History, Russian Academy of Sciences.

Maria O. Troyanovskaya is Assistant Professor in the Department of Modern and Contemporary History, Moscow State University.

V. L. Ushakov is the leading researcher of the St. Petersburg branch of the Institute of Russian History, the Russian Academy of Sciences.

AMERICAN CONTRIBUTORS

Richard Buel Jr. is Professor of History at Wesleyan University.

Jack P. Greene is Andrew W. Mellon Professor of Humanities at Johns Hopkins University.

Ronald Hoffman is Director of the Institute of Early American History and Culture in Williamsburg, Virginia.

James A. Henretta is Burke Professor of History at the University of Maryland, College Park.

Pauline Maier is William R. Kenan Jr. Professor of History at the Massachusetts Institute of Technology.

John M. Murrin is Professor of History at Princeton University.

Linda K. Kerber is May Brodbeck Professor in the Liberal Arts and Professor of History at the University of Iowa.

Jack Rakove is Professor of History at Stanford University.

Richard A. Ryerson is Editor-in-Chief of the *Adams Papers,* Massachusetts Historical Society.

Gordon S. Wood is the University Professor and Professor of History at Brown University.

Louise G. Wood is former head, Department of English, Lincoln School, Providence, Rhode Island.

INDEX

Adams, "Deacon" John, 98
Adams, John, 119, 126; family, 79, 98; at
  Harvard, 79–80 passim; legal practice
  in Massachusetts, 79, 82, 83, 98; rise to
  prominence in Boston, 80–84; pamphlets in
  Stamp Act crisis, 80–81; on relations with
  England, 81, 83; elected to Massachusetts
  legislature, 83; in Boston Tea Party crisis,
  84; delegate to Continental Congresses, 85,
  86, 87, 91, 92, 183; stance toward England,
  88, 223–24, 240; on state governments, 89,
  90, 102; on separation of powers, 89–90;
  as diplomat to France, 92, 93, 99; in peace
  negotiations, 94–95; on aristocracies in
  Europe, 99–100
Adams, Samuel: and Sons of Liberty, 54, 61
  passim, 70, 75; influence on John Adams,
  79, 102; correspondence, 171; in Congress,
  193, 223; on draft of Federal Constitution,
  227; on Shays's Rebellion, 277
Age of Reason, 141
"Agrarian Justice," 110, 141
Albany County (N.Y.), 30, 56
Alden, John Richard, 208
Allen, Ethan, 62, 63, 64, 68, 74
American Historical Association (AHA),
  1–2 passim, 19
American Historical Review, 16
Ancien regime in America, 25, 36; critique
  by John Adams, 80, 284
Andover (Mass.), 74
Andrews, Charles M., 22
Anglican Church, 150, 161–62, 169
Anglo-Saxon common law, 150, 163
Anson County (N.C.), 71
Antifederalists, 132, 140, 154, 265, 275
Appleby, Joyce O., 186
Appleton family, 36
Aptheker, Herbert, 1, 7; on main trends in
  American Revolution, 33, 47; on farmers,
  40, 49, 154
Arbatov, Georgii, 8
Aristotle, 102
Arminianism, 268
Armstrong, John, 194

Articles of Confederation, 3, 16, 132–34
  passim, 205, 215, 217, 227; and slavery,
  229; shortcomings, 230–31; factors in
  framing it, 234, 238–39, 244–45
Austria, 93

Bailyn, Bernard, 13, 19, 25; on cultural
  context of American Revolution, 4, 135,
  142, 184; on Paine's "Common Sense,"
  26, 41
Baltimore, Lord, 50
Bank of North America, 121, 204, 211, 214
Barrow, Thomas C., 23–24 passim
Baskin, M. P., 135
Beard, Charles, 3, 4, 8; criticized, 16, 30,
  120; on conservatism of Constitution, 218
Beccaria, Cesare, "On Crimes and
  Punishments," 161
Becker, Carl: on American Revolution, 3, 16,
  30, 73; on Association, 171, 186
Belcher, Sarson, 196, 214
Bemis, Samuel F., 78
Berkshire County (Mass.), 251, 253, 260
"Bill for Establishing Religious Freedom,"
  153, 168
"Bill for the More General Diffusion of
  Knowledge," 156
Bill of Rights, 134, 154
Bland, Richard, 159
Bolingbroke, Lord, 150
Bolkhovitinov, Nikolai N., 6, 8, 9
Bolles, Albert S., 190
Bonds: issued by Congress, 200–201
Bonomi, Patricia, 22
Boorstin, Daniel, 15, 24, 39, 246
Boston Bar: admission of John Adams, 80
Boston Gazette, 67, 80
Boston Tea Party (1773), 65, 84
Bowdoin, James, 253–55 passim, 258, 259
Bowen, Catherine D., 78
Boycotts: Boston trade, 61, 62, 171, 184. *See
  also* Townshend Acts
Boyd, Julian P., 160, 168
Braintree (Mass.), 79